MAJORITY RULE OR MINORITY WILL

ADHERENCE TO PRECEDENT ON THE U.S. SUPREME COURT

This book examines the influence of precedent on the behavior of U.S. Supreme Court justices throughout the Court's history. Under the assumption that for precedent to be an influence on the behavior of justices it must lead to a result they would not otherwise have reached, the results show that when justices disagree with the establishment of a precedent, they rarely shift from their previously stated views in subsequent cases. In other words, they are hardly ever influenced by precedent. Nevertheless, the doctrine of *stare decisis* does exhibit some low-level influence on the justices in the least salient of the Court's decisions. The book examines these findings in light of several leading theories of judicial decision making.

Harold J. Spaeth is Professor of Political Science at Michigan State University.

Jeffrey A. Segal is Professor of Political Science at SUNY Stony Brook.

MAJORITY RULE
OR MINORITY WILL

ADHERENCE TO PRECEDENT
ON THE U.S. SUPREME COURT

HAROLD J. SPAETH

JEFFREY A. SEGAL

CAMBRIDGE
UNIVERSITY PRESS

PUBLISHED BY THE PRESS SYNDICATE OF THE UNIVERSITY OF CAMBRIDGE
The Pitt Building, Trumpington Street, Cambridge, United Kingdom

CAMBRIDGE UNIVERSITY PRESS
The Edinburgh Building, Cambridge CB2 2RU, UK
40 West 20th Street, New York, NY 10011-4211, USA
10 Stamford Road, Oakleigh, Melbourne 3166, Australia
Ruiz de Alarcón 13, 28014 Madrid, Spain
Dock House, The Waterfront, Cape Town 8001, South Africa

http://www.cambridge.org

First published 1999
First paperback edition 2001
Reprinted 2000

Printed in the United States of America

Typeface Times Roman, 10/12 pt   *System* Macintosh [BTS]

A catalog record for this book is available from the British Library.

Library of Congress Cataloging in Publication data is available.

ISBN 0 521 62424 X hardback
ISBN 0 521 80571 6 paperback

for Jean, for forty-five years
Harold J. Spaeth

for Larry Segal and Sharon Schorr
Jeffrey A. Segal

Contents

Tables and Figures

TABLES

FIGURES

Preface

The publication of our first book together, *The Supreme Court and the Attitudinal Model* (1993), argued that the decisions of the Supreme Court could be overwhelmingly explained by the attitudes and values of the justices, and that traditional legal factors, such as precedent, text, and intent, had virtually no impact.

The book met, not unexpectedly, with a variety of criticisms from jurisprudentially inclined scholars. Though few doubted that we had provided clear and convincing evidence of the influence the justices' attitudes had on their decisions, our analysis of the legal model was far less systematic and relied almost exclusively on anecdotal evidence.

At the time, we argued that the components of the legal model were so vague that they could not be subject to falsifiable tests. That is, if factors such as precedent can be used to support any position that a justice could take, such that one could not predict *a priori* how precedent might influence a decision, then precedent is completely meaningless as an explanation of the Court's decisions.

After the publication of our book, we began to consider possible falsifiable hypotheses that could be made about the influence of precedent on Supreme Court decisions. We began with the notion that for precedent to be such an *influence*, it must lead justices to decisions that they would not otherwise have reached. That is, if a justice supports abortion rights and continues to do so following the establishment of pro-choice precedents, we cannot claim that the justice was influenced by those precedents. But we can test the influence of precedent on those who disagree with the established position.

We first developed this idea in a 1996 article in the *American Journal of Political Science* and simultaneously provided some preliminary tests. The journal published a forum centered on our article, and we have since been able to benefit from the comments, criticisms, and analyses of Jack Knight and Lee Epstein, Saul Brenner and Marc Stier, Donald Songer and Stephanie Lindquist, and Richard Brisbin. For this book we have refined our measures and provided a comprehensive analysis of the influence of precedent over the history of the Supreme Court, examining the population of the Court's landmark decisions as identified by Witt (1990) and a random sample of the Court's ordinary cases.

Chapter 1 introduces the subject matter of the book and explains why the notion of *stare decisis* is important for the Court and for our theoretical understanding of the Court. Chapter 2 describes in great detail our methodology for examining the influence of *stare decisis*. Chapters 3 through 8 examine precedential behavior chronologically through the history of the Court, focusing on landmark cases, but providing information on the often-neglected ordinary litigation facing the Court as well. Chapter 9 summarizes the results and provides tests for a variety of hypotheses we have derived.

In addition to the critics we mentioned earlier, we thank Ken Meier for publishing our original work in the *AJPS* and creating the forum on that article in the same issue. Lee Epstein deserves additional mention, for without fail she makes her insights available to us whenever we need assistance, which is more often than we would like to admit. She and Larry Baum of Ohio State University also read the entire manuscript, thereby appreciably enhancing its accuracy and readability. Aneu Greene provided research assistance for some of the materials in Chapter 1, and Kevin McDonnell put together the data set used for the statistical analyses in Chapter 9. Some of those data were gathered with support from NSF grants SES8313773, SES9211452, SBR9320509, SBR9515335, and SBR9614000.

Segal would like to thank his chair, Mark Schneider, for all of the support he has provided through the years, and the rest of his colleagues at the State University of New York at Stony Brook for providing what must be one of the most exceptional work environments anywhere. He also thanks his wife, Christine – not, as is typically done in these circumstances, for graciously accepting the time it took to write this book, but for just the opposite: for always wanting him to come home early.

Spaeth thanks the National Science Foundation for the support needed to construct archived databases. Without such support, the collection and compilation of the data on which work such as this rests would not be feasible.

We thank our Cambridge editor, Alex Holzman, who allows his authors to work without hindrance or interference. Andrew Roney and Susan Thornton ably performed the demanding and thankless tasks of production editor and copy editor, respectively.

Finally, the inverse alphabetical order of our names does not indicate that Spaeth wrote more of this book than Segal. Responsibility for its contents is equally divided. The order serves only to distinguish this book from its cowritten predecessor, *The Supreme Court and the Attitudinal Model*, which Cambridge University Press also published.

1

Precedent and the Court

INTRODUCTION:

THE CASE OF *PLANNED PARENTHOOD V. CASEY*

That the Court was ready to overturn *Roe v. Wade* (1973) in June 1992 appeared indisputable. Three years earlier, Justice Antonin Scalia concurred with a judgment of the Court that he and Justice Harry Blackmun believed effectively overturned *Roe* (*Webster v. Reproductive Services* 1989, p. 532). And while the plurality judgment in *Webster*, written by Rehnquist and joined by White and Kennedy, declared that *Roe* was "unsound in principle and unworkable in practice" (p. 518), it left the 1973 decision standing, claiming that the limited impact of the Missouri statute on abortion rights "affords no occasion to revisit the holding of *Roe*" (p. 521).[1]

Thus, with four justices ready to overturn *Roe*, the replacement of the pro-choice justices William Brennan and Thurgood Marshall with David Souter and Clarence Thomas, respectively, made a fifth vote to overturn *Roe*, and possibly a sixth, all but certain. Souter kept his views on abortion secret, but few believed that President George Bush would nominate to the Supreme Court a man who supported abortion rights (Lewis 1990). Thomas, on the other hand, had gone so far as to suggest not only that *Roe* was wrong, but also that constitutional mandates actually prohibited states from allowing abortions (Lewis 1991).

The 1992 decision upholding abortion rights (*Planned Parenthood of Southeastern Pennsylvania v. Casey*) surprised more than a few Court watchers, with the *New York Times* headlining Linda Greenhouse's article with the phrase "SURPRISING DECISION" (Greenhouse 1992a; see also Barrett 1992, Marcus 1992, and Savage 1992).

The plurality's explanation of why it voted the way it did focused heavily on the doctrine of *stare decisis*. Opening with the stirring claim

---

[1] Rehnquist actually had little choice in the matter, as the fifth vote to uphold the statute belonged to Justice O'Connor, who, as we shall see, generally supports abortion rights.

"Liberty finds no refuge in a jurisprudence of doubt" (p. 844), the Court declared, "After considering the fundamental constitutional questions resolved by *Roe*, principles of institutional integrity, and the rule of *stare decisis*, we are led to conclude this: the essential holding of *Roe v. Wade* should be retained and once again reaffirmed" (pp. 846–847). While noting that *stare decisis* in constitutional questions is far from an inexorable command (p. 854), the Court explained why *Roe* differed:

Where, in the performance of its judicial duties, the Court decides a case in such a way as to resolve the sort of intensely divisive controversy reflected in *Roe* and those rare, comparable cases, its decision has a dimension that the resolution of the normal case does not carry. It is the dimension present whenever the Court's interpretation of the Constitution calls the contending sides of a national controversy to end their national division by accepting a common mandate rooted in the Constitution.

The Court is not asked to do this very often, having thus addressed the Nation only twice in our lifetime, in the decisions of *Brown* and *Roe*. But, when the Court does act in this way, its decision requires an equally rare precedential force to counter the inevitable efforts to overturn it and to thwart its implementation. Some of these efforts may be mere unprincipled emotional reactions; others may proceed from principles worthy of profound respect. But whatever the premises of opposition may be, only the most convincing justification under accepted standards of precedent could suffice to demonstrate that a later decision overruling the first was anything but a surrender to political pressure, and an unjustified repudiation of the principle on which the Court staked its authority in the first instance. So to overrule under fire in the absence of the most compelling reason to reexamine a watershed decision would subvert the Court's legitimacy beyond any serious question. (pp. 866–867)

Throughout the opinion, the commands of *stare decisis* ring, as if requiring the Court to reach a decision that it would not otherwise have reached on its own. This is, in a sense, as it should be, as "adherence to precedent must be the rule rather than the exception if litigants are to have faith in the evenhanded administration of justice" (Cardozo 1921, p. 34).

Journalists and scholars alike were quick to accept the triumvirate's explanation that *stare decisis* influenced its decision. Linda Greenhouse's (1992b) analysis accepts at face value the claim that adhering to *Roe v. Wade* was necessary even for justices who continued to have doubts about the decision. The *Chicago Tribune* declared that the "decision relied on the time-honored doctrine of respecting legal precedent" (Neikirk and Elsasser 1992, p. A1; also see Daly 1995, Howard 1993, and Maltz 1992).

At the risk of flouting the conventional wisdom, we would at least like to question the *influence* of *stare decisis* on the Court's decision. We do so by starting with the notion that those wishing to assess systematically the influence of precedent must recognize that in many cases Supreme Court decision making would look exactly the same whether justices were influenced by precedent or not. Consider the Court's decision in *Roe v. Wade* (1973). The majority found a constitutional right to abortion that could not be abridged without a compelling state interest. The dissenters found no such right. In subsequent cases, Justices Blackmun, Brennan, Marshall, and others, continued to support abortion rights. While we could say that choices in these cases were based on the precedent set in *Roe*, it is just as reasonable – if not more so – to say that those justices would have supported abortion rights in subsequent cases even without the precedent in *Roe*. Thus, even in a system without a rule of precedent Justice Scalia would continue to support the death penalty, nonracial drawing of congressional districts, limited privacy rights, and so on. When prior preferences and precedents are the same it is not meaningful to speak of decisions as being determined by precedent. For precedent to matter as an *influence* on decisions, it must achieve results that would not otherwise have been obtained. As Judge Jerome Frank stated, "Stare decisis has no bite when it means merely that a court adheres to a precedent that it considers correct. It is significant only when a court feels constrained to stick to a former ruling although the court has come to regard it as unwise or unjust" (*United States ex rel. Fong Foo v. Shaughnessy* 1955, p. 719).

Did the plurality opinion in *Casey* give any indication that its authors considered the ruling in *Roe* to be unwise or unjust? For the most part, the answer is no. While the authors[2] pointed out that "time has overtaken some of *Roe*'s factual assumptions" (p. 860), and that some parts of *Roe* were unduly restrictive, the decision "has in no sense proven 'unworkable'" (p. 855), has facilitated "the ability of women to participate equally in the economic and social life of the nation" (p. 856), and fits comfortably with doctrinal developments before and after 1973 (pp. 857–8). Indeed, the Court refers to *Roe* as an "exemplar of Griswold liberty" (p. 857).

While it is true that there are instances where the Court finds fault with *Roe*, each and every time it does it substitutes its own judgment for that of *Roe!* Thus the Court supplants the trimester framework with viability (p. 870) and exchanges the compelling interest standard for an undue burden standard (p. 876). Additionally, the Court reversed holdings in *Akron v. Akron Center for Reproductive Health* (1983) and *Thornburgh v. American College of Obstetricians and Gynecologists* (1986). In sum,

---

[2] Sandra Day O'Connor, Anthony Kennedy, and David Souter. For what appears to be the first time in history, a prevailing opinion was jointly written by less than all the justices. An opinion listing each justice as an author has occurred a time or two, however.

nowhere in the plurality opinion does the Court clearly substitute *Roe*'s judgment, or that of any other case, for its own contemporary preference.

Our answer about the *influence* of *Roe* changes a bit if we look to the past for the views of the justices. Perhaps, the strongest case for precedential impact can be made for Justice Kennedy. As noted previously, Kennedy joined Rehnquist's opinion in *Webster* (1989), which, among other things, questioned why the "State's interest in protecting human life should come into existence only at the point of viability" (p. 436). But as a federal court of appeals judge, Kennedy "only grudgingly upheld the validity of naval regulations prohibiting homosexual conduct," citing *Roe v. Wade* and other "privacy right" cases very favorably in the process (Yalof 1997, p. 353). According to the dossier Deputy Attorney General Steven Matthews prepared on Kennedy for the Reagan Justice Department, "This easy acceptance of privacy rights as something guaranteed by the constitution is really very distressing" (Yalof 1997, pp. 353–54). Thus his opposition to *Roe* was never as strong as popularly believed.

Even more ambiguous is the position of justice Souter. Though appointed by a purportedly pro-life President,[3] Souter had sat on the Board of Directors of a New Hampshire hospital that performed voluntary abortions, with no known objections from Souter. Without any clear indications of his prior beliefs about *Roe*, it is nearly impossible to determine the extent to which *Roe* influenced his position in *Casey*.

Alternatively, no ambiguity surrounded Justice Sandra Day O'Connor's preferences. She supported abortion rights while a legislator in Arizona ("It's About Time" 1981) and, once on the Court, frequently found problems with the trimester format of *Roe* but never doubted that a fundamental right to abortion existed (e.g., *Webster v. Reproductive Services* 1989, and *Thornburgh v. American College of Obstetricians and Gynecologists* 1986). Indeed, *Casey*'s attacks on *Roe*'s trimester framework and its adoption of the undue burden standard come directly from O'Connor's *dissent* in *Akron v. Akron Center for Reproductive Services* (1983). So too, *Casey*'s overuling of *Akron* and *Thornburgh* comport perfectly with her dissents in those cases. It is extraordinarily difficult to argue that *stare decisis* influenced O'Connor in any manner in the *Casey* case. Where *Roe* and her previously expressed preferences met, she followed *Roe*. But where any majority opinion in any abortion case

---

[3]   Bush supported abortion rights until Ronald Reagan nominated him to be Vice President in 1980. He had even been an active supporter of Planned Parenthood (Lewis 1988).

differed from her previously expressed views, she stuck with her views. Justice O'Connor "followed" precedent to the extent that she used it to justify results she agreed with, but there is no evidence whatsoever that these precedents influenced her positions.

MEASURING THE INFLUENCE OF PRECEDENT

While we believe our position on the justices' votes to be reasonable, we are struck by a lack of hard evidence as to how Justices O'Connor, Kennedy, and especially Souter actually felt about *Roe*. For example, O'Connor's early Court positions on abortion, which generally accepted a right to abortion, could readily have been affected by the precedent established in *Roe*. But for *Roe*, she might not have taken that position. Thus, the best evidence about whether justices are influenced by a precedent would come not from justices who joined the Court after the decision in question, for we usually cannot be certain about what their position on the case would have been as an original matter. Nor can we gather such evidence from those on the Court who voted with the majority, for the precedent established in that case coincides with their revealed preferences (whatever their cause). Rather, the best evidence for the influence of precedent must come from those who dissented from the majority opinion in the case under question, for we *know* that these justices disagree with the precedent. If the precedent established in the case influences them, that influence should be felt in that case's progeny, through their votes and opinion writing. Thus, determining the influence of precedent requires examining the extent to which justices who disagree with a precedent move toward that position in subsequent cases.

This is not an unobtainable standard. Examples of justices' changing their votes and opinions in response to established precedents clearly exist. In *Griswold v. Connecticut* (1965), Stewart rejected the creation of a right to privacy and its application to married individuals. Yet in *Eisenstadt v. Baird* (1972) he accepted *Griswold*'s right to privacy and was even willing to apply it to unmarried persons. Justice White dissented when the Court established First Amendment protections for commercial speech (*Bigelow v. Virginia* [1975]);[4] he thereafter supported such claims. (See *Virginia Pharmacy Board v. Virginia Citizens Con-*

---

[4] Rehnquist's dissent, which White joined, emphasized the fact that the advertisement in question pertained to abortion providers rather than commercial speech per se. Arguably, White's objection rested on his opposition to abortion (he and Rehnquist had dissented in *Roe v. Wade*) rather than to commercial speech.

sumer Council [1976], and *Bates v. Arizona State Bar* [1977]). And while Justice Rehnquist dissented in the jury exclusion cases *Batson v. Kentucky* (1986) and *Edmonson v. Leesville Concrete Co.* (1991), he concurred in *Georgia v. McCollum* (1992), providing an explicit and quintessential example of what it means to be constrained by precedent: "I was in dissent in *Edmonson v. Leesville Concrete Co.* and continue to believe that case to have been wrongly decided. But so long as it remains the law, I believe it controls the disposition of this case. . . . I therefore join the opinion of the Court" (p. 52).[5]

We believe that this operational definition of precedential influence is both reasonable and, unlike other definitions, falsifiable. Compare our definition to one that counts a justice as following precedent as long as she cites some case or cases that are consistent with that justice's vote. Since there are always some cases supporting both sides in virtually every conflict decided by the Court, such a definition turns *stare decisis* into a trivial concept, at least for explanatory purposes. Moreover, a justice-centered view of precedent makes precedent a personal decision, not the institutional decision that it so clearly is supposed to be.

Analyzing precedent from our perspective should yield important substantive and theoretical insights into the nature of judicial decision making.[6] The doctrine of *stare decisis* is a fundamental part of the American legal system. Lawyers fill their briefs with previously decided cases; jurists at all levels of the federal and state court systems cite cases in virtually all of their written opinions; law school professors dissect these citations in the pages of their journals; and most important for our study, justices of the Supreme Court of the United States make mention of them in their private discussions (Epstein and Knight 1997) and endorse them in their opinions.

Indeed, one could readily claim that to the justices *stare decisis* remains the heart of the rule of law. In *Payne v. Tennessee* (1991), Thurgood Marshall argued in dissent that "this Court has repeatedly stressed that fidelity to precedent is fundamental to 'a society governed by the rule of law.' . . . Stare decisis . . . 'is essential if case-by-case judicial decision-making is to be reconciled with the principle of the rule of law, for when governing standards are open to revision in every case, deciding cases becomes a mere exercise of judicial will'" (p. 849). The

---

[5]   Also see Schubert (1963) for an examination of Justice Clark's changing his position in three court-martial cases decided in the 1959 term in response to newly established precedents. Clark also dissented in *Miranda v. Arizona* (1966) before acceding to it in his opinion in *United States v. Wade* (1967).

[6]   Lee Epstein contributed language and ideas to the following three paragraphs. We thank her for her assistance.

majority opinion's "debilitated conception of *stare decisis* would destroy the Court's very capacity to resolve authoritatively the abiding conflicts between those in power and those without" (p. 853). Justices O'Connor, Kennedy, and Souter noted in *Planned Parenthood v. Casey* (1992) that "no judicial system could do society's work if it eyed each issue afresh in every case that raised it. . . . Indeed, the very concept of the rule of law underlying our own Constitution requires such continuity over time that a respect for precedent is, by definition, indispensable" (p. 854). In short, appeal to precedent is the primary justification justices provide for the decisions they reach.[7]

But with all this attention to *stare decisis*, a critical question has gone unaddressed, at least in a systematic fashion, for far too long: Do previously decided cases influence the decisions of Supreme Court justices? That is, does precedent actually cause justices to reach decisions that they otherwise would not have made? Of course, as we have shown, in some cases, the answer clearly appears to be yes. But we still do not know how frequently such behavior occurs. The real question is not whether such behavior exists at all, for surely it does, but whether it exists at systematic and substantively meaningful levels.

This is the central question we address in this book, and it is of no small consequence, at least in part because the legal and scholarly communities disagree over its answer. At one end of the spectrum are those who herald the importance of *stare decisis* as perhaps the single most important factor influencing judicial decisions. These are supporters of what we will call "precedential" models. At the other end of the spectrum are those who argue that precedent is not influential, that it merely cloaks the justices' personal policy preferences. These are supporters of what we will call "preferential" models. Finally, in the middle are those who argue that precedent can occasionally influence the justices but also believe that nonlegal factors can be just as important. We label these scholars "legal moderates."

While this study can theoretically and empirically advance our understanding of how the Supreme Court makes decisions, it is important as well to highlight some of the claims we will not be able to make:

- Our approach does not and cannot speak to normative arguments about precedent, those suggesting what judges should and should not do.
- Our approach does not and cannot examine the role of *stare decisis* as

---

[7]   One recent study, for example, found that over 80 percent of the constitutional arguments raised by Justices Brennan and Rehnquist in majority opinions were based on precedent (Phelps and Gates 1991, p. 594).

a tool used to enhance the legitimacy of courts as adjudicative bodies (Shapiro 1972).

• Though our approach could be used to examine vertical *stare decisis*, where lower courts appear to be influenced by higher court commands (Songer, Segal, and Cameron 1994), such inquiries are beyond the scope of this study. Indeed, we readily recognize that Supreme Court justices might be *the* set of judges least likely to be influenced by *stare decisis* (Segal and Spaeth 1993), so conclusions from this study may not be generalizable to the judicial system as a whole.[8] But conclusions about the Supreme Court, even if not generalizable, are important enough to merit the careful consideration we provide.

With these caveats in mind, we conclude this chapter with a further exploration of the differing views of the influence of *stare decisis*.

PRECEDENTIAL AND PREFERENTIAL MODELS

In this section we examine a variety of different views that attempt to explain the conditions under which *stare decisis* will influence the decisions of judges and justices: those of precedentialists, preferentialists, and legal moderates.

Precedentialists

We begin with the precedentialists, and clearly the least defensible doctrine within this camp, mechanical jurisprudence. Edward Levi, though no believer in mechanical jurisprudence, describes it well as a three-step process "in which a proposition descriptive of the first case is made into a rule of law and then applied to a next similar situation. The steps are these: similarity is seen between cases; next, the rule of law inherent in the first case is announced; then the rule of law is made applicable to the second case" (1949, pp. 1–2).[9] As Cardozo notes, "Some judges seldom

---

[8] Even on the Supreme Court, we cannot conduct a complete test of *stare decisis*. *Stare decisis* could shore up votes of justices who might otherwise stray from rulings they once liked. Or precedent might influence justices who come on the Court after a landmark case is decided. Unfortunately, in these cases we simply do not know that the justices' "preferences" differ from the precedent in question. We can only systematically examine precedent in situations where falsifiable tests can be created.

[9] Precedentialists, unfortunately, do not tell us how to proceed when the rule of law is itself undefinable, as not uncommonly is the situation. For example,

Articulating precisely what "reasonable suspicion" and "probable cause" mean is not possible. They are commonsense, nontechnical conceptions that deal with "the factual and practical considerations of everyday life on which reasonable and prudent men, not legal technicians, act." . . . As such, the standards are "not readily, or even usefully, reduced to a neat set of legal rules." . . . We have cautioned that these

get beyond that process in any case. Their notion of their duty is to match the colors of the case at hand against the colors of many sample cases spread out along their desk. The sample nearest in shade provides the applicable rule" (1921, p. 21).

Mechanical jurisprudence traces its roots at least as far back as the eighteenth-century jurist Sir William Blackstone, who wrote that judges "are the depositories of the laws; the living oracles who must decide all cases of doubt" (Blackstone 1979, p. 69). They are sworn

to determine, not according to (their) own private judgment, but according to the known laws and customs of the land; not delegated to pronounce a new law, but to maintain and expound the old one. Yet this rule admits of exception, where the former determination is most evidently contrary to reason; much more if it be clearly contrary to the divine law. But even in such cases the subsequent judges do not pretend to make a new law, but to vindicate the old law from misrepresentation. For if it be found that the former decision is manifestly absurd or unjust, it is declared, not that such a sentence was *bad law*, but that it was *not law*. (pp. 69–70)

If Blackstone's following among legal scholars has waned, his following among judges has not. No history of mechanical jurisprudence would be complete without Justice Roberts's statement for the Court in *U.S. v. Butler* (1936):

It is sometimes said that the court assumes a power to overrule or control the action of the people's representatives. This is a misconception. The Constitution is the supreme law of the land ordained and established by the people. All legislation must conform to the principles it lays down. When an act of Congress is appropriately challenged in the courts as not conforming to the constitutional mandate, the judicial branch of Government has only one duty, to lay the article of the Constitution which is invoked beside the statute which is challenged and to decide whether the latter squares with the former. (p. 62)

Though it might be difficult to find modern legal scholars who believe that this is all judges do,[10] it is not difficult to find modern justices who so profess. In one recent case, Justice Scalia declared, "To hold a governmental act to be unconstitutional is not to announce that we forbid it, but that the *Constitution* forbids it" (*American Trucking Associations v. Smith*, p. 174).

> two legal principles are not "finely-tuned standards," comparable to the standards of proof beyond a reasonable doubt or of proof by a preponderance of the evidence.... They are instead fluid concepts that take their substantive content from the particular contexts in which the standards are being assessed. (*Ornelas v. United States* 1996, p. 918)

> To assert that the undefinable standard of proof beyond a reasonable doubt is nonetheless "finely tuned" accords with the mindset of those who believe that words speak more authoritatively than actions.

[10] Dworkin (1978, p. 16) argues that even Blackstone was not really a mechanical jurisprude.

Modern precedentialists instead often tend to fall into a category that can be called neolegalism. While recognizing that a variety of factors might influence the decisions of judges and justices, they still consider traditional legal factors, including adherence to precedent, to be important, if not primary.

We emphasize the writings of Ronald Dworkin, who is arguably this generation's preeminent legal theorist. Though Dworkin arguably emphasizes normative claims over empirical assertions, in fact he often intermixes the two, as we will see. In doing so, he represents the empirical side of the neolegalist position exceedingly well.

In *Taking Rights Seriously* (1978), Dworkin critiques legal positivism in general and the writings of H. L. A. Hart in particular. While Dworkin's larger goal is to demonstrate that certain rights inhere in civil society regardless of constitutional or statutory commands, his attack on positivism disputes the notion that judges are free to exercise discretion. While recognizing that precedent only inclines judges toward certain answers, rather than commands them, he nevertheless disputes the notion that judges are free to "pick and choose amongst the principles and policies that make up (this) doctrine" (p. 38), or that each judge applies "extra-legal" principles (e.g., no man shall profit from his own wrong) "according to his own lights" (p. 39). He insists instead that judges "do not have discretion in the matter of principles" (p. 47).

Precedent plays an important role in *Taking Rights Seriously* (Dworkin 1978, pp. 110–15; see also Dworkin 1986, p. viii, for a brief reflection on his precedential views in the earlier book), and needless to say that role is most important in hard cases, those where no preexisting rule of law exists. Dworkin argues that legal positivists err in claiming that judges legislate new rights in such cases, and again disputes the notion that in doing so they exercise discretion. "It remains the judge's duty, even in hard cases, to *discover* what the rights of the parties are, not to invent new rights retrospectively" (p. 81, emphasis added).

When a new case falls clearly within the scope of a previous decision, the earlier case has an "enactment force" that binds judges. But even when novel circumstances appear, earlier decisions exert a "gravitational force" on judges (p. 111). This is not mechanical jurisprudence, as judges may disagree as to what the gravitational force is. Yet to Dworkin, there is a *correct* answer to that question that judges must *find*. And though his theory of precedent requires that a judge's answer will "reflect his own intellectual and philosophical convictions in making that judgment, that is a very different matter from supposing that those convictions have some independent force in his argument just because they are his" (p. 118).[11]

Dworkin (1986) tells more or less the same story in *Law's Empire*. In hard cases, judges find the correct answer by discovering the most coherent explanation for the previous relevant cases.[12]

We do not wish to overstate Dworkin's position. He is not a pure legalist by any means. While the requirement of finding a fit between past cases and the current one will "eliminate interpretations that some judges would otherwise prefer, so that the brute facts of legal history will in this way limit the role any judge's personal concoctions can play in his decisions," "different judges will set this threshold differently" (1986, p. 255). Nor is he oblivious to institutional factors. Higher courts are generally exempt from strict precedent (1986, p. 401), the *obligation* to follow past decisions, but nevertheless are subject to the gravitational pull of weak precedent. Overall, though, the notions that there are correct answers to hard legal questions, that the judge's job is to find these answers, and that precedents constitute major guideposts of this search indicate a vital role for *stare decisis* in judicial decision making.

Though we have focused on the influential works of Ronald Dworkin, it is possible to illustrate more broadly (though not necessarily demonstrate) the primacy of precedent as an explanation of judicial decisions. To do so, we sought to determine how law review articles attempted to explain judicial decisions. We began by examining all articles published in 1993 by the *Columbia Law Review*, *Harvard Law Review*, *Michigan Law Review*, and *Yale Law Journal*. Because our interest was in explanations of judicial decisions, and not, for example, book reviews, proposed policy initiatives, and retrospectives on justices' careers, and so forth, we then selected all articles that contained the name of one or more judicial decisions in its title. Following the lead of Phelps and Gates (1991), who sampled the content of judicial opinions, we sampled the content of these articles in an attempt to find the focus of attempts to explain the decisions.[13] Though our sample size consists of only 31 paragraphs and was

[11] This quotation concerns Dworkin's mythical judge Hercules, but Dworkin applies the technique to human judges as well (p. 130). It might also be argued that we are turning a normative argument into an empirical one. In our defense, Dworkin frequently mixes and matches what he thinks judges actually do with what he thinks they ought to do. For example, "Judges are agreed that earlier decisions have gravitational force" (1978, p. 112) and "Judges characteristically feel an obligation to give what I call 'gravitational force' to past decisions" (Dworkin 1986, p. viii) are empirical statements, not normative ones.

[12] This, of course, assumes that even a single coherent explanation of a series of decisions by a series of judges over varying times and factual circumstances exists, much less a number of such explanations.

[13] We sampled the first paragraph of every tenth page of each relevant article.

not randomly selected, we are reasonably confident that the findings from different samples would not markedly change our conclusions. Briefly, of the nine paragraphs that attempted to explain the decision, seven and a half focused on previous cases, half focused on intent of the framers, and one focused on plain meaning.[14] Perhaps there is evidence that precedent is not the dominant explanation that law schools provide for judicial decisions, but we are unaware of it.

Legal Moderates

Support for precedent, though to a lesser degree, survives not just in Ronald Dworkin's world, but in that of a disparate set of modern legal scholars. While we do not review these scholars' works in detail, we note the following:

Bruce Ackerman's *We the People* argues that the Supreme Court's role in American history has been to provide a synthesis between constitutional transformations (such as that following the Civil War) and past practices (e.g., the Founders' Constitution). Thus, to Ackerman, the notorious *Lochner* decision (*Lochner v. New York* 1905) represents not conservative justices reaching conservative results, but justices "exercising a preservationist function, trying to develop a comprehensive synthesis of the meaning of the Founding and Reconstruction out of the available legal materials" (p. 101). Though Ackerman does not focus on precedent per se, these are among the legal materials that drive judicial decisions.

Herman Pritchett, who "blazed a trail" (Schubert 1963, p. v) that behavioral judicial scholars have followed for fifty years, retreated from his assumption that the justices' votes are "motivated by their own preferences" (Pritchett 1948, p. xii).

[P]olitical scientists, who have done so much to put the "political" in "political jurisprudence," need to emphasize that it is still "jurisprudence." It is judging in a political context, but it is still judging; and judging is still different from legislating or administering. Judges make choices, but they are not the "free" choices of congressmen. . . . There is room for much interpretation in the texts of constitutions, statutes, and ordinances, but the judicial function is still interpretation and not independent policy making. It is just as false to argue that judges freely exercise their discretion as to contend they have no policy functions at all. Any accurate analysis of judicial behavior must have as a major purpose a full clarification of the unique limiting conditions under which judicial policy making proceeds. (Pritchett 1969, p. 42)

---

[14] Most of the paragraphs (ten and a half) dealt with descriptions of the main case, five dealt with the impact of the decisions, three and a half dealt with scholarly opinion, two dealt with empirical findings, and one explained how a map was drawn.

Walter Murphy, the most influential strategic-choice scholar in judicial politics, argues from the viewpoint of institutional stability that "a tribunal that frequently reversed itself could not expect others to respect its decisions. Not surprisingly, then, *stare decisis* is the normal guide even in the Supreme Court. Overrulings come, but they come infrequently" (Murphy, Fleming, and Harris 1986, p. 308).[15] In a related vein, Knight and Epstein (1996) argue that following precedent is a legitimacy enhancing norm that must be observed, even by justices whose goal is to maximize their policy preferences. Indeed, we provide later, in the section on cooperative models, a simple game theoretic explanation why policy maximizing justices might follow precedents of which they disapproved in a repeated game.

Prominent positive political theorists, who typically conceive of justices as primarily interested in policy outcomes (see later discussion), clearly hold open the possibility that judges have legal considerations as goals, and not just constraints (Ferejohn and Weingast 1992).

We note as well that that other nonlegal scholars, including methodologically sophisticated behavioral scientists, also accept the operational accuracy of various tenets of the legal model, including precedent. Thus, one scholar has noted that "legal rules" are treated as producing "legal and normative constraints on judicial decisionmaking" (Knight 1994, p. 6), while another asserts that "judges apply a set of interpretive canons, a set of principles that guide them in interpreting the Constitution, statutes, precedent, and derive an outcome. They are driven not by outcomes but by interpretive philosophy" (Rosenberg 1994, p. 7). As for specific references to precedent, Knight and Epstein (1996) argue that precedent constrains Supreme Court decision making; Brenner and Stier (1996) claim that precedent influences at least the Court's center justices; while Songer and Lindquist (1996) assert that precedent typically controls the justices' policy positions.

Cooperative Models. Returning to Murphy's approach, what we find most interesting is his view that justices support *stare decisis* not because they normatively feel that they ought to, but because the long-term survival of their policy goals depends on it. In the following paragraphs we provide an alternative mechanism whereby respect for *stare decisis* could evolve among policy motivated justices.

Respect for precedent could evolve not out of any inherent desire to defer to the past, but through cooperative behavior among justices. To

---

[15] See Epstein and Knight (1997) for a presentation of the institutional stability argument in greater detail.

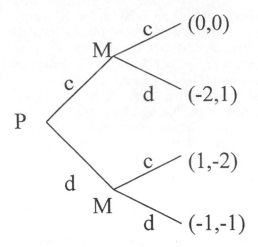

Figure 1.1. The precedent game.

see how this might work, we start with two hypothetical justices, whom we'll call Murphy and Pritchett. Assume that overturning any particular precedent involves some small institutional loss in prestige and/or legitimacy, or that Murphy and Pritchett, like virtually all human decision makers, subjectively feel that losses weigh more than gains (Kahneman and Tversky 1979, 1984; Tversky and Kahneman 1986). Thus, other factors being equal, they prefer saving a precedent they like to overturning one they dislike. Now let's say that there are two precedents that will be overturned unless Murphy and Pritchett cooperate (*c*), one that Murphy likes and one that Pritchett likes. Figure 1.1 presents the games and the payoffs, where Pritchett first votes on the precedent that Murphy likes, and Murphy subsequently votes on the precedent that Pritchett likes. We assume as part of this game that Murphy and Pritchett will each vote for his own favored precedent.

The first bracketed number at the end of each branch represents Pritchett's payoff; the second represents Murphy's. If both players cooperate (i.e., vote to uphold each other's precedents), then the status quo is maintained and each receives a payoff of 0. If Pritchett cooperates but Murphy defects, Pritchett maintains the status quo on his bad precedent (payoff = 0) and loses his good precedent (payoff = −2) for a total payoff of −2. Murphy gains as his bad precedent is overturned (payoff = 1) and he retains the status quo on the good precedent (payoff = 0) for a total payoff of 1.

If both players defect, both precedents are overturned, leading to a +1 payoff for the bad precedent, a −2 payoff for the good precedent, and a total payoff of −1 for each player.

If Pritchett defects but Murphy cooperates, the payoffs are symmetrical to Pritchett's cooperating and Murphy's defecting, as discussed.

Pritchett could cooperate (*c*) and vote for Murphy's favored precedent under an implicit or explicit, but in any event nonbinding, understanding that Murphy would reciprocate in the next round; or he could defect (*d*) and vote his own preferences in that case. But if Murphy goes last, there is nothing that would necessarily keep him to his word. And if Pritchett did not trust Murphy, Pritchett wouldn't cooperate in the first vote. The backward-induced equilibrium of this game is (*d*, *d*), with both players ending up with a payoff of −1.[16] Indeed, as long as the number of cases is known and finite, formal theoretical results demonstrate a lack of cooperation from the first move (Morrow 1994, p. 157). This result may seem counterintuitive, but it is crucial that the theoretical results do not hold when the game does not have a definite end (ibid.).[17] Thus, in repeated games, cooperation can readily evolve even when the players do not trust each other (Axelrod 1984).

The fact that cooperation can evolve does not necessarily mean that it will last (Bendor and Swistak 1997). Court changes that place dissenters into majority positions may lead to justices' having more to gain than lose from overturning precedents. Or cooperation could break down once a justice has decided to leave the Court. Under these and other such circumstances, precedential cooperation could quickly erode (see also Walker, Epstein, and Dixon 1988).

Preferential Models

In contrast to the precedential and moderate models, we examine the jurisprudential theories that would not expect much support for precedent, beginning with those of the legal realists (Frank 1930; Llewellyn 1951).

Legal Realism. The realist movement grew from the works of John Chipman Gray (1931) and Oliver Wendell Holmes (1897), who argued

---

[16] If Pritchett first cooperated, Murphy would still have an incentive to defect, preferring a payoff of 1 to a payoff of 0. That would leave Pritchett with −2, which is worse than any outcome he could have obtained by defecting. And if Pritchett does defect on the first move, Murphy is better off defecting and receiving a payoff of −1 than cooperating and receiving a payoff of −2.

[17] We might also point out that in long-term but finite games, experimental research demonstrates that the results do not hold either (Morrow 1994, p. 157).

that the reigning orthodoxy, mechanical jurisprudence, poorly described what judges actually did. The leaders of the resulting movement found discretion and choice inhering in all levels of judicial decision making. According to Karl Llewellyn, the first principle of legal realism is the "conception of law in flux, of moving law, and of judicial creation of law" (Llewellyn 1931, p. 1237).

Judicial creation of law did not result because bad jurists sought power for themselves, but was inevitable fallout from an ever-changing society. According to Jerome Frank:

The layman thinks that it would be possible so to revise the law books that they would be something like logarithm tables, that the lawyers could, if only they would, contrive some kind of legal slide-rule for finding exact legal answers. . . .

But the law as we have it is uncertain, indefinite, subject to incalculable changes. This condition the public ascribes to the men of law; the average person considers either that lawyers are grossly negligent or that they are guilty of malpractice, venally obscuring simple legal truths in order to foment needless litigation, engaging in a guild conspiracy of distortion and obfuscation in the interest of larger fees. . . .

Yet the layman errs in his belief that this lack of precision and finality is to be ascribed to lawyers. The truth of the matter is that the popular notion of the possibilities of legal exactness is based upon a misconception. The law always has been, is now, and will ever continue to be, largely vague and variable. And how could this be otherwise? The law deals with human relations in their most complicated aspects. The whole confused, shifting helter-skelter of life parades before it – more confused than ever, in our kaleidoscopic age.

Even in a relatively static society, men have never been able to construct a comprehensive, eternalized set of rules anticipating all possible legal disputes and settling them in advance. Even in such a social order no one can foresee all the future permutations and combinations of events; situations are bound to occur which were never contemplated when the original rules were made. How much less is such a frozen legal system possible in modern times. . . . Our society would be straight-jacketed were not the courts, with the able assistance of lawyers, constantly overhauling the law and adapting it to the realities of ever-changing social, industrial and political conditions. (Frank 1949, pp. 5–7)

If judges necessarily create law, how do they come to their decisions? To the legal realists, the answer clearly is not to be found in "legal rules and concepts insofar as they purport to *describe* what either courts or people are actually doing" (Llewellyn 1931, p. 1237). According to Frank:

the judge often arrives at his decision before he tries to explain it. . . . After the judge has so decided, then the judge writes his "opinion." The D[ecision] has been fixed. The judge's problem is now to find an R[ule] and an F[acts] that will equal this already determined D. . . .

Opinions then, disclose little of how judges come to their conclusions. . . .

How then does a judge arrive at his decision? In terse terms, he does so by a "hunch" as to what is fair and just and wise and expedient. (1932, pp. 652–55)

Judicial opinions containing such rules merely rationalize decisions; they are not the cause of them.

Without clear answers to how judges actually made decisions, the legal realists called for an empirical, scientific study of law (Yntema 1934), taking as dictum the statement of Oliver Wendell Holmes, Jr., that "the prophecies of what courts will do in fact, and nothing more pretentious, are what I mean by law" (Holmes 1897, pp. 460–61). "The object of our study, then, is prediction" (p. 457). Thus as far back as 1922 we can find Charles Grove Haines creating quantitative evidence on judicial behavior, noting, for example, that while one judge dismissed 79 percent of intoxication cases, another discharged but 18 percent (Haines 1922, pp. 105–6), concluding that "the process of judicial decision is determined to a considerable extent by the judges' views of fair play, public policy, and their general consensus as to what is right and wrong" (p. 106).

Haines found discretion pushed "to its utmost limits" in constitutional law, where "the conclusions reached were largely controlled by influences, opinions, and prejudices to which the justices had been subjected" (p. 107).

Critical Legal Theory. So too do the modern day critical legal studies proponents remain completely unpersuaded by arguments that discretion is anything but complete in judicial decision making. For example, Tushnet (1988) argues, as have more mainstream analysts and jurists (e.g., Brennan 1985), that originalist history, devotion to the intent of the Framers, "requires definite answers (because it is part of a system in which judgment is awarded to one side or another) and clear ones (because it seeks to constrain judges)" (p. 36). Yet "the universal experience of historians belies the originalist effort" (ibid.).

Of more immediate interest to us is critical thought on precedent. Precedent, it seems, is no more tractable to Crits than it is to realists:

At the moment a decision is announced we cannot identify the principle that it embodies. Each decision can be justified by many principles, and we learn what principle justified Case 1 only when a court in Case 2 tells us. . . . The theory of neutral principles thus loses almost all of its constraining force. We have only to compare Case 2, which is now decided, to Case 1 to see if a principle from Case 1 has been neutrally applied in Case 2. If the demand is merely that the opinion in Case 2 deploy some reading of the earlier case from which the holding in Case 2 follows, the openness of the precedents means that the demand can always be satisfied. And if the demand is rather that the holding be derived from the principles actually articulated in the relevant precedents, differences between Case 2 and the precedents will inevitably demand a degree of reinterpretation of the old principles. New cases always present issues different from those settled by prior cases. Thus, to decide a new case a judge must take some liberties with the old principles if they are to be applied at all. There is, however, no principled way to determine how many liberties can be taken; hence this reading of the theory provides no meaningful constraints. (Tushnet 1988, pp. 49–50)

What then distinguishes the Crits from the realists, for our purposes, is not their view of the validity of the legal model, but the purposes to which justices with discretion act. It is typically the case that Crits expect to find a conservative, if not reactionary bias to the Court's decisions (Kairys 1982). According to Tushnet, "Law in a class society is a form of incomplete hegemony of the ruling class" (Tushnet 1979, p. 1346). To Gabel (1980), "legal thought originates within the consciousness of the dominant class" (p. 26). This does not necessarily result from the mere conservative bias of judges but through legal consciousness itself, conceptions of what law is, and how it is to be derived (Kennedy 1980).

Neoinstitutionalism. Next we examine neoinstitutional theories, which argue that the degree of discretion exercised by judges is determined at least in part by their institutional environment. For example, the decision that a state supreme court judge facing reelection makes in a prominent death penalty case might not be the same decision she would make if she were a life tenured federal judge (Brace and Hall 1990). Nor would the decision of a life tenured lower court federal judge subject to higher court reversal necessarily be the same as her decision if she were on the Supreme Court (Songer, Segal, and Cameron 1994).

One neoinstitutional theory, the attitudinal model, argues that the peculiar institutional factors facing the Supreme Court allow the justices almost always to vote their sincere policy preferences in the decision on the merits. Five institutionally related factors stand out to help the justices do so.

First, the justices have life tenure. Like other federal judges, but unlike most state judges, Supreme Court justices cannot be removed from office for unpopular decisions (Rohde and Spaeth 1976, p. 72; Segal and Spaeth 1993, pp. 69–71).

Second, there is no court above the Supreme Court that can overrule it (Rohde and Spaeth p. 72; Segal and Spaeth pp. 71–72). Thus, while federal district court judges must constrain their policy preferences to prevent being overturned by the courts of appeals, and federal circuit court judges must constrain their policy preferences to prevent being overturned by the Supreme Court, Supreme Court justices have no similar concerns.

Third, Supreme Court justices typically, if not exclusively in the modern era, lack ambition for higher office (Rohde and Spaeth 1976, pp. 72–73; Segal and Spaeth 1993, p. 71). Empirical evidence amply demonstrates that ambition can alter sincere behavior (Schlesinger

1966). Alternatively, the absence of higher ambition "means that personal policy preferences are more freely expressed" (Rohde and Spaeth 1976, p. 72).

Fourth, the Supreme Court has docket control and thus can weed out legally frivolous cases. The legal realists argue that all judicial decisions tender plausible legal arguments on both sides,[18] allowing all judges to render decisions based on their personal policy preferences. Segal and Spaeth, alternatively, allow that legally frivolous cases that no judges could decide on the basis of their policy preferences no doubt exist (1993, p. 70).[19] Such cases, though, could never make it past the Court's screening process.

Fifth, though Congress can override the Court's statutory interpretation decisions, several factors lessen the likelihood that Congress will or could react to such situations:[20] the median justice usually is located within the set of irreversible decisions; the Court can counter congressional overrides if it so chooses by reinterpreting the override; opportunity and transaction costs make override unlikely; and finally, the Court lacks the information it needs to know when it would have to trim its sails to avoid override (Segal 1997).

Another neoinstitutional theory, the separation-of-powers (SOP) theory, typically agrees with the attitudinal notion that justices are motivated primarily, if not exclusively, by their policy preferences. Where the proponents of this approach (who are typically known as positive political theorists) differ from the attitudinalists is their notion that the political environment places far greater constraints on the Supreme Court than attitudinalists allow. Thus, according to the SOP theory, justices will attempt to make decisions not at their ideal points, but as close as possible to their ideal points without getting overturned (Eskridge 1991; Epstein and Knight 1997).

Figure 1.2 provides an illustration of the model. In this example, the House (*H*), Senate (*S*), and Court (*C*) all have ideal points that represent their preferred outcome of a two-dimensional policy issue. The game is played as follows: First, the Court makes a decision in ($x1$, $x2$) policy

---

[18] Support for this position can be found in economic theories of law. The federal judge Frank Easterbrook rhetorically asked Linda Greenhouse of the *New York Times*, "Given that litigation is so expensive, why are parties willing to take their cases up? It's because precedent doesn't govern. Precedent covers the major premise. But the mindset of the judge covers the minor premise" (Greenhouse 1988, p. 12).

[19] In partial answer to Easterbrook, even when the law is clear, losing parties might endure the cost of litigation in order to delay adverse civil and criminal rulings.

[20] In his dissent in *Burnet v. Coronado Oil & Gas Co.* (1932, pp. 406–9), Brandeis identified forty instances in which the Court altered statutory precedents that Congress could have corrected but did not.

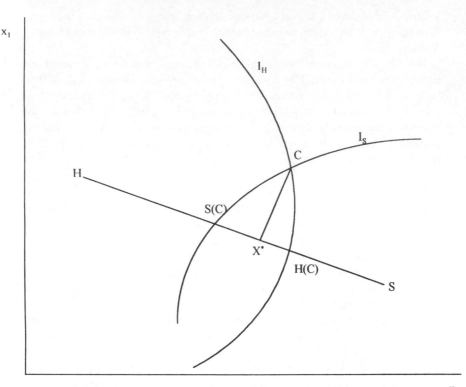

Figure 1.2. The separation of powers model: H = House ideal point; S = Senate ideal point; C = Court ideal point; I_H = House indifference curve; I_S = Senate indifference curve; S(C) = Point on Pareto Optimals where Senate is indifferent to Court ideal point; H(C) = Point on Pareto Optimals where House is indifferent to Court ideal point; X* = equilibrium.

space. Second, the House and Senate can override the Court decision if they can agree on an alternative. The line segment *HS* represents "the set of Pareto Optimals." That is, no decision on that line can be overturned by Congress, because improving the position of one player by moving closer to its ideal point necessarily worsens the position of the other. Alternatively, any decision off *HS*, call it x, can be overturned, because there will necessarily be at least one point on *HS* that both *H* and *S* prefer to x. Imagine, for example, a decision at the Court's ideal point, *C*. The arc I_S represents those points where the Senate is indifferent to the Court's decision. And obviously, the Senate prefers any point inside the arc to any point on the arc (or, obviously, outside the arc).

Similarly, I_H represents those points where the House is indifferent to the Court's decision. Thus, both the House and the Senate prefer any point between $S(C)$ (the point on the set of Pareto Optimals where the Senate is indifferent to the Court's decision) and $H(C)$ (the point on the set of Pareto Optimals where the House is indifferent to the Court's decision) to a decision at C.

If the assumptions of this model are correct, then if the Court rules at its ideal point, or indeed anyplace off the set of Pareto Optimals, Congress will overturn the Court's decision and replace it with something that is necessarily worse from the Court's perspective. For example, if the Court rules at C, then Congress's result will be someplace between $S(C)$ and $H(C)$. The trick for the Court is to find the point on the set of Pareto Optimals that is closest to its ideal point. By the Pythagorean theorem, it accomplishes this by dropping a perpendicular onto the line. Thus, rather than voting sincerely at C and ending up with a policy someplace between $S(C)$ and $H(C)$, the Court rules at X^*, the point between $S(C)$ and $H(C)$, indeed, the point between H and S, that it most prefers.

Thus, unlike in the attitudinal model, in the separation-of-powers game justices cannot always vote their sincere policy preferences. But even when they must cast votes off their policy preferences, they are simply concerned with placating Congress and are not influenced by previous decisions per se. Thus we might see occasional flips in voting positions as the political environment changes, but as in the attitudinal model we would not expect systematic deference to precedent.

THEORETICAL EXPECTATIONS

These models obviously were not derived with our particular tests in mind, so sharp distinctions as to what we would expect under each model do not exist. Thus while low levels of precedential voting would not invalidate precedential models, they would make it less likely that such models are true. Similarly, low levels of precedential voting would not prove that any of the preferential models are true, but would make it more likely that such models captured something useful about Supreme Court decision making.

In the following chapter we will establish specific decision rules for determining whether a justice's decision in any particular case was influenced by precedent. With such rules, we can determine for any justice his or her level of support for precedent. If we seek to apply these results to our models, we must recognize that where we set cutoffs for support for our various models is perhaps arbitrary. But if we have models suggesting high, medium, and low support, it is arguably least arbitrary to set the levels as follows: 0–33 percent as low levels, thus supporting preferential models; 34–67 percent as moderate levels, thus supporting the legal moderates; and 68–100 percent as high levels, thus supporting the precedential models.

Needless to say, this does not cover all jurisprudential theories. We leave to others far braver than we are to determine what hermeneuticists, aestheticists, and others might argue. Nor are our tests definitive; we expect, rather, that they will provide evidence for the continuing evaluation of such models.

2
Measuring Precedential Behavior

Our goal for this book is to determine the extent to which precedent influences the decisions of Supreme Court justices. We start with the proposition that "influence" requires people to do what they otherwise would not. Just as friends, neighbors, and spouses cannot influence you to vote for a Presidential candidate you would have voted for anyway, we cannot find precedential influence among justices who would have supported a particular position even without the prior existence of that precedent. In terms of our research, this means that we cannot claim that justices who joined the original majority that established a precedent decided future cases as a result of that precedent. Moreover, while justices who joined the Court after the establishment of a precedent could be influenced by that precedent in future cases, we cannot know what their prior preferences were. We only can make a relatively clean inference for those justices who opposed the establishment of the precedent in the original case. Their original preferences conflict with the precedent, so if they subsequently support the precedent, we can make a strong presumption, or at least a prima facie case, that the established precedent influenced their votes.

In this chapter we explain how we will determine whether the decisions of the justices more closely represent preferential behavior or more closely represent precedential behavior. This requires an elaboration of two sets of decision rules: how to determine the progeny of a case and how to evaluate the decisions of the relevant justices in those progeny. We begin, though, with a discussion of our sampling of cases.

SAMPLING PRECEDENTS

If our goal is to examine the decisions of the justices in the progeny of established precedents, we must sample the precedents that we examine.

Major Decisions

We initially limit our search for progeny to those that pertain to the Court's major decisions. We do so because major cases are most likely to be cited as precedents and hence most likely to spawn progeny. We operationalize major cases quite simply as those listed in Congressional Quarterly's *Guide to the U.S. Supreme Court* as "Major Decisions."[1] While no list is definitive, Witt's is more broadly based than others and has been employed in earlier research (Segal and Spaeth 1996a). Common alternatives, such as constitutional law books, almost completely ignore statutory cases. We exclude from Witt's list unanimously decided cases. Only dissenters can experience conflict between their stated preferences and the precedent the majority established in that case.[2]

Because the number of landmark cases on Witt's list is manageable for a book-length project, we sampled 100 percent of the cases with dissent.

Minor Decisions

While the Court's decisions in the progeny of landmark cases form the backbone of our study, we would be remiss if we did not attempt to ascertain whether our findings are generalizable to run-of-the-mill cases.

Because the Court has decided thousands of cases with dissent (Epstein, Segal, Spaeth, and Walker 1994, ch. 3), sampling becomes necessary. Though the ideal would be a pure random sample, two factors prevent this. First, dissent rates vary substantially across the Court's history. Several terms during the Court's first half century contain no cases with dissent, while in recent years as many as three-quarters of all cases have contained dissents (ibid.). Second, to our knowledge, there exists no published source or sources where the population of all cases with dissent can readily be obtained. To solve these problems, we rely on a stratified random sample using multiple methods.

[1] Elder Witt, *Guide to the U.S. Supreme Court* (Washington, D.C.: Congressional Quarterly Press, 1990), pp. 883–929.

[2] Because Witt mistakenly identifies certain cases as containing dissents, while indicating that others are unanimous, we have independently checked all items on her list. Thus, she lists McKenna and Pitney as dissenters in *Brushaber v. UP R. Co.* (1916); they dissented in the succeeding case, but *Brushaber* was only an opinion of the Court. In *Wood v. Broom* (1932), the four justices specified as dissenting actually specially concurred. Conversely, Justice Johnson partially dissented in *Fletcher v. Peck* (1810). In other cases, Witt incorrectly identifies the dissenters, for example, *Aptheker v. Secretary of State* (1964) and *Harper v. Virginia State Board of Elections* (1966), which were decided by 6 to 3 rather than 7 to 2 votes, while the vote in *Duncan v. Louisiana* (1968) was 7 to 2 rather than 8 to 1.

Perusal of the Epstein et al. (1994) data on dissents suggests three periods within which to sample: 1793 through 1867, when the Court rarely issued more than ten dissents per term; 1868 through 1936, when dissent rates increased to moderate levels; and 1937 through the present, when high levels of dissent are the norm.[3] For the most recent period, we simply took a 1 percent random sample of all cases with dissent from Spaeth's U.S. Supreme Court Judicial Database (including the Vinson Court), supplemented by data collected by Epstein, Mershon, Segal, and Spaeth (NSF grant SBR-9320509) on the 1936 through 1945 terms.

Prior to 1936, creating a sample of cases with dissent proves more difficult, as there are no preexisting databases to use. Instead, we searched HoweData's electronic U.S. Reports for all cases that used the words "dissent," "dissenting," or "dissented." The search yielded 500 cases in the first period (1793–1867) and 2,119 cases in the second period (1868–1936). We then examined about 200 of the cases, finding that about 85 percent of them actually contain dissents. We set as our goal a 100-case sample for each period, so we randomly selected a 120-case sample from each. Though we focus on the progeny of landmark cases, we will examine the progeny of these ordinary cases as well.

IDENTIFICATION OF PROGENY

With our 100 percent sample of landmark cases with dissent and our stratified sample of ordinary cases with dissent, we must now determine what the progeny of these cases are.[4]

We treat as progeny decisions subsequent to the precedent whose issue(s) and factual circumstances closely resemble those of the precedent itself. While factual *identity* between cases never occurs, especially at the Supreme Court level, correspondence between the legal provisions on which the decision rests and the policy questions at issue does obtain, as do varying degrees of factual *similarity*. Determination of the connection between a precedent and succeeding decisions is, of course, far from an exact science. Nonetheless, we believe that the procedures described in the following discussion enable us to specify reasonably accurately the decisions that substantially rely on a particular previously

---

[3] On the basis of the data alone, we might have split the second and third periods at 1941 or so (Walker, Epstein, and Dixon 1988), but 1937 begins the modern era of Supreme Court decision making and coincides with reliable data on the cases containing dissents (see later discussion).

[4] Note that we use the word "progeny" unconventionally to mean only cases in which dissenters from the precedent cast a subsequent vote in a case that qualifies as a "progeny" according to the criteria we specify in this chapter.

decided case. Readers who remain dubious about the adequacy of our procedures will find the progeny of each precedent listed in the various tables of Chapters 3–8. These tables, of course, omit cases that we do not consider progeny. Readers who wish to check our accuracy in this regard may do so by using LEXIS to identify the pages in the Court's Reports that *Shepard's Citations* references. As explained later, this is the source we use to identify progeny.

We begin explication of progeny by limiting consideration to orally argued decisions.[5] We primarily rely on the case syllabus, or summary. A reference therein to a previous decision generally qualifies it as a precedent,[6] but not always. Some syllabi cite a case only because the lower

[5]   While this seems a fairly obvious step, two published sets of criticisms (Brenner and Stier 1996; Songer and Lindquist 1996) argue that such procedures bias our sample by excluding summary decisions. These critics base their argument on the plausible but false notion that summary dispositions are simply smaller versions of full decisions and can be treated as such.

The overwhelming majority of the summary decisions that reach the merits of the case are summary reversals without opinions. On the rarest of occasions the Court may issue summary affirmances as well. Additionally, on "rare and exceptional occasions" (Stern, Gressman, and Shapiro 1986, p. 281), the Court issues per curiam decisions. In these, the Court disposes of the merits of the case without briefing or oral argument. The Court does produce a short per curiam opinion discussing the facts of the case, the issue or issues involved, and the rationale for its decision. These cases usually involve lower court decisions that are so clearly erroneous that briefing the case is a waste of time. The problem with including summary reversals is that one cannot tell how the justices voted in the case from the reversal order. As Baum notes, "The dearth of recorded dissents in summary cases . . . may indicate only an accepted Court practice of eschewing dissents in summary cases" (1997, ch. 3).

Also included in the types of cases Brenner/Stier and Songer/Lindquist believe we should have included are grant–vacate–remand (GVR) cases, which are also known as summary reconsideration orders or "hold" cases. Not only are these dispositions not minutely sized versions of full decisions, they do not even dispose of the merits of the case. We share this view with (1) the leading authority on summary decisions: "This kind of summary order and the process by which it came about bears no resemblance to merits decisions and the process that leads to them" (Epstein 1996, 4); (2) the leading authority on Supreme Court practice and procedure: "it seems fairly clear that the Court does not treat the summary reconsideration order as the functional equivalent of the summary reversal order" (Stern, Gressman, and Shapiro 1986, p. 280); and (3) the justices themselves: GVR orders are an "appropriate exercise of our *certiorari* jurisdiction," and "It is not customary, but quite rare, to record dissents from *certiorari*, including 'GVR's'" (*Lawrence v. Chater* 1996, 553, 568). And even if we chose to mix apples and oranges by including nonmeritorious decisions, we might find the deck stacked against precedent. Under such a decision rule we would have to include the *thousands* of opinions written by Brennan and Marshall during the Burger Court alone adhering to their dissenting position in the death penalty case, *Gregg v. Georgia* (1976), as well as the more than 400 opinions written between 1973 and 1975 supporting the dissents in the obscenity case *Paris Adult Theatre I v. Slaton* (1973).

[6]   Reference to a test or rule does not qualify a case as a precedent unless the test or rule is used synonymously, for instance, *Plessy v. Ferguson* and the separate but equal doctrine.

court relied on it in reaching its decision. Other cases are distinguished in such a way that the prevailing opinion treats them as irrelevant to its decision. Apart from being distinguished, a case may differ sufficiently from the issue addressed in the precedent to warrant exclusion. Thus, for example, the syllabus of *Griffith v. Kentucky* (1987) makes four separate references to *Batson v. Kentucky* (1986). Yet *Griffith* lacks the status of progeny for our purposes because it turns on the matter of *Batson's* retroactivity, a consideration completely absent from the *Batson* opinions themselves. Finally, syllabi occasionally reference a precedent only as an item in a string of citations. Thus, *Crowell v. Randell* (1836) cites the precedent *Craig v. Missouri* (1830) as one of a string of thirteen cases, all of which pertain to Section 25 of the Judiciary Act of 1789, a matter peripheral to the ruling in *Craig*.

LEXIS and Shepard's Citations

The absence of an appearance in the syllabus does not necessarily disqualify a case as a precedent even for the justices joining the prevailing opinion in the progeny. How, then, do we ascertain what cases may be progeny of our precedents? We do so by using LEXIS to identify the pages in the various editions of the Court's Reports that cite the precedent. *Shepard's Citations*, the most widely used and the most authoritative citator, provide these data.[7]

Notwithstanding its reputation, *Shepard's* is not fully accurate. It does not include shorthand citations to decided cases. Typically, it lists only those in which the full name of the case appears, as distinct from textual references to only the petitioner or the respondent. And occasionally it even overlooks the full cite. Thus, citations to *Monell v. New York City Dept. of Social Services* (1978) neither reference 480 U.S. 266, *Springfield v. Kibbe* (1987), which contains the formal title, nor 267 or 268, where the case is identified only as *Monell*. Indeed, one egregious example, *First National Bank v. Bellotti* (1978), lacked any reference in *Austin v. Michigan State Chamber of Commerce* (1990), even though an earlier LEXIS search produced nine separate citations. More distressing, however, are the failure of *Shepard's* to include *Harlow v. Fitzgerald* (1982), among the cases citing *Nixon v. Fitzgerald* (1982), notwithstanding that *Harlow* actually cites *Nixon* on 14 different pages, and the failure of *Texas v. Johnson*, the flag desecration case, to reference *United States v. Eichman* (1990), its sequel, even though *Johnson* is mentioned on

---

[7] On the use of *Shepard's Citations*, see Melone (1990, pp. 26–30). For a discussion of their validity and reliability, see Kemper (1998).

every page of the *Eichman* majority opinion and all but one page of the dissent!

Because LEXIS at the time of our search infrequently cited any decision beyond volume 492 of the *United States Reports*, the last volume of the 1988 term, we supplement citations to the official reports with those LEXIS provides to the *Lawyers' Edition*. These, however, do not appear to be systematically listed. Some decisions are cited to the current term; others appear to omit at least a portion of cases decided during the 1990s. Nonetheless, citations are sufficiently numerous that the omission of some of the more recent decisions does not plausibly skew our findings. Its only effect is that we lack progeny with which to assess the behavior of the most recently appointed justices: Kennedy, Souter, Thomas, Ginsburg, and Breyer.

In our search for progeny, we especially focus on those citations that contain an entry in the *Shepard's* analysis column, particularly if the entry reads "followed," "questioned," or "overruled."[8] We also examine all the other entries that *Shepard's* uses. Except for "dissenting opinion," all of these others – "explained," "distinguished" – pertain to the prevailing opinion. No separate reference, for example, appears for concurring opinions. We also examine all citations to which *Shepard's* lists at least two unidentified entries – those without any entry in the *Shepard's* analysis column. We so restrict our examination of the unidentified entries for two reasons. First, a single entry will not likely warrant a syllabus reference, and second, it will likely be part of a string of citations, thereby further minimizing any controlling impact the cited case may putatively have. However, because of the paucity of Supreme Court citations found in the decisions of the Marshall Court and its predecessors, we did examine all *Shepard's* entries without exception for cases decided prior to the January 1836 term.

Not uncommonly, a single precedent may produce more than a hundred citations; *Gregg v. Georgia* (1976), for example, lists more than 700. Because of the time it took to determine whether the cases cited by *Shepard's* qualified as a progeny of Witt's (1990) nonunanimous precedents, no fixed concluding date governs our research. Cases Shepardized earlier are less current than those Shepardized most recently. We are confident these differences do not affect the validity of our findings. Minimizing these differences is the fact that our operational definition of progeny is time bound. When no dissenter from the precedent remains

---

[8] "Followed" doesn't necessarily mean adhered to. It may merely indicate that a lower court or even a nonjudicial official verbalized the Court's ruling, for example, *United States v. Watson* (1976), at 413, where postal inspectors read the defendant the *Miranda* warnings.

on the Court, inquiry ceases even though the precedent is extensively cited thereafter. Hence, any impact from this procedure affects only the Rehnquist Court and the Burger Court holdovers, Stevens and O'Connor, in addition to Rehnquist himself. To control for this situation, we analyzed the Rehnquist Court most recently.

Progeny as Precedents

Our decision rules do not preclude a case from being a precedent for certain progeny, and for those progeny to serve as precedents for still other progeny. Given the Court's penchant for citing more recent cases in a line of precedents, rather than the original ones, as authority for its decisions, progeny readily become precedents themselves. Moreover, nothing precludes a given case from serving as progeny for more than a single precedent, for example, *Allegheny County v. Greater Pittsburgh ACLU* (1989) as a progeny of *Lynch v. Donnelly* (1984), as well as *Wallace v. Jaffree* (1985). *Allegheny County* itself serves as precedent for four progeny: *Westside Community Board of Education v. Mergens* (1990), *Lee v. Weisman* (1992), *Kiryas Joel Board of Education v. Grumet* (1994), and *Capital Square Review Board v. Pinette* (1995).

Though a precedent is not identified in the syllabus, we nonetheless consider it such if the majority or prevailing opinion emphasizes the precedent as impacting its decision. Thus, we consider the seven distinct page references in *New York v. Burger* (1987) to *Marshall v. Barlow's Inc.* (1978) more than sufficient to make *Burger Barlow's* progeny. We reach the same conclusion because of the six separate page references to *Davis v. Passman* (1979) in *United States v. Stanley* (1987). Needless to say, it is less likely that a precedent on which a dissenting or concurring opinion rests will find its way into the case syllabus unless the prevailing opinion also focuses on it.

Issue Identity

We do not require the issue in a progeny to be on all fours with that in the precedent. The greater the issue identity the less the need for unequivocal references that the previously decided case controls the outcome in the case we are considering as a progeny. Where issue discrepancy prevails, we require greater verbal dependence on the precedent as the basis for the special opinion. Thus, Harlan's dissenting opinion and that of White in *Miranda v. Arizona*, a self-incrimination case, served as the basis for Harlan's and Stewart's votes in *Schmerber v. California* (1966), which involved no testimonial privilege. Similarly, Stewart relied on

Miranda as authority for his dissent in the juvenile case, *In re Gault* (1967), while Clark used his *Miranda* dissent as authority for adhering to precedent in *United States v. Wade* (1967), a police line-up case.

On the other hand, the fact that a subsequent decision addresses the same issue as a case referenced in its syllabus does not necessarily make the referenced case a precedent. Again, *Batson* illustrates. Clearly, *Edmonson v. Leesville Concrete Co.* (1991) and *Georgia v. McCollum* (1992) also pertain to racially based peremptory challenges. But the opinion in Edmonson that the only holdover dissenter from *Batson* joined – Justice Rehnquist – makes absolutely no reference to *Batson*, while his concurrence in *McCullom* references only *Edmonson.*[9]

Miscellaneous Criteria

If we find on the basis of these criteria that the syllabus and/or majority opinion creates a progeny of the original decision, then we attempt to evaluate the behavior of all justices who dissented from the original opinion, whether or not they joined the majority or prevailing opinion of the progeny. But if a concurring or dissenting justice reaches her decision on grounds unrelated to the precedent, then that justice's vote cannot be evaluated: thus, the votes of Justices Brown and White in *Spreckels Sugar Refining Co. v. McClain* (1904), a progeny of the Income Tax Case, *Pollock v. Farmers' Loan and Trust Co.* (1895). They did not address the question of direct taxation, but rather the finality of the lower court's decision.

As a further example, imagine that Justice Stewart was on the Court and had dissented from *Wolf v. Colorado* (1949). His opinion in *Mapp v. Ohio* (1961), striking the conviction on First and Fourteenth Amendment grounds, could not have been evaluated as a progeny of *Wolf*. Nevertheless, concurring and dissenting justices who do not mention the precedent, but decide the case on the same issues as the majority, will be evaluated in terms of the precedent. In other words, not all the dissenters from a precedent will necessarily treat a subsequent decision as a progeny. Some of them may consider other cases as precedential, with the result that they view the case before them as progeny to these other cases, rather than the one deemed precedential by their

---

[9]   Viewing Rehnquist's opinion in *Edmonson* as a self-contained entity rather than a regular concurrence, his vote would count as preference rather than precedent, but because he joined the Court's opinion, which did rest on *Batson*, we count it as adhering to precedent: "I was in dissent in Edmonson ... and continue to believe that case to have been wrongly decided. But so long as it remains the law, I believe that it controls the disposition of this case" (505 U.S. at 59).

colleagues. In no way is such behavior time bound. For example, *Shepard's* lists as "connected" with *Texas v. White* (1868) two cases – *Huntington's Executors v. Texas* (1872) and *First National Bank v. Texas* (1873) – which have absolutely no relationship to the basis of Swayne's dissent in *White*, which Miller joined. We exclude such cases from consideration.

Relatedly, if *Shepard's* or the prevailing opinion clearly indicates adherence to a precedent of which the dissent or special concurrence disapproves, we consider the case to be a progeny – for example, *Cleavinger v. Saxner* (1985) as progeny of *Butz v. Economou* (1978).

Alternatively, we sometimes find cases where concurring and dissenting justices explicitly and unequivocally rest their decisions on a previous case even when the majority opinion does not. In such cases, only the pertinent subset of the original dissenters will be identified as voting precedent or preferences in the progeny. Thus, Justice Holmes called for the overruling of *Lochner v. New York* (1905) in *Coppage v. Kansas* (1915) even though the majority opinion made no reference to it whatsoever. Also consider that of the four dissenters in *New York v. Quarles* (1984), only Brennan and Marshall viewed it as a precedent to the Court's decision in *Oregon v. Elstad* (1985). The other *Quarles* dissenters, O'Connor, who wrote the Courts *Elstad* opinion, and Stevens, who dissented, viewed *Miranda v. Arizona* (1966) as the relevant precedent.[10] In such situations, we count the case in question as a "progeny" for the appropriate dissenting and concurring justices, even if the controlling opinion does not mention the case.

But where a justice votes his or her preferences in a progeny while failing to mention the relevant precedent in the dissenting or concurring opinion that he or she wrote or joined, and if, in addition, the case's prevailing opinion does not meet our definition of precedent, the preferentially voting justice is excluded from consideration. We omit such a justice even though it is perfectly clear that he or she rejects the precedent in question. Justice White's behavior in a set of parochiaid cases provides an excellent illustration. He, along with Burger and Rehnquist, dissented from *Wallace v. Jaffree* (1985). Burger and Rehnquist voted preferentially in *Grand Rapids v. Ball* (1985) and *Aguilar v. Felton* (1985) by basing their dissents in these cases on those in *Jaffree*. But not White. He cited two other cases as his authority for having "long disagreed with the Court's interpretation of the Establishment Clause in the context of

---

[10] *Marshall v. Barlow's Inc.* (1978) provides a further example. Rehnquist, Blackmun, and Stevens dissented. But only Stevens referenced his *Barlow's* dissent in *Michigan v. Clifford* (1984), thereby making this case a progeny for him. By contrast, Rehnquist's dissenting opinion, which Blackmun joined, makes nary a reference to *Barlow's*.

state aid to private schools" (p. 400). Hence, White's votes are counted as neither precedent nor preference.

We adopt this excessively formalistic stance for two interrelated reasons. First, our determination of whether a case is progeny of a particular precedent depends on the justices' own words. Second, to disregard the judicial language or otherwise read between the lines would subject us to warranted criticism. Thus, even though no one would dispute the consistency with which a justice adheres to personal – as distinguished from institutional – *stare decisis* (as White's behavior in the parochiaid cases illustrates), said justice's failure to articulate the basis for that behavior precludes us from rendering an independent judgment. Hence, we sacrifice one level of objectivity in order to achieve another: that is, a systematically even-handed approach to the specification of precedent.

Consider as well the situation where a majority opinion takes pains to distinguish a precedent from its decision and holding. Such opinions will not be considered progeny of the precedent for the justices who join it. *Federal Election Comn. v. National Conservative PAC* [*NCPAC*] (1985) illustrates the matter. Marshall and White dissented on the basis that the government's interest in campaign expenditures met strict scrutiny and thereby overrode the First Amendment. One year later, Marshall silently joined the majority in *Federal Election Comn. v. Massachusetts Citizens for Life* (1986), which distinguished *NCPAC* at 259–63 and held that the First Amendment overrode the relevant provision of the Federal Election Campaign Act. Justice White dissented again, citing his *NCPAC* opinion as his basis for doing so. Inasmuch as White considered his *NCPAC* dissent controlling, we count his vote as preference. Marshall's vote, however, counts as neither preference nor precedent because the opinion which he joined considered *NCPAC* irrelevant to its decision. If Marshall had not shared this opinion, he would, of course, have cast a vote sustaining precedent. In sum, the controlling opinion can create a progeny for the entire Court, but concurring and dissenting justices, under much stricter standards, can create progeny only for themselves.[11]

To summarize: only formally decided cases are treated as progeny. We identify progeny by finding citations in the case syllabus, or summary, that pertain to the issue the case concerns. Such citations qualify as precedents. Absent a syllabus reference, we consult *Shepard's Citations*

---

[11] As mentioned, we do not exclude from consideration justices who dissent from a precedent and subsequently join the majority opinion. Depending on which of our decision rules they adhere to they may vote either preferences or precedent.

Thus, a dissenter who subsequently joins an opinion of the Court that favorably cites the precedent from which the justice dissented has voted precedentially.

to ascertain the precedents of our cases. We examine all citations in *Shepard's* analysis column as well as all cases that are cited at least twice. A case may be precedent for certain progeny, and for those progeny to serve as precedents for still other progeny. Issue discrepancy between putative progeny and precedents requires verbal dependence on the precedent, a lesser amount where issue identity prevails.

If these criteria create progeny of the original decisions, we evaluate the behavior of all justices who dissented from the original decision. We assess each dissenter's opinion and voting behavior to determine whether or not the dissent adheres to the precedent. Most critical to such determinations is the wording to which the justice subscribes.

Hurtado v. California (1884) illustrates the foregoing procedures. Harlan alone dissented from the ruling that the Fourteenth Amendment's due process clause does not require grand jury indictments. Consequently, our assessment of potential progeny ceases with his departure from the Court. We do not include as progeny *Hagar v. Reclamation District* (1884), a case decided later the same year, for two reasons. The sole reference to the precedent is dicta, and *Hagar* pertains to civil proceedings. The Court held that a special assessment for governmentally provided health improvement did not violate due process. Harlan relied on *Hurtado* in its progeny, *Baldwin v. Kansas* (1889), where the Court ruled that the procedures used to try and convict a person for capital murder were not federal questions; *Hallinger v. Davis* (1892), which upheld the constitutionality of a guilty plea; and *Talton v. Mayes* (1896), which held that the courts of the Cherokee Indians did not require indictment by a grand jury. We exclude from consideration a memo decision of December 14, 1896, referencing *Hurtado,* along with *American Publishing Co. v. Fisher* (1897). The latter declared unconstitutional a territory's civil jury of nine persons because it violated the Seventh Amendment. Because *Holden v. Hardy* (1898) involved freedom of contract in the context of an eight-hour day, we also exclude it from consideration. *Hurtado*'s other progeny are *Maxwell v. Dow* (1900), involving an eight-member jury; *Dorr v. United States* (1904), excluding the Philippine Islands from jury trials; *Twining v. New Jersey* (1908), exempting states from the self incrimination clause; and *Dowdell v. United States* (1910), reiterating, *inter alia*, that the Constitution does not require grand jury indictments in the Philippine Islands.

EVALUATING PROGENY

The fact that a fully objective determination of which decisions are progeny of a precedent cannot be made impacts our evaluation of progeny. Hard and fast decision rules of whether a dissenter from a precedent conforms to it are somewhat problematical. But, as with progeny themselves, the tables in the next six chapters identify the dissenters' behavior in each of the progeny in which they participate, thereby enabling readers so minded to check the accuracy of our judgments.

Once we determine which cases can reliably be considered progeny of a landmark case, we must evaluate the positions taken in the progeny by the justices who dissented from the landmark. As we explain later, the issue in the case, the basis for the dissenting justice's subsequent vote(s), and the direction of these votes all guide our judgment of whether or not we categorize the justice's position as comporting with either the established precedent or the justice's preferences. Simplistic decision rules cannot apply. If they did, we would arrive at irrational results. To wit: *West Coast Hotel Co. v. Parrish* (1937), which overruled *Adkins v. Children's Hospital* (1923), would nonetheless be supportive of *Adkins* because *Parrish* used the *Adkins* rational basis standard to uphold, rather than to void, the minimum wage law at issue.

In formulating the foregoing decision rules to help us determine whether justices dissenting from the precedents we consider accept them or continue to vote their preferences, we also recognize that the individual justices sometimes use their language bearing on the matter in very unusual and creative ways. Two examples suffice. In *California v. Brown* (1987), Justice Blackmun quotes his pro–death penalty dissent in *Furman v. Georgia* (1972, p. 413) to support the precedent his *Furman* dissent opposed! Similarly, Justice Stevens's dissent in *Atascadero State Hospital v. Scanlon* (1985, 304) reports that he initially rejected a precedent, then accepted it, and now again repudiates it:

> "Because my decision to join JUSTICE BRENNAN's dissent is a departure from the opinion I expressed in *Florida Dept. Of Health v. Florida Nursing Home Assn.*, 450 U.S. 147, 151 (1981), a word of explanation is in order. As I then explained, notwithstanding my belief that *Edelman v. Jordan*, 415 U.S. 651 (1974), was incorrectly decided . . . I then concluded that the doctrine of *stare decisis* required that *Edelman* be followed. Since then, however, the Court has not felt constrained by *stare decisis* in its expansion of the protective mantle of sovereign immunity . . . and additional study has made it abundantly clear that . . . *Edelman* . . . can be properly characterized as "egregiously incorrect." . . . I am now persuaded that a fresh example of the Court's Eleventh Amendment jurisprudence will produce benefits that far outweigh "the consequences of further unraveling the doctrine of *stare decisis*" in this area of the law.

In our earlier work, we coded the relevant justices' positions as following either precedent or preferences (Segal and Spaeth, 1996a). Although this approach produced a high level of intercoder reliability (we separately coded the cases), it resulted more from our decision rules than from a case-by-case application of our concept of progeny to a series of cases decided over a long period. Careful reading of cases that may qualify as progeny has led us to identify different manifestations of *stare decisis* that might properly be considered an ordinal scale.

Levels of Precedential/Preferential Behavior

Strong Precedential. At the highest level, a precedentially behaving justice formally accedes to the precedent in approximately so many words. Thus, Justice Harlan in *Ashe v. Swenson* (1970) at 448: "Having acceded in *North Carolina v. Pearce* . . . to the decision in *Benton v. Maryland* . . . which, over my dissent, held that the Fourteenth Amendment imposes on the States the standards of the Double Jeopardy Clause . . . I am satisfied that on this present record Ashe's acquittal in the first trial brought double jeopardy standards into play." We label these opinions "Strong Precedential."

But a close reading of opinion language is frequently necessary. Thus, the words of Justice Harlan in *Hadley v. Junior College District* (1970, p. 60) with reference to the precedent cited in the syllabus, *Avery v. Midland County* (1968):[12] "While I deem myself bound by *Reynolds* and *Avery* – despite my continued disagreement with them as constitutional holdings . . . – I do not think that either of these cases, or any other in this Court, justifies the present decision. I therefore dissent." If this language were found in our datasets it would not qualify as a precedential vote, but rather as a preferential one. To take a live example supporting an opposite outcome, we count Harlan's special opinion in *United Transportation Union v. Michigan State Bar* (1971) as strongly supporting his dissent in the precedent, *NAACP v. Button* (1963). Although he says he complies with the result in the two other progeny of *Button,* he also states that he would not extend them further. He cites his *Button* dissent to minimize the First Amendment interests at stake in the case.

Moderate Precedential. At a moderate level, precedentially voting justices join or write an opinion that specifically supports and cites the precedent in question as authority for their vote, for example, Stewart's opinion of the Court in *Crist v. Bretz* (1978, p. 32), in which he cites *Benton v. Maryland* (1969) as controlling. Stewart had dissented in *Benton.* Stewart's opinion of the Court in *Ashe v. Swenson* (1970) further exemplifies his acceptance of *Benton* as a precedent binding his vote. We label such behavior "Moderate Precedential."

---

[12] Neither case appears in Witt's list or in our set of sampled cases.

Weak Precedential. Dissenters from a precedent can accede to it indirectly by voting in a progeny compatibly with the direction of the decision in the precedent (e.g., liberal or conservative) where the issue in the progeny is effectively the same as that of the precedent. We include in this definition cases in which the syllabus/summary either does not cite the precedent or the text of the prevailing opinion only cites the precedent incidentally. But we do require the relevant justices to rely substantially on the precedent with which the progeny is associated. For example, we treat the votes of Black and Harlan in *Graham v. Richardson* (1971) as precedential to *Shapiro v. Thompson* (1969), from which they dissented. Although one may debate the applicability of the latter to the former, both concern the eligibility of nonresidents for welfare benefits. We label such behavior "Weak Precedential."

Weak Preferential. The weakest example of preferential behavior occurs when a dissenter from the precedent writes or joins an opinion opposite in direction from that of the precedent, for example, a liberal precedent used as authority for a conservative progeny, or vice versa, that nevertheless does not explicitly repudiate the precedent. Harlan's membership in the conservative majority of *Cameron v. Johnson* (1968) and *Younger v. Harris* (1971), progeny of the liberally decided *Dombrowski v. Pfister* (1965), from which he had dissented, illustrates this form of weak preferential voting. The position such votes espouse implicitly narrows the precedent. For example, the votes of Powell and Burger in *Lake Carriers' Assn. v. MacMullan* (1972) curbed the preemptive effect of *Younger v. Harris* (1971).

Frequently justices who disagree with a precedent will argue that "even under" the precedent, results consistent with the original dissenters' preferences obtain. Not uncommonly, those who originally supported the precedent will chastise such justices for improper use of the precedent. As an example, consider the dissenters in *Swisher v. Brady* (1978), who allege at 219 that the majority opinion "is at odds" with the precedent, *Benton v. Maryland* (1969). Incidentally, Justice Stewart, who dissented in Benton, voted precedentially by joining the Swisher majority. Justice White's conservative opinion of the Court in *Maryland v. Buie* (1990) further illustrates this feature of our broad definition of preferences. His opinion limited the applicability of the liberal precedent, *Chimel v. California* (1969), from which he had dissented.[13] We label such positions "Weak Preferential."

---

[13] For further examples, note Burger's behavior in the precedent, *Harlow v. Fitzgerald* (1982), and its progeny, *Davis v. Scherer* (1984), at 197–98; and White's behavior in the precedent, *Federal Election Comn. v. National Conservative PAC* (1985), and its progeny, *Austin v. Michigan Chamber of Commerce* (1990), at 701, 703, 705, 711.

This weak definition, however, does not require a dissent or special concurrence in the progeny chastising the majority for improper use of the precedent. Unanimity may prevail, as is the case in two of the progeny of the short-lived *National League of Cities v. Usery* (1976): *Hodel v. Virginia Surface Mining* (1981) and *United Transportation Union v. Long Island R. Co.* (1982).

Not uncommonly, the Court will distinguish a precedent in which (1) the dissenter(s) will write the majority opinion in the progeny, and (2) the dissenters in the progeny – members of the precedent's majority – will strongly assert that the precedent controls. As an example, consider the liberally decided child welfare case *Jimenez v. Weinberger* (1974), from which Rehnquist dissented. Rehnquist wrote the Court's opinion in the progeny, *Weinberger v. Salfi* (1975), and joined the conservative majority in *Mathews v. Lucas* (1976). Douglas, Brennan, and Marshall strongly objected to the treatment the *Salfi* majority accorded the precedent; Stevens, Brennan, and Marshall, the action of the *Mathews* majority. Throughout, of course, Rehnquist behaved preferentially.

Infrequently, the converse obtains: a precedent is extended beyond its original context to govern a different issue. *INS v. Cardoza-Fonseca* (1987), a deportation case, provides a good example. Although *NLRB v. Food & Commercial Workers* (1987) concerned an unfair labor practice, the majority opinion cited *Cardoza-Fonseca* as authority, while its remaining dissenters – Rehnquist and White – joined a concurring opinion disparaging its dicta.[14]

Moderate Preferential. When justices support their original position by either dissenting from or concurring in a decision or prevailing opinion that cites the precedent from which they had dissented as authority for the Court's decision, they fall in a middle standard of preferential voting. We label this level "Moderate Preferential." This position differs from the "Strong Preferential" position in that the preferentially voting justices do not cite their opinion in which they originally dissented from the establishment of the precedent. Note that the majority opinion in such cases need not meet our definition of a precedent. Thus, for example, in inveighing against Justice O'Connor's position with respect to the excessive entanglement test under the establishment clause, the dissent that Justice Rehnquist joined in *Kiryas Joel Board of Education v. Grumet* (1994) cites his *Wallace v. Jaffree* dissent, at 591.

Somewhat arbitrarily perhaps, we also assign justices who dissent without opinion to this intermediate category. Similarly, justices who

---

[14] Note that Rehnquist's and White's votes illustrate moderate preferential voting, discussed in the succeeding paragraph, rather than weak preferential.

conform to precedent without articulating reasons therefore are also classified as "Moderately Precedential."

An alternative aspect of this level insofar as preferences are concerned is exemplified by justices who cite the precedent supportively to sustain their dissent or special concurrence from the direction of the controlling decision. Thus, for example, Justice Scalia, writing in dissent for himself and Rehnquist in *Edwards v. Aguillard* (1987), repeatedly cites the majority opinion in *Wallace v. Jaffree* (1985) as authority for their *Edwards* votes at 613–14. But this use of *Jaffree* certainly does not indicate they approve of that decision voiding Alabama's minute of school silence. They rather use it to hoist the majority on its own petard, by taking language therein to support Louisiana's law for balanced treatment of creation science.[15] This aspect of the middle position occurs quite often. It is clearly an effective way for a dissenter to appear to support precedent while actually voting preferences.

Strong Preferential. Finally, the strongest preferential votes will belong to justices who either reassert adherence to their dissent from the precedent in the progeny, again in approximately so many words, or cite a dissent from the precedent. Alternatively, a strongly preferentially voting justice may flatly reject the precedent. Thus, Chief Justice Rehnquist in *Webster v. Reproductive Health Services* (1989), at 518: "*Stare decisis* is a cornerstone of our legal system, but it has less power in constitutional cases, where, save for constitutional amendments, this Court is the only body able to make needed changes.... We think the *Roe* trimester framework falls into that category." So, too, Justice Brennan in *Oregon v. Elstad* (1985), at 349: "The Court today finally recognizes these flaws in the logic of [*Michigan v.*] *Tucker* and [*New York v.*] *Quarles*. Although disastrous in so many other respects, today's opinion at least has the virtue of rejecting the inaccurate assertion . . . that confessions extracted in violation of Miranda are not presumptively coerced for Fifth Amendment purposes." We label such behavior "Strong Preferential."

Note that the prevailing opinion in cases manifesting strong preferential voting need not meet our definition of precedent if the dissent or concurrence rejects its precedential character. Thus, Justice Scalia in his *Kiryas Joel* (1994, p. 591) dissent emphatically states that *Grand Rapids School District v. Ball* (1985) and *Aguilar v. Felton* (1985), "so hostile to our national tradition of accommodation, should be overruled at the earliest opportunity."

---

[15] Because this opinion subsequently cites Rehnquist's *Jaffree* dissent, it falls under our strongest level of preferences, rather than the moderate level. But sans any reference to the *Jaffree* dissent, it would fully illustrate the moderate level.

We recognize that though we have striven mightily, our decision rules lack verbal – to say nothing of mathematical – precision. We will therefore identify debatable votes and opinions in the succeeding chapters that deal with the justices' behavior and justify our treatment of them. This approach opens our judgment about specific votes to detailed scrutiny and readily provides readers with the opportunity to critique our categorization of votes as precedent and preference.

To summarize: We divide precedential and preferential behavior into three exclusive categories: strong, moderate, and weak. Strong precedential behavior formally accedes to the precedent in question. Moderate precedential sees a justice writing or joining an opinion that specifically supports the precedent as authority for his or her vote. Weak precedential involves a vote that supports the direction of the precedent's decision where the progeny's issue is effectively identical to that of the precedent. Preferential behavior parallels that which supports precedent. Thus, weak preferential behavior occurs when a dissenter from a precedent writes or joins an opinion opposite in direction from that of the precedent. Moderate preferential behavior occurs when justices support their original position by dissenting from or concurring with the prevailing opinion in a progeny that cites the precedent as authority. Justices' votes are strongly preferential when they reassert adherence to their disapproval of the precedent either in approximately so many words or in their citing of a dissent from the precedent as their authority.

In designing our research strategy, we recognize that changes in judicial behavior (by dissenting justices) that follow the establishment of a precedent toward the position taken in that precedent merely establish a rebuttable presumption that the switch was due to the precedent. Undoubtedly we will code some votes as precedential when other factors may have intervened. When such factors are obvious to us, we will note the possibility of alternative explanations. But we do not and cannot attempt the sort of intensive case study of alternative factors that would be necessary to finalize our assessment of each instance of precedential behavior that we find. Nevertheless, in the final chapter we compare the precedentially consistent switching we observe to a baseline of precedentially inconsistent switching, so as to derive an aggregate estimate of pure precedential behavior.

We will, in other words, take a sample of the landmark and ordinary cases to ascertain the extent to which the justices who establish the precedent continue to adhere to it in its progeny. Some justices from the original majority will for a variety of reasons, much like those who dissented, no longer adhere to their inceptive position. But if precedent really matters, justices initially opposed to the precedent should be substantially more likely to switch to it than justices initially supportive of it should be to switch from it. Comparing the amount of changing behavior of those initially opposed to the precedent to a baseline of changing behavior from those initially favorable to it provides a crucial test of whether we can infer that dissenting justices who move toward the precedent really were influenced by preferential concerns, and what percentage of those changes really were precedentially induced.

This part of our analysis moves the scope of our study from pure description into the realm of a quasi experiment. By comparing majority and dissenting behavior in the same cases with the same progeny in the same periods, we will go a long way toward assuring that the precedential behavior we find is really precedential. Moreover, we will subject our purportedly precedential behavior to a series of specific tests designed to test alternative explanations for such actions.

Alternative Approaches

We also recognize that alternative approaches to assessing precedential impact might exist, both narrowly and broadly. Narrowly, alternative approaches to our coding of the cases clearly exist. In our view, though, proffered alternatives do not accord with the realities of the Court's decision making. Thus, we could have counted justices as supporting precedent anytime they agreed with an opinion that cited it as authority. This, of course, completely ignores the strategic ability of justices to use (and misuse) precedents for their own ideological purposes as well as the Court's institutional rules for writing and forming opinions. To illustrate: the Court standardly uses language from the World War II internment cases to void racial discrimination: for example, racial categorizations are "by their very nature odious to a free people" (*Hirabayashi v. United States* 1943, 100), and "courts must subject them to the most rigid scrutiny" (*Korematsu v. United States* 1944, 216). If the *Korematsu* dissenters had still been alive to participate in the unanimous opinion that voided bans on interracial marriage (*Loving v. Virginia* 1967), is it likely that joining the majority would have signified support for the *Korematsu* precedent? Hardly.

On other occasions, the justices so severely limit or distinguish precedents that they become irrelevant to a succeeding decision. To count such behavior as precedentially supportive countenances frigidity as a temperature below seventy degrees Fahrenheit. Given the reluctance of a court to overturn a precedent unnecessarily, litigants realize they need not ask the Court to do so when they can win if an objectionable precedent is held inapplicable. Thus, the Legal Defense Fund's initial strategy focused on the inequality of segregated southern schools before it sought overruling of the separate but equal doctrine (*Plessy v. Ferguson* 1896). Judicial statements that various systems could not meet the separate but equal standard hardly meant, on the eve of *Brown v. Board of Education* (1954), that they accepted that doctrine.

Furthermore, although justices disagree with a precedent, they will commonly write that in the case at hand their policy preferences are accommodated "even under" the objectionable precedent. Thus, for example, no rational person would allege that Justices Rehnquist and White ever supported *Roe v. Wade* (1973). With one debatable exception, they have invariably voted against a woman's right to abortion.[16] In doing so, they follow a simple strategy: if *Roe* sustains the decision, attack *Roe*. If the case does not implicate *Roe*, assert that even *Roe* does not support the pro-choice position. Thus, in *Harris v. McRae* (1979) the Court permitted states to terminate Medicaid funding for abortions, holding that the cutoff did not violate *Roe*. That certainly does not imply that the majority opinion writer and those acceding to it supported *Roe* as a precedent for this decision.

Finally, justices need to form majority opinions. Assume, for example, that three justices wish to limit a rule, while two others wish to overrule it. The latter pair could join the other set or could concur specially. The latter option precludes formation of a majority opinion. The pair of justices would thereby gain very little, except perhaps a sense of rectitude. But if they join the other three they will have moved the Court close to their most preferred position. In such situations, we do not automatically code the justices as voting preference or precedent. Rather, we analyze the behavior case by case on the basis of doctrinal movement toward or away from the position the original dissenters took in the case establishing the precedent.

To exemplify, consider the positions taken by the four dissenters – Burger, Blackmun, Powell, and Rehnquist – in *Furman v. Georgia*, the 1972 decision outlawing the death penalty. When the Court reconsidered the matter in 1976 in *Gregg v. Georgia*, the judgment of the Court, which Powell cowrote with Stewart, a member of the *Furman* majority, and the newly seated Stevens held that the capricious and arbitrary elements of Georgia's procedure were remedied. *Furman* had been decided *seriatim*,

---

[16]   Rehnquist's vote in *Bellotti v. Baird* (1979), in which the Court required judicial bypass for minors seeking parentally unapproved abortions. He adhered to his anti-*Roe* position *in Planned Parenthood v. Danforth* (1976) that a state could constitutionally impose a blanket parental consent requirement, but willingly joined the *Bellotti* opinion limiting *Danforth* by allowing a judicial bypass as an alternative to parental consent.

with the only commonality a per curiam statement that the procedures at issue "constituted cruel and unusual punishment" (1972, 40).

Positive references to *Furman* in the plurality opinion of *Gregg* are limited to Burger's and Powell's dissenting opinions. Blackmun concurred in *Gregg's* judgment, citing only the four *Furman* dissents as justification. White, Burger, and Rehnquist focused on the new Georgia statutory scheme and, compatibly with their original support for capital punishment, held it constitutional. To rely on the disposition in *Gregg* as determinative of whether the *Furman* dissenters voted preferences or precedent is eminently reasonable.

We also could have expanded our inquiry to include justices who dissent from a precedent their votes initially helped establish. The classic example here is the second flag salute case, *West Virginia State Board of Education v. Barnette* (1943). We do not do so, however, because the shift from initial support for a precedent to opposition may trigger institutional and attitudinal considerations different from those governing initial disapproval. Complicating such an enterprise is the fact that not all such votes result in the overruling of precedent. Justice White, for example, was a member of the majority opinion coalition in the affirmative action case *Steelworkers v. Weber* (1979). In *Johnson v. Transportation Agency* (1987), he said he would overrule it (at 657). Systematic identification of all cases in which members of a majority subsequently sought to overrule their prior action would entail extremely meticulous and time-consuming labor. One case in which the Court "reconsidered" but chose not to overrule a precedent is *Helvering v. Griffiths* (1942). The precedent was *Eisner v. Macomber* (1920), in which the Court held that dividends paid on common stock were not income within the meaning of the Sixteenth Amendment. None of the four dissenters – Brandeis, Clarke, Day, and Holmes – was still on the Court when *Griffiths* was decided. Three justices dissented from the failure to overrule *Eisner*: Black, Douglas, and Murphy. Rutledge did not participate. For a more recent example, consider *United States v. IBM* (1996), which the justices accepted "to decide whether we should overrule" a precedent (p. 130). The precedent in question antedated the most senior justice's service by some 55 years, however. Two justices dissented from the failure to overrule the precedent: Kennedy and Ginsburg. Stevens did not participate.

More broadly, alternative measures of the influence of *stare decisis* might exist. For example, Knight and Epstein (1996) assert that precedent is a norm that constrains Supreme Court justices to adopt policies less favorable than they might otherwise. We agree, of course, that precedent is a norm, but no one heretofore has provided evidence that it has inhibited justices or otherwise precluded them from achieving optimal outcomes. Merely showing the existence of citations to precedent in decisions, briefs, and so on, as do Knight and Epstein, does not demonstrate that precedent has any particular function, or even any function at all. Valid inference requires demonstration that as precedent changes, so also does – or does not – the justices' behavior.

This being so, Knight and Epstein nonetheless inquire why lawyers cite precedent in their briefs and justices cite precedent in their interoffice memos and in their opinions.

Two alternative explanations comport with the view that though precedent is a norm, it does not constrain their policies.[17] First, because of a real need for legitimacy the justices must cloak their policy preferences with legal language, including rules of law and precedents. The need for legitimacy operates as much within the Marble Palace as among the public at large. Rehnquist could not have sent Marshall a memo stating he supported capital punishment because he believes in retribution, nor Blackmun a memo to Scalia explaining his support for abortion on the basis of zero population growth. So even citation of precedent in internal memos hardly evidences adherence thereto. Moroever, legitimacy enhancing factors, such as intent and plain meaning, in addition to precedent, are so broad, nebulous, and ill defined that justices rarely if ever need worry about justifying their chosen policies. (For documentation, see Solan 1993.) These devices effectively support policy choices; in no meaningful way do they constrain them.

Second, if human beings have an unlimited capability, it is the ability to rationalize our druthers. We ought never underestimate our talent for motivated reasoning. For all we know, justices may actually believe they resolve disputes by legal analysis. Nevertheless, they often assert that their colleagues are not so motivated, for example, White's dissent in *Roe v. Wade* (1973, 221) and Marshall's dissent in *Payne v. Tennessee* (1991, 844). Classic sociopsychological findings demonstrate that the ability to convince oneself of the propriety of what one prefers to believe psychologically approximates the human reflex (Baumeister and Newman 1994; Kunda 1990).

Yet, not every preferred argument is credible. "There is considerable evidence that people are more likely to arrive at conclusions that they want to arrive at, but their ability to do so is constrained by their ability to construct seemingly reasonable justifications for these conclusions" (Kunda 1990, 480). Thus, even if legal arguments play no part in a

---

[17]   Other factors constrain realization of optimal policies, not the least of which is the desire to form a majority opinion coalition.

conscious game, lawyers must provide precedents. "When one wants to draw a particular conclusion, one feels obligated to construct a justification that would be plausible to a dispassionate observer" (Kunda 1990, 493). Thus, internal and external citations to precedent – or its equivalent – would exist, regardless of whether or not they influenced judges. We, of course, do not suggest that the justices are in any way irrational. Rather, we believe that they are human and, as such, subject to the fallible reasoning processes that are our lot.

CONCLUSION

Though we do not argue that we have found the only means of testing the influence of *stare decisis*, we believe that the methods and standards proposed in this chapter represent a reliable and valid test of the influence of the doctrine.

The remainder of this book will examine the votes and opinions of the justices in light of the substantive, theoretical, and methodological concerns described.

3

Precedential Behavior
from the Beginning
Through the Chase Court

In assessing the extent to which the justices of the Supreme Court have adhered to precedent over its history, we proceed chronologically Court by Court. We initially consider each Court's landmark decisions, then a sample of its common cases. We limit our discussion to the more interesting manifestations of precedent and preferences. However, for readers interested in replicating our work, we provide complete tables detailing each of our precedents, their progeny, and the level of precedential or preferential behavior of each relevant justice.

Note that though each Court's precedents were established during the lifetime of that Court, the progeny of these precedents may extend beyond the establishing Court's lifetime. The progeny of any precedent end with the departure from the Court of the last remaining justice who dissented from the precedent's creation. Thus, for example, the last of the progeny of *Ogden v. Saunders* (1827) is *Suydam v. Broadnax* (1840), decided five years after Marshall's death while Smith Thompson, one of the two *Ogden* dissenters, was still on the Court.

Because only a single landmark and no common decisions antedate the Marshall Court, we include *Chisholm v. Georgia* (1793) with the Marshall Court.[1]

BEGINNINGS THROUGH THE MARSHALL COURT

Notwithstanding the eminence of the first chief justice, John Jay, the earliest Supreme Court lacked the power and prestige attached to it today. Jay resigned from the Court to become Governor of New York, and upon renomination to the Court in 1800, declined, citing among other reasons, the fact that the Court lacked "the energy, weight, and dignity which are essential to its affording due support to the national government" (Witt 1981, p. 114).

[1] Actually, one common case also antedates the Marshall Court, *Cotton v. Wallace* (1796). It has no progeny, however, in which the dissenter, Paterson, participated.

Nevertheless, the Jay Court (1789–95) did provide one historic decision, *Chisholm v. Georgia* (1793). Chief Justice John Jay wrote the prevailing opinion, over Iredell's dissent, that residents of one state may sue another state in federal court without the consent of the sued state. The adoption of the Eleventh Amendment nullified this ruling. In *Hollingsworth v. Virginia* (1797), the Court unanimously accepted the language of the Eleventh Amendment that federal jurisdiction did not apply to suits by nonresidents against a state.[2]

The Ellsworth Court (1796–1800) also rendered at least one indisputably landmark case, *Calder v. Bull* (1798), which authoritatively limited the Constitution's ban on *ex post facto* laws to criminal cases. This decision, plus decisions upholding Congress's authority to tax carriages[3] and declaring that U.S. treaties overrode the provisions of conflicting state laws,[4] were reached unanimously.

With Ellsworth's resignation, President John Adams made what might be the single most important appointment in the history of the United States: John Marshall to chief justice. Indeed, if we think in terms of Congresses, presidents, and chief justiceships, Marshall's reign might rank with Lincoln's as the most influential in American history. Under Marshall, the Court established three enduring legacies: judicial supremacy,[5] national supremacy,[6] and an expansive view of federal power.[7] At the same time it also set protections of individual rights, at least where property interests were at stake.[8] All but one of these decisions were unanimously decided, though other Witt landmarks, discussed later, were not.

Given the hagiographic treatment accorded justices of the formative

---

[2] Given that the amendment accorded with Iredell's original position, he obviously did not recant his *Chisholm* vote.

[3] *Hylton v. United States* (1796).

[4] *Ware v. Hylton* (1798).

[5] *Marbury v. Madison* (1803) not only established judicial review, but authoritatively declared it the judiciary's responsibility to determine what the Constitution means.

[6] In a series of decisions culminating in *Cohens v. Virginia* (1821), the Supreme Court ruled that federal courts, and not state courts, were the ultimate arbiters of the meaning of federal law.

[7] *M'Culloch v. Maryland* (1819) gave Congress broad powers under the necessary and proper clause and simultaneously limited state authority to limit such actions. *Gibbons v. Ogden* (1824) expanded Congress's power over interstate commerce to all behavior that is not "completely internal . . . and does not extend to or affect other states" (9 Wheaton 1, at 189).

[8] *Fletcher v. Peck* (1810) prevented legislatures from rescinding land grants, even when they were obtained via bribery. Nine years later, over the solo dissent of Duvall, the Court prohibited states from altering private corporate charters (*Dartmouth College v. Woodward* [1819]).

era – such as Marshall, Johnson, and Story – and the general deification conferred on the Marshall Court, according to the conventional wisdom precedent should manifest itself to a pronounced degree. We find this not to be the case for either its landmark or its ordinary litigation. As Tables 3.1 and 3.2 show, dissenting justices adhered to their preferences with over 80 percent of their votes in progeny of landmark decisions, and with more than three-quarters of their votes in progeny of common cases. Admittedly the number of progeny votes is small, 15 and 13, respectively, plus the single vote in *Chisholm*'s progeny, *Hollingsworth v. Virginia* (1797). Nonetheless, the preferential proportion is sufficiently high to belie much adherence to precedent. Granted the distribution of votes is not dispersed among the justices, with William Johnson and Smith Thompson accounting for 12 of the 15 landmark votes, and five of the 13 in common cases. On the other hand, only two of the eight Marshall Court landmarks containing a dissent produced no progeny in which a dissenter participated: *Dartmouth College v. Woodward* (1819) and *Mason v. Haile* (1827). The latter held that modification of the remedies for defaulting on a contract does not necessarily violate the contract clause. Washington dissented. Duvall was the *Dartmouth College* dissenter.

That William Johnson accounts for five of the votes in progeny of the Marshall Court's landmark occasions no surprise, given his reputation as the Court's first great dissenter (Morgan 1954). What does surprise is that Smith Thompson, who sat during the final 13 years of the Marshall Court and thereafter until 1843, cast seven. Johnson, by comparison, served more than twice as long, 1805–1833. Rectifying this imbalance, however, are Johnson's four ordinary case votes, compared with Thompson's one. (See Table 3.2.)

The first leading decision in which a dissenter adhered to precedent occurs in a progeny of *Ogden v. Saunders* (1827): *Boyle v. Zacharie* (1832). In *Saunders*, the justices delivered their opinions *seriatim* with Johnson writing two separate opinions(!), each of which comprises a different majority. One deals with the contract clause, the other the extraterritorial effect of a state bankruptcy discharge. Toward the former issue, Johnson adheres to his dissent in *Fletcher v. Peck* (1810), narrowly construing the clause. We do not count *Saunders* as *Fletcher*'s progeny, however, because Johnson's opinion does not reference *Fletcher*. But we do count *Boyle v. Zacharie* (1832) as *Saunders*'s progeny, even though the Court itself did not recognize Johnson's opinion on the constitutionality of state insolvent laws as controlling until it so announced in *Boyle*, five years later. The entirety of the *Boyle* opinion reads as follows:

Table 3.1.
Voting and opinion behavior: Marshall Court landmarks

| | | | Level of Expression | | | | | |
| | | | Preferences (%) | | | Precedent (%) | | |
Justice	Prefs/prec	%Prefs	Strong (1)	Moderate (2)	Weak (3)	Strong (1)	Moderate (2)	Weak (3)
Johnson	5	0	100.0	2 (40.0)	3 (60.0)				
Iredell	1	0	100.0	1 (100)					
Washington	1	0	100.0	1 (100)					
Thompson	5	2	71.4	1 (20.0)	2 (40.0)	2 (40.0)	1 (50.0)	1 (50.0)	
McLean	1	1	50.0		1 (100)			1 (100)	
Totals	13	3	81.3	5 (38.5)	6 (46.2)	2 (15.4)	1 (33.3)	2 (66.7)	0

Precedent/progeny	Preferences	Precedent
Chisholm v. Georgia (1793) **c**	Iredell-1	Iredell-1
Hollingsworth v. Virginia (1797)		
Fletcher v. Peck (1810) **c**		
Satterlee v. Matthewson (1829)	Johnson-1	
Osborn v. Bank of the United States (1824) **c**	Johnson-1	
Bank of United States v. Planter's Bank (1824)	Johnson-2	
Sundry African Slaves v. Medrano (1828)	Johnson-2	
Cherokee Nation v. Georgia (1831)	Johnson-2	
Ex parte Crane (1831)	Johnson-2	
Ogden v. Saunders (1827) **c**		
Mason v. Haile (1827)	Washington-1	
Boyle v. Zacharie (1832)	Thompson-1	Thompson-1
Beers v. Haughton (1835)	Thompson-1	
Suydam v. Broadrax (1840)	Thompson-3	
Brown v. Maryland (1827) **c**		
Mayor of New York City v. Miln (1837)	Thompson-2	
Weston v. Charleston (1829) **c s**		
Holmes v. Jennison (1840)	Thompson-2	
Craig v. Missouri (1830) **c**		Thompson-2
Byrne v. Missouri (1834)		McLean-2
Briscoe v. Bank of Commonwealth (1837)	Thompson-3 McLean-2	

Legend: **c** = constitutional decision

       s = statutory decision

       = decision neither constitutionally nor statutorily based

Note: All progeny rest on the same decisional basis as the precedent unless otherwise indicated.

Table 3.2.
Voting and opinion behavior: Marshall Court ordinary cases

| | | | Level of Expression | | | | | |
| | | | Preferences (%) | | | Precedent (%) | | |
Justice	Prefs/prec	%Prefs	Strong (1)	Moderate (2)	Weak (3)	Strong (1)	Moderate (2)	Weak (3)
Story	2	0	100.0			2 (100)			
Baldwin	1	0	100.0		1 (100)				
Livingston	1	0	100.0			1 (100)			
Thompson	1	0	100.0			1 (100)			
Johnson	3	1	75.0	1 (33.3)		2 (66.7)		1 (100)	
McLean	2	2	50.0		2 (100)			1 (50.0)	1 (50.0)
Totals	10	3	76.9	1 (10.0)	3 (30.0)	6 (60.0)	0	2 (66.7)	1 (33.3)

Precedent/progeny	Preferences	Precedent
Ex parte Bollman (1807) **s**		
Ex parte Kearney (1822)	Johnson-3	
Ex parte Watkins (1830)	Johnson-3	
Ex parte Watkins (1833)	Johnson-1	
Croudson v. Leonard (1808)		
The Mary (1815)	Livingston-3	
Brig Short Staple v. United States (1815) **s**		
The William King (1817)	Story-3	
Daly's Lessee v. James (1823)		
Jackson, ex. dem. St. John v. Chew (1827)		Johnson-2
Parsons v. Bedford (1830) **s**		
Livingston v. Story (1835) **s**	McLean-2	
Minor v. Tillotson (1844)		
Phillips v. Preston (1847)		
United States v. King (1849)	McLean-2	
Society for the Propagation of the Gospel v. Pawlet (1830)		
Lessee of Clark v. Courtney (1831)	Baldwin-2	McLean-2
Cherokee Nation v. Georgia (1831) **c**		McLean-3
Worcester v. Georgia (1831)	Thompson-3	
	Story-3	

Legend: **c** = constitutional decision
       s = statutory decision
       = decision neither constitutionally nor statutorily based
Note: All progeny rest on the same decisional basis as the precedent unless otherwise indicated.

The judges who were in the minority of the court upon the general question as to the constitutionality of state insolvent laws, concurred in the opinion of Mr. Justice *Johnson* in the case of Ogden v. Saunders. That opinion is therefore to be deemed the opinion of the other judges who assented to that judgment. Whatever principles are established in that opinion, are to be considered no longer open for controversy, but the settled law of the court. (1832, 348; also see Morgan 1954, 234–35)

Of the three *Saunders* dissenters – Washington, Trimble, and Thompson – only the last still sat when *Boyle* was decided. The unequivocal character of the quoted language indicates not only Thompson's support of the precedent, but also his doing so in so many words. But Thompson's and the Court's puzzling behavior does not end here: in two subsequent progeny, Thompson voted compatibly with the direction of his *Saunders* dissent: that a bankruptcy discharge does have extraterritorial effect in the federal courts of another state. In the first, *Beers v. Haughton* (1835), he dissented in an opinion in which he inappositely observed that the majority's interpretation of a federal statute "is certainly overruling [*Ogden v. Saunders*]. So far as that goes, I can have no particular objection, as I was in the minority in that case" (364). In the other case in which he reverted to a preferential posture, *Suydam v. Broadnax* (1840), he simply joined a majority compatible with the direction of his *Ogden* dissent.

Saunders also produced a progeny, *Mason v. Haile* (1827), in which another dissenter, Bushrod Washington, maintained his original position. After alleging, "It has never been my habit to deliver dissenting opinions where it has been my misfortune to differ from those pronounced by a majority of this court," he baldly accords preference primacy: "A regard for my own consistency, and that, too, upon a great constitutional question, compels me to . . . dissent" (377). In effect: precedent be damned; my will be done.

Such an attitude does not always prevail. Dissimulation also occurs. Thus, Thompson begins his dissent in *Brown v. Maryland* (1827), the famous original package doctrine case, as follows:

> It is with some reluctance, and very considerable diffidence, that I have brought myself publicly to dissent from the opinion of the court in this case; and did it not involve an important constitutional question relating to the relative powers of the general and state governments, I should silently acquiesce in the judgment of the court, although my own opinion might not accord with theirs. (449–50)[9]

Craig v. Missouri (1830), the last of the nonunanimous Marshall Court landmarks, holds that the constitutional ban on state bills of credit

---

[9] Thompson sustained his preferences by writing a pro-state concurrence in *Mayor of New York v. Miln* (1837) ten years later.

encompasses state issuance of interest bearing loan certificates. In separate opinions, Thompson and McLean dissented, arguing that the constitutional prohibition does not deny the states the power to issue any and all paper currency. In *Byrne v. Missouri* (1830), a connected case, Thompson and McLean silently acquiesce in Marshall's opinion for a unanimous Court that "Craig ... is expressly in point, and on its authority the judgment in this case must also be reversed" (43). Marshall, however, does note that only a "majority of the court" (43) voided the state law at issue in *Craig*.

The precedential voting manifest in the connected case of *Byrne* commonly occurs. Dissenters from precedents often fail to reassert their objections in separately decided companion or connected cases. It seems most unlikely that such behavior indicates acceptance of the precedent in question, especially when, as here, the precedential dissenters reassert their preferences in subsequent unconnected cases as Thompson and McLean do in *Briscoe v. Bank of the Commonwealth* (1837). Nonetheless, our decision rules require us to count such votes as precedential. Over the dissent of Justice Story in *Briscoe*, *Craig*'s other progeny, McLean's opinion of the Court upholds the constitutionality of notes circulated by a state-chartered bank, whose officers and directors were appointed by the state legislature; its stock, funds, and profits were state owned; and private interests were expressly excluded. Thompson concurred, emphasizing that the bank notes do not fall under the bills of credit that the Constitution prohibits.[10]

Although it does not affect our tally of either precedential or preferential votes, *Ex parte Bollman* (1807), a nonlandmark decision, further exemplifies our reluctance to deviate from our decision rules. In his dissent, Johnson remarks that he is "supported by the opinion of one of my brethren, who is prevented from indisposition from attending" (1807, 107). Morgan (1954, 56) surmises that this colleague is Chase. The failure of the Reports so to state precludes our counting Chase as a dissenter, however.

Bollman further illustrates the disrepute in which Johnson held precedent. In dissent in a progeny decided a quarter of a century later, *Ex parte Watkins* (1833), he severely chastises his colleagues for their

---

[10] We parenthetically note our exclusion of *Crowell v. Randall* (1836) from the progeny of *Craig v. Missouri* (1830), notwithstanding the citation of the latter in the summary of the former. The mere appearance of a citation to a precedent in a case summary does not invariably make the citing case a progeny. *Crowell's* summary cites some 13 cases, including *Craig*, as a string. Not uncommonly, an opinion of the Court will, as in *Crowell*, review a set of cases as collective authority for its decision. Without more, we exclude such cited cases as precedents for subsequent decisions.

decision, "which is a distinct augury . . . of the conclusions to which we are finally to be led by precedent. I have always opposed the progress of this exercise of jurisdiction, and will oppose it as long as a hope remains to arrest it" (1833, 581).[11]

A dissent of Justice Story from Marshall's opinion in *The Brig Short Staple* provides us with our only example of a peculiar basis for a dissenting vote. The decision held that the crew of a captured vessel have no duty to free themselves even though they could readily overpower their captors. Story dissents because he "adhered to the opinion which he gave in the court below" (1815, 64).[12] We find it more than passing strange to find a justice as eminent as Story rationalizing a dissent on the basis of the position he espoused as a lower court judge, especially when confronted with the disagreement of all the other justices. Story's position, however, must have been meritorious. Two years later, when the same vessel reappeared in further litigation, the Court acceded to Story's position: *The William King* (1817). Refusing to consider its earlier decision conclusive, the Court unanimously reversed itself and held that the capture of *The Short Staple* was fictitious and collusive.

As a final example of the treatment Marshall Court justices accord precedent, consider William Johnson's solo dissent in *Daly's Lessee v. James* (1823). The case concerned the convoluted disposition of real property following the death of a testator and the executors of his estate. Johnson's disagreement with the majority concerns the extent to which the Court considers itself bound by the decision of the state supreme court. The majority did. Johnson demurred: "As precedents entitled to high respect, the decisions of the state courts will always be considered. . . . But a single decision on the construction of a will cannot be acknowledged as of binding efficacy, however it may be respected as a precedent. In the present instance, I feel myself sustained in my opinion upon the legacy . . . by the opinion of one of the three [*sic!*] learned judges who composed the state court" (1823, 542). Johnson, however, accedes to this precedent four years later by silently joining the Court's opinion in *Jackson, ex dem. St. John v. Chew* (1827). Perhaps Johnson's rationale for complying with precedent was that "in the case under consideration,

---

[11] Although it is not grist for our analysis, we note Livingstone's language denigrating precedent in his dissent in *The Edward* (1816), an admiralty case:

> I have thought it a duty to express my dissent from the judgment which has just been rendered.
>
> But were the case doubtful, I should still arrive at the same conclusion, rather than execute a law so excessively penal, about whose existence and meaning such various opinions have been entertained. (1816, 277)

[12] Neither Story nor the Reports specify the reasons for his circuit court decision.

there have been two decisions in the two highest courts of the state upon the identical question now in judgment" (1827, 169), not merely one.[13]

Perchance Johnson's position is best captured in language from his concurrence in *Gibbons v. Ogden* (1824), a landmark decided without dissent, in which the justices first assayed a definition of interstate commerce: "In questions of great importance and great delicacy, I feel my duty to the public best discharged by an effort to maintain my opinions in my own way" (1824, 223).

The Justices' Behavior

The record reported previously and in Tables 3.1 and 3.2 hardly sustains the Marshall Court's putative reputation for staunch adherence to precedent. Indeed, by merely changing the justices' names, critics of any of the modern Courts could use our summary as evidence of judicial willfulness.

Consider, as well, the likelihood that Thompson's and McLean's silent acquiescence in the unanimously decided *Byrne v. Missouri* (1830), a case connected to *Craig v. Missouri* (1829), does not indicate accession to the latter, given adherence to their dissenting position in the unconnected case of *Briscoe v. Bank of the Commonwealth* (1837). A similar pattern characterizes Thompson's behavior in the progeny of *Ogden v. Saunders* (1827). He supports the precedent in *Boyle v. Zacharie* (1832), but he votes his preferences in the last two, as noted (also see Table 3.1). Although not previously discussed, McLean behaved similarly. He followed his two precedential votes in progeny of the nonlandmark decision *Parsons v. Bedford* (1830), a Seventh Amendment case, with one that reaffirms his original dissent.

Also noteworthy is the fact that dissenters' expressions of preferences are much more emphatic in the landmark decisions than in ordinary litigation. Almost 85 percent are either strong or moderate, as compared with only 40 percent in the common cases. Conversely, weak expressions occur four times more frequently in the common cases than in the landmarks.

THE TANEY COURT

John Marshall, nominated to the Supreme Court shortly before Jefferson's inaugural, joined a Supreme Court populated only with

---

[13] Morgan (1954) makes no reference to either of these cases, evidencing perhaps their trivial character.

Federalists. But after Jefferson's defeat of Adams in 1800, no Federalist was again elected President, and after Marshall no Federalist was again nominated to the Court. Thus, the Court Taney inherited consisted of two Democratic-Republicans (Story and Thompson) and three Jacksonian Democrats (McLean, Baldwin, and Wayne), though both Baldwin and Taney had at one time been Federalists (Epstein, Segal, Spaeth, and Walker 1996, p. 314). Yet no more than the Burger Court undid the decisions of the Warren Court did the Taney Court (1836–1864) undo those of the Marshall Court. Expectations that the leveling influences of Jacksonian democracy would curtail vested property rights and commercial interests and expand the sphere of states' rights went largely unrealized.

Two rulings typify the Taney Court's handling of the policy issues that characterized the Marshall Court. In *Charles River Bridge v. Warren Bridge* (1837) Taney ruled that states could reserve the right to alter, amend, or repeal corporate charters and that no implied powers exist in the provisions of a public grant to a private organization. A corporation has only those specifically bestowed. Any ambiguity should be resolved in favor of the public. In drawing the foregoing line between private enterprise and government regulation, the Taney Court did not markedly deviate from Marshall's position. Marshall himself had observed that corporations are artificial entities created by law. As creatures of the law, they have only the powers their charters expressly confer.

In *Cooley v. Board of Port Wardens* (1852) the Taney Court spelled out the Marshall Court's ruling in *Gibbons v. Ogden* (1824). Labeling their common position "selective exclusiveness," the majority held that Congress's power to regulate commerce was complete and to some extent exclusive. Only those subjects that "are in their nature national, or admit of only one uniform system, or plan of regulation, may justly be said to be of such a nature as to require exclusive regulation by Congress" (p. 319). The states might regulate other matters if their regulations did not conflict with those of Congress.

Its moderation on economic issues notwithstanding, the Taney Court is rightly reviled for the most disgraceful decision ever rendered by the United States Supreme Court: *Scott v. Sandford* (1857), which made the nation's racism the Court-sanctioned law of the land.[14]

---

[14] Under this decision blacks were not, and could not become, citizens of the United States. The Missouri Compromise, which banned slavery in certain territories, was unconstitutional. Blacks were "a subordinate and inferior class of beings ... [having] no rights and privileges but such as those who held the power and government might choose to grant them" (60 U.S. 393, at 404–5).

Although the Taney Court justices cast almost twice as many votes in progeny as do those who dissent from leading decisions of the Marshall Court (28 versus 15), all but three pertain to progeny of *Kendall v. United States ex rel. Stokes* (1838), *Prigg v. Pennsylvania* (1842), and *Dodge v. Woolsey* (1856) (see Table 3.3). This concentration, in contrast with the dispersal of progeny among all but two of the Marshall Court's landmarks, is also reflected in the number and importance of the Taney Court landmarks from which justices dissented but which lack progeny: *Mayor of New York v. Miln* (1837), *Briscoe v. Bank of Kentucky* (1837), *Charles River Bridge v. Warren Bridge* (1837), *Holmes v. Jennison* (1840), *Rhode Island v. Massachusetts* (1846), *Luther v. Borden* (1849), *The Passenger Cases* (1849), *Cooley v. Board of Wardens* (1851), and *Scott v. Sandford* (1856).

Although little difference exists between the Marshall and Taney Courts' dissenters from their respective leading decisions (<3 percent), we do note that the six precedential votes cast by Taney Court dissenters occur in the last of the progeny in which the dissenter participated. Thus, *Kendall v. United States ex rel. Stokes* (1838) holds that federal courts may issue writs of mandamus to compel performance of ministerial acts. Taney disagrees, alleging an absence of such a power, and also agrees with Barbour and Catron, Jackson's final two appointees, that Congress had not invested the trial courts with the authority to issue such writs. In a series of four decisions, the dissenters are part of anti-mandamus majorities.[15] But in the last of this series, *United States ex rel. Crawford v. Addison* (1858), Taney and Catron switch positions and accede to the *Kendall* precedent that jurisdiction does exist.

The same pattern prevails in *Dodge v. Woolsey* (1852), which concerns the constitutionality under the contract clause of a state's revocation of a tax exemption. In dissent, Campbell, Catron, and Daniel deny the existence of federal court jurisdiction. Without opinion, they vote the same in *Mechanics' and Traders' Bank v. Debolt* (1855) and *Mechanics' and Traders' Bank v. Thomas* (1855). After the death of Daniel in 1860 and the resignation of Campbell in 1861, Catron twice votes as part of unanimous majorities upholding the exercise of federal jurisdiction and the unconstitutionality of state banking legislation: *Franklin Branch of the Bank of Ohio v. Ohio* (1862) and *Wright v. Sill* (1863). In the latter case, after citing *Dodge v. Woolsey*, *Debolt*, and *Franklin Bank*, the Court states: "Whatever difference of opinion may have existed in this

---

[15] *Decatur v. Paulding* (1840), *Brashear v. Mason* (1848), *United States ex rel. Tucker v. Seaman* (1855), and *United States v. Guthrie* (1854). Only the first was decided prior to Barbour's death in 1841.

Table 3.3.
Voting and opinion behavior: Taney Court landmarks

| | | | | Level of Expression | | | | | |
| | | | | Preferences (%) | | | Precedent (%) | | |
Justice	Prefs	/prec	%Prefs	Strong (1)	Moderate (2)	Weak (3)	Strong (1)	Moderate (2)	Weak (3)
Daniel (Dan)	5	0	100.0	1 (40.0)	3 (60.0)	1 (20.0)			
Campbell (Cm)	2	0	100.0		2 (100)				
McLean (McL)	2	0	100.0	1 (50.0)	1 (50.0)				
Barbour (Bar)	1	0	100.0			1 (100)			
Taney (Ta)	6	1	85.7		1 (16.7)	5 (83.3)		1 (100)	
Catron (Cat)	6	3	66.7		2 (33.3)	4 (66.7)	1 (33.3)	2 (66.7)	
Clifford (Cl)	0	2	0				1 (50.0)	1 (50.0)	
Totals	22	6	78.6	2 (9.1)	9 (40.9)	11 (50.0)	2 (33.3)	4 (66.7)	0

Precedent/progeny	Preferences	Precedent
Kendall v. United States ex rel. Stokes (1838) s		
Decatur v. Paulding (1840)	Bar-3	
	Cat-3	
	Ta-3	
Brashear v. Mason (1848)	Cat-3	
	Ta-3	
United States ex rel. Tucker v. Seaman (1854)	Cat-3	
	Ta-3	

Case	Codes
United States v. Guthrie (1854)	Cat-3, Ta-3
United States ex rel. Crawford v. Addison (1858)	Cat-2, Ta-2
Prigg v. Pennsylvania (1842) **c**	
Passenger Cases (1849)	Dan-2, Ta-2, Dan-3, McL-1, Ta-3
Moore v. Illinois (1852)	
Scott v. Sandford (1856)	McL-1
Pennsylvania v. Wheeling & Belmont Bridge Co. (1851) **c**	Dan-1
PA v. Wheeling & Belmont Bridge Co. (1855)	
Dodge v. Woolsey (1855) **c**	Cm-2, Cat-2, Dan-2
Mechanics' & Traders' Bank v. DeBolt (1855)	
Mechanics' & Traders' Bank v. Thomas (1855)	Cm-2, Cat-2, Dan-2
Franklin Bank of Ohio v. Ohio (1861)	Cat-2, Cat-1
Wright v. Sill (1862)	
Prize Cases (1862) **c**	Cl-1, Cl-2
Williams v. Bruffy (1877)	
Ford v. Surget (1878)	

Legend: **c** = constitutional decision
   s = statutory decision
   = decision neither constitutionally nor statutorily based

Note: All progeny rest on the same decisional basis as the precedent unless otherwise indicated.

court originally in regard to these questions, or might now exist if they were open for reconsideration, it is sufficient to say that they are concluded by these deliberations" (1862, 545). Although Catron did not write this language, his agreement clearly indicates a repudiation of his original position.

The final Taney Court landmark in which a dissenter repudiates his original position is *The Prize Cases* (1863), which involves the legality of a presidential proclamation of a naval blockade absent a declaration of war. Fifteen years later, the sole remaining dissenter, Clifford, adhered to the *Prize Cases*'s majority opinion in his concurring opinion in *Williams v. Bruffy* (1877, 193), and he reiterated it a year later in another concurrence in *Ford v. Surget* (1878, 608, 613, 621).

A pattern similar to that of the Taney Court's landmarks, though not as complete, prevails in the sample of ordinary Taney Court litigation (see Table 3.4):

- Justice Catron vigorously dissents from the decision in *Nelson v. Carland* (1843), objecting to the lack of uniformity prevailing in the administration of the bankruptcy laws. He reaffirms his position by dissenting again in *Ex parte City Bank of New Orleans* (1845).[16] But in *Carland*'s final progeny, *Crawford v. Points* (1851), he silently accedes to the Court's unanimous opinion citing both the precedent and *Ex parte Christy* as authority for its decision.
- Catron again reverts to precedent in the progeny of *Pollard v. Hagan* (1845), a case that applies an early variant of the equal footing doctrine to uphold Alabama's title to certain soil under navigable waters. He concludes his dissent from the decision with the following language:

  > I have expressed these views ... because this is deemed the most important controversy ever brought before this court [*sic!*], either as it respects the amount of property involved, or the principles on which the present judgment proceeds. (1845, 235)

  Catron's rhetoric, however, did not deter repudiation of his initial behavior in *Goodtitle v. Kibbe* (1850) and *Doe v. Beebe* (1851), where the Court unanimously affirmed Alabama court decisions voiding title to land on the shore of a navigable tidewater river under an act of Congress.
- McLean's votes and opinions in *Lessee of Gantly v. Ewing* (1845), *Planters' Bank v. Sharp* (1848), and *West River Bridge v. Dix* (1848), progeny of *Bronson v. Kinzie* (1843), maintain his original narrow view of the scope of the contract clause. But in *Howard v. Bugbee*

---

[16]   The Reports also refer to this case as *Ex parte Christy.*

(1861), three weeks before his death, he joined a unanimous opinion citing *Bronson*, the precedent from which he had dissented, as authority for voiding a state law authorizing a judgment creditor of a mortgagor to redeem the land within two years after the sale under the mortgage.[17]

- McKinley, Van Buren's first appointee, joins McLean in dissent in *Harris v. Robinson* (1846), a decision involving notice of nonpayment of a note. They object to the holder's failure to exercise due diligence. But they silently agree with their fellows in *Lambert v. Ghiselin* (1850) that due diligence was provided compatibly with the *Harris* precedent.

- Justices Grier and Wayne join Justice Nelson, who came to the Court only after four previous nominations by Tyler were rejected,[18] in dissent on the question of costs in *O'Reilly v. Morse* (1853), upholding the validity of Samuel Morse's patent of the telegraph. In *Seymour v. McCormick* (1857), Justice Nelson wrote the Court's opinion, joined by Wayne, to the effect that an unreasonable delay of disclaimer before instituting suit did not occur, thus warranting the award of costs. Grier, however, continues to dissent, indicating fidelity to his preferences, as does the language of his dissent in *Silsby v. Foote* (1858).[19]

- Catron, a stalwart defender of states' rights (Scheb 1992), joins two likeminded brethren dissenting in *Piqua Branch of the Bank of Ohio v. Knoop* (1853), where the majority holds that an increase in the rate of taxation to which a bank is subject violates the contract clause. In the first four *Knoop* progenies the dissenters adhere to their *Knoop* dissent. (See Table 3.4.) But in the final three, after the death of Daniel and the departure of Campbell, Catron joins a unanimous Court affirming the ruling in *Knoop* and its progeny: *Jefferson Branch Bank v. Skelly* (1862), *Franklin Branch of the Ohio Bank v. Ohio* (1862), and *Wright v. Sill* (1863).[20] The Court's brief opinion in

[17] We note in passing the language in the Court's opinion stating that the judges of the Alabama Supreme Court "felt bound by a decision of their predecessors, which they admitted to be in direct conflict with the case of *Bronson v. Kinzie*, and that the two decisions could not be reconciled" (1861, 465).

[18] Only two of these were for the seat that Nelson ultimately filled. The other two were for Henry Baldwin's open position, which eventually received a third unsuccessful nomination by Tyler, a spurned offer of the position by Polk to the future President James Buchanan (Witt 1990, p. 824), and a rejection by the Senate of Polk's next choice, before the seat was filled by Grier.

[19] Nelson's opinion of the Court, which Wayne joined, is inapposite to the precedent and excluded from consideration.

[20] The fifteen votes cast in progeny by the *Knoop* dissenters are the most of any Taney Court decision.

Table 3.4.
Voting and opinion behavior: Taney Court ordinary cases

Justice	Prefs/prec	%Prefs	Level of Expression					
			Preferences (%)			Precedent (%)		
			Strong (1)	Moderate (2)	Weak (3)	Strong (1)	Moderate (2)	Weak (3)
Daniel (Dan)	14	100.0	9 (64.3)	2 (14.3)	3 (21.4)			
Campbell (Cm)	5	100.0	3 (60.0)	2 (40.0)				
Taney (Ta)	1	100.0			1 (100)			
McLean (McL)	7	70.0	1 (11.1)	2 (28.6)	4 (57.1)		3 (100)	
Catron (Cat)	8	57.1	6 (75.0)	1 (12.5)	1 (12.5)		6 (100)	
Grier (Gr)	3	50.0	1 (33.3)	1 (33.3)	1 (33.3)		3 (100)	
Nelson (Ne)	2	50.0			2 (100)		2 (100)	
Wayne (Way)	2	50.0			2 (100)		2 (100)	
Clifford (Cl)	1	50.0	1 (100)				1 (100)	
McKinley (McK)	0	0.0						1 (100)
Totals	43	70.5	21 (48.8)	8 (18.6)	14 (32.6)	0	17 (94.4)	1 (5.6)
	18					–		–

Precedent/progeny	Preferences	Precedent
Nelson v. Carland (1843) **s**		
Ex parte City Bank of New Orleans (1845)	Cat-1	Cat-2
Crawford v. Points (1851)		
Bronson v. Kinzie (1843) **c**		
M'Cracken v. Hayward (1844)		McL-2
Lessee of Gantly v. Ewing (1845)	McL-3	
Planters' Bank v. Sharp (1848)	McL-2	
West River Bridge v. Dix (1848)	McL-2	McL-2
Howard v. Bugbee (1861)		

Case		
Gwin v. Breedlove (1844) c	Dan-3	Cat-2
Gwin v. Barton (1848)		Cat-2
Pollard v. Hagan (1845) s		McL-2 McK-2
Goodtitle v. Kibbe (1850)		
Doe v. Beebe (1851)		
Harris v. Robinson (1846)		
Lambert v. Ghiselin (1850)		
Fox v. Ohio (1847) c		
United States v. Marigold (1850)	McL-3	
Moore v. Illinois (1852)	McL-1	
Prentice v. Zane's Administrator (1850)		
Graham v. Bayne (1855)	McL-3 Way-3	
Guild v. Fontin (1856)	McL-3 Way-3	
Williamson v. Ball (1850)		
Suydam v. Williamson (1861)	Cat-Ne-Ta-3	
Williamson v. Suydam (1868)	Ne-3	
O'Reilly v. Morse (1853) s		Ne-2 Way-2
Seymour v. McCormick (1857)	Gr-2	
Silsby v. Foote (1858)	Gr-1	
Piqua Branch Bank of Ohio v. Knoop (1853) c	Cm-2 Cat-Dan-1	
Ohio Life Ins. & Trust Co. v. DeBolt (1853)	Cm-Cat-Dan-1	
Dodge v. Woolsey (1856)	Cm-Cat-Dan-1	
Mechanics' & Traders' Bank v. DeBolt (1856)	Cm-Cat-Dan-1	
Mechanics' & Traders' Bank v. Thomas (1856)		
Jefferson Bank v. Skelly (1862)		Cat-2
Franklin Bank v. Ohio (1862)		Cat-2
Wright v. Sill (1863)		Cat-2
Deshler v. Dodge (1853) c		
Ohio Life Ins. & Trust Co. v. DeBolt (1853)	Cat-1	
Dodge v. Woolsey (1856)	Cm-Cat-Dan-2	
Propeller Monticello v. Mollison (1855) c		
Providence v. Clapp (1855)	Dan-1	
Bank of Tennessee v. Horn (1855)	Dan-1	

Table 3.4 (cont.)

Precedent/progeny	Preferences	Precedent
Providence v. Clapp (1855) **c**		
Propeller Monticello v. Mollison (1855)	Dan-1	
Bank of Tennessee v. Horn (1855)	Dan-1	
Burchell v. Marsh (1855)		
NY&C R. Co. v. Myers (1856)		Ne-2
United States v. Peralta (1857)		
United States v. Cambuston (1858)	Dan-3	
Fuentes v. United States (1860)	Dan-3	
Covington Drawbridge Co. v. Shepherd (1858) **c**		
Covington Drawbridge Co. v. Shepherd (1858)	Dan-1	
Maguire v. Card (1859)		
Meyer v. Tupper (1862)		Way-2
Knox County v. Aspinwall (1859) **c**		
Knox County v. Wallace (1859)	Dan-2	
Lytle v. Arkansas (1860) **s**		
Magwire v. Tyler (1862)		Cl-3
Orient Mutual Ins. Co. v. Wright (1860)		
Sun Mutual Ins. Co. v. Wright (1860)	Cl-1	
Gaines v. Hennen (1861)		
Gaines v. New Orleans (1868)		Gr-2
Gaines v. De La Croix (1868)		Gr-2
Gaines v. Lizardi (1868)		Gr-2
Bridge Proprietors v. Hoboken Co. (1864) **s**		
Steamboat Victory v. Boylan (1868)	Gr-3	

Legend: **c** = constitutional decision
   s = statutory decision
   = decision neither constitutionally nor statutorily based
Note: All progeny rest on the same decisional basis as the precedent unless otherwise indicated.

the last of these stated that "Whatever difference of opinion may have existed in this court originally . . . are concluded by these adjudications. The argument upon both sides was exhausted in the earlier cases" (1863, 545). Given Catron's support for states' rights, his belated adherence to precedent is especially telling.

- Justice Nelson dissents in *Burchell v. Marsh* (1854). The majority ruled that the arbitrators' award was not so outrageous as to be conclusive evidence of fraud or corruption. Nelson viewed the award as "so extravagant, disproportioned and gross as to afford evidence of passion and prejudice" (1854, 352). Nelson, however, joined the majority opinion in *NY&C R. Co. v. Myers* (1856), notwithstanding his strong language objecting to the precedent. The majority's language is equally unequivocal: "This conclusion of his [the arbitrator] is a final decision on the question, for this court cannot revise his mistakes, either of law or fact, if such had been established" (1856, 253).

- Justice Wayne dissents without opinion in *Maguire v. Card* (1859). The Court revoked an admiralty rule of its own creation, authorizing the federal district courts to hear proceedings *in rem* against domestic vessels engaged in navigation and trade among ports in a single state.[21] Wayne subsequently joins a unanimous Court in *Meyer v. Tupper* (1862) applying the new rule. Because Wayne's vote occurs without opinion we cannot determine whether he objects to the Court's rule making or to the jurisdictional merits of the precedent. Either way, however, we consider his vote precedential.

- As in the preceding case, it is difficult to ascertain the basis for the dissenter's vote (Clifford) in *Magwire v. Tyler* (1862), the progeny of *Lytle v. Arkansas* (1860). Clifford had dissented from the decision in the precedent in an opinion written by McLean. Their dissent appears not to pertain to the merits of the controversy, but rather to the refusal of a state supreme court to defer to a U.S. Supreme Court decision. In the progeny, Clifford silently joins the majority opinion – McLean having died – that states, "The case falls within the principle declared in *Lytle v. Arkansas*" (1862, 203). Although the progeny turns on the question of the Supreme Court's jurisdiction, it bears no relevance to state court noncompliance. Indeed, the majority affirms the decision of the Missouri Supreme Court. Nonetheless, we consider Clifford's vote as one sustaining precedent. Though it is the only progeny, it also illustrates the tendency of Taney Court

---

[21] The case exemplifies an early example of the Court's exercise of rule making under the authority of acts of Congress. Congress delegated such power to the Court in its Acts of May 8, 1792 (1 Stat. 275), and August 23, 1842.

dissenters to vote precedentially in the last progeny of the precedent (see Table 3.4).

- The final instance of a Taney Court justice's voting precedentially in the last of the progeny in which he participated involves Justice Grier, the sole dissenter remaining when the progeny of *Gaines v. Hennen* (1861) were decided. Because it illustrates exceptionally well the ongoing nature of at least some Supreme Court litigation, as well as a human interest dimension alien to modern Supreme Court decision making, we provide a degree of superfluous detail. The *Gaines* precedent was itself the *sixth* in a line of cases that began with *Ex parte Whitney* (1839), *Gaines v. Relf* (1841), and *Gains v. Chew* (1844) and extended through *Patterson v. Gaines* (1848) to *Gaines v. Relf* (1851). The litigation, involving marital infidelity, illegitimacy, and bigamy, reads like a nineteenth-century soap opera. Justice Grier indicates in his one paragraph dissent that he deems it unnecessary to "vindicate my opinion by again presenting to the public a history of the scandalous gossip which has been buried under the dust of a half century" (1861, 631). He therefore hoped that this would be "the last time" he would confront the case and "the dim recollections, imaginations, or inventions of anile gossips" who, "after forty-five years . . . disturb the titles, and possessions of bona fide purchasers" (Id.). Grier's hope was dashed, seven years later, in a set of three companion cases that reaffirmed the precedent's decision without further objection from him or any of his colleagues: *Gaines v. New Orleans* (1868), *Gaines v. De La Croix* (1868), and *Gaines v. Lizardi* (1868).[22] The Court ends its *New Orleans* opinion by reaffirming "on mature consideration" its decision in the precedent, *Gaines v. Hennen*. It concludes on a most atypically plaintive note: "Can we not indulge the hope that the rights of Myra Clark Gaines in the estate of her father, Daniel Clark, will now be recognized?" (1868, 718).[23]

The votes pertaining to these bulleted precedents and their progeny account for 17 of the 18 precedential votes cast by dissenters (94.4

---

[22] Technically, only the first of these three companion cases references the precedent. The other two reference the first of its companions, *Gaines v. New Orleans*. To exclude the latter pair from consideration would, however, elevate form over substance, in addition to reducing the number of precedential votes.

[23] The Court answered its question for itself by ruling against Myra Clark Gaines in *Davis v. Gaines* (1881). She did, however, win in *Gaines v. Fuentes* (1876). The final nail was figuratively driven into her coffin in *New Orleans v. Christmas* (1889), when, after her death, her administrator unsuccessfully sustained her claims. For anyone interested, the opinion in *Christmas* coherently recounts the entire history of the litigation.

If any other litigation received more Supreme Court attention over a longer period we are unaware of it.

percent).[24] We note that the overall proportion of preferences/precedential votes (70.5 percent) is six and a half points lower than that of the common Marshall Court sample.

The Justices' Behavior

As for the justices themselves, given the heightened partisanship that the sectional crisis produced, both inside and outside the Court, one might have thought that the Taney Court justices would have displayed a higher proportion of preferential voting than the reputedly cohesive Marshall Court. In the ordinary litigation, for example, six of the ten participating Taney Court justices vote preferences less than 60 percent of the time. And although none of these justices other than Catron voted very often, they collectively cast half of the votes in common cases (31 of 61). Aside from Taney's single vote, only two justices cast more than 70 percent of their votes preferentially: Daniel and Campbell. Accordingly, the Taney Court appears split between a group of six justices who rather evenly divide their votes between precedent and preference and three, plus McLean,[25] who do not.

The increase in precedential voting cannot, however, be attributed entirely to the lack of salience that these ordinary cases possess. Thus, for example, we find Justice Daniel asserting in dissent in *Rich v. Lambert* (1851), a decision not in our sample, that the case is one in which he has "heretofore repeatedly expressed" his objections (1851, 360).[26] While Daniel is perhaps the most unyielding among the Taney Court justices in sustaining his preferences, we have noted other examples where justices adhere to their preferences notwithstanding the mundane character of the litigation.[27]

---

[24] The sole exception is McLean's vote in *M'Cracken v. Hayward* (1844), the initial progeny of *Bronson v. Kinzie* (1843).

[25] Adding McLean's two votes in the Taney Court landmarks raises his preferential percentage to 75 percent. On the Marshall Court, he split his six votes equally between preferences and precedent.

[26] The case concerns the effort by different shippers of goods damaged at sea to join their claims so as to meet the jurisdictional amount of $2000. The majority accepted as a given that admiralty jurisdiction applies. Daniel, however, demurs on this point, viewing the remedy as one at common law.

Another example of Daniel's willful adherence to preferences is his opinion in *Propeller Monticello v. Mollison* (1855), where he dissents because "of a want of jurisdiction in this court," rather than on the merits, adding that the reason for dissent "is simply to maintain my own consistency in adhering to convictions which are in nowise weakened" (1855, 156).

Also see Daniel's reiteration of his objection to the treatment of corporations as citizens in *Covington Drawbridge Co. v. Shepherd* (1858, 234).

[27] A clever example of the Court's use of precedent to sustain preferences – and simultaneously overrule a precedent *sub silentio* – occurs in *Suydam v. Williamson* (1861), a progeny of *Williamson v. Ball* (1850). *Ball* involves construction of a private act of the New York legislature enacted to remove obstacles to the execution of a trust under a

Somewhat surprisingly perhaps, given the extent of precedential voting, the level at which the Taney Court justices expressed themselves in the sample of ordinary litigation is quite high (see Table 3.4). By contrast, their level of preferential expression in landmark litigation produces a pattern even more strongly tilted in the opposite direction: over 90 percent of the votes are moderate or weak. All but one of the common precedential votes falls into the moderate category, a pattern reflective of the justices' overall behavior in ordinary litigation.

THE CHASE COURT

Salmon Chase, an ardent abolitionist, became Secretary of the Treasury in 1861. Responsible for financing the war effort, he oversaw the national government's first issuance of paper money. After disputes with Lincoln and unsuccessful attempts to receive the Republican presidential nomination in 1864, Chase resigned from the cabinet. In an effort to secure judicial support for Civil War and planned Reconstruction policies, and perhaps to remove a rival from the political scene, Lincoln nominated Chase to the Supreme Court upon Taney's death.

The Chase Court (1864–73) was a transitional Court that began with Civil War cases, moved on to Reconstruction, and ended with the earliest cases on the scope of the Fourteenth Amendment as a limit on the states' power to regulate business.

Perhaps the Court's most remarkable rulings came in the *Legal Tender Cases*.[28] Though Chase, as Secretary of Treasury, proposed and implemented the issuance of paper money as legal tender, he joined a majority of the Court in voting against its constitutionality. One year later the

---

will. Relief was to be provided by the famous Chancellor Kent. Over the dissents of three of the justices, the majority ruled that Kent lacked authority under New York law to administer the trusts in question. The dissenters – Catron, Nelson, and Taney – vigorously assert that only New York's courts could determine Kent's authority, and that – because they had done so – it was most inappropriate for the majority to disregard the state's own determination (1850, 558–60). Although the *Suydam* Court does not say that it overruled – but rather that it only reexamined – the decisions in the three *Williamson* cases (the third was *Williamson v. Berry* [1850]), one may nevertheless conclude that it effectively did so. The Court sustained the state court's decision notwithstanding plaintiffs' accurate assertion that under the three *Williamson* cases "every material question in this case is *res judicata*," and "Every principle by which our law of precedents is justified, tends against the reopening of the case in this court." (1861, 431). The Court disagreed, ruling that where property is concerned state law prevails, even though the Supreme Court has rendered a contradictory decision. Moreover, the Court will not reexamine its earlier opinion or "attempt to account for or to reconcile the difference," but "without any hesitation" it will apply the state's rule (1861, 434).

[28] *Hepburn v. Griswold* (1870) and the *Legal Tender Cases* (1871).

three dissenters, Lincoln appointees all, joined two new Grant appointees and upheld Congress's power to issue the currency under the necessary and proper clause.

In another set of Civil War–related decisions, the Court, after refusing to decide the constitutionality of military tribunals during the Civil War on the basis that Congress had not given it jurisdiction to do so,[29] effectively reversed itself once the war was over. In a two-part ruling, the Court unanimously held in *Ex parte Milligan* (1866) that the President lacks power to try civilians by military tribunals during wartime in places where the civil courts are open and functioning, and by a 5-to-4 vote that the combined war powers of President and Congress did not constitutionally authorize such tribunals where the regular courts were open.

The Radical Republicans responded to this decision by restricting the Court's jurisdiction to hear such cases (Epstein and Walker 1995). In *Ex parte McCardle* (1869) the Court, in a unanimous decision, deferred to Congress and upheld the law limiting its jurisdiction even though the case was already argued and awaiting decision.

By the end of the Chase Court the Civil War and Reconstruction were no longer major judicial issues, but in a portent of the type of case that would soon dominate the Court's agenda, the Chase Court was faced with one of the results of the war, the Fourteenth Amendment. The *Slaughterhouse Cases* (1873) had nothing to do with protections offered liberated blacks, but rather with a monopoly that Louisiana had granted to a slaughterhouse. Other butchers complained that the act put them out of business. Although the due process and equal protection clauses are among the most litigated constitutional provisions, the clause of the Fourteenth Amendment on which the majority focused – privileges and immunities – has been little used. The amendment created no new rights, said the Court, but allowed Congress, if it is so minded, to protect legislatively only the handful of privileges and immunities that peculiarly derive from federal rather than state citizenship. The right to own and operate a butcher shop was not among them.

Like those of the Taney Court, the votes of justices who dissent from the precedents in this Court's leading cases are concentrated in the progeny of only a couple of decisions: specifically the two sets of legal tender cases, *Hepburn v. Griswold* (1870) and the *Legal Tender Cases* (1871). Of the 40 votes that dissenters from the Chase Court's leading decisions cast, 29 occur in progeny of these two decisions (72.5 percent). See Table 3.5. By contrast, 25 of the 28 Taney Court votes occur in three cases (89.3 percent). Lessening the appearance of Taney Court

---

[29]   *Ex parte Vallandigham* (1864).

Table 3.5.
Voting and opinion behavior: Chase Court landmarks

| | | | Level of Expression | | | | | |
| | | | Preferences (%) | | | Precedent (%) | | |
Justice	Prefs/prec	%Prefs	Strong (1)	Moderate (2)	Weak (3)	Strong (1)	Moderate (2)	Weak (3)
Field (Fld)	6	0	100.0	3 (50.0)	2 (33.3)	1 (16.7)			
Clifford (Cl)	4	0	100.0	1 (25.0)	2 (50.0)	1 (25.0)			
Bradley (Brd)	1	0	100.0	1 (100)					
Chase (Ch)	5	1	83.3	2 (40.0)	2 (40.0)	1 (20.0)		1 (100)	
Davis (Dav)	5	2	71.4	5 (100)				2 (100)	
Swayne (Sw)	5	2	71.4	5 (100)				2 (100)	
Miller (Mil)	4	2	66.7	4 (100)				2 (100)	
Nelson (Ne)	1	2	33.3			1 (100)		2 (100)	
Totals	31	9	77.5	21 (67.7)	6 (19.4)	4 (12.9)	0	9 (100)	0

Precedent/progeny	Preferences	Precedent
Cummings v. Missouri (1867) **c**	Ch-Dav-Mil-Sw-1	
Ex parte Garland (1367)		Ch-Dav-Mil-Sw-2
Pierce v. Carskadon (1872)		
Hepburn v. Griswold (1870) **c**		Dav-Mil-Sw-2
McGlynn v. Magraw (1870)		
Legal Tender Cases (1871)	Dav-Mil-Sw-1	
Dooley v. Smith (1872)	Dav-Mil-Sw-1	
N&W R. Co. v. Johnson (1873)	Dav-Mil-Sw-1	
Juillard v. Greenman (1883)	Dav-1	
Legal Tender Cases (1871) **c**	Ch-Cl-Fld-Ne-3	
Trebilcock v. Wilson (1872)	Ch-Cl-Fld-2	Ne-2
Dooley v. Smith (1872)	Ch-Cl-Fld-2	Ne-2
SS Telegraph v. Gordon (1872)	Ch-Cl-Fld-2	
N&W R. Co. v. Johnson (1873)	Ch-Cl-Fld-1	
Juillard v. Greenman (1883)	Fld-1	
Slaughterhouse Cases (1873) **c**		
Bartemeyer v. Iowa (1874)	Brd-Fld-Sw-1	

Legend: **c** = constitutional decision

     s = statutory decision

     = decision neither constitutionally nor statutorily based

Note: All progeny rest on the same decisional basis as the precedent urless otherwise indicated.

concentration is the fact that the Congressional Quarterly *Guide to the U.S. Supreme Court* (Witt 1990) identifies 14 nonunanimous leading Taney Court decisions, as compared with nine decided by the Chase Court. Thus, 22 percent of the Chase Court's leading decisions generated a per precedent average of 36 percent of the progeny, as compared with 21 percent of the Taney Court's generating a per precedent average of 30 percent.

With regard to the *Legal Tender Cases*, which overruled *Hepburn v. Griswold* (1870), the behavior of the justices is preferentially consistent, with the exception of that of Justice Nelson, who dissents from the overruling of *Hepburn* and that of the three *Hepburn* dissenters in a case companion thereto: *McGlynn v. Magraw* (1870). Nelson silently accedes to the overruling of *Hepburn* in the two progeny of the *Legal Tender Cases* (1871) in which he participated: *Dooley v. Smith* (1872) and *The Steamship Telegraph v. Gordon* (1872). The *Hepburn* dissenters – Davis, Miller, and Swayne – silently join a unanimous Court in a brief opinion in *McGlynn v. Magraw* (1870), a case on all fours with *Hepburn* and decided the same day. Given Davis's, Miller's, and Swayne's votes to overrule *Hepburn* fifteen months later, we may safely assume they simply did not bother to repeat their objections, rather than recanting them. Their majority participation in the progeny of the overruling of *Hepburn* – *Dooley v. Smith* (1872), *Norwich & Worcester RR. Co. v. Johnson* (1873), and *Juilliard v. Greenman* (1883)[30] – supports this interpretation. Nonetheless, we adhere to our decision rules and count these votes as precedential. The four dissenters from the *Legal Tender Cases* – Chase, Clifford, Field, and Nelson – constitute part of the majority in *Trebilcock v. Wilson* (1872), holding the legal tender acts inapplicable. Excluding Nelson, they reaffirmed their opposition to the overruling of *Hepburn* in *Dooley*, *Steamship v. Gordon*, and *Norwich & Worcester RR.* Accordingly, 24 votes in the progeny of these cases support the justices' preferences, and either two or five adhere to precedent. A subjectively more accurate accounting suggests that only Nelson's two votes accede to precedent, but as Table 3.5 shows, we count all five.

The other two important Chase Court decisions that occasion participation in progeny by dissenters are *Cummings v. Missouri* (1867), the loyalty test oath case, and the *Slaughterhouse Cases* (1873). The four *Cummings* dissenters – Chase, Davis, Miller, and Swayne – adhere to their position in *Ex parte Garland* (1867) but vote precedentially in *Pierce v. Carskadon* (1872). The *Slaughterhouse Cases* beget a progeny in *Bartemeyer v. Iowa* (1874), in which Field, Swayne, and Bradley, the

---

[30]   Only Davis was still a member of the Court when *Juilliard* was decided.

holdover dissenters, specifically adhere to their original position in their special concurrences.

Only three ordinary Chase Court cases generate any progeny (see Table 3.6). To some substantial extent this is a function of this Court's brief life, a total of eight and a half years. Among chief justices, only Stone, five years, and Vinson, seven years, served for a shorter period during the nineteenth and twentieth centuries.

One of the three common cases, however, warrants extended discussion: *Riggs v. Johnson County* (1868). For a Court reputedly scarred by the *Dred Scott* decision and its aftermath, the holding in *Riggs* appears as dismissive of state autonomy as any decision in the Court's entire history, arguably, even more so. The Court held (1) that state courts cannot prevent federal courts from resolving the same dispute and (2) that a federal court sitting in the same state and deciding the same issue can disregard and overrule the construction the state court gives to its own constitutions and statutes. Justice Miller, joined by Chase and Grier, dissented on the second point, observing that as a result of the majority's decision, "state officers are commanded to disobey an injunction of a state court, rendered in regular judicial proceedings, to which they were proper parties, in a matter in which that court had undoubted jurisdiction" (1868, 200). The majority did back off from its holding, however, in the first of *Riggs*'s progenies, *United States ex rel. Morgan v. Gates* (1869). Notwithstanding specific reference to *Riggs*, the Court unanimously enforces a decision of the Wisconsin Supreme Court applying the letter of the state's relevant law.[31]

A month before he retired, Grier parted company with Miller and Chase and voted with the majority in *United States ex rel. Butz v. Mayor of Muscatine* (1869), who held that the Supreme Court determines for itself the construction and effect of a state statute without reference to decisions of the state supreme court. Swayne's language for the Court is mindbogglingly instructive:

> There are several adjudications of the highest court of the State. . . . We do not deem it necessary . . . to advert to them. . . . It is alike the duty of that court and of this to decide the questions involved in this class of cases. . . . It cannot be performed on our part by blindly following the footsteps of others. . . .
>
> Were we to accept such a solution we should abdicate the performance of a solemn duty, betray a sacred trust committed to our charge, and defeat the wise

---

[31] We do not consider *United States ex rel. Moses v. Keokuk* (1868), *United States ex rel. Thomas v. Keokuk* (1868), *Cox v. United States ex rel. McGarrahan* (1870), or *Graham v. Norton* (1873) as progeny of *Riggs* because the decisions in these cases rest exclusively on the first prong of the *Riggs* decision, not the aspect on which Miller and company dissent.

Table 3.6.
Voting and opinion behavior: Chase Court ordinary cases

Justice	Prefs/prec	%Prefs	Level of Expression					
			Preferences (%)			Precedent (%)		
			Strong (1)	Moderate (2)	Weak (3)	Strong (1)	Moderate (2)	Weak (3)
Miller (Mil)	8	0	100.0		2 (25.0)	6 (75.0)			
Field (Fld)	3	0	100.0			3 (100)			
Chase (Ch)	2	0	100.0		2 (100)				
Grier (Gr)	1	1	50.0		1 (100)			1 (100)	
Totals	14	1	93.3	0	5 (35.7)	9 (64.3)	0	1 (100)	0

Precedent/progeny	Preferences	Precedent
United States v. Circuit Judges (1866) **s**		
In re Zellner (1870)		
Riggs v. Johnson County (1868)	Fld-Mil-3	
United States ex rel. Morgan v. Gates (1869)	Ch-Gr-Mil-2	
United States v. Mayor of Muscatine (1869)	Ch-Mil-2	Gr-2
Rees v. Watertown (1874)	Mil-3	
Heine v. Board of Levee Commissioners (1874)	Mil-3	
Rosenbaum v. Bauer (1887)	Mil-3	
United States v. Hartwell (1868) **s**		
United States v. Germaine (1879)	Fld-Mil-3	
United States v. Smith (1888)	Fld-Mil-3	

Legend: **c** = constitutional decision
s = statutory decision
= decision neither constitutionally nor statutorily based

Note: All progeny rest on the same decisional basis as the precedent unless otherwise indicated.

Table 3.7.
Preferential voting on the early Courts

	Landmarks		Common cases	
Court	N	%	N	%
Marshall	13–3	81.3	10–3	76.4
Taney	22–6	78.6	43–18	70.5
Chase	31–9	77.5	14–1	93.3
Totals	66–18	78.6	67–22	75.3

and provident policy of the Constitution which called this court into existence. (1869, 582)

After Chase's death, Miller continued to vote his preferences in *Rees v. Watertown* (1874), *Heine v. Board of Levee Commissioners* (1874), and *Rosenbaum v. Bauer* (1887).

The Justices' Behavior

The 15 votes cast by justices of the Chase Court in our random sample of ordinary cases clearly deviates from that of the Marshall and Taney Courts. Only a single vote of Grier adheres to precedent. Not only are these votes distributed among only four justices, over half (eight) are cast by Miller alone, as Table 3.6 shows. Moreover, none of the preferential votes is strongly expressed; by contrast, nine of the 14 are weakly so. As a result, we discount the behavior displayed in these few votes, especially since the preferential/precedential ratio varies so starkly from the percentages in the landmark cases. Although Field behaves completely preferentially in both components, Miller does not, casting two of his six landmark progeny votes precedentially. Inasmuch as both these justices served throughout the succeeding Court, we will qualify judgment about the Chase Court pending analysis of the Waite Court.

Notwithstanding that the Chase Court justices cast more than twice as many votes in their landmarks as in their common cases, their preferential proportion falls appreciably below the latter, 16 points. In further contrast, the justices express themselves much more vigorously in their landmarks than in the ordinary litigation. Over two-thirds of the former votes receive strong support, none of the votes in the common cases. But even these lower ratios preclude support for precedential voting. Any

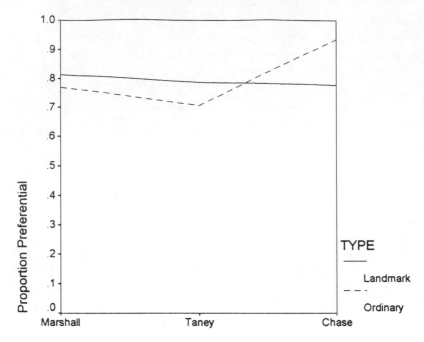

Figure 3.1. Precedential/preferential behavior on the Marshall, Taney, and Chase Courts.

support for precedent that the Taney Court displays has been dashed by the behavior of the Chase Court justices.

Figure 3.1 and Table 3.7 display these results in a summary fashion. We include the Marshall and Taney Courts in order to provide a comparative perspective. From a theoretical standpoint, then, we find some moderate levels of precedential support, but overall the findings are most consistent with preferential models. In subsequent chapters, we provide parallel figures that extend the data from Figure 3.1 to include the same data from the more recent Courts.

4

Precedential Behavior
Bridging the Nineteenth
and Twentieth Centuries

We begin this chapter with an examination of the sleepy Waite Court (1874–88), followed by the more activist Fuller (1888–1910), White (1910–21), and Taft (1921–30) Courts.[1] The post-Waite Courts may properly be characterized as protectors of propertied interests in the United States by whatever means necessary, be it the taxation, commerce, spending, or due process clause.[2]

THE WAITE COURT

On January 19, 1874, President Ulysses S. Grant nominated Morrison Waite to the position of Chief Justice of the United States. The Senate confirmed two days later. Thus ended the most unsuccessful run of Supreme Court nominations for any president whose party controlled the Senate.[3]

Grant's troubles began in 1869 when he nominated his Attorney General, Ebenezer Hoar, for a newly re-created ninth seat on the Court.[4] To appease a Senate unhappy with Hoar's nomination, he then nominated Edwin M. Stanton.[5] The Senate responded by confirming Stanton (who then died four days later) and decisively rejecting Hoar. Grant ultimately succeeded in filling these vacancies with the nominations of William Strong, a former justice on the Pennsylvania Supreme Court,

---

[1] But see Warren (1923) for evidence of restraint on these Courts.

[2] Gillman (1993) has a more benign take on *Lochner* era jurisprudence: "The decisions and opinions that emerged from state and federal courts during the LOCHNER era represented a serious, principled effort to maintain one of the central distinctions in nineteenth-century constitutional law – the distinction between valid economic regulation, on the one hand, and invalid 'class' legislation, on the other – during a period of unprecedented class conflict" (p. 10). See also Ackerman (1991).

[3] This excludes Presidents John Tyler and Andrew Johnson, who, while elected on Whig and Union tickets, respectively, were both Democrats.

[4] Congress had reduced the size of the Court from 10 to 8 in order to prevent Andrew Johnson from filling vacancies. It re-created the ninth seat early in Grant's term.

[5] Johnson's firing of Stanton as Secretary of War instigated Johnson's impeachment.

and Joseph Bradley, a Radical Republican. Both were selected in large part to overturn the original legal tender decisions, and both lived up to expectations.[6]

Grant's troubles began anew on Salmon Chase's death in 1873. First, Senator Roscoe Conkling (Republican of New York) declined nomination. A few months later, Grant nominated his Attorney General, George H. Williams, only to be forced to withdraw the nomination one month later in the face of Senate opposition over an apparent lack of qualifications. Grant followed Williams's nomination with the nomination of Caleb Cushing, who too would see his name withdrawn.[7] Grant finally settled on Morrison Waite, who had no judicial experience, but had gained some degree of prominence for his service on the Geneva Arbitration Commission.[8] The Senate confirmed Waite 63–0.

With Civil War litigation drawing to a close and calls for regulation of the economy largely unheeded, the Waite Court busied itself with the most mundane commercial litigation, rendering few exceptional decisions. A few, though, stand out.

- In 1876 the Supreme Court gutted congressional legislation designed to protect blacks who exercised their right to vote under the Fifteenth Amendment.[9] Then in the *Civil Rights Cases* of 1883, the same fate befell congressional legislation designed to outlaw discrimination in places of public accommodation. The Fourteenth Amendment does not apply to private discrimination, said the justices, but only that produced by affirmative state action. Discrimination by privately owned public utilities, though they are heavily regulated by government, does not constitute state action.

  Over the solo dissent of a former Kentucky slave owner, John M. Harlan, the majority held that "Individual invasion of individual rights is not the subject-matter of the Amendment." The power to enforce the Amendment "does not invest Congress with power to legislate upon subjects which are within the domain of state legisla-

---

[6] Bradley later cast the crucial votes on the Presidential Election Commission of 1876, securing the fraudulent election of Rutherford B. Hayes. Beyond the clear vote fraud against Tilden in the southern states of Florida, Louisiana, and South Carolina, Bradley allegedly switched his commission vote to favor the Republicans after pressure "from leading Republican and railroad interests, to which he was supposedly beholden" (Schwartz 1993, p. 172).

[7] Among other things, Cushing was 74 years old and had shifted political parties four times.

[8] The commission helped settle arbitration claims against England stemming from the Civil War.

[9] In *United States v. Reese* (1876) and *United States v. Cruikshank* (1876).

tion," but only provides "relief against state legislation or state action" (p. 111).

- Such literalism was not apparent when the Supreme Court declared that corporations were "persons" within the meaning of the Fourteenth Amendment, as the Court declared in *Santa Clara County v. Southern Pacific R. Co.* (1886). After the Court received briefs on the question, Chief Justice Waite simply announced that "The court does not wish to hear oral argument on the question whether the provision in the Fourteenth Amendment to the Constitution . . . applies to these corporations. We are all of [the] opinion that it does" (p. 396).
- This decision would have extraordinary import when the Court began striking economic regulation as violating the "right to contract" it found inherent in the Fourteenth Amendment, but the Waite Court was not ready for such action. In *Munn v. Illinois* (1876) the Court agreed that due process limited state interference with property rights, but ruled that such rights were limited by the state's power to regulate businesses "affected with a public interest" (p. 130). In this case, the state's interest in regulating grain elevators overrode the owners' property interests.

Eighteen of the 39 votes cast by dissenters in progeny of leading Waite Court decisions locate – not surprisingly – in progeny of *Munn*. Justice Field in dissent, joined by Strong, took the opportunity to argue for a substantive concept of due process that a majority of the Court would soon embrace. Strong, equally ardent in his support of both capitalistic and Christian principles, adhered to his *Munn* position, as did Field, except Field failed to dissent in the unanimously decided *Dow v. Beidelman* (1888). Given his language in opinions such as that in *Ruggles v. Illinois* (1883),[10] his failure to dissent in *Dow* can only be described as an anomaly. Nonetheless, we count it as a precedential vote.

Field also accounts for the second of the three precedential votes cast in progeny of Waite Court landmarks. *Mugler v. Kansas* (1886) upheld a state prohibition law. But in *Kidd v. Pearson* (1888), the third of four progeny, he silently joined his colleagues in upholding Iowa's right to abate a distillery as a nuisance. Field apparently viewed the Iowa abatement as applying exclusively to intrastate liquor, unlike his specification of the situation in the third of the three cases combined for decision in *Mugler*. Although this explanation is a plausible one, Field's failure to articulate it warrants viewing his *Kidd* vote as precedential.

---

[10] "I do not give any weight to *Munn v. Illinois.* . . . My objections to the decision in that case were expressed at the time it was rendered, and they have been strengthened by subsequent reflection" (541, 1883).

Although one landmark produced a disproportionate number of the votes in progeny, this does not explain the Waite Court's extremely high proportion of preferential votes (92.3 percent) – 36 of 39 (see Table 4.1). Moreover, the three precedential votes are succeeded by a return to preferential voting by the pertinent justices – Field and Harlan. Approximately half of the preferential votes are strongly such (17). Nine classify as moderate, ten as weak. Although these proportions do not incline as precipitously toward the strong end as do those of the Chase Court (21 of 31), neither does the Waite Court reflect Chase's higher proportion of precedential votes.

On the other hand, only four of the 15 justices who served on the Waite Court participated in progeny of the Court's landmark decisions; that figure matches the Marshall Court's proportion and is below the seven of twenty on the Taney Court and the eight of twelve on the Chase Court. This low proportion may possibly explain the high level of preferential voting. Although Field anchors the scale of preferential Waite Court voters,[11] he led the Chase Court justices. His overall proportion on these two Courts is 91.7 percent (22 of 24).

In frequency of dissenters' votes in progeny, the sample of the Waite Court's ordinary litigation corresponds much more closely to the Taney than to the Chase Court even though its length was half that of the Taney Court (29 versus 14 years). On the other hand, the number of precedents producing dissenters' votes in progeny was much smaller than was true of the Taney Court, whose 61 votes are scattered among 22 precedents; the 80 of the Waite Court among only ten.

Dissenters from *Coloma v. Eaves* (1876) produce more votes in progeny than is true of any of the sampled Waite Court decisions, 27.[12] They also produce more precedential votes than any other Waite Court case, eight (of a total of 18; see Table 4.2). Davis, Field, and Miller dissented without opinion from the majority's decision that bonds issued by a municipal corporation reciting the condition precedent that the authorizing state statute required is conclusive and obligates the corporation to holders in due course. The same trio reiterated their opinionless dissent in *Genoa v. Woodruff* (1876), *Venice v. Murdock* (1876), and *Marcy v. Oswego* (1876). But in a final 1876 case, *Humboldt Township v. Long*, the dissenters terminated their silence in a Miller opinion abjuring the precedent. Given this emphatic dissent, as well as those written in subse-

---

[11]   A percentage of 88.9 hardly qualifies as an "anchor." Nonetheless, no one is lower.
[12]   A substantial number of cases cite *Coloma*. Compatibly with the decision rules specified in Chapter 2, we include as progeny only those citing *Coloma* in their summary or as more than a part of a string of citations. The included cases all pertain to the issue in *Coloma*: the issuance of bonds by local governments and their obligations to holders of these bonds.

quent cases, their votes in *County Commissioners v. Bolles* (1877) supporting the precedent come as a surprise. Perhaps the Reporter overlooked their dissent. No plausible reason suggests deviation from their opposition to the *Coloma* precedent. Eleven weeks later the dissenters reaffirmed their preferences in *South Ottawa v. Perkins* (1877), a case decided on reargument. Bradley and Hunt switched sides, voting with the *Coloma* dissenters, with the other members of the erstwhile majority – Clifford, Strong, Swayne, and Waite – in dissent. After Davis's departure, Field and Miller continued to vote antibondholder in *Buchanan v. Litchfield* (1880) and *Dixon County v. Field* (1884). But in *County Commissioners v. Beal* (1885) and *County Commissioners v. Potter* (1892) they silently joined pro-bondholder majorities, as did Field, after Miller's death, in *Evansville v. Dennett* (1896).

In a railroad case, *CM&St.P R. Co. v. Ackley* (1877), Field, joined by Strong, continued to express opposition to *Munn v. Illinois* (1877), an opposition that they applied to *W&St.P R. Co. v. Blake* (1877) and *Stone v. Wisconsin* (1877). After Strong's resignation, Field adhered to his preferences in dissent in *Budd v. New York* (1892). Field's reference to *Munn* in *Ackley* epitomizes the hostility of laissez-faire economics toward unsympathetic business regulation: "That decision . . . practically destroys all the guaranties of the Constitution and of the common law invoked by counsel for the protection of the rights of the railroad companies. . . . It sanctions intermeddling with all business and pursuits and property in the community, leaving the use and enjoyment of property and the compensation for its use to the discretion of the Legislature" (1877, 186–87).

Although peripheral to our concern with precedent, *Cannon v. United States* (1885) warrants attention. The case pertained to the construction of a federal criminal law relating to polygamy. Disregarding any pretense of strict construction – or even common sense – the majority defined the operative verb, "cohabits," as living in the same house with two or more women whom the defendant held to be his wives and with whom he ate occasionally. It did not require that he sleep or have intercourse with either of them (1885, 74). Field joined Miller's terse dissent that cohabitation requires "actual sexual connection" (1884, 80). One year later, in *Snow v. United States* (1886), the Court – perhaps realizing that its ruling left the emperor sans clothing – used its status as a court of limited jurisdiction and unanimously reversed itself "in order that the reported decision [*Cannon*] may not appear to be a precedent" (1886, 355).[13] The Court's decision arguably amounts to its most egregious confession

---

[13] The Court need not await a motion to this effect by either party. It may dismiss for want of jurisdiction on its own authority.

Table 4.1.
Voting and opinion behavior: Waite Court landmarks

Justice	Prefs/prec		%Prefs	Level of Expression					
				Preferences (%)			Precedent (%)		
	Prefs	prec		Strong (1)	Moderate (2)	Weak (3)	Strong (1)	Moderate (2)	Weak (3)
Gray (Gra)	5	0	100.0			5 (100)			
Strong (Stg)	5	0	100.0	5 (100)					
Harlan (Har)	10	1	90.9	3 (30.0)	7 (70.0)				1 (100)
Field (Fld)	16	2	88.9	9 (56.3)	2 (12.5)	5 (31.3)	–	2 (100)	–
Totals	36	3	92.3	17 (47.2)	9 (25.0)	10 (27.8)	0	2 (66.7)	1 (33.3)

Precedent/progeny	Preferences	Precedent
Munn v. Illinois (1877) **c**		
CB&Q R. Co. v. Cutts (1877)	Fld-Stg-1	
Peik v. CNW R. Co. (1877)	Fld-Stg-1	
CMStP&P R. Co. v. Ackley (1877)	Fld-Stg-1	
W&StP R. Co. v. Blake (1877)	Fld-Stg-1	
Stone v. Wisconsin (1877)	Fld-Stg-1	
Ruggles v. Illinois (1883)	Fld-1	
WStL&P R. Co. v. Illinois (1886)	Fld-3	
Dow v. Beidelman (1888)		Fld-2
CM&StP R. Co. v. Minnesota (1890)	Fld-3	
Budd v. New York (1892)	Fld-1	
Brass v. North Dakota (1894)	Fld-1	
Covington & Cinti Bridge Co. v. KY (1894)	Fld-3	
MP R. Co. v. Nebraska (1896)	Fld-3	

Case		
Ex parte Siebold (1879) **s**		
Ex parte Coy (1888)	Fld-2	
Civil Rights Cases (1883) **c**		
Baldwin v. Franks (1887)	Har-2	
Robertson v. Baldwin (1897)	Har-2	
Hodges v. United States (1906)	Har-2	
Patterson v. Colorado (1907)	Har-2	
Hurtado v. California (1884) **c**		
Baldwin v. Kansas (1889)	Har-1	
Hallinger v. Davis (1892)		Har-3
Talton v. Mayes (1896)	Har-2	
Maxwell v. Dow (1900)	Har-1	
Dorr v. United States (1904)	Har-1	
Twining v. New Jersey (1908)	Har-2	
Dowdell v. United States (1910)	Har-2	
WStL&P R. Co. v. Illinois (1886) **c**		
Covington & Cinti Bridge Co. v. KY (1894)	Gra-3	
Adams Express Co. v. Ohio State Auditor (1897)	Gra-3	
Henderson Bridge Co. v. Kentucky (1897)	Gra-3	
LS&MS R. Co. v. Ohio (1899)	Gra-3	
Austin v. Tennessee (1900)	Gra-3	
Mugler v. Kansas (1887) **c**		
Bowman v. CNW R. Co. (1888)	Fld-1	
Powell v. Pennsylvania (1888)	Fld-2	
Kidd v. Pearson (1888)		Fld-2
Leisy v. Hardin (1890)	Fld-3	

Legend: **c** = constitutional decision
       s = statutory decision
       = decision neither constitutionally nor statutorily based

Note: All progeny rest on the same decisional basis as the precedent unless otherwise indicated.

Table 4.2.
Voting and opinion behavior: Waite Court ordinary cases

Justice	Prefs/prec		%Prefs	Preferences (%) Strong (1)	Moderate (2)	Weak (3)	Level of Expression Precedent (%) Strong (1)	Moderate (2)	Weak (3)
Harlan (Har)	5	0	100.0		4 (80.0)	1 (20.0)		1 (100)	
Swayne (Sw)	8	1	88.9		4 (50.0)	4 (50.0)		1 (100)	
Strong (Stg)	6	1	85.7	2 (33.3)	2 (33.3)	2 (33.3)		1 (100)	
Davis (Dav)	5	1	83.3	1 (20.0)	3 (60.0)	1 (20.0)		1 (100)	
Field (Fld)	19	5	79.2	3 (15.8)	12 (63.2)	4 (21.1)		5 (100)	
Bradley (Brd)	7	2	77.8		3 (42.9)	4 (57.1)		2 (100)	
Miller (Mil)	9	5	64.3	1 (11.1)	5 (55.6)	3 (33.3)		5 (100)	
Clifford (Cl)	3	3	50.0			3 (100)		2 (66.7)	1 (33.3)
Totals	62	18	77.5	7 (11.3)	33 (53.2)	22 (34.9)	0	17 (94.4)	1 (5.6)

Precedent/progeny	Preferences	Precedent
Nashville Mayor & Council v. Ray (1874)		Cl-Sw-Stg-2
Nashville v. Lindsay (1874)		
Hitchcock v. Galveston (1878)	Cl-Sw-Stg-3	
Little Rock v. Merchants' Nat'l Bank (1878)	Cl-Sw-Str-3	
Wall v. Monroe County (1881)		Cl-3
Murdock v. Memphis (1875) s		
B&O R. Co. v. Maryland (1875)	Brd-Cl-Sw-3	
Tennessee v. Davis (1880)	Brd-Sw-3	Cl-2
New Jersey v. Wright (1886)	Brd-3	
Barnes v. District of Columbia (1876)		
Maxwell v. District of Columbia (1876)	Brd-Fld-Sw-Stg-2	
Dant v. District of Columbia (1876)	Brd-Fld-Sw-Stg-2	
Johnston v. District of Columbia (1886)	Brd-Fld-3	

Case		
District of Columbia v. Woodbury (1890)		
Coloma v. Eaves (1876)		Brd-Fld-2
Genoa v. Woodruff (1876)	Dav-Fld-Mil-2	
Venice v. Murdock (1876)	Dav-Fld-Mil-2	
Marcy v. Oswego (1876)	Dav-Fld-Mil-2	
Humboldt Township v. Long (1876)	Dav-Fld-Mil-1	
County Commissioners v. Bolles (1877)		Dav-Fld-Mil-2
South Ottawa v. Board of Supervisors (1877)	Dav-Fld-Mil-3	
Buchanan v. Litchfield (1880)	Fld-Mil-2	
Dixon County v. Field (1884)	Fld-Mil-3	
County Commissioners v. Beal (1885)		Fld-Mil-2
County Commissioners v. Potter (1892)		Fld-Mil-2
Evansville v. Dennett (1896)		Fld-2
LS&M R. Co. v. United States (1877) s		
AT&SF R. Co. v. D&NO R. Co. (1884)	Mil-3	
CM&StP R. Co. v. Ackley (1877) c		
W&StP R. Co. v. Blake (1877)	Fld-Stg-1	
Stone v. Wisconsin (1877)	Fld-Stg-1	
Budd v. New York (1892)	Fld-2	
Cass County v. Johnston (1877)		Mil-2
Cass County v. Jordan (1877)	Brd-2	
Carroll County v. Smith (1884)		Brd-Mil-2
Casey v. Cavaroc (1878)		
Casey v. National Park Bank (1878)	Fld-Har-Sw-2	
Casey v. Schuchardt (1878)	Fld-Har-Sw-2	
Cannon v. United States (1885) s		
Snow v. United States (1886)	Fld-Mil-2	
Railroad Commission Cases (1886) c		
Stone v. IC R. Co. (1886)	Fld-Har-2	
Stone v. NO&NE R. Co. (1886)	Fld-Har-2	
WStL&P R. Co. v. Illinois (1896)	Fld-Har-3	

Legend: c = constitutional decision
         s = statutory decision
            = decision neither constitutionally nor statutorily based

Note: All progeny rest on the same decisional basis as the precedent unless otherwise indicated.

of error in history. Rarely if ever does the Court find a want of jurisdiction after its decision is publicly announced, but that was the situation here:

The question of jurisdiction was not considered in fact in that case [*Cannon*], nor alluded to in the decision, nor presented to the court by the counsel for the United States, nor referred to by either party at the argument or in the briefs. Probably both parties desired a decision on the merits. The question was overlooked by all the members of the court. (1886, 354)

In comparison with the Taney Court, which, in number of votes and preferential proportion, most closely approximates the Waite Court, we find much less extreme voting. The preferential proportion of four of the eight Waite Court justices falls within ten points of the Court's mean, as opposed to but one of the Taney Court's ten. Two others – Swayne and Miller – are within 13 points, as Table 4.2 shows. But in expressing preferences, the Waite Court justices fall substantially below the strength with which those on the Taney Court did so. In this regard, the Waite Court reflects the behavior of the Marshall and Chase Court justices. On the other hand, adherence to precedent overwhelmingly produces moderate expression, 94.4 percent – the same percentage as the Taney Court attains.

Given this behavior and the rather inexplicable waffling between preferences and precedent that dissenters from such precedents as *Coloma v. Eaves* (1876) and *Cass County v. Johnston* (1877) display in the progeny of these cases, it appears that such reputedly doctrinaire justices as Field, Bradley, and Miller may have voted more pragmatically than might have been expected, given their behavior on the preceding Court. Field and Miller cast none but preferential votes in the sample of ordinary Chase Court litigation – three and eight votes, respectively. In landmark decisions, Field regularly voted his preferences (6 of 6), Miller much less so (4 of 6). Though it is only speculation, the beginning of the process whereby the justices wrote laissez-faire economics into the Constitution may possibly explain the apparent lack of firm attachment to either precedent or preference.

THE FULLER COURT

The Waite Court, by allowing corporations to have the same Fourteenth Amendment rights as people, and by accepting limits on state regulatory power over businesses "not affected with a public interest," set the stage for a judicial chokehold on efforts to limit the effects of laissez-faire capitalism.

We start with taxation. In 1894, Congress enacted the Wilson-Gorman

Tariff Act, which placed a tax of two percent on the income of individuals and corporations from rents, interest, dividends, salaries, and profits over $4,000. Progressive and Populist elements hailed the tax as a great victory. So much did the plunderbund fear the tax that they told the Court that the act was part of a "'Communist march' against the rights of property" (Pritchett 1977, p. 68). In April 1895, the Court declared in *Pollock v. Farmers' Loan and Trust* that the tax on rents was in reality a tax on land and thus a direct tax that must be apportioned. Taxes on municipal bonds were invalidated on the grounds of intergovernmental immunity. With Justice Jackson ill, the Court split 4 to 4 on the constitutionality of the income tax. When Jackson recovered, the case was reargued. Jackson joined those who thought the income tax constitutional, but Justice Shiras switched, invalidating the tax.[14] According to the Supreme Court historian Robert McCloskey, the direct tax clause "provided the judges with an objective formulation of their prejudice in favor of wealth" (1960, p. 141).

In a final blow to the act, the Court also struck the tax on business profits and employment income. It did not find such taxes unconstitutional; rather, it asserted that Congress would not have taxed these sources of income if it could not also tax dividends, interest, and rent. The *Pollock* decisions led to the ratification of the Sixteenth Amendment, one of four times an amendment undid a decision of the Court. The Amendment simply states that "The Congress shall have power to lay and collect taxes on incomes, from whatever source derived, without apportionment among the several States, and without regard to any census or enumeration." As we shall see, the Amendment also did not prevent the White and Taft Courts from voiding taxes by labeling them constitutionally prohibited *nontaxes*.

The same year that the Supreme Court ruled the income tax unconstitutional, 1895, it severely limited federal power to regulate interstate commerce. The first relevant case, *United States v. E.C. Knight Co.*, involved enforcement of the Sherman Antitrust Act, enacted by Congress in 1890, which made "every contract, combination . . . or conspiracy in restraint of trade or commerce among the several states, or with foreign nations . . . illegal." The Department of Justice sought to break up the American Sugar Refining Company, which, through acquisitions, controlled over 98 percent of the nation's sugar refining.

The Court conceded that the sugar trust was an illegal monopoly; the relevent question, rather, was whether Congress had the authority to suppress monopolies. The Court said it did not. First, the Court asserted

---

[14] *Pollock v. Farmers' Loan and Trust Co.* (1895). Also see King (1967, pp. 193–221).

that the protection of life, health, and property is part of the police power, which belongs exclusively to the states. When monopolies burden the citizens of a state, the state's legislature must remedy the wrong. Second, while the Court recognized that Congress had plenary authority to regulate interstate commerce, it denied that the manufacture of 98 percent of the nation's sugar in several different states by one company constituted commerce. Drawing a distinction between manufacturing and commerce, the Court declared that "Commerce succeeds to manufacture, and is not a part of it" (p. 12). Monopolistic production affects commerce only indirectly, and thus is beyond the power of Congress to regulate.[15]

When the federal government tried to regulate the economy, the Court's answer typically was that such regulation was up to the states, but when the states tried to regulate the economy, the Court adopted a new legal device to protect capitalism: substantive due process. The first case in which the Supreme Court struck down a state law on substantive due process grounds was the 1897 decision in *Allgeyer v. Louisiana*. The Court invalidated a Louisiana statute that prohibited Louisiana companies from purchasing marine insurance from out-of-state businesses that did not comply with Louisiana regulations. The Court overturned Allgeyer's conviction for purchasing the insurance because

the statute is a violation of the fourteenth amendment of the federal constitution, in that it deprives the defendants of their liberty without due process of law. . . . The "liberty" mentioned in that amendment means, not only the right of a citizen to be free from the mere physical restraint of his person, as by incarceration, but the term is deemed to embrace the right of the citizen to be free to . . . enter into all contracts which may be proper, necessary and essential to his carrying out to a successful conclusion the purposes above mentioned. (p. 589)

However nugatory the substance of the *Allgeyer* decision might seem – allowing companies to let out-of-state contracts hardly seems momentous – the scope of the new right to contract became apparent in *Lochner v. New York* (1905). Under its police powers, the State had enacted a maximum-hour law limiting bakers to ten hours of work per day and sixty hours of work per week. In a 5-to-4 decision the Court ruled that

---

[15]   The Court's commerce clause decisions did not invariably support business. In 1905, for example, it ruled that fixing prices through collusion at a stockyard violated the Sherman Act even though the activity took place within a single state. The Court held the activity to be part of "a current of commerce among the States" (*Swift and Co. v. United States* at 398–399) that started with the raising of cattle and ended with the final retail sale. Other businesses did not deserve protection because of their incompatibility with the Puritan ethic that underlay laissez-faire economics. Thus, the Court held the commerce clause a perfectly appropriate vehicle for prohibiting the interstate sale of lottery tickets (*Champion v. Ames* [1903]). But such decisions were exceptions to the rule.

the law necessarily interfered with freedom of contract. Rejecting evidence that long hours were injurious to bakers, the Court declared such efforts beyond the police power.

The Fuller Court even held certain economic protections in the Bill of Rights binding on the states,[16] but not procedural protections.[17] Finally, the Court enshrined Jim Crow into law with its acceptance of the separate-but-equal doctrine in *Plessy v. Ferguson* (1896).

Although the Fuller Court existed for 22 years (1888–1910), longer than any of its predecessors save Marshall, dissenters from its landmark and ordinary precedents cast a markedly higher number of dissents in progeny – 119 and 106 votes, respectively – than any of its predecessor Courts (see Tables 4.3 and 4.4). Indeed, only the Burger Court justices voted as frequently in the progeny of the sampled precedents from which they had dissented.

Like those of the Taney, Chase, and Waite Courts, a small fraction of the Fuller Court's progeny produced a disproportionate number of the dissenters' votes: 42 from the two insular cases of 1901, *De Lima v. Bidwell* and *Downes v. Bidwell* (see King 1967, pp. 262–77). A distinctive set of four justices dissented in each case: Gray, McKenna, Shiras, and White from *De Lima*; Brewer, Fuller, Harlan, and Peckham from *Downes*. Only Justice Brown, the Michigander who wrote the Court's opinion in *Plessy v. Ferguson*, was in the majority in both cases, writing the opinion of the Court in each of them. The *De Lima* majority ducked the constitutional question that the case presented, the constitutionality of duties on goods shipped from Puerto Rico to the United States, and instead said that the relevant statute did not authorize the duties in question. The dissenters cited as their authority the holding of *Downes*: that constitutional limits apply to territories only after Congress has "incorporated" them into the United States. The nationalistic fervor of McKenna's dissent, which Shiras and White joined, could well have accompanied the most jingoistic rendition of a Sousa march:[18]

It vindicates the government from national and international weakness. It exhibits the Constitution as a charter of great and vital authorities . . . which . . . enable

---

[16] *CB&Q R. Co. v. Chicago* (1897).

[17] *Hurtado v. California* (1884), *Maxwell v. Dow* (1900), and *Twining v. New Jersey* (1908).

[18] McKenna, the son of an Irish immigrant who fled the potato famine of the 1840s, filled the seat vacated by his California predecessor, Stephen Field. Shiras, the son of a wealthy brewery merchant, was born and died in Pittsburgh. Like McKenna, White was a Catholic, educated in Catholic schools. Captured by Union forces during the Civil War, he built a lucrative law practice thereafter and served as an able promoter of Louisiana's sugar interests during his service in the U.S. Senate. Cleveland appointed him to the Court after the Senate's rejection of his two previous nominees – William Hornblower and Wheeler Peckham.

the United States to . . . do all "Acts and Things which Independent States may of right do," – and confidently do. . . . All powers of government . . . put to no hazard of loss or impairment; the power of the nation also secured in its great station, enabled to move with strength and dignity and effect among the other nations of the earth to such purpose as it may undertake or to such destiny as it may be called. (1901, 220)

Over the holding of the *Downes* majority that constitutional limits apply only after Congress "incorporates" the territory into the United States, the dissent asserted that subjection to U.S. authority suffices to make a territory part of the United States.

Both sets of dissenters used their respective position to justify their votes in the pair of *Dooley v. United States* (1901) decisions. Brewer and company reiterated their opposition to *Downes* in its progeny: *Hawaii v. Mankichi* (1903), *Dorr v. United States* (1904), and *Rasmussen v. United States* (1905). *Mankichi* and *Dorr* nicely illustrate the casuistic games that the justices may play with precedent. The former upheld a Philippine conviction in a trial without a jury. In the latter case, Peckham, a judicially active laissez-fairist, acceded to *Mankichi* in a concurrence joined by Fuller and Brewer, unequivocally proclaiming that he would simultaneously have his cake and eat it:

> I concur . . . simply because of the decision in *Hawaii v. Mankichi*. . . . That case was decided by . . . a majority of this court, and *although I did not and do not concur* in those views, yet *the case in my opinion is authority* for the result arrived at in the case now before us, to wit, that a jury trial is not a constitutional necessity in a criminal case in Hawaii or in the Philippine Islands. But, while concurring in this judgment, *I do not wish to be understood as assenting to the view that* Downes v. Bidwell . . . *is to be regarded as authority* for the decision herein. (1904, 153–54, emphasis added)[19]

Harlan, the fourth *Downes* dissenter, also persisted in his opposition to *Downes* and its progeny, articulating it in *Rasmussen v. United States* (1904, 528–29), unlike his colleagues, even when the majority reached a result compatible with Harlan and company's pro-incorporation position.

In addition to the two *Dooley* (1901) decisions, the *De Lima* dissenters adhered to their position in *Bidwell, The Diamond Rings* (1901), and *Lincoln v. United States* (1906). Although only two of the original dissenters – White and McKenna – still sat when *Lincoln* was reargued, their opinion, written by the soon-to-be chief justice, White, utilized an interesting variation on the precedent/preferences dichotomy. After

---

[19] We count the concurrers as voting their preferences. If *Mankichi* had been the precedent, we would have counted them as adhering to this precedent on the basis of the quoted language. But *Downes v. Bidwell* is the precedent, and their language makes clear they do not accede to it.

remarking on his string of dissents, he stated that he had been "constrained" to adhere to precedent in *Lincoln* I (1905) because he had concluded that "they were binding on me under the rule of *stare decisis*." He had so voted in *Lincoln* I (1905),[20] but on reargument in *Lincoln* II (1906) White and McKenna found reasons again to vote preferentially, namely, "additional public reports and documents" to which "my attention was not directed" in the original argument (1906, 500).

Given this history, it comes as no surprise that all 42 votes that the respective dissenters cast in the progeny of these two insular cases were preferential, all but seven of them strongly so. Further evidencing the justices' consistency are the dissents of Brewer, Fuller, Harlan, and Peckham in two memorandum cases affirming lower federal court decisions on the authority of *Downes v. Bidwell* (1901), *Czarnikow, MacDougall & Co. v. Bidwell* (1903), and *Warner, Barnes & Co. v. Stranahan* (1903). Dissents in memorandum decisions were vitually unheard of prior to the modern era. Given our decision rules, we exclude both from consideration.

From a modern perspective, the votes and opinions in *United States v. Wong Kim Ark* (1898), the famous Chinese exclusion case, illustrate the vagaries of ideological consistency from one era to another. Although the chief justice's dissent occasions no surprise, that of the incorporationist and sole dissenter from the separate but equal doctrine of *Plessy v. Ferguson* Justice Harlan does. Disregarding the plain language of the Fourteenth Amendment, they asserted that citizenship by place of birth was feudalistic in origin and that the common law provided no guide for the relevant constitutional language. "In other words, the 14th Amendment does not . . . arbitrarily [*sic*] make citizens of children born in the United States of parents who, according to the will of their native government and of this government, are and must remain aliens" (1898, 732). On the other hand, two outspoken devotees of laissez faire and the gospel of wealth, Fuller and Peckham, coupled their pro–civil liberty vote in *Wong Kim Ark* with vigorous dissents in its anti–civil liberty progeny: *United States v. Sing Tuck* (1904) and *United States v. Ju Toy* (1905). They note in the former case that they "have heretofore dissented in several cases involving the exclusion or the expulsion of the Chinese" and that their "views on the questions are unchanged" (1904, 170–71). Fuller and Harlan, by contrast, preferentially acceded to the majority opinion in both *Sing Tuck* and *Ju Toy*.

Harlan, however, did adhere to his pro–civil liberty incorporationist

---

[20] We do not list this decision as a progeny of *De Lima* because it is cited only as a source of additional information. The authority for *Lincoln* I rests on *Dooley* I. See 197 U.S. at 428, 429.

postion in the progeny of *Maxwell v. Dow* (1900), which held that a twelve-member jury was not among the privileges and immunities of United States citizenship: *West v. Louisiana* (1904), *Dorr v. United States* (1904), and *Twining v. New Jersey* (1908).

The last of the Fuller Court's landmark decisions that spawned a progeny in which a dissenter participated, *Ex parte Young* (1908), has been celebrated for both illogic and irony (Orth, 1992). These characteristics afflict the behavior of the majority as well as that of the dissenter, Harlan. Disregarding the prohibition of the Eleventh Amendment restricting the jurisdiction of the federal courts to hear suits against states, the majority asserted that the federal court could grant an injunction against the effort of a state attorney general to enforce one of his own state's laws in its own courts. Peckham, for the Court, asserted that such action stripped the officer of his official character. Peckham, however, did not bother to explain how the action of such a denuded official could constitute state action for the purposes of the Fourteenth Amendment, which the state law in question – setting railroad rates – allegedly violated. In the nonlandmark decisions of *In re Ayers* (1887) and *Fitts v. McGhee* (1889), on all fours with *Young,* the Court had ruled that the attorney general in the former case had acted officially and that the federal court in the latter had no authority to enjoin state criminal action. Peckham distinguished these two cases by denying federal court jurisdiction only to cases in which an effort was made to compel a state to adhere to its contractual obligations.[21]

Harlan begins his *Young* dissent by "frankly admit[ting] embarrassment arising from certain views stated in [my] dissenting opinions . . . which did not . . . meet the approval of my brethren, and which I do not now entertain" (1908, 169). Harlan then proceeds to state his adherence to what the Court formerly had held while – accurately – accusing his colleagues of abandoning precedent:

What I shall say in this opinion will be in substantial accord with what the court has heretofore decided, while the opinion of the court departs . . . from principles previously announced by it upon full consideration. (1908, 169)

Harlan reaffirmed his no-federal-court-jurisdiction position in *Hunter v. Wood* (1908), but in *Western Union Telegraph Co. v. Andrews* (1910) and *Herndon v. CRI&P R. Co.* (1910) Harlan joined a unanimous Court upholding the exercise of federal court jurisdiction. We can only con-

---

[21] The implicit rationale for *Young* rests on the need for federal courts to be able to void unconstitutional state action. As a corollary, federal courts also need to be able to enjoin state officials from violating federal law. The ultimate irony is that a policy forged by upperdogs and a conservative Court is today used by underdogs against unresponsive state governments (Orth 1992).

clude that at the end of his career Harlan returned to his pre-*Young* position of no Eleventh Amendment immunity, a position he apparently held except for his embarrassing dissent in *In re Ayers* (1888). If one were to examine the history of Eleventh Amendment jurisprudence in the period after the Civil War, we suspect that the justices would display attachment neither to precedent nor to their initial preferences. To say that they vacillated understates the obvious.[22]

The Justices' Behavior

Because the progeny of *Ex parte Young* produce only a minor blip on the tally of precedent and preference votes (along with the fact that we do not concern ourselves with *Young*'s antecedents), 110 of the 119 votes cast by dissenters from the Fuller Court's landmark decisions uphold the dissenters' preferences, 92.4 percent. This proportion, 0.1 percent higher than that of its predecessor Court, exceeds that of the other earlier Courts by more than ten percentage points. Moreover, as noted, the Fuller Court produced almost as many analyzable votes as its predecessors combined. Of the 22 landmark decisions, 18 produced countable votes. Of the four that did not, two involved its last two landmark cases – *Twining v. New Jersey* (1908) and *Weems v. United States* (1910) – with *Plessy v. Ferguson* (1896) accounting for another. Harlan alone dissented from the first and last, with White joining him in *Weems*.

As Table 4.3 shows, the preferential votes are distributed among the three categories as follows: 44 strong, 20 moderate, and 46 weak. All but nine of the strong preference votes locate in the two 1901 insular cases, indicating perhaps an intensity of views beyond that of most of the other decisions. Seven of the nine precedential votes fall into the moderate category, with the other two weak. Twelve of the 20 justices who sat on the Fuller Court dissented from one of its landmarks and participated in at least one progeny. Half of them cast only preferential votes.

Fuller Court Ordinary Litigation

Inexplicably, dissenters from the ordinary precedents of the Fuller Court cast far more votes in progeny (106) than any other Court save that of

---

[22] We hypothesize that the vacillation may be more apparent than real if considered from the standpoint of the attitudinal model. Measures of judicial attitudes may display an underlying consistency in the justices' votes based on more salient issues – for instance, economic regulation in the context of laissez-faire economics – than the more instrumentally oriented value of considerations of federalism. If, however, our expectation proves to be false, we would suggest that the Eleventh Amendment might be fruitfully analyzed from a strategic game theoretic standpoint.

Table 4.3.
Voting and opinion behavior: Fuller Court landmarks

| Justice | Prefs/prec | | %Prefs | Preferences (%) | | | Level of Expression | | |
				Strong (1)	Moderate (2)	Weak (3)	Precedent (%) Strong (1)	Moderate (2)	Weak (3)
Brewer (Brw)	15	0	100.0	3 (20.0)	6 (40.0)	6 (40.0)			
Peckham (Pec)	11	0	100.0	4 (36.4)	4 (36.4)	3 (27.3)			
Gray (Gra)	7	0	100.0	5 (71.4)		2 (28.6)			
Shiras (Shi)	6	0	100.0	5 (83.3)		1 (16.7)			
Day (Day)	2	0	100.0		1 (50.0)	1 (50.0)			
Lamar (Lam)	1	0	100.0			1 (100)			
Harlan (Har)	22	2	91.7	7 (31.8)	2 (9.1)	13 (59.1)		2 (100)	
White (Whi)	11	1	91.7	6 (54.5)	1 (9.1)	4 (36.4)			1 (100)
Holmes (Hol)	8	1	88.9	3 (37.5)		5 (62.5)		1 (100)	
Fuller (Ful)	13	2	86.7	4 (30.8)	4 (30.8)	5 (38.5)		2 (100)	
McKenna (McK)	11	2	84.6	6 (54.5)	1 (9.1)	4 (36.4)		1 (50.0)	1 (50.0)
Brown (Bro)	3	1	75.0	1 (33.3)	1 (33.3)	1 (33.3)		1 (100)	
Totals	110	9	92.4	44 (40.0)	20 (18.2)	46 (41.8)	0	7 (77.8)	2 (22.2)

Precedent/progeny	Preferences	Precedent
CM&StP R. Co. v. Minnesota (1890) **c**	Gra-Lam-3	
Budd v. New York (1892)	Gra-3	
San Diego Land & T Co. v. National City (1899)		Ful-2
United States v. Texas (1892) **c**		
Minnesota v. Hitchcock (1902)	Ful-2	
South Dakota v. North Carolina (1904f)	Har-3	
United States v. E.C. Knight Co. (1895) **s**	Har-3	
Addyston Pipe & Steel v. United States (1899)	Har-3	
Northern Securities v. United States (1904)	Har-3	
Swift & Co. v. United States (1905)	Har-3	
Loewe v. Lawlor (1908)	Har-3	
Standard Oil Co. v. United States (1911)		
California v. Southern Pacific Co. (1895) **c**	Brw-Har-3	
South Dakota v. North Carolina (1904)		
Pollock v. Farmers' Loan & Trust Co. (1895) **c**	Bro-Whi-2, Har-3	
Nicol v. Ames (1899)	Bro-Whi-Har-3	
Knowlton v. Moore (1900)	Har-3	
Spreckles Sugar Refining Co. v. McClain (1904)	Har-Whi-3	
Flint v. Stone Tracy Co. (1911)		
CB&Q R. Co. v. Chicago (1897) **c**	Brw-2	
Backus v. Fort Street Depot (1898)	Brw-3	
MK&T R. Co. v. Haber (1898)	Brw-2	
Norwood v. Baker (1898)	Brw-2	
Taylor v. Beckham (1900)	Brw-3	
Raymond v. Chicago Union Traction Co. (1907)		
Holden v. Hardy (1898) **c**	Brw-Pec-2	
Lochner v. New York (1907)		

Table 4.3 (*cont.*)

Precedent/progeny	Preferences	Precedent
United States v. Wong Kim Ark (1898) **c**		
United States v. Sing Tuck (1904)	Ful-Har-3	
United States v. Ju Toy (1905)	Ful-Har-3	
Maxwell v. Dow (1900) **c**		
West v. Louisiana (1904)	Har-2	
Dorr v. United States (1904)	Har-1	
Twining v. New Jersey (1908)	Har-1	
Knowlton v. Moore (1900) **s**		
Flint v. Stone Tracy Co. (1911)	Har-McK-3	
Brushaber v. UP R. Co. (1916)	McK-3	
New York Trust Co. v. Eisner (1921)	McK-3	
Greiner v. Lewellyn (1922)	McK-3	
De Lima v. Bidwell (1901) **s**		
Dooley v. United States (1901)	Gra-McK-Shi-Whi-1	
Downes v. Bidwell (1901)	Gra-McK-Shi-Whi-1	
Downes v. Bidwell (1901)	Gra-McK-Shi-Whi-1	
Dooley v. United States (1901)	Gra-McK-Shi-Whi-1	
The Diamond Rings (1901)	Gra-McK-Shi-Whi-1	
Lincoln v. United States (1906)	McK-Whi-1	
Downes v. Bidwell (1901) **c**		
Dooley v. United States (1901)	Brw-Ful-Har-Pec-2	
Dooley v. United States (1901)	Brw-Ful-Har-Pec-1	
Hawaii v. Mankichi (1903)	Brw-Ful-Har-Pec-1	
Dorr v. United States (1904)	Brw-Ful-Har-Pec-1	
Rasmussen v. United States (1905)	Brw-Ful-Pec-3, Har-1	

Case		
Champion v. Ames (1903) **c**	Brw-Ful-Pec-Shi-3	
Francis v. United States (1903) **s**	Brw-Ful-Pec-2	
Howard v. IC R. Co. (1908) **c**	Brw-Ful-Pec-3	
Adair v. United States (1908)		
Northern Securities v. United States (1904) **s**	Hol-Whi-3	
United States v. United Shoe Co. (1918)	Hol-Whi-3	
United States v. US Steel (1920)		
United States v. Southern Pacific Co. (1922)		Hol-2
McCray v. United States (1904) **c**		
Schick v. United States (1904)	Bro-Ful-Pec-1	
Cliff v. United States (1904)	Ful-Pec-2	Bro-2
Maxley v. Hertz (1910)		Ful-2
Lochner v. New York (1905) **c**	Day-2, Hol-1	
Coppage v. Kansas (1915)	Day-Hol-3	Whi-3
Prudential Ins. Co. v. Cheek (1922)	Hol-1	
Adkins v. Children's Hospital (1923)		
Adair v. United States (1908) **c**	Hol-1	
Coppage v. Kansas (1915)	Hol-3, McK-2	McK-2
Wilson v. New (1917)	Hol-3	
Arizona Copper Co. v. Hammer (1919)		McK-3
Ex parte Young (1908) **c**		
Hunter v. Wood (1908)	Har-1	
Western Union Telegraph Co. v. Andrews (1910)		Har-2
Herndon v. CRI&P R. Co. (1910)		Har-2

Legend: **c** = constitutional decision
  s = statutory decision
  = decision neither constitutionally nor statutorily based

Note: All progeny rest on the same decisional basis as the precedent unless otherwise indicated.

Warren Burger, 123. Granted that the Fuller Court existed for 22 years (1888–1910), longer than any other save that of John Marshall, norms of consensus had by no means broken down. Nonetheless, 18 of this Court's precedents produce votes in progeny by justices who dissented in the decision that initially established the precedent. On the other hand, we do not deal with a pure random sample. Hence, it behooves us not to make too much, if anything, of these numbers.

Among the more interesting decisions in our sample of ordinary Fuller Court litigation are the following:

- Justice Brewer, joined by Field and Brown, delivered a characteristically laissez-faire dissent, complete with an *argumentum ad horrendum*, in *Budd v. New York* (1892). The majority held grain elevators to be businesses affected with a public interest. Said Brewer:

   The paternal theory of government is to me odious. The utmost possible liberty to the individual, and the fullest possible protection to him and his property, is both the limitation and duty of government. If it may regulate the price of one service, which is not a public service, or the compensation for the use of one kind of property which is not devoted to a public use, why may it not with equal reason regulate the price of all service, and the compensation to be paid for the use of all property? And if so, "Looking Backward" is nearer than a dream. (1892, 551)[23]

   Brewer reiterated his objections, joined by Field but not by Brown, in *Brass v. North Dakota* (1894). The majority upheld a statute fixing the price of grain stored in privately owned and operated elevators.[24] The dissenters were in the majority in opinions written by Justice Brown voiding a Kentucky law fixing tolls and fare on an interstate bridge: *Covington & Cincinnati Bridge Co. v. Kentucky* (1894) and *Covington & Cincinnati Elevated R. & Transfer & Bridge Co. v. Kentucky* (1894).

- In *NP R. Co. v. Hambly* (1894), the majority stretched the fellow servant rule to apply to a gandy dancer hit by a train as a result of the engineer's negligence. Field, Fuller, and Harlan dissented without opinion. They did the same in objecting to the application of the fellow servant rule in *Central R. Co. of NJ v. Keegan* (1895), *NP R. Co. v. Peterson* (1896), and *NP R. Co. v. Charles* (1896). Harlan

---

[23]   Brewer defended social and economic inequality and viewed the popular movements of his day as a threat to civilization. See Fiss (1992).

[24]   No reason suggests itself for Brown's adherence to precedent, given his preferentially consistent votes in the other two progeny of *Budd*. The case clearly is on all fours with *Budd*. In addition to Field, Jackson and White joined Brewer's dissent.

continued his silent oppostion in *Oakes v. Mase* (1897) and *Martin v. AT&SF R. Co.* (1897). But Field and Fuller did not, joining the majority instead.[25] Fuller persisted in adhering to precedent in *New England R. Co. v. Conroy* (1899), notwithstanding that Shiras, in his opinion of the Court, specifically referenced Fuller's anti–fellow servant voting record, particularly with reference to the case that the majority overruled, *CM&St.P R. Co. v. Ross* (1884). Harlan, voting consistently, broke his silence and expressly adhered to his *Ross* views. In the last of *Hambly*'s progeny, *NP R. Co. v. Dixon* (1904), Fuller returned to the preferential fold that he abandoned in *Oakes, Martin,* and *Conroy* by joining White's dissenting opinion, which stated that "the ruling now made . . . reverses many previous decisions of this court" (1904, 347).[26] Although White's statement does not withstand scrutiny – *Dixon* overruled at most one precedent, *B&O R. Co. v. Baugh* (1893) – it does indicate that Fuller's precedential voting was a temporary aberration. Nonetheless, we count his discrepant votes as precedential.

• Fuller behaved similarly in the next randomly selected ordinary case, *NP R. Co. v. Peterson* (1896).[27] The same three justices dissented as in the preceding precedent, *NP R. Co. v. Hambly,* and again they did so without opinion. Like *Hambly, Peterson* involved application of the fellow servant rule – the facts of which are summarized in footnote 25 – and, with one exception, *Peterson*'s progeny are identical to those of *Hambly* that were decided after the date of the *Peterson* decision. Given the identity of the progeny of the two cases, Field and Fuller acceded to precedent in *Oakes v. Mase* (1897) and *Martin v. AT&SF R. Co.* (1897). In the progeny unique to *Peterson, Alaska Treadwell Co. v. Whelan* (1897), decided within one and one-half months of Field's resignation, Fuller and Harlan voted their preferences, but

---

[25] The former case held that an engineer on one train and a conductor on another are fellow servants; the latter, that the assurance of a foreman that he would watch for an oncoming train did not affect the duty of the employer to furnish a safe work environment for a common laborer injured because the foreman negligently did not watch for the oncoming train. The fellow servant rule overrode the duty to furnish a safe workplace.

These two decisions occurred eleven months before Field left the Court. Given his overall support for private property, his willingness to hold railroads liable for employee injuries and death indicates less than ideological consistency.

[26] Harlan and McKenna also joined White's dissent.

[27] *Peterson* also was a progeny of the preceding precedent, *NP R. Co. v. Hambly* (1894). Fuller's and Field's voting in the progeny of *Hambly* and *Peterson* produced half the number of precedential votes cast by all the Fuller Court justices, 11 of 22 (see Table 4.4).

not Field. In the two remaining progeny, *New England R. Co. v. Conroy* (1899) and *NP R. Co. v. Dixon* (1904), Harlan and Fuller reflect the assessment we made with respect to these decisions as progeny of *Hambly*. Overall, then, as between these two precedents, *Hambly's* progeny produced 14 preferential and five precedential votes; *Peterson's* ten and six, respectively.

- Given the short shrift accorded state tax laws affecting interstate commerce, the Court's decision in *Hennington v. Georgia* (1896) could hardly stand in starker contrast. With Brewer not participating, the majority – in an opinion by Justice Harlan – held a Sunday closing law prohibiting the running of any freight train on any railroad in the state *not* to violate the commerce clause. The train in question originated in Chattanooga and was destined for Meridian, Mississippi. Its route took it through a single minuscule county in the northwestern corner of Georgia.[28] The majority denied that the law's enacted "purpose" was to regulate interstate commerce (1896, 304), but rather, "that the best interests of all required that one day in seven be kept for the purposes of rest from ordinary labor" (Id.). Totally eschewing any consideration of the law's economic impact, the majority continued by stating that "the state committed these matters to the determination of the legislature. If the law-making power errs in such matters, its responsibility is to the electors, and not to the judicial branch" (Id.). Fuller's dissent, which White joined, states the obvious: that the power of Congress is exclusive because it "is a matter national in its character and admitting of uniform regulation" (1896, 318). Alternatively, if the matter be a police regulation, "when a power of a state and a power of the general government come into collision, the former must give way" (Id., 318–19).

In *Hennington*'s progeny, White voiced his preferences in *LS&MS R. Co. v. Ohio* (1899), in which the majority upheld a state law requiring all passenger trains to stop at stations serving 3000 or more people as a police power regulation promoting public convenience and not a regulation of interstate commerce. Fuller, however, acceded to precedent by silently voting with the majority and by writing the Court's opinion in *Petit v. Minnesota* (1900), a case that does not involve interstate commerce, but rather the police power aspects of a regulation closing barber shops on Sundays. Fuller used the precedent to sustain the statute on police power grounds.[29]

---

[28] Violators were subject to a $1000 fine and/or a year on a chain gang.

[29] Inasmuch as the case does not concern interstate commerce, the primary focus of White's objection to *Hennington*, we exclude him from consideration.

The Justices' Behavior

The precedent–preferences proportion of the Fuller Court does not appreciably differ from that of its predecessor, 79.2 versus 77.5 percent, for the Waite Court (see Table 4.4).[30] Marked differences, however, do manifest themselves in level of expression. The Fuller Court favored strong expression much more than did the Waite Court – 32 percent versus 11 percent – and a corresponding diminution of a weak posture: 23 versus 35 percent.

As for the votes of the individual justices, only two Waite Court holdovers, Harlan and Field, participated. Both behave more precedentially than on the Waite Court, Field especially. His support for precedent increases from 20.8 to 41.7 percent. In addition to Field, three of the other nine participants support precedent with a third or more of their votes – Fuller, Peckham, and Brown. This contrasts with only two of eight on the Waite Court.[31]

The Fuller Court justices cast approximately the same number of votes in the landmark as in the ordinary litigation set (119 versus 106). Nine of the ten justices who voted in progeny of ordinary litigation precedents from which they had dissented also participated in the landmark set, the exception being Field. As a result, we may compare the justices' behavior between the two sets.[32] Table 4.3 provides the Fuller Court justices' behavior in the landmark cases. Of the nine justices who appear on both Fuller Court tables, only three adhere to precedent more in the minor than in the landmark cases: Harlan, Holmes, and McKenna. The differences, however, are ephemeral. Harlan's percentages differ by barely 2 points: 93.9 to 91.7 percent. Holmes cast only one vote, which was preferential, in the minor cases, thereby exceeding his preferential proportion of 88.9 percent in the landmarks. McKenna cast two precedential votes out of 13 in the landmarks, and none out of seven in the ordinary cases. Much more meaningful is the record of the other Fuller Court justices, excluding Harlan and Peckham. All eleven of Peckham's landmark votes sustained his preferences, but only one of his two in ordinary litigation. The 50 percent increase in precedential voting arguably results from the randomness inherent in but a pair of votes.

---

[30] We compare the Waite and Fuller Courts, not only because they followed each other, but, more importantly, because a substantial number of their justices cast a reasonably approximate total number of votes, 80 and 106. Not until we reach the Burger Court do we again find any Court casting as many as 40 total votes in the sample of ordinary litigation.

[31] Bradley and Field come close, with 22.2 and 20.8 percent, respectively.

[32] We were not able to make such a comparison for earlier Courts because of the paucity of votes, or the participation of only a few of a given Court's justices, or both.

Table 4.4.
Voting and opinion behavior: Fuller Court ordinary cases

| | | | Level of Expression | | | | | |
| | | | Preferences (%) | | | Precedent (%) | | |
Justice	Prefs/prec	%Prefs	Strong (1)	Moderate (2)	Weak (3)	Strong (1)	Moderate (2)	Weak (3)
McKenna (McK)	7	0	100.0	5 (71.4)	1 (14.3)	1 (14.3)			
Gray (Gra)	4	0	100.0		1 (25.0)	3 (75.0)			
Holmes (Hol)	1	0	100.0	1 (100)					
Harlan (Har)	31	2	93.9	11 (35.5)	18 (58.1)	2 (6.5)		2 (100)	
Brewer (Brw)	6	1	85.7	1 (16.7)	2 (33.3)	3 (50.0)		1 (100)	
White (Whi)	9	2	81.8	6 (66.7)	2 (22.2)	1 (11.1)		2 (100)	
Fuller (Ful)	16	8	66.7	2 (12.5)	9 (56.3)	5 (31.3)		8 (100)	
Field (Fld)	7	5	58.3	1 (14.3)	4 (57.1)	2 (28.6)		5 (100)	
Peckham (Pec)	1	1	50.0		1 (100)			1 (100)	
Brown (Bro)	2	3	40.0			2 (100)		3 (100)	
Totals	84	22	79.2	27 (32.1)	38 (45.2)	19 (22.6)	0	22 (100)	0

Precedent/progeny	Preferences	Precedent
McCall v. California (1890) **c**		
N&W R. Co. v. Pennsylvania (1890)	Brw-Ful-Gra-2	
Ficklin v. Shelby County District (1892)	Brw-Ful-Gra-3	
Peake v. New Orleans (1891)		
Warner v. New Orleans (1897)	Ful-Har-3	
New Orleans v. Warner (1899)	Ful-Har-3	
Crutcher v. Kentucky (1891) **c**		
Maine v. GT R. Co. (1891)	Ful-Gra-3	
Ficklin v. Shelby County District (1892)	Ful-Gra-3	
Western Union Telegraph Co. v. Kansas (1910)	Ful-2	
Pullman Co. v. Kansas ex rel. Coleman (1910)	Ful-2	
Ludwig v. Western Union Telegraph Co. (1910)	Ful-2	
Budd v. New York (1892) **c**		
Brass v. North Dakota (1894)	Brw-Fld-1	Bro-2
C&C Bridge Co. v. Kentucky (1894)	Bro-Brw-Fld-3	
C&C Elevated R.&T. & Bridge v. Kentucky (1894)	Bro-Brw-Fld-3	
NP R. Co. v. Hambly (1894)		
Central R. Co. of New Jersey v. Keegan (1895)	Fld-Ful-Har-2	
NP R. Co. v. Peterson (1896)	Fld-Ful-Har-2	
NP R. Co. v. Charles (1896)	Fld-Ful-Har-2	
Oakes v. Mase (1897)	Har-2	Fld-Ful-2
Martin v. AT&SF R. Co. (1897)	Har-2	Fld-Ful-2
New England R. Co. v. Conroy (1899)	Har-1	Ful-2
NP R. Co. v. Dixon (1904)	Ful-Har-1	

Table 4.4 (cont.)

Precedent/progeny	Preferences	Precedent
NP R. Co. v. Peterson (1896)	Fld-Ful-Har-2	
NP R. Co. v. Charles (1896)	Har-2	Fld-Ful-2
Oakes v. Mase (1897)	Har-2	Fld-Ful-2
Martin v. AT&SF R. Co. (1897)	Ful-Har-2	Fld-2
Alaska Treadwell Co. v. Whelan (1897)	Har-1	Ful-2
New England R. Co. v. Conroy (1899)	Ful-Har-1	
NP R. Co. v. Dixon (1904)		
Hennington v. Georgia (1896) c		
LS&MS R. Co. v. Ohio (1899)	Whi-1	Ful-2
Petit v. Minnesota (1900)		Ful-2
Muse v. Arlington Hotel Co. (1897) s		
Filhiol v. Maurice (1902)		Har-Whi-2
Sloan v. United States (1904)		Har-Whi-2
Savings & Loan Society v. Multnomah County (1898) c		
New Orleans v. Stempel (1899)	Har-Whi-2	
Bolln v. Nebraska (1900) c		
Maxwell v. Dow (1900)	Har-2	
Hawaii v. Mankichi (1903)	Har-2	
Dorr v. United States (1904)	Har-1	
Twining v. New Jersey (1908)	Har-2	
B&O SW R. Co. v. Voigt (1900)		
NP R. Co. v. Adams (1904)	Har-2	

Case		
Tonawanda v. Lyon (1901) **c**	Har-McK-Whi-1	
Webster v. Fargo (1901)	Har-McK-Whi-1	
Cass Farm Co. v. Detroit (1901)	Har-McK-Whi-1	
Detroit v. Parker (1901)	Har-McK-Whi-1	
Wormley v. District of Columbia (1901)	Har-McK-Whi-1	
Shumate v. Heman (1901)	Har-McK-Whi-2	
CCC&StL R. Co. v. Porter (1908)		Brw-Pec-2
Booth v. Illinois (1902) **c**	Brw-Pec-2	
Otis & Gassman v. Parker (1903)		Bro-2
Gatewood v. North Carolina (1906)		Bro-2
NP R. Co. v. Townsend (1903) **s**	Har-2	
NP R. Co. v. Ely (1905)	Har-2	
NP R. Co. v. Hasse (1905)		
Western Union Telegraph Co. v. Pa R. Co. (1904) **s**	Har-1	
Western Union Telegraph Co. v. Pa R. Co. (1904)		
NP R. Co. v. Ely (1905) **s**	Har-2	
NP R. Co. v. Hasse (1905)		
Lincoln v. United States (1906) **s**	McK-Whi-3	
United States v. Heinszen (1907)		
Kuhn v. Fairmont Coal Co. (1910) **c**	Hol-1	
Black & White Taxi v. Brown & Yellow Taxi (1928)		

Legend: **c** = constitutional decision
        s = statutory decision
        = decision neither constitutionally nor statutorily based

Note: All progeny rest on the same decisional basis as the precedent unless otherwise indicated.

Harlan, by contrast, shows little variation between the two sets: 6.1 percent upholding ordinary precedent, 8.3 percent in landmark cases. Given that these proportions stem from 33 and 24 votes, respectively, we may conclude that Harlan effectuates his preferences regardless of case salience.[33]

The other four justices' increased support for precedent in the common cases does appear significant. They upheld precedent by an average of 22 points more in this sample. Brewer declines from 100 to 85.7 percent, White from 91.7 to 81.8, Fuller from 86.7 to 66.7, and Brown from 75.0 to 40.0. Although Brown's record results from votes in four landmarks and five common cases, admittedly a slim basis for judgment, the votes of the others range from seven to 24. The behavior of these justices suggests a strong correlation between salience and preferential voting. This is not to say that precedent characterizes the behavior of justices who vote in progeny of precedents from which they dissented. As the data reported thus far clearly establish, this is not the situation. Support for precedent that rarely reaches as little as 50 percent hardly evidences adherence to this norm. As for justices who vary little in their behavior between landmark and common cases, this results because their preferences – rather than any attachment to precedent – dominate both sets of cases.

THE WHITE COURT

As President, William Howard Taft made no secret of the fact that he would have preferred to be Chief Justice (Rohde and Spaeth 1976, p. 73).[34] Thus it comes as no surprise that he "devoted more attention to the choice of justices than any other President" (Schwartz 1993, p. 204). This careful selection led to more cross-party appointments than those of any other President: Horace Lurton, his close friend and former colleague from the Court of Appeals; Joseph Lamar, who had served on the Georgia Supreme Court; and Edward White, the first associate justice promoted to chief justice. These of course were not Bryan Democrats, but Southern Democrats.

The White Court (1910–21) stayed the course laid out by Fuller. In its most infamous decisions, the White Court blocked congressional attempts to limit child labor, either through the interstate commerce clause[35] or through the Sixteenth Amendment.[36] State efforts to regulate

---

[33] Harlan behaved the same on the Waite Court. All five of his ordinary case votes bolstered his preferences, as did ten of eleven landmark votes.

[34] This wish, of course, was later fulfilled.

[35] *Hammer v. Dagenhart* (1918).   [36] *Bailey v. Drexel Furniture* (1922).

the economy typically met with similar rebukes.[37] In the *Coppage* case, the Court noted that "It is impossible to uphold freedom of contract without at the same time recognizing as legitimate those inequalities of fortune that are a necessary result of those rights" (p. 17).

It was also during Chief Justice White's reign that the Supreme Court, in an opinion by Holmes, issued the clear and present danger doctrine in free speech cases. Though nominally considered a broad reading of First Amendment rights, the doctrine resulted in prison terms for those who dared to speak out against U.S. military efforts during World War I and the Bolshevik Revolution.[38]

The number of votes cast in progeny by dissenters from the White Court's leading decisions contrasts sharply with that of the Fuller Court while approximating the number cast by the Taney, Chase, and Waite Courts. Four cases generate all but six of the 33 total votes, with two, *Bunting v. Oregon* (1917) and *Duplex Printing Press Co. v. Deering* (1921), accounting for 16. *Bunting* provided for a maximum workday of ten hours. The dissenters who participated in its progeny – McReynolds and Van Devanter[39] – adhered to their position in *Adkins v. Children's Hospital* (1923), *Ribnik v. McBride* (1928), *Morehead v. New York ex rel. Tipaldo* (1936), and *West Coast Hotel v. Parrish* (1937). The dissenters in *Duplex Printing Press Co. v. Deering* (1921), which narrowly construed the Clayton Act's union antitrust exemption – Brandeis, Clarke,[40] and Holmes – also produced eight preferential votes in *Deering*'s progeny: *American Steel Foundries v. Tri-City Trades* (1921), *Truax v. Corrigan* (1921), *San Francisco Industrial Assn. v. United States* (1925), and *Bedford Cut Stone Co. v. Stone Cutters' Assn.* (1927).

The Justices' Behavior

The White Court's landmarks produce 28 preference votes and five precedential ones (84.8 percent) as Table 4.5 indicates. This proportion

---

[37] For example, *Coppage v. Kansas* (1915), striking laws prohibiting "yellow dog" contracts (agreements not to join unions as a condition of employment). But see *Muller v. Oregon* (1908) and *Bunting v. Oregon* (1917) for decisions limiting contractual rights. *Bunting* upheld a maximum hours law for factory workers without even mentioning *Lochner.*

[38] *Schenck v. United States* (1917), *Debs v. United States* (1919), and *Abrams v. United States* (1919). Holmes dissented from the (mis)use of his doctrine in the *Abrams* case.

[39] McReynolds, Wilson's attorney general, was perhaps the most intolerant individual to sit on the Court. A lifelong bachelor, he displayed hostility toward women and his two Jewish colleagues, Brandeis and Cardozo. Van Devanter was the intellectual leader of the conservative wing of the Court during his quarter century of service.

[40] Like McReynolds, Clarke was a bachelor and Wilson nominee. Unlike him, he occupied the liberal end of the White Court. McReynolds's nastiness precipitated Clarke's resignation in 1922.

Table 4.5.
Voting and opinion behavior: White Court landmarks

Justice	Prefs/prec		%Prefs	Preferences (%)			Level of Expression		Precedent (%)	
				Strong (1)	Moderate (2)	Weak (3)	Strong (1)	Moderate (2)	Weak (3)	
McReynolds (McR)	4	0	100.0		1 (25.0)	3 (75.0)				
Clarke (Clr)	3	0	100.0		1 (33.3)	2 (66.7)				
Harlan (Har)	1	0	100.0	1 (100)						
Hughes (Hu)	1	0	100.0			1 (100)				
Pitney (Pit)	1	0	100.0			1 (100)				
Van Devanter (VD)	6	1	85.7		1 (14.3)	5 (85.7)		1 (100)		
Brandeis (Br)	4	1	80.0	1 (25.0)	1 (25.0)	2 (50.0)		1 (100)		
Holmes (Hol)	7	2	77.8	1 (14.3)	1 (14.3)	5 (71.4)		2 (100)		
McKenna (McK)	1	1	50.0			1 (100)		1 (100)		
Totals	28	5	84.8	3 (10.7)	5 (17.9)	20 (71.4)	0	5 (100)	0	

Precedent/progeny	Preferences	Precedent
Standard Oil Co. v. United States (1911) **s**	Har-1	
United States v. American Tobacco Co. (1911) **c**		
Coyle v. Smith (1911)		
Ex parte Webb (1912)	Hol-McK-3	
HE&W R. Co. v. United States (1914) **c**	Pit-3	
Wisconsin RR Commission v. CB&Q R. Co. (1922) **c**		
Frank v. Mangum (1915) **c**	Hol-Hu-3	
Moore v. Dempsey (1923)		
Clark Distilling Co. v. WM R. Co. (1917) **c**	Hol-VD-3	
United States v. Hill (1919)		
Williams v. United States (1921)		Hol-VD-2
Washington v. Dawson & Co. (1924)	Hol-VD-3	
Bunting v. Oregon (1917) **c**	McR-VD-3	
Adkins v. Children's Hospital (1923)	McR-VD-3	
Ribnik v. McBride (1928)	McR-VD-3	
Morehead v. New York ex rel. Tipaldo (1936)	McR-VD-2	
West Coast Hotel v. Parrish (1937)		
Hammer v. Dagenhart (1918) **c**	Clr-3	
Bailey v. Drexel Furniture Co. (1922)	Br-3	
Kentucky Whip & Collar Co. v. IC R. Co. (1937)		Br-Hol-McK-2
Duplex Printing Press Co. v. Deering (1921) **s**	Clr-3	
American Foundries v. Tri-City Trades (1921)	Br-Clr-Hol-2	
Truax v. Corrigan (1921)	Br-Hol-3	
San Francisco Assn. v. United States (1925)	Br-Hol-1	
Bedford Cut Stone Co. v. Stone Cutters (1927)		

Legend: **c** = constitutional decision
    s = statutory decision
    = decision neither constitutionally nor statutorily based

Note: All progery rest on the same decisional basis as the precedent unless otherwise indicated.

falls approximately 7.5 points below those of its predecessors, Waite and Fuller, but several points higher than those of the earliest Courts. Eight of the eleven precedents produce progeny, with 20 of the preference votes falling into the weakest category, three and five into the strong and moderate ones. All five precedent votes are moderately so. With over two-thirds of the preference votes in the weakest category, the White Court arguably manifests a lesser inclination toward preferential behavior than any of its predecessors, none of which has more than half of their votes in this category. Relatedly, only the Taney Court has a lower proportion than the 10.7 percent of the White Court in the strongest preference category.

As Table 4.5 indicates, the 33 votes are scattered among nine of the 13 White Court justices. Notwithstanding, Holmes and Van Devanter cast almost half these votes (16), including three of the five precedential ones.

The White Court Common Case Sample

Only 17 relevant votes result from the White Court sample, barely half the number that the landmarks produce. In *SAL R. Co. v. Blackwell* (1917) the Court held a Georgia law requiring a train to slow sufficiently as to be able to stop at any obstructed grade crossing to violate interstate commerce. The train in question crossed 124 roads in the 123 miles between Atlanta and the South Carolina line. Compliance would double the time needed to traverse the route. Brandeis, Pitney,[41] and White nonetheless dissented on the ground that the regulation was one that a state could permissibly make absent congressional action. And Congress had not acted. In the only progeny, Brandeis, the sole remaining dissenter did so in *Di Santo v. Pennsylvania* (1927), which voided a state law licensing travel agents engaged in foreign commerce. In place of Pitney and White, Holmes and Stone also dissented.

Schaefer v. United States (1920) produces the only precedential votes cast in this small set of ordinary cases – those of Clarke and Holmes in *Gilbert v. Minnesota* (1920). *Schaefer* holds that the publication of articles in German during World War I disparaging the war effort violated the Espionage Act of 1917. Brandeis, along with Clarke and Holmes, dissented. The latter pair voted with the majority in *Gilbert*, however, holding that a state law criminalizing the teaching or advocacy of nonenlistment in the armed forces or nonassistance in the war effort does not violate the First Amendment. Holmes rejoined Brandeis in liberally dissenting in *Gitlow v. New York* (1925), while after Holmes's retirement

---

[41]   Pitney, the last of Taft's six conservative nominees to the Court, read the due process clauses as providing liberty of contract. Although not a friend of organized labor, he did support state workers' compensation laws.

Brandeis again dissented in *Herndon v. Georgia* (1935), which bars on procedural grounds a conviction for an attempt to incite insurrection against a state.

The Justices' Behavior

Seventeen votes in progeny are too few to base conclusions on. Nonetheless, fifteen of these votes support the dissenters' preferences (88.2 percent), a proportion 10–15 points higher than that for any other Court's ordinary cases except Chase, all but one of whose sixteen votes support preferences (93.3 percent). The White Court's behavior reaffirms the proximity in the total preferential proportions of landmark and common decisions that the Marshall and Taney Courts also achieve. Here the difference is 3.4 points. Table 4.6 displays the votes.

Though the votes are too few from which to draw conclusions, we may note in passing that Holmes ranks at the precedential end of the rankings as he does in the White Court's landmark decisions. This, however, was not true of the Taft Court landmarks, in which nine of his ten votes sustained his preferences. Expressions of preference were predominantly moderate and weak, with a combined proportion of 86.7 percent. Of the six Courts considered thus far, an inverse correlation exists between high preference behavior and weak expression thereof. This association is somewhat suspect, however, because all three Courts displaying this pattern saw few votes cast in progeny by dissenters from the precedents: Marshall, Chase, and White. By contrast, well over half the preferential votes of justices on the Taney, Waite, and Fuller Courts were expressed strongly or moderately.

THE TAFT COURT

As noted previously, the only job William Howard Taft really wanted was Chief Justice of the United States. When White died in 1921, Taft set out to make sure it would happen, lobbying successfully for his own appointment (Pringle 1939, vol. II, ch. 50).

With the economy roaring and Republicans in charge, there was little national economic legislation for the Taft Court (1921–30) to consider under the commerce clause. The Court, though, did continue to protect the right to contract, whether infringed by the state or national governments.[42] Interestingly, a Court that found this right inherent in the Fourteenth Amendment was unwilling to consider wiretapping protected by

---

[42] See *Wolff Packing Co. v. Court of Industrial Relations* (1923), requiring binding arbitration in certain labor-management disputes, and *Adkins v. Children's Hospital* (1923), striking minimum wage laws for women and children in the District of Columbia.

Table 4.6.
Voting and opinion behavior: White Court ordinary cases

| | | | | Level of Expression | | | | | |
| | Prefs/prec | | %Prefs | Preferences (%) | | | Precedent (%) | | |
Justice				Strong (1)	Moderate (2)	Weak (3)	Strong (1)	Moderate (2)	Weak (3)
Brandeis (Br)	5	0	100.0	1 (20.0)	4 (80.0)				
Day (Day)	2	0	100.0			2 (100)			
Pitney (Pit)	2	0	100.0			2 (100)			
McReynolds (McR)	1	0	100.0			1 (100)			
Clarke (Cla)	3	1	75.0		1 (33.3)	2 (66.7)		1 (100)	
Holmes (Hol)	2	1	66.7	1 (50.0)	1 (50.0)			1 (100)	
Totals	15	2	88.2	2 (13.3)	6 (40.0)	7 (46.7)	0	2 (100)	0

Precedent/progeny	Preferences	Precedent
SAL R. Co. v. Blackwell (1917) **c**		
DiSanto v. Pennsylvania (1927)	Br-2	
Eagle Glass & Mfg Co. v. Rowe (1917)		
Hitchman Coal & Coke v. Mitchell (1917)	Br-Cla-Hol-2	
United States v. United Shoe Machinery (1918) **s**		
American Column & Lumber v. United States (1921)	Cla-Day-Pit-3	
United Shoe Machinery v. United States (1922)	Cla-Day-Pit-3	
Schaefer v. United States (1920) **c**		
Gilbert v. United States (1920)	Br-2	Cla-Hol-2
Gitlow v. New York (1925)	Br-Hol-1	
Herndon v. Georgia (1935)	Br-2	
MC R. Co. v. Mark Owen & Co. (1921)		
C&NW R. Co. v. Durham Co. (1926)	McR-3	

Legend: **c** = constitutional decision
    s = statutory decision
    = decision neither constitutionally nor statutorily based

Note: All progeny rest on the same decisional basis as the precedent unless otherwise indicated.

the Fourth Amendment, because protections of such communications were not explicitly covered by the constitutional text.[43] The Court did, however, hold the First Amendment's protection of freedom of speech binding on the states through the Fourteenth Amendment,[44] but only in a form so watered down that any speech with a "bad tendency" could be prohibited.

Perhaps the major accomplishment during the Taft Court was Congress's passage, at Taft's urging, of the Judiciary Act of 1925,[45] which relieved the Court of most of its obligatory jurisdiction, freeing the justices to hear more important cases.

Six of the nine landmark decisions of the Taft Court account for all 44 votes that the dissenters from these decisions cast in their progeny. The number of progeny votes per precedent range from 5 to 10, with an average of 7.3, appreciably higher than that for any previous Court.

Brandeis and Holmes consistently supported the exercise of freedom of communication in their ten votes in the progeny of *Gitlow v. New York* (1925): *Whitney v. California* (1927), *Fiske v. Kansas* (1927), *Stromberg v. California* (1931), *Near v. Minnesota* (1931), *Herndon v. Georgia* (1935), and *Herndon v. Lowry* (1937). Brandeis, Holmes, and McReynolds adhered to their dissenting positions in the progeny of *Myers v. United States* (1926) dealing with the President's power to remove federal officials: *Springer v. Philippine Islands* (1928) and *Humphrey's Executor v. United States* (1935). The three *Olmstead v. United States* (1928) dissenters who participated in its progeny – Brandeis, Butler, and Stone – cast another five preferential votes in other Fourth Amendment cases: *Nardone v. United States* (1937), *Goldstein v. United States* (1942), and *Goldman v. United States* (1942). In the last of these, Stone's opinion reads as follows:

> Had a majority of the Court been willing at this time to overrule the Olmstead Case, we should have been happy to join them. But as they have declined to do so, and as we think this case is indistinguishable in principle from Olmstead's, we have no occasion to repeat here the dissenting views in that case with which we agree. (1942, 136)

Another quarter century would pass before the Court interred the *Olmstead* cadaver in *Katz v. United States* (1967).

The other three Taft Court precedents collectively spawned markedly more precedential than preferential votes.

- The three dissenters in the second child labor case, *Adkins v. Children's Hospital* (1923) – Taft, Holmes, and Sanford[46] – reversed

---

[43]   *Olmstead v. United States* (1928).   [44]   *Gitlow v. New York* (1925).
[45]   43 Stat. 936.
[46]   Sanford, a Tennessee Republican, gained his seat on the Court through the lobbying

themselves in *Wolff Packing Co. v. Industrial Relations Court* (1923) and joined their colleagues in a decision that meat packing was not a business clothed with a public interest; hence freedom of contract obtained with regard to employee wages. In *Radice v. New York* (1924), they reverted to their *Adkins* position and agreed that a state could prohibit women from working nights. In *Tyson & Brothers v. Banton* (1927), Holmes and Sanford wrote separate dissents, Holmes labeling the concept of businesses affected with a public interest "as little more than a fiction intended to beautify what is disagreeable to the sufferers" (1927, 446). Four years earlier, of course, he had agreed with its use in *Wolff Packing Co.* One year later, in *Ribnik v. McBride* (1928), Taft again voted precedentially, as did Sanford. The latter explicitly acceded to the *Tyson* precedent from which he had dissented, rather than that of *Adkins*.[47] Nonetheless, it makes no difference to us: a vote based on a progeny of a precedent is no less precedential than if based on the precedent itself. Although Taft maintained his consistency, again voting in support of the precedent from which he had dissented, Holmes did not, either here or in the final progeny, *O'Gorman & Young v. Hartford Insurance Co.* (1931).

- Two unlikely justices, the staunchly conservative McReynolds and Sutherland, dissented from *Carroll v. United States* (1925), which authorized warrantless searches of automobiles based on a loose definition of probable cause. The dissenters characterized the search as "ill-founded" "mere suspicion" (1925, 163). A few months later a unanimous Court used *Carroll* as a precedent to void the conviction of an individual subject to a warrantless narcotics search at a place several blocks distant from the place of his arrest (*Agnello v. United States* [1925]). Thereafter, McReynolds and Sutherland voted precedentially, joining their colleagues in a decision holding that probable cause existed to search an automobile prior to the arrest of the accused (*Husty v. United States* [1931]). After Sutherland's retirement, McReynolds wrote the Court's opinion in *Scher v. United States* (1938), also decided unanimously, upholding the reasonableness of a warrantless search of an automobile conducted some time after the arrest of the accused.

- The final Taft Court case, *Euclid v. Ambler Realty Co.* (1926), which upheld the constitutionality of zoning against a takings clause chal-

efforts of Taft himself, who prevailed on President Harding to nominate him. Interestingly, Taft and Sanford died on the same day.

47   "I concur in this result upon the controlling authority of Tyson & Bro. . . . which, as applied to the question in this case [an employment agency as a business affected with a public interest], I am unable to distinguish" (1928, 359).

lenge, saw the opinionless dissenters – Butler, McReynolds, and Van Devanter – accede to the precedent in its two unanimously decided progeny: *Zahn v. Los Angeles Board* (1927) and *Gorieb v. Fox* (1927). We parenthetically, but nonetheless significantly, note that, apart from *Euclid*, in only one landmark decision since the Court's beginning did no dissenter from the precedent fail to adhere to his preferences in at least one of the progeny of the landmark. Clifford, the sole remaining dissenter from *The Prize Cases* (1862), fifteen years later expressly adhered to its precedent in *Williams v. Bruffy* (1877) and also in *Ford v. Surget* (1878). We deem such behavior rather conclusive evidence of the domination of preferential models over the strength of precedent in the Court's leading decisions during the first 150 years of its existence.

The Justices' Behavior

To the extent that precedential models show any operational relevance, the behavior of the Taft Court manifests it markedly more than any of its predecessor Courts. More than one-third of its dissenters' votes adhered to institutional precedent (see Table 4.7). This increase of 11.6 points over the next most precedentially inclined Court – Chase – amounts to a 50 percent increase in precedential voting. Supporting this increase is the distribution of the votes across the levels of precedential/preferential voting: 59 percent of the preference votes fall into the weakest category, with only 17 and 24 percent in the strongest and moderate categories, respectively. Conversely, 13 of the 15 precedential votes (87 percent) manifest themselves as moderately strong. From a theoretical perspective, if precedential voting at a level of one-third of the votes is defined as moderate, we may consider the behavior of the Taft Court moderately precedential.

But, on the other hand, if two-thirds of the votes remain high enough to support a preferential model, we may initially note that 60 percent (9) of the precedential votes were contributed by the conservative "Four Horsemen": Butler, McReynolds, Sutherland, and Van Devanter. Conversely, they collectively cast only five preferential votes.[48] If we add Taft to this group, the numbers increase to twelve precedential votes and six preferential.

We also note, albeit in passing, that Taft shows himself to be the first justice whom we have encountered who literally adheres to precedent.

---

[48]   This behavior, however, fails to characterize their voting in the Hughes Court, as we point out in the beginning section of the next chapter.

Although he cast but four votes in progeny of a precedent from which he had dissented, three supported the precedent to which he objected. Mitigating this judgment to some extent is the fact that all three of his votes supporting precedent occurred in progeny of *Adkins v. Children's Hospital* (1923). Taft had joined Holmes and Sanford, Brandeis not participating, in a liberal dissent in *Adkins*.[49] Arguably, his votes in progeny actually reflected his true views better than *Adkins* itself. Nonetheless, his record, such as it is, is clear. Unfortunately, he cast no votes in our sample of ordinary litigation. Hence, we cannot judge whether his precedential behavior applies across the board.

In comparison with the votes in the sample of the White Court's common cases (17), the Taft Court justices cast only 26. Interestingly, these two Courts differ in their level of precedent–preference support by only 0.3 percentage point. Especially noteworthy is the fact that the Taft Court justices support their common case preferences at a rate 23 percent higher than they did those in their landmarks!

Of the three Taft Court precedents in which dissenters participated in progeny, *Jaybird Mining Co. v. Weir* (1926) held that land leased from the federal government was not subject to state taxation. Brandeis and McReynolds dissented in separate opinions. They again dissented separately in *Panhandle Oil Co. v. Mississippi ex rel. Knox* (1928). The majority ruled that a state may not tax gas sold to the federal government for use in activities authorized by the Constitution.

Jaybird's next progeny, *Burnet v. Coronado Oil & Gas Co.* (1932), presents the opposite side of the intergovernmental tax immunity coin from that of the precedent: a federal tax on the states. Brandeis adhered to his preferences, while McReynolds in the Court's opinion sustained the *Jaybird* precedent from which he had dissented. In adhering to his preferences, Brandeis wrote some words of more than passing interest:

> Stare decisis is not, like the rule of res judicata, a universal, inexorable command. . . . Whether it shall be followed or departed from is . . . entirely within the discretion of the court. . . . Stare decisis is usually the wise policy, because in most matters it is more important that the applicable rule of law be settled than it be settled right. . . . This is commonly true even where the error is a matter of serious concern, provided correction can be had by legislation. (1932, 405–6)

Brandeis then proceeds to footnote some forty instances where the Court altered its precedents, "although correction might have been secured by legislation" (Id. 406).

In *Jaybird*'s final progeny, *Helvering v. Mountain Producers* (1938),

---

[49] Holmes wrote his own dissent. Sanford joined Taft's.

Table 4.7.
Voting and opinion behavior: Taft Court landmarks

Justice	Prefs/prec		%Prefs	Level of Expression					
				Preferences (%)			Precedent (%)		
				Strong (1)	Moderate (2)	Weak (3)	Strong (1)	Moderate (2)	Weak (3)
Brandeis (Br)	9	0	100.0	1 (11.1)	2 (22.2)	6 (66.7)			
Stone (Sto)	3	0	100.0	1 (33.3)	1 (33.3)	1 (33.3)			
Holmes (Hol)	9	1	90.0	2 (22.2)	2 (22.2)	5 (55.6)		1 (100)	
Sanford (San)	2	2	50.0		1 (50.0)	1 (50.0)	1 (50.0)	1 (50.0)	
Sutherland (Su)	1	1	50.0			1 (100)		1 (50.0)	
McReynolds (McR)	3	4	42.9	1 (33.3)	1 (33.3)	1 (33.3)		4 (100)	
Butler (But)	1	2	33.3			1 (100)		2 (100)	
Taft (Taf)	1	3	25.0			1 (100)		2 (66.7)	1 (33.3)
Van Devanter (VD)	0	2	0.0					2 (100)	
Totals	29	15	65.9	5 (17.2)	7 (24.1)	17 (58.6)	1 (6.7)	13 (86.7)	1 (6.7)

Precedent/progeny	Preferences	Precedent
Adkins v. Children's Hospital (1923) **c**		
Wolff Packing Co. v. Industrial Court (1923)	Hol-San-Taf-3	Hol-San-Taf-2
Radice v. New York (1924)	Hol-1 San-2	Taf-2
Tyson & Bros v. Banton (1927)	Hol-2	San-1 Taf-3
Ribnick v. McBride (1928)	Hol-3	
O'Gorman & Young v. Hartford Ins. Co. (1931)		

Case		
Carroll v. United States (1925) **c**		
Agnello v. United States (1925)	McR-Su-3	
Olmstead v. United States (1928)		McR-Su-2
Scher v. United States (1938)		McR-2
Gitlow v. New York (1925) **c**		
Whitney v. California (1927)	Br-Hol-1	
Fiske v. Kansas (1927)	Br-Hol-3	
Stromberg v. California (1931)	Br-Hol-3	
Near v. Minnesota (1931)	Br-Hol-3	
Herndon v. Georgia (1935)	Br-3	
Herndon v. Lowry (1937)	Br-2	
Myers v. United States (1926) **c**		
Springer v. Philippine Islands (1928)	Br-Hol-McR-2	
Humphrey's Executor v. United States (1935)	Br-3 McR-1	
Euclid v. Ambler Realty Co. (1926) **c**		
Zahn v. Los Angeles Board (1927)		But-McR-VD-2
Gorieb v. Fox (1927)		But-McR-VD-2
Olmstead v. United States (1928) **c**		
Nardone v. United States (1937)	Br-But-St-3	
Goldstein v. United States (1942)	St-2	
Goldman v. United States (1942)	St-1	

Legend: **c** = constitutional decision

        s = statutory decision

        = = decision neither constitutionally nor statutorily based

Note: All progeny rest on the same decisional basis as the precedent unless otherwise indicated.

Table 4.8.
Voting and opinion behavior: Taft Court ordinary cases

				Level of Expression					
				Preferences (%)			Precedent (%)		
Justice	Prefs/prec		%Prefs	Strong (1)	Moderate (2)	Weak (3)	Strong (1)	Moderate (2)	Weak (3)
Brandeis (Br)	3	0	100.0		2 (66.7)	1 (33.3)			
Butler (But)	3	0	100.0		1 (33.3)	2 (66.7)			
Sutherland (Su)	3	0	100.0		1 (33.3)	2 (66.7)			
Van Devanter (VD)	7	1	87.5	1 (14.3)	2 (28.6)	4 (57.1)		1 (100)	
McReynolds (McR)	7	2	77.8	1 (14.3)	3 (42.9)	3 (42.9)		2 (100)	
Totals	23	3	88.5	2 (8.7)	9 (39.1)	12 (52.2)	0	3 (100)	0

Precedent/progeny	Preferences	Precedent
Rockefeller v. United States (1921) **s**	McR-VD-2	
United States v. Phellis (1921)		McR-VD-2
Cullinan v. Walker (1923)		
Weiss v. Stearn (1924)	McR-VD-3	
Marr v. United States (1925)	McR-VD-1	
Koshland v. Helvering (1936)	McR-VD-3	
Jaybird Mining Co. v. Weir (1926) **c**		
Panhandle Oil Co. v. Mississippi (1928)	Br-McR-2	
Burnet v. Coronado Oil & Gas (1932)	Br-2	McR-2
Indian Territory Oil Co. v. Tulsa Board (1933)	Br-McR-3	
Helvering v. Mt. Producers (1938)	McR-2	
Bromley v. McCaughn (1929) **c**		
Heiner v. Donnen (1932)	But-Su-VD-3	
Burnet v. Wells (1933)	But-Su-VD-2	
Helvering v. St. Louis Union Trust (1935)	But-Su-VD-3	

Legend: **c** = constitutional decision
      s = statutory decision
         = decision neither constitutionally nor statutorily based

Note: All progeny rest on the same decisional basis as the precedent unless otherwise indicated.

Table 4.9.
Preferential voting during the middle years

Court	Landmarks		Common cases	
	N	%	N	%
Waite	36–3	92.3	62–18	77.5
Fuller	110–9	92.4	84–22	79.2
White	28–5	84.8	15–2	88.2
Taft	29–15	65.9	23–3	88.5
Totals	203–32	86.4	184–45	80.3

Figure 4.1. Precedential/preferential behavior on the Marshall through Taft Courts.

the Court – overruling *Burnet v. Coronado Oil & Gas* (1932) – held that neither immunity nor *Jaybird* applied to state taxation of oil on Indian lands leased with the approval of the Secretary of the Interior. McReynolds joined a dissent of Butler citing the *Jaybird* precedent as authority for their dissent. As noted, McReynolds had written the now overruled *Burnet* opinion in which he had cited the *Jaybird* precedent from which he had dissented as authority. Consistency may be the hobgoblin of small minds, but this sort of inconsistency provides no enlargement.[50]

As was true of the sample of ordinary White Court cases, we confront too few votes in progeny to render much in the way of judgment. As with the Taft Court, expression of preferences is muted. Over 90 percent of the votes are either moderate or weak (see Table 4.8). Especially note-worthy – though it may be skewed by the concentration of votes in the progeny of only three precedents – is the discrepancy between voting in the Taft Court's landmark and common cases. No Court supported precedent *more* than the justices in Taft Court landmarks. Only the Chase Court among Courts to date supported precedent *less* than the justices in ordinary Taft Court litigation. Also note that the Four Horsemen – Butler, McReynolds, Sutherland, and Van Devanter – voted their preferences in 20 of their 23 ordinary case votes, as contrasted with only 5 of their 14 landmark votes.

CONCLUSION

As Table 4.9 shows, the four Courts we consider in this chapter continue the pattern of preferential/precedential behavior that we documented for the Marshall, Taney, and Chase Courts. Figure 4.1 presents these data graphically. Their collective preferential behavior, however, uni-formly rises 8 percentage points in the landmark cases above that of Marshall, Taney, and Chase. Even the common cases produce a prefer-ential proportion exceeding 80 percent. We do note, however, a mono-tonic pattern of *decreasing* support for preferences from the Waite to the Taft Court in the landmarks.[51] But only in the last of these four Courts is the decrease at all precipitous, from 84.8 percent in the White Court to 65.9 percent in the Taft Court. Consideration of the Hughes (1930–41), Stone (1941–46), and Vinson (1945–53) Courts in the next chapter will indicate whether or not this trend continues.

Contrasting with behavior in the landmarks is that in the common cases. Here an exactly opposite pattern prevails: one that without excep-

---

[50]   Included in this melange of tax cases which our sample uncovered is *Compania General De Tabacos v. Collector* (1927) in which Holmes uttered his oft-quoted remark "Taxes are what we pay for civilized society" (1927, 100). This case, however, in which Holmes and Brandeis dissented, generated no progeny.

[51]   The Fuller Court's landmarks slightly break the monotonic patern, increasing one percentage point above that of its predecessor, Waite, to 92.4 from 92.3 percent.

tion monotonically *increases* the preferential proportion beginning with the Waite Court. The variance, however, is not as marked as in the landmarks. The proportion increases only 11 points, from 77.5 to 88.5 percent. Preferential voting, however, remains overwhelming.

5

Precedential Behavior in the Hughes, Stone, and Vinson Courts

At the beginning of the Hughes Court in 1930, belief in the operation of the legal model and adherence to precedent were basically unquestioned except by a handful of legal realists crying in the wilderness (e.g., Frank 1930). But by the end of the Vinson Court in 1953, belief in the descriptive accuracy of the legal model was under severe attack, though not without its academic defenders (e.g., Bickel 1962; Mendelson 1961; Wechsler 1961). Legalistic normative pronouncements continued to fill the pages of the law reviews, of course, arguing perhaps for reform of the legal model, but not its displacement. Assessment of the Court's leading decisions over the quarter century of the Hughes, Stone, and Vinson Courts should go far to document the extent to which the justices' behavior continued to bypass the strictures of the legalists and the assertions of defenders of the various precedential models.

THE HUGHES COURT

Charles Evans Hughes, nominated to the Supreme Court by William Howard Taft in 1910, resigned from the Court in 1916 to run for President on the Republican and Progressive tickets. After his defeat he returned to his lucrative private law practice and then served as Secretary of State for Harding and Coolidge. When Hoover nominated Hughes to the Chief Justice's position after Taft's retirement in 1930, Senator Norris declared that "No man in public life so exemplifies the influence of powerful combinations in the political and financial world as does Mr. Hughes."[1] Despite opposition from Democratic and Republican progressives, the Senate confirmed Hughes by a 52 to 26 vote.

The Hughes Court (1930–41) contained extraordinarily clear ideological divisions. On the Right were the so-called Four Horsemen – Van Devanter, McReynolds, Sutherland, and Butler – who could be counted

---

[1] *Congressional Record*, 71 Cong., 2nd Session, vol. 72, p. 3373.

on to limit most attempts to regulate the economy. On the Left were Holmes (replaced in 1932 by Cardozo), Brandeis, and Stone, who were willing to let the nation make its economic judgments. In the center with the balance of power stood Hughes and Roberts.

With the onset of the Great Depression in 1929, the demand for federal regulation increased. When Franklin Roosevelt took office in 1933, he immediately proposed "New Deal" legislation to revive the national economy. Although the legislation sailed through Congress, it failed to receive Court approval.

In quick succession the Supreme Court limited congressional authority, stiking the following laws: the National Industrial Recovery Act (NIRA);[2] the Railroad Retirement Act of 1934, which had established a mandatory retirement plan for railroad employees covered by the Interstate Commerce Act; the Agricultural Adjustment Act of 1933;[3] and the Bituminous Coal Conservation Act. Thus by an idiotropic reading of the commerce clause, the Court throttled much of the New Deal.

Needless to say, decisions rendered on state regulations were no more enlightened. In 1934 Hughes and Roberts aligned themselves with the liberals to uphold a New York law regulating the price of milk,[4] but in 1935 and 1936 they joined forces with the conservatives in a series of important cases. Shortly after concluding in *Carter v. Carter Coal Co.* (1936) that the national government infringed on states' rights by regulating wages and prices, the Court ruled that New York's attempt to regulate minimum wages for women violated due process. By a 5-to-4 vote (Hughes split with Roberts and voted with the dissenters) the Court declared that "the State is without power by any form of legislation to prohibit, change or nullify contracts between employers and adult women workers as to the amount of wages to be paid."[5] Robert McCloskey later remarked that the five *Morehead* majority justices were "thoroughly deluded by the notion that the welfare state could be judicially throttled and the brave old world of their youth restored" (1960, pp. 166–67).

By the middle of 1936 it was obvious that the Court would allow neither the federal nor the state governments to relieve the misery caused by the Depression. President Roosevelt made little issue of the Supreme Court in his 1936 reelection campaign, but after his landslide victory he made a bold move. On February 5, 1937, he proposed a Court reform bill, ostensibly designed to improve judicial efficiency. The bill

---

[2] *Panama Refining Co. v. Ryan* (1935) and *Schechter Poultry v. United States* (1935).
[3] *United States v. Butler* (1936).
[4] *Nebbia v. New York.*
[5] *Morehead v. New York ex rel. Tipaldo* (1936) at 611.

would allow the President to appoint one new justice for each gerontocratic member over 70 who chose not to resign. Given the ages of the justices, this would have amounted to six new appointments. Though many of the Court's decisions were unpopular, the notion of judicial independence was not. The press vilified the plan and the public opposed it. Progressive forces failed to rally behind the bill; Southern Democrats joined Republicans in opposition to it (Adamany 1973).

The Court itself played no small role in defusing the plan. On March 29, 1937, by a 5-to-4 vote the justices overturned forty years of freedom-of-contract doctrine.[6] Then on April 12, another 5-to-4 vote upheld the National Labor Relations Act, which guaranteed the right of labor to bargain collectively and authorized the National Labor Relations Board to prevent unfair labor practices. The case, *National Labor Relations Board v. Jones and Laughlin Steel Corp.* (1937), declared that a steel company centered in Pittsburgh with coal mines in Michigan, Minnesota, and Pennsylvania; warehouses in Chicago, Detroit, Cincinnati, and Memphis; and factories in New York and New Orleans conducted business in interstate commerce. Rejecting the dichotomy between manufacture and commerce, the Court instead asked whether steel production had a substantial effect on commerce. Clearly it did.

Finally, on May 24, 1937, a third 5-to-4 vote declared the Social Security Act to be within the tax powers of Congress.[7] This effectively overruled the limits on the taxing power decreed by the *Butler* case. In all three cases, Hughes and Roberts joined the three liberals to uphold the state or federal action in question. Because of the negative impact these decisions had on support for Roosevelt's plan, they have since become known as "the switch in time that saved nine."

Roosevelt's plan became fully superfluous when Justice Van Devanter resigned on May 18, 1937. Instead of a shaky 5-to-4 majority, the Court would soon have its first Roosevelt appointee and with it a 6-to-3 majority. Roosevelt lost the battle to enlarge the Court, but of course, he had won the war.

With regard to precedent, these decisions help highlight the reputed breakdown in the consensual norms that had governed the Court's decisional process since John Marshall's time. Initially manifesting itself in the struggle over the constitutionality of New Deal legislation in the mid-1930s, the normative breakdown reached a peak in the early 1940s (Walker, Epstein, and Dixon 1988). Consequently, we expect an increase in dissents in the landmark decisions construing their constitutionality. Because of the recalcitrance of the Old Guard, their opposition to the

[6] *West Coast Hotel Co. v. Parrish.*   [7] *Steward Machine Co. v. Davis.*

so-called revolution in federalism, and the concomitant narrowness of the decisions that ultimately upheld the New Deal, we expect preferential behavior to return to, and perhaps exceed, that antedating the Taft Court.

Landmarks

The increase in the number of landmark decisions spawned by the New Deal is reflected in a huge increase in the number of votes dissenters from these precedents cast in their progeny. Only the 119 Fuller Court votes approximate the 141 cast by dissenters from the Hughes Court's landmarks. Most of these votes, not surprisingly, pertain to the economic issues that were the heart of the New Deal reforms. Most productive was *Nebbia v. New York* (1934), whose progeny produced thirty votes – more than 20 percent of the total. Given that *Nebbia* not only abandoned the hoary doctrine of *Munn v. Illinois* (1877), but also upheld the constitutionality of price fixing, the dissenters unfailingly voted their preferences.[8]

Among the 104 votes that the four conservatives cast in progeny of Hughes Court landmarks are those of *Steward Machine Co. v. Davis* (1937). Sutherland and Van Devanter viewed the unemployment compensation provisions of the Social Security Act as administratively violating the Tenth Amendment, while Butler and McReynolds held the tax unconstitutional because unemployment did not fall within the scope of the commerce power. They all voted their preferences in *Carmichael v. Southern Coal & Coke* (1937), while Sutherland and Van Devanter split with the other dissenters and upheld the tax sustaining the Social Security Act's retirement benefits in *Helvering v. Davis* (1937). Given that the act does not involve the states in financing and providing old age pensions, Sutherland and Van Devanter's votes probably should be excluded from consideration rather than counted as precedential. But their silence in *Helvering*, coupled with Cardozo's extremely heavy reliance

---

[8] The progeny are *Borden's Farm Products Co. v. Baldwin* (1934), *Baldwin v. Seelig* (1935), *Borden's Farm Products Co. v. Ten Eyck* (1936), *Mayflower Farms v. Ten Eyck* (1936), *Morehead v. New York ex rel. Tipaldo* (1936), *West Coast Hotel v. Parrish* (1937), *Highland Farms Dairy v. Agnew* (1937), and *United States v. Rock Royal Coop* (1939).

  In *Borden's Farm Products v. Ten Eyck*, the *Nebbia* dissenters not only "adhere[d] to what we there said" (1936, 264), but also objected to deviation from the fixed price accorded to dealers with a less well-advertised trade name. Interestingly, they did so on a basis reprised by opponents of modern-day affirmative action programs: a person or institution "who through merit has acquired a good reputation, can be deprived of the consequent benefit in order that another may trade successfully. Thus the statute destroys equality of opportunity – puts appellant at a disadvantage because of merit" (1936, 265).

on *Steward Machine* as authority for the Court's *Helvering* opinion, cause us to count these two votes as supporting precedent.

The Hughes Court's Old Guard cast 104 of the 141 votes in progeny of leading decisions from which members of that Court had dissented – almost three-quarters of the total, 73.8 percent. This despite the fact that all the votes in the progeny were cast in a span of ten years (1931–41), since none of the quartet served beyond the end of the Hughes Court itself. By contrast, seven different justices accounted for the progeny votes in the other quarter of the total cast. The 104 votes cast by the conservative quartet pertain to twelve precedents; the 37 cast by the seven other justices derive from only seven. If we also consider the ten leading decisions of the Hughes Court that generated no progeny in which a dissenter from the precedent participated, we find that dissent here was confined exclusively to members of the conservative quartet.[9]

The Justices' Behavior

Not surprisingly, the Hughes Court behaved markedly differently from its predecessor, the Taft Court, and conformed to the extremely high level of preferential voting that the other predecessor Courts had displayed since the time of John Marshall. Notwithstanding the harsh rhetoric that characterized many of the Hughes Court's landmark decisions, dissenters – perhaps surprisingly – voted preferences approximately 4 percent less often than did those on the Waite and Fuller Courts, 88 versus 92 percent.

Although the Hughes Court displayed a fairly high level of preferential voting, it is not as high as might have been expected, nor as high as that of the Chase, Waite, or Fuller Court. An equal number of votes, 34, attained the strongest and weakest levels; the other 57 were moderate. Fourteen of the 16 precedential votes were moderately so, with the other two weak.

Eleven of the 16 justices participated in a progeny from which they had dissented. As Table 5.1 indicates, only Justice Murphy's two precedential votes produced a preferential percentage lower than 83.3. Especially interesting is the behavior of the holdover justices from the Taft Court. The liberal Brandeis and Stone, who invariably voted preferentially on

---

[9] These ten decisions and their dissenters are Butler and McReynolds in *Powell v. Alabama* (1932), *Helvering v. Davis* (1937), *Johnson v. Zerbst* (1938), *Missouri ex rel. Gaines v. Canada* (1938), *Graves v. New York ex rel. O'Keefe* (1939), and *Lane v. Wilson* (1939); the quartet in *West Coast Hotel v. Parrish* (1937); McReynolds in *United States v. Curtiss-Wright Export Corp.* (1936) and *Sunshine Anthracite Coal Co. v. Adkins* (1940); and Butler in *Palko v. Connecticut* (1937).

Table 5.1.
Voting and opinion behavior: Hughes Court landmarks

| | | | | Level of Expression | | | | | |
| | | | | Preferences (%) | | | Precedent (%) | | |
Justice	Prefs/prec		%Prefs	Strong (1)	Moderate (2)	Weak (3)	Strong (1)	Moderate (2)	Weak (3)
Hughes (Hu)	4	0	100.0	1 (25.0)	1 (25.0)	2 (50.0)			
Black (Blk)	2	0	100.0		2 (100)				
Douglas (Dou)	2	0	100.0		2 (100)				
Butler (But)	28	2	93.3	8 (28.6)	12 (42.9)	8 (28.6)		2 (100)	
Stone (Sto)	14	1	93.3	4 (28.6)	6 (42.9)	4 (28.6)		1 (100)	
McReynolds (McR)	34	3	91.9	9 (26.5)	17 (50.0)	8 (23.5)		2 (66.7)	1 (33.3)
Sutherland (Su)	16	3	84.2	5 (31.3)	5 (31.3)	6 (37.5)		3 (100)	
Van Devanter (VD)	15	3	83.3	4 (26.7)	5 (33.3)	6 (40.0)		3 (100)	
Cardozo (Car)	5	1	83.3	2 (40.0)	3 (60.0)			1 (100)	
Brandeis (Br)	5	1	83.3	1 (20.0)	4 (80.0)			1 (100)	
Murphy (Mur)	0	2	0.0				—	1 (50.0)	1 (50.0)
Totals	125	16	88.7	34 (27.2)	57 (45.6)	34 (27.2)	0	14 (87.5)	2 (12.5)

Precedent/progeny	Preferences	Precedent
Stromberg v. California (1931) c		
Near v. Minnesota (1931)	But-McR-2	
Herndon v. Lowry (1937)	But-McR-2	
Thornhill v. Alabama (1940)	McR-2	
Carlson v. California (1940)	McR-2	
Near v. Minnesota (1931) c		
Herndon v. Lowry (1937)	But-McR-Su-VD-2	
Nixon v. Condon (1932) c		
Grovey v. Townsend (1935)	But-McR-Su-VD-3	
Home Bldg & Loan Assn. v. Blaisdell (1934) c		
Nebbia v. New York (1934)	But-McR-Su-VD-1	
W.B. Worthen Co. v. Thomas (1934)	But-McR-Su-VD-1	
W.B. Worthen Co. v. Kavanaugh (1935)	But-McR-Su-VD-3	
Veix v. 6th Ward Bldg & Loan Assn. (1940)		McR-3
Nebbia v. New York (1934) c		
Borden's Farm Products Co. v. Baldwin (1934)	But-McR-Su-VD-3	
Baldwin v. Seelig (1935)	But-McR-Su-VD-3	
Borden's Farm Products Co. v. Ten Eyck (1936)	But-McR-Su-VD-1	
Mayflower Farms v. Ten Eyck (1936)	But-McR-Su-VD-3	
Morehead v. New York ex rel. Tipaldo (1936)	But-McR-Su-VD-3	
West Coast Hotel Co. v. Parrish (1937)	But-McR-Su-VD-2	
Highland Farms Dairy v. Agnew (1937)	But-McR-Su-VD-1	
United States v. Rock Royal Co-op (1939)	But-McR-2	
Panama Refining Co. v. Ryan (1935) c		
Schechter Poultry Co. v. United States (1935)	Car-1	

Table 5.1 (cont.)

Precedent/progeny	Preferences	Precedent
Norman v. B&O R. Co. (1935) **c**		
Holyoke Water Co. v. American Paper Co. (1937)	But-McR-Su-VD-2	
Smyth v. United States (1937)	But-McR-Su-1	
Guaranty Trust v. Homewood (1939)	But-McR-2	
Railroad Retirement Board v. Alton R. Co. (1935) **c**		
Mulford v. Smith (1939)	Hu-Sto-3	
United States v. Rock Royal Co-op (1939)	Hu-Sto-3	
United States v. Lowden (1939)	Hu-Sto-2	
United States v. Butler (1936) **c**		
Rickert Rice Mills v. Fontenot (1936)		Br-Car-Sto-2
Carter v. Carter Coal Co. (1936)	Br-Car-Sto-2	
Steward Machine Co. v. Davis (1937)	Br-Car-Sto-2	
Mulford v. Smith (1939)	Sto-3	
Ashwander v. TVA (1936) **c**		
Tennessee Electric Power Co. v. TVA (1939)	McR-2	
United States v. Appalachian Power (1940)	McR-2	
Carter v. Carter Coal Co. (1936) **c**		
NLRB v. Jones & Laughlin Steel Crop. (1937)	Br-Car-Sto-2	
Santa Cruz Fruit Co. v. NLRB (1938)	Br-Sto-2	
NLRB v. Fainblatt (1939)	Sto-3	
Sunshine Coal Co. v. Adkins (1940)	Sto-1	
United States v. Darby (1941)	Sto-1	
Morehead v. New York ex rel. Tipaldo (1936) **c**		
West Coast Hotel Co. v. Parrish (1937)	Br-Car-Hu-Sto-1	

Case			
NLRB v. Jones & Laughlin Steel Corp. (1937) **c**	But-McR-Su-VD-2		But-McR-Su-VD-2
Associated Press v. NLRB (1937)			But-McR-Su-VD-2
WA, VA & MD Coach Co. v. NLRB (1937)			
Myers v. Bethlehem Shipbuilding (1938)			
Santa Cruz Fruit Co. v. NLRB (1938)	But-McR-1		
Consolidated Edison v. NLRB (1938)	But-McR-1		
NLRB v. Fansteel (1939)	But-McR-3		
NLRB v. Columbian Enameling Co. (1939)	But-McR-3		
NLRB v. Fainblatt (1939)	But-McR-2		
Apex Hosiery Co. v. Leader (1940)	McR-2		
Steward Machine Co. v. Davis (1937) **c**	But-McR-Su-VD-2		
Carmichael v. Southern Coal & Coke (1937)	But-McR-2	Su-VD-2	
Helvering v. Davis (1937)			
Mulford v. Smith (1939) **c**			
Hood & Sons v. United States (1939)	But-McR-2		
Coleman v. Miller (1939) **c**			
Chandler v. Wise (1939)	But-McR-1		
Hague v. CIO (1939) **c**			
Hines v. Davidowitz (1941)			
Minersville School District v. Gobitis (1940) **c**	McR-1		
Jones v. Opelika (1942)	Sto-2		
West Virginia Bd. of Education v. Barnette (1943)	Sto-1		
United States v. Classic (1941) **c**			
United States v. Saylor (1944)	Blk-Dou-2		Mur-3
Screws v. United States (1945)	Blk-Dou-2		Mur-3

Legend: **c** = constitutional decision

      s = statutory decision

      = decision neither constitutionally nor statutorily based

Note: All progeny rest on the same decisional basis as the precedent unless otherwise indicated.

the Taft Court (12 of 12), continued to do so at a slightly lower level on the Hughes Court (10 of 12 votes). But the conservative Old Guard, who had appeared supportive of precedent on the Taft Court with 9 of their 14 votes, completely reversed their behavior on the Hughes Court by casting 93 of 104 votes preferentially (89.4 percent).

Ordinary Cases

Dissenters from the ordinary Hughes Court precedents cast approximately the same number of votes in its progeny as Taft Court dissenters: 23 versus 26. Four Hughes Court precedents spawn such votes as compared with three from the Taft Court. (See Tables 5.2 and 4.8.) The two Courts differ, however, in the proportion of preferential votes: 88.5 percent for Taft Court dissenters, only 69.6 percent for the Hughes Court. No other Court to date has so high a precedential proportion. Only the Taney Court comes close, 0.9 percent lower. Interestingly, the Taft Court's landmarks contain the highest proportion of precedential votes of any Court, 34.1 percent; the Hughes Court, by contrast, has only one-third as many: 11.3 percent.

The first of the Hughes Court decisions in our sample that produces any progeny is *United States v. Bland* (1931), one of three related decisions that the majority overruled; the others were *United States v. Schwimmer* (1929) and *United States v. MacIntosh* (1931), the latter a companion to *Bland.* All three cases hold that Congress could deny naturalization to conscientious objectors. Stone joined three other justices in dissent. Fifteen years later, on the very day he died, he wrote the dissenting opinion in *Girouard v. United States* (1946) upholding the precedent from which he had dissented. As we have seen, justices do occasionally accede to precedent. But in none of our other cases does a dissenter from a precedent dissent from its overruling. Because of its uniqueness, Stone's rationale warrants extensive quotation.

> With three other Justices of the Court I dissented in the MacIntosh and Bland Cases, for reasons which the Court now adopts as ground for overruling them. Since this Court . . . rejected the construction of the statute for which the dissenting Justices contended, the question, which for me is decisive of the present case, is whether Congress has likewise rejected that construction by its subsequent legislative action, and has confirmed the Court's earlier construction of the statutes in question. A study of Congressional action . . . since the decision in the Schwimmer Case, leads me to conclude that Congress had adopted and confirmed this Court's earlier construction of the naturalization laws. (1946, 72–73)

We count Stone's vote as adhering to precedent. But do note that what Stone arguably supported was Congress's ratification of the Court's ear-

lier decisions. He did not repudiate his vote in *Bland*. Indeed, he states
that his language quoted summarizes the sole reason for his vote.[10]

The third of the four ordinary Hughes Court precedents saw its progeny produce only one precedential vote out of eight, as opposed to five
of eleven in the second case on Table 5.2. *Sibbach v. Wilson & Co.* (1941)
held that the Court could notice *sua sponte* the lower courts' failure to
comply with a Federal Rule of Civil Procedure prohibiting a party from
being cited for contempt for refusing to submit to a physical examination. Frankfurter, in an opinion that Black, Douglas, and Murphy joined,
redefined the issue as "whether the authority which Congress gave to this
Court to formulate rules of civil procedure for the district courts allows"
for the overruling of one of the Court's own precedents (1944, 17).[11]
Because bodily integrity has "historic roots in Anglo-American law," an
examination requires "explicit legislation" (Id. 17–18). The dissenters
voted preferences in *Mississippi Publishing Corp. v. Murphree* (1946), a
unanimous decision, asserting the Court's right to deviate from the Rules
of Civil Procedure, notwithstanding that the Court itself promulgated
them. In *Schlagenhauf v. Holder* (1964), Black adhered to the dissent he
joined in *Sibbach*, while Douglas expressly accepted that decision "as
one governed by *stare decisis*" (1964, 125). But both Black and Douglas
voted preferences in *Hanna v. Plumer* (1965), broadly construing the
congressional legislation providing the Court with the power to specify
the civil procedure of the federal district courts.[12]

The Justices' Behavior

As Table 5.2 shows, the votes of the justices in this small set of cases are
much too widely scattered to allow any conclusions to be drawn about
specific members. At the summary level, we can note that a greater
proportion of both the preferential and precedential votes cast by this
Court were more weakly expressed than is true of any previous Court.
The overall preferences/precedent voting is the lowest of any Court's
common case sample, 69.6 percent. Only the Taney Court approximates
it at 70.5 percent. We shall be interested to ascertain whether this pattern
of relatively high adherence to precedent manifests itself in the run-of-
the-mill litigation of subsequent Courts, or whether the Hughes Court's
behavior is simply a blip on the screen.

---

[10] "For that reason alone I think that the judgment should be affirmed" (Id.).
[11] That case was *UP R. Co. v. Botsford* (1891), which held that a court may not, at
      respondent's request, require the plaintiff prior to trial to submit to a physical exami-
      nation to determine the extent of the injury sued for.
[12] The statute was the 1958 version of the Rules Enabling Act, 28 USC §2072.

Table 5.2.
Voting and opinion behavior: Hughes Court ordinary cases

Justice	Prefs/prec	%Prefs	Level of Expression					
			Preferences (%)			Precedent (%)		
			Strong (1)	Moderate (2)	Weak (3)	Strong (1)	Moderate (2)	Weak (3)
Black (Blk)	4 0	100.0	1 (25.0)		3 (75.0)			
Frankfurter (Fk)	1 0	100.0			1 (100)			
McReynolds (McR)	1 0	100.0		1 (100)				
Murphy (Mur)	1 0	100.0			1 (100)			
Reed (Re)	1 0	100.0			1 (100)			
Douglas (Dou)	3 1	75.0			3 (100)	1 (100)		
Roberts (Rob)	4 3	57.1		2 (50.0)	2 (25.0)		1 (33.3)	2 (66.7)
Hughes (Hu)	1 2	33.3		1 (100)				2 (100)
Stone (Sto)	0 1	0.0				1 (100)		
Totals	16 7	69.6	1 (6.3)	4 (25.0)	11 (68.8)	2 (28.6)	1 (14.3)	4 (57.1)

Precedent/progeny	Preferences	Precedent
United States v. Bland (1931) **s**		Sto-1
Girouard v. United States (1946)		
Helvering v. Horst (1940)	Hu-McR-Rob-2	
Helvering v. Eubank (1940)		Hu-Rob-3
Harrison v. Schaffner (1941)		Hu-Rob-3
Hort v. Commissioner (1941)		
Pearce v. Commissioner (1942)	Rob-3	
Helvering v. Stuart (1942)	Rob-3	
Rogers' Estate v. Helvering (1943)	Rob-2	
Commissioner v. Harmon (1944)		Rob-2
Sibbach v. Wilson & Co. (1941) **s**	Blk-Dou-Frk-Mur-3	
Mississippi Publishing Co. v. Murphree (1946)	Blk-1	
Schlagenhauf v. Holder (1964)	Blk-Dou-3	
Hanna v. Plumer (1965)		Dou-1
United States v. Cooper Corp. (1941) **s**		
Georgia v. Evans (1942)	Blk-Dou-Re-3	

Legend: **c** = constitutional decision
       s = statutory decision
       = decision neither constitutionally nor statutorily based

Note: All progeny rest on the same decisional basis as the precedent unless otherwise indicated.

THE STONE COURT

The short-lived Stone Court (1941–46) had the briefest existence – five years – of any Court since those of the eighteenth century. The battle over the New Deal had been won, and every member of the Court except Justice Roberts owed his position to Franklin Roosevelt. Nonetheless, the contentiousness of the Stone Court reached a new high. Over its life the proportion of cases with at least one dissenting opinion approximated 50 percent, more than double that of the strife ridden Hughes Court (Epstein et al. 1996, 197–98).

Though the Stone Court gave us the repugnant Japanese exclusion cases,[13] it was that Court that first breathed life into a little noticed doctrine buried in *United States v. Carolene Products* (1938). The case involved the constitutionality of the Filled Milk Act of 1923, which prohibited the interstate shipment of skimmed milk with oil-based fillers. Justice Stone, then an associate justice, writing for the majority, made it clear that the Court would only minimally scrutinize such statutes. But in footnote 4 he declared:

There may be a narrower scope for operation of the presumption of constitutionality when legislation appears on its face to be within a specific prohibition of the Constitution, such as those of the first ten amendments, which are deemed equally specific when held to be embraced within the Fourteenth. . . .

It is unnecessary to consider now whether legislation which restricts those political processes which can ordinarily be expected to bring about repeal of undesirable legislation, is to be subjected to more exacting judicial scrutiny under the general prohibitions of the Fourteenth Amendment than are most other types of legislation. . . .

Nor need we inquire whether similar considerations enter into the review of statutes directed at particular religious . . . or national . . . or racial minorities . . . whether prejudices against discrete and insular minorities may be a special condition, which tends seriously to curtail the operation of those political processes ordinarily thought to be relied upon to protect minorities, and which may call for a correspondingly more searching judicial inquiry. (pp. 152–53)

Thus the formulation of what is known as the "preferred freedoms doctrine." Under this doctrine, the Court assumes legislation constitutional unless it facially abridges a provision of the Bill of Rights, restricts access to normal political processes (e.g., the right to vote), or violates the equal protection rights of "insular minorities." If so, then the presumption of constitutionality does not obtain. The state can overcome the presumption of unconstitutionality if a law is "narrowly tailored" to sustain a "compelling" governmental interest.

[13] *Hirabayashi v. United States* (1943) and *Korematsu v. United States* (1994).

In a Court filled with Roosevelt appointees such as Douglas, Black, and Murphy, and with economic matters no longer a prime concern of the Court, it began, however slowly and contentiously, to focus its attention on matters of civil liberties. In 1943, it overturned a two-year-old precedent that had allowed states to require flag salutes.[14] In 1944 it overruled a 1935 decision and held that (white) primaries were part of the state election apparatus and thus were subject to the requirements of the Fourteenth and Fifteenth Amendments.[15]

Landmarks

Notwithstanding its contentiousness and the fact that two of its more outspoken justices – Douglas and Black – served long after Stone's death the Stone Court did not produce an inordinate number of progeny in which the dissenters from the precedents participated: a grand total of 78 votes in 39 progeny, an average of two per progeny. By contrast, the 141 votes cast by Hughes Court dissenters occurred in only 55 progeny, an average of half a vote more per progeny (2.56).

Well over half the votes (45 of 78) cast by dissenters from Stone Court landmark decisions appear in the progeny of *Betts v. Brady* (1942) and *Murdock v. Pennsylvania* (1943).[16] We consider *Betts* first.

Beginning with *Foster v. Illinois* (1947) and continuing until *Gideon v. Wainwright* (1963) overruled *Betts*, Black consistently voices his continued opposition, joined by Douglas and Murphy, the other *Betts* dissenters, to the Court's refusal to require the states to supply counsel to indigents accused of serious crime. Thus, referring to *Betts* as precedent to *Foster*, he wrote, "It is the kind of precedent that I had hoped this Court would not perpetuate" (1947, 140). One year later, Douglas, speaking for himself and the others, refers to *Betts* as "ill-starred" (*Bute v. Illinois* 1948, 677). In *Gibbs v. Burke* (1949, 782) Black and Douglas explicitly call for the overruling of *Betts,* a request Black reiterated in *Carnley v. Cochran* in 1962 (519), a year before the feat was accomplished.[17]

---

[14] The original case was *Minersville School District v. Gobitis* (1940); the overruling case was *West Virginia Board of Education v. Barnette* (1943).

[15] *Smith v. Allwright* (1944) overruling *Grovey v. Townsend* (1935).

[16] Indeed, with but a single exception, *Korematsu v. United States* (1944), every Stone Court precedent that generated any votes at all produced at least six by dissenters in progeny. *Korematsu* produced only one, Murphy's vote in *Takahashi v. Fish and Game Commission* (1948).

[17] *Betts*'s other progeny are *Gryger v. Burke* (1948), *Gibbs v. Burke* (1949), *Quicksall v. Michigan* (1950), *Crooker v. California* (1958), and *McNeal v. Culver* (1961).

Murdock v. Pennsylvania (1943) produces the most numerous set of progeny votes among the Stone Court's leading decisions, 24, three more than *Betts*. Articulating the preferred position doctrine (1943, 115), the majority ruled that the licensing of door-to-door religious solicitors amounts to a tax on the free exercise of religion. In three separate opinions, Justices Frankfurter, Jackson, Reed, and Roberts dissent. They adhere to their position with various levels of preferential voting in *Jones v. Opelika* (1943), *Martin v. Struthers* (1943), *Prince v. Massachusetts* (1944), and *Poulos v. New Hampshire* (1953). Reed upholds precedent in *Follett v. McCormick* (1944), while the other three vote their preferences. Reed does so in language akin to that employed by Justice Harlan when he acceded – as we shall see – to Warren Court decisions of which he disapproved:

My views on the constitutionality of ordinances of this type . . . remain unchanged but they are not in accord with those announced by the Court.

As I see no difference in respect to the exercise of religion between an itinerant distributor and one who remains in one general neighborhood or between one who is active part time and another who is active all of his time, there is no occasion for me to state again views already rejected by a majority of the Court. Consequently, I concur. (1944, 578)

With Roberts gone and Jackson not participating, Reed reaffirmed his original *Murdock* position in *Marsh v. Alabama* (1946). Frankfurter, however, did what Reed had done in *Follett*, concurring while professing adherence to his original dissent. Frankfurter manifested his original sentiments by acerbically denigrating the preferred position doctrine that he had originally condemned in his *Murdock* dissent. Though Reed's and Frankfurter's votes conform to their preferences to at least as great an extent as they do to precedent, we nonetheless count them as precedential. Finally, all four of the *Murdock* dissenters disregard their preferences and join their colleagues in the orally argued one paragraph per curiam, *Busey v. District of Columbia* (1943), which vacated and remanded the decision of the District's court of appeals "to enable it to reexamine its rulings . . . in the light of those decisions [*Murdock* and *Opelika*]" (1943, 580). As we have documented elsewhere (Segal and Spaeth 1996b, 1077–80), cursory grant, vacate, and remand decisions (GVRs) pattern themselves after summary decisions rather than the full-blown orally argued signed opinion variety. Nonetheless, *Busey,* though but a single paragraph in length, was orally argued. Hence, without more, it meets our criteria for inclusion in our dataset. Therefore, we count it.

A badly fractured Court in *Colegrove v. Green* (1946) ruled that congressional reapportionment was a political question, one not appropriate for judicial resolution.[18] The dissenters adhere to their position in *Colegrove*'s progeny, most immediately *MacDougall v. Green* (1948) and *South v. Peters* (1950). Although Justice Frankfurter in dissent in *Baker v. Carr* (1961) declared *Colegrove* a dead letter, Brennan, writing for the majority, adroitly avoided doing so (Brenner and Spaeth 1995, 125). In their *Colegrove* dissent, Douglas, Black, and the now deceased Murphy had not only held that reapportionment is a justiciable matter, they also asserted that population inequities should be rectified. *Baker* and its sequels – *Gray v. Sanders* (1963) and *Wesberry v. Sanders* (1964) – address the latter concern. Hence, for Black and Douglas, their *Colegrove* position remained relevant.[19]

Another leading decision of the Stone Court in which dissenters voted in its progeny is *United States v. South-Eastern Underwriters Assn.* (1944). Frankfurter and the Chief Justice demurred on the applicability of the Sherman Act to the insurance business. Jackson, unable to distinguish between insurance and other interstate transactions, nonetheless held that the total absence of congressional legislation dealing with insurance counseled restraint, given "this important and complicated enterprise," and "will require an extensive overhauling of state legislation relating to taxation and supervision. The whole legal basis will have to be reconsidered" (1944, 590). After Congress's overruling of *South-Eastern Underwriters* by the passage of the McCarran Act and the Court's affirmation of the Statute in *Prudential Insurance Co. v. Benjamin* (1946), Frankfurter acceded to Jackson's dissent in *Connecticut Mutual Life Insurance Co. v. Moore* (1948) that the federal courts should continue to stay out of insurance controversies even if the McCarran Act permits. They took the same position in *Maryland Casualty Co. v. Cushing* (1954) with respect to the applicability of the Limited Liability Act in a Louisiana workers' compensation case. After Jackson's death, Frankfurter continued to adhere to a no federal jurisdiction position in *SEC v. Variable Annuity Co.* (1959), "declin[ing] to give a niggardly construction to the McCarran Act" (1959, 96–97). He reasserted this view one year later in *FTC v. Travelers Health Assn.* (1960).

[18] Technically, *Colegrove* was not a Stone Court decision. The Chief Justice died on April 22, 1946; the case was not decided until June 10, the last day of the 1945 term. Stone's successor, Fred Vinson, was not confirmed until June 20. Inasmuch as Vinson had not yet taken the center chair, we ascribe *Colegrove* to the Stone Court.

[19] Compatibly with our decision rules, we count Douglas's vote in *Gomillinon v. Lightfoot* (1960) a progeny of *Colegrove* even though the case concerned the redrawing of a city's boundaries to exclude blacks in violation of the Fifteenth Amendment. In joining the majority opinion, Douglas specifically adhered to the *Colegrove* dissents (1960, 348).

The Justices' Behavior

Of a total of 78 votes, the Stone Court justices voted their preferences 71 times, a percentage of 91.0. Only the 92.3 percent and 92.4 percent of the Waite and Fuller Courts, respectively, exceed it. Compatible with the high proportion of preference votes is a similarly high level of expression: 37 strongly preferential, 25 moderate, and only nine weakly so, as Table 5.3 shows. Conversely, five of the seven precedential votes are weak, the other two moderate.

No justice cast less than 80 percent of his votes preferentially. All but three of the eleven members of this Court participated in progeny of precedents from which they had dissented: Stone, Byrnes, and Burton. The latter two served only a year. We may properly split the eight participants into exclusive sets of liberals (Black, Douglas, Murphy, and Rutledge) and conservatives (Frankfurter, Jackson, Reed, and Roberts). Doing so documents lesser attachment to precedent by the liberals – only 1 of 38 votes (2.6 percent) – than by the conservatives – 6 of 40 (15.0 percent). Theoretically, these percentages continue to belie the operational relevance of any of the precedential models.

Ordinary Litigation

In the number of common precedents in which dissenters cast votes in progeny and in the total number of such votes cast, the Stone Court varies but little from its predecessor. Whereas the Hughes Court contained four precedents, the Stone Court has five. Hughes Court dissenters cast 23 votes in the progeny of these precedents; those of the Stone Court, 27. Moreover, one of the Stone Court precedents spawns almost half the 27 votes, *Colorado Interstate Gas Co. v. FPC* (1945).

The only one of the common precedents that warrants discussion is *United States v. Waddill, Holland & Flinn* (1945), from which Jackson dissented. The Court gave priority to the federal government's lien for unpaid taxes over the unperfected and imprecisely specified lien of a lessor for rent due. Jackson again dissented in *Illinois v. Campbell* (1946), where the majority gave priority out of the property of an insolvent debtor to unemployment compensation taxes due the United States rather than those owed the state. Three other justices joined his dissent in *Massachusetts v. United States* (1948), a case factually similar to *Campbell.* Jackson labeled the majority's decision "unnecesarily ruthless" (Id., 635) given the U.S. claim for 100 percent of the unemployment compensation taxes even though the debtor paid the state because the Social Security Act provides for a 90 percent credit against the federal

Table 5.3.
Voting and opinion behavior: Stone Court landmarks

| | | | Level of Expression | | | | | | |
| | | | Preferences (%) | | | Precedent (%) | | |
Justice	Prefs/prec	%Prefs	Strong (1)	Moderate (2)	Weak (3)	Strong (1)	Moderate (2)	Weak (3)
Black (Blk)	14 0	100.0	6 (42.9)	6 (42.9)	2 (14.3)			
Douglas (Dou)	14 0	100.0	8 (57.1)	5 (35.7)	1 (7.1)			
Rutledge (Ru)	2 0	100.0	2 (100)					
Jackson (Jac)	7 1	87.5	4 (57.1)	1 (14.3)	2 (28.6)			1 (100)
Murphy (Mur)	7 1	87.5	4 (57.1)	2 (28.6)	1 (14.3)			1 (100)
Reed (Re)	13 2	86.7	3 (23.1)	8 (61.5)	2 (15.4)		1 (50.0)	1 (50.0)
Roberts (Rob)	6 1	85.7	4 (66.7)	2 (33.3)				1 (100)
Frankfurter (Fnk)	8 2	80.0	6 (75.0)	1 (12.5)	1 (12.5)	–	1 (50.0)	1 (50.0)
Totals	71 7	91.0	37 (52.1)	25 (35.2)	9 (12.7)	0	2 (28.6)	5 (71.4)

Table 5.3 (cont.)

Precedent/progeny	Preferences	Precedent
Betts v. Brady (1942) **c**		
Adamson v. California (1947)	Blk-Dou-Mur-1	
Bute v. Illinois (1948)	Blk-Dou-Mur-1	
Gryger v. Burke (1948)	Blk-Dou-Mur-2	
Gibbs v. Burke (1949)	Blk-Dou-1 Mur-3	
Quicksall v. Michigan (1950)	Blk-2	
Crooker v. California (1958)	Blk-Dou-2	
McNeal v. Culver (1961)	Blk-3 Dou-1	
Carnley v. Cochran (1962)	Blk-Dou-1	
Gideon v. Wainwright (1963)	Blk-Dou-1	
McNabb v. United States (1943)		
Anderson v. United States (1943)	Re-2	
United States v. Mitchell (1944)	Re-1	
Malinski v. New York (1945)	Re-2	
Haley v. Ohio (1948)	Re-2	
Townsend v. Burke (1948)	Re-2	
Upshaw v. United States (1948)	Re-1	
United States v. Carignan (1951)	Re-2	
Gallegos v. Nebraska (1951)	Re-2	
Murdock v. Pennsylvania (1943) **c**		
Jones v. Opelika (1943)	Frk-Jac-Re-Rob-1	
Martin v. Struthers (1943)	Frk-Jac-Re-Rob-2	
Busey v. District of Columbia (1943)		Frk-Jac-Re-Rob-3
Prince v. Massachusetts (1944)	Frk-Jac-Rob-1	Re-3
Follett v. McCormick (1944)	Frk-Jac-Rob-1	Re-2
Marsh v. Alabama (1946)	Re-2	Frk-2
Poulos v. New Hampshire (1953)	Jac-Re-3	

Yakus v. United States (1944) **c**		
Bowles v. Willingham (1944)	Rob-1	
Steuart v. Bowles Co. (1944)	Rob-2	
Porter v. Werner Holding Co. (1946)	Ru-1	Mur-3
Sunal v. Large (1947)	Ru-Mur-1	
United States v. South-Eastern Underwriters (1944) **s**		
Connecticut Mutual Life Ins. Co. v. Moore (1948)	Frk-Jac-3	
Maryland Casualty Co. v. Cushing (1954)	Frk-Jac-1	
SEC v. Variable Annuity Co. (1959)	Frk-1	
FTC v. Travelers Health Assn. (1960)	Frk-1	
Korematsu v. United States (1944) **c**		
Takahashi v. Fish & Game Commission (1948)	Mur-1	
Colegrove v. Green (1946)		
MacDougall v. Green (1948)	Blk-Dou-Mur-2	
South v. Peters (1950)	Blk-Dou-2	
Gomillion v. Lightfoot (1960)	Dou-1	
Baker v. Carr (1962)	Blk-Dou-1	
Gray v. Sanders (1963)	Blk-Dou-3	
Wesberry v. Sanders (1964)	Blk-Dou-2	

Legend: **c** = constitutional decision

       s = statutory decision

       = decision neither constitutionally nor statutorily based

Note: All progeny rest on the same decisional basis as the precedent unless otherwise indicated.

tax if that amount was paid into an approved state unemployment compensation fund, as was the case here.

The concluding portion of Jackson's dissent warrants quoting. It provides an infrequently stated rationale for deviating from precedent:

> The Court's opinion . . . goes to some lengths to show that the Court as a whole and without dissent . . . has become committed to the interpretation it adopts, and by unusual deference to the doctrine of stare decisis declares itself bound hand and foot to full federal priority. . . . If I have agreed to any prior decision which forecloses what now seems to be a sensible construction of this Act, I must frankly admit that I was unaware of it. However, no rights have vested and no prejudicial action has been taken in reliance upon such a ruling. It does not appear to have been called to the attention of Congress and in effect approved by failure to act. Under these circumstances, except for any personal humiliation involved in admitting that I do not always understand the opinions of this Court, I see no reason why I should be consciously wrong today because I was unconsciously wrong yesterday. (Id. 639–40)

Jackson, however, did adhere to precedent in *United States v. Gilbert Associates* (1953), joining the majority in a decision giving priority of payment out of an insolvent taxpayer's estate to a federal rather than a town lien. The town failed to perfect its lien and under federal law the mere assessment of a tax did not make the town a judgment creditor.

Finally, Jackson reverted to his original preferences by joining a unanimous Court in *United States v. New Britain* (1954) refusing to give the federal government absolute priority where the debtor is not insolvent. Instead, it applied the rule, First in time, first in right.

The Justices' Behavior

The 85.2 percent proportion of preferential voting shown in Table 5.4 substantially exceeds that of the Hughes Court. An extremely high proportion of the preferential votes cast by the Stone Court justices are moderately expressed, 73.9 percent. The 53 percent of the Waite Court comes closest. This and the overall proportions contrast with those of the Hughes Court: the Stone Court justices expressed their preferences more strongly than did those of the Hughes Court. Precedential voting displayed an opposite pattern.

THE VINSON COURT

Upon Harlan Fiske Stone's death in 1946, Justice Jackson, on leave from the Court in Nuremberg to prosecute Nazi war criminals, accused Justice Black of attempting to block Jackson's promotion to Chief Justice. According to Truman, both threatened to resign if the other were promoted to Chief (Gerhart 1958, p. 260). Truman instead followed the practice he established in his earlier nomination of Harold Burton to the Court: name a close personal friend. Thus, Truman nominated Fred Vinson, a former congressman and appellate court judge, who was Truman's Treasury Secretary.[20]

The Vinson Court's (1946–53) most momentous decision stemmed from Truman's seizure of the nation's steel mills during the Korean War in order to prevent a strike.[21] The Court, with Vinson, Reed, and Minton dissenting, ruled that Truman had exceeded his executive authority.

Many other decisions of the Vinson Court similarly resulted from the Cold (and occasionally hot) War: the Court upheld requirements that union officials[22] and public employees[23] swear to loyalty oaths and upheld the convictions of leading members of the Communist Party for teaching and advocating the overthrow of government.[24]

On civil rights, the Court unanimously struck down judicial enforceability of racially restrictive covenants[25] and started chipping away at the separate-but-equal doctrine.[26] Indeed, the Court originally heard oral arguments in *Brown v. Board of Education* (1954) in December 1952. According to Richard Kluger's (1975) analysis of the conference discussion following oral argument, two to four justices would have dissented had the decision come down in the 1952 term, with the most likely dissenters being Vinson, Clark, and Reed. Frankfurter, realizing the importance of a unanimous decision, strategically called for reargument focusing on the intent of the framers of the Fourteenth Amendment. The Court unanimously agreed. When Vinson died unexpectedly that summer, Frankfurter remarked, "This is the first indication I have ever had that there is a God" (Kluger 1975, p. 656).

The Vinson Court, in existence only two years longer than the Stone Court (seven versus five), saw dissenters from its landmark decisions cast only eleven votes more than its predecessor in their progeny (89 versus 78). But whereas the Stone Court's progeny votes were concentrated

---

[20] Truman followed this appointment with that of two more close friends, Tom Clark and Sherman Minton, both in 1949.

[21] *Youngstown Sheet and Tube Co. v. Sawyer* (1952).

[22] *American Communications Association v. Douds* (1950). Black dissented, with Douglas, Clark, and Minton not participating.

[23] *Garner v. Board of Public Works* (1951). Burton, Frankfurter, Douglas, and Black dissented.

[24] *Dennis v. United States* (1951), Black and Douglas dissenting. Cold War decisions of the Vinson Court weren't limited to First Amendment cases. The Court's final decision upheld the death sentences of Julius and Ethel Rosenberg.

[25] *Shelley v. Kraemer* (1948).

[26] *Sweatt v. Painter* (1950) and *McLaurin v. Oklahoma State Regents* (1950).

Table 5.4.
Voting and opinion behavior: Stone Court ordinary cases

| | | | Level of Expression | | | | | |
| | | | Preferences (%) | | | Precedent (%) | | |
Justice	Prefs/prec	%Prefs	Strong (1)	Moderate (2)	Weak (3)	Strong (1)	Moderate (2)	Weak (3)
Black (Blk)	3　0	100.0	1 (33.3)	2 (66.7)				
Douglas (Dou)	3　0	100.0	1 (33.3)	2 (66.7)				
Roberts (Rob)	2　0	100.0		2 (100)				
Stone (Sto)	2　0	100.0		2 (100)				
Frankfurter (Frk)	5　1	83.3		4 (80.0)	1 (20.0)			1 (100)
Jackson (Jac)	4　1	80.0	1 (25.0)	2 (50.0)	1 (25.0)			1 (100)
Reed (Re)	3　1	75.0		2 (66.7)	1 (33.3)			1 (100)
Murphy (Mur)	1　1	50.0		1 (100)			1 (100)	
Totals	23　4	85.2	3 (13.0)	17 (73.9)	3 (13.0)	0	1 (25.0)	3 (75.0)

Precedent/progeny	Preferences	Precedent
United States v. Bethlehem Steel Corp. (1942)		
Muschany v. United States (1945)	Frk-2	
Priebe & Sons v. United States (1947)	Frk-2	
Penn Dairies v. Milk Control Commission (1943) **s**		
Pacific Coast Dairy v. California Dept. (1943)	Blk-Dou-Jac-1	
Paul v. United States (1963)	Blk-Dou-2	
United States v. Georgia PSC (1963)	Blk-Dou-2	
United States v. Waddill Holland & Flinn (1945) **s**		
Illinois v. Campbell (1946)	Jac-2	
Massachusetts v. United States (1948)	Jac-2	
United States v. Gilbert Assoc. (1953)		Jac-3
United States v. New Britain (1954)	Jac-3	
Colorado Interstate Gas Co. v. FPC (1945) **s**		
Colorado-Wyoming Gas Co. v. FPC (1945)	Frk-Re-Rob-Sto-2	
Panhandle Eastern Pipe Line v. FPC (1945)	Frk-Re-Rob-Sto-2	
FPC v. Panhandle Eastern Pipe Line (1949)	Frk-Re-3	
Phillips Petroleum v. Wisconsin (1954)		Frk-Re-3
Mabee v. White Plains Publishing Co. (1946) **s**		
Oklahoma Press Publishing v. Walling (1946)	Mur-2	
Morris v. McComb (1947)		Mur-2

Legend: **c** = constitutional decision
  s = statutory decision
  = decision neither constitutionally nor statutorily based
Note: All progeny rest on the same decisional basis as the precedent unless otherwise indicated.

among seven precedents, with all but one of these votes in six precedents, the Vinson Court required 12 precedents to account for the progeny votes. Moreover, the progeny votes in these 12 precedents are much more evenly distributed than in the Stone Court, ranging downward from a maximum of fifteen in *Garner v. Board of Public Works* (1951), twelve in *Wolf v. Colorado* (1949) and *United States v. Rabinowitz* (1950), and ten in *Dennis v. United States* (1951).

Landmarks

Among the fifteen votes cast by *Garner*'s dissenters in its progeny are four of the ten precedential votes that the Vinson Court justices produce. Each of the four *Garner* dissenters wrote his own opinion asserting that the municipal loyalty oath at issue was unconstitutional on various grounds. Burton stated that it was a bill of attainder and an ex post facto law; Frankfurter, that the oath's lack of *scienter* violated due process; and Black and Douglas on these bases, plus freedom of speech and assembly and redress of grievances. In the first of *Garner*'s four progeny, *Adler v. Board of Education* (1952), Black and Douglas dissent, while Burton silently agrees with the majority upholding a New York law prohibiting the continued employment of public school teachers who advocate or are members of organizations promoting the forcible overthrow of government.[27]

In *Slochower v. Board of Higher Education* (1956), Black, Douglas, and Frankfurter adhere to their original positions, but Burton again votes precedent, joining Reed and Clark in a dissent upholding the summary dismissal of a city's employees for invoking self-incrimination in response to congressional inquiries into national security. Burton, now joined by Frankfurter, continued to adhere to precedent in the third of *Garner*'s progeny, *Beilan v. Board of Education* (1958). The majority used the precedent to sustain dismissal of a teacher who refused to answer the superintendent's questions concerning Communist affiliations, Black and Douglas dissenting. In the final progeny, *Speiser v. Randall* (1958), all four justices adhere to their original position, voting liberally in a decision distinguishing *Garner* and declaring unconstitutional as a violation of procedural due process and freedom of speech a California provision that denied veterans a tax exemption for failing to file a loyalty oath.

---

[27] Frankfurter dissented on jurisdictional grounds. Hence, his vote counts as neither precedent nor preference.

Along with *Wolf v. Colorado* (1949), the progeny of *United States v. Rabinowitz* (1950) contain more votes by its dissenters – twelve – than any other Vinson Court landmark except *Garner v. Board of Public Works* (1951). But unlike *Wolf*, not all of these votes support the dissenters' preferences. Overruling a two-year-old precedent of its own creation, *Trupiano v. United States* (1948), the *Rabinowitz* majority said that the proper test of a warrantless search "is not whether it is reasonable to procure a search warrant," as *Trupiano* had held, "but whether the search was reasonable" (1950, 66). Black, Frankfurter, and Jackson dissented, Douglas not participating. The dissenters held their ground in *United States v. Jeffers* (1951) and, after Jackson's death, in *Giordenello v. United States* (1958) and *Jones v. United States* (1958).

Frankfurter, however, supported the *Rabinowitz* precedent in *Abel v. United States* (1960). In writing the opinion of the Court, he distinguished the facts in Abel's case from that of Rabinowitz, asserting, "The search here was less intrusive than . . . the deliberately exhaustive quest . . . [in] *Rabinowitz*, and its purpose not less justifiable" (1960, 237). "It would, under these circumstances, be unjustifiable retrospective lawmaking for the Court . . . to reject the authority of [*Rabinowitz*]" (1960, 235–36). A more likely explanation for Frankfurter's switch is the fact that Abel's case involved the deportation of an alien involved in an alleged Cold War conspiracy. He permissively supported both deportation and efforts to strengthen internal security.[28]

In *Chapman v. United States* (1961), however, Frankfurter reverted to his original preferences, asserting, "In joining the Court's judgment, I do so on the basis of the views set forth in my dissents in . . . *United States v. Rabinowitz*" (1961, 619). *Chapman*, noteworthily, concerns neither aliens nor internal security, but rather a moonshiner and his still. The final progeny, *Chimel v. California* (1969), overruled *Rabinowitz*. Black, surprisingly, dissented,[29] in an opinion written by Justice White. Noting that "few areas of the law have been as subject to shifting constitutional

---

[28] Frankfurter upheld the deportation in the other two orally argued Warren Court deportation cases in which he participated, *Niukkanen v. McAlexander* (1960) and *Kimm v. Rosenberg* (1960), both of which concern internal security. He also never voted against a legislative investigation nor objected to the application of federal internal security legislation in any orally argued Warren Court case that was nonunanimously decided; neither, with one exception, *Green v. McElroy* (1959), did he fail to vote to sanction an alleged security risk.

[29] A justice who opposes the establishment of a precedent typically rejoices at its overthrow, especially if he has systematically voted against its progeny. Thus, Black himself consistently objected to the Stone Court's decision in *Betts v. Brady* (1942), as we have seen, until it was eventually repudiated in *Gideon v. Wainwright* (1963), with Black himself writing the Court's opinion.

standards," White said that the Court "should not now abandon the old [*Rabinowitz*] rule" (1969, 770). Seeking to differentiate Chimel's situation from Rabinowitz's, White concluded, "An arrested man, by definition conscious of the police interest in him, . . . is in an excellent position to dispute the reasonableness of his arrest and contemporaneous search in a full adversary proceeding" (1969, 783). The same, of course, was true of Rabinowitz. Both were "provided almost immediately with . . . a judge" (Id.). What apparently made a difference for Black was the intervening *Miranda v. Arizona* (1966) decision requiring the almost immediate provision of a judge. Given the opinion that he joined, if this not be the explanation for Black's belated support for precedent, it must result from his increased conservatism toward the Fourth Amendment.

Two additional Vinson Court precedents garnered seven and eight votes, respectively, in progeny from their dissenters: *Everson v. Board of Education* (1947) and *United States v. California* (1947). The four *Everson* dissenters – Burton, Frankfurter, Jackson, and Rutledge – who objected to public provision of bus transportation to parochial school students, referenced their opinion one year later in *Illinois ex rel. McCollum v. Board of Education* (1948), which voided Illinois's program of released time religious instruction authorizing such for public school students during regular school hours by non–public school teachers. Four years later the Court upheld a slightly altered program in *Zorach v. Clauson* (1952), Burton silently finding a constitutional difference between an off- and an on-campus program, both occurring during regular school hours. The other dissenters, Frankfurter and Jackson, viewed the two programs as no different from Tweedle-dum and Tweedle-dee.[30]

United States v. California (1947), whose progeny occasioned eight votes by its dissenters, concerned the matter of tideland ownership: the adjacent state or the United States. The two dissenters differ on their reasons for disagreement. Reed, effectively voicing the equal footing doctrine, holds California to be equal to the original thirteen states, which claimed ownership of the littoral to a three-mile limit. Frankfurter, the other dissenter, argues that the Court should not resolve the question of title. In *United States v. Louisiana* (1950), the Court, without dissent, states that the precedential case controlled, *a fortiori*, Louisiana's claim to lands 27 miles seaward from its coast. Speaking for himself, Frankfurter states that "the issue there decided [in *United States v. California*] is no longer open for me" (1950, 723). Reed echoes: "Insofar as Louisi-

---

[30] Jackson's exact language was "The distinction attempted between that case [*McCollum*] and this is trivial, almost to the point of cynicism. . . . Today's judgment will be more interesting to students of psychology and of the judicial processes than to students of constitutional law" (1952, 325).

ana is concerned, I see no difference between its situation and that passed upon in the California Case" (1950, 720). But in *United States v. Texas* (1950), decided companionably to *United States v. Louisiana*, Reed readheres to his *California* preference that Texas owns the submerged offshore land in question, while Franfurter's explanation for his preferential vote reads as follows:

I must leave it to those who deem the reasoning of that decision [*California*] right to define its scope and apply it, particularly to the historically very different situation of Texas. As is made clear in the opinion of Mr. Justice Reed, the submerged lands now in controversy were part of the domain of Texas when she was on her own. The Court now decides that when Texas entered the Union she lost what she had and the United States acquired it. How that shift came to pass remains for me a puzzle. (1950, 724)

In the three remaining progeny, *Alabama v. Texas* (1954), *United States v. Louisiana* (1960), and *United States v. Florida* (1960), Frankfurter and Reed vote preferences. In *Alabama*, Reed expressly references the equal footing doctrine to support retention of his original view. Frankfurter also adheres to his original pro-state view, albeit silently. In the 1960 cases construing the Submerged Lands Act, Frankfurter finds support therein for his pro-state views.

The Justices' Behavior

Overall, the Vinson Court's proportion of preferential to precedential voting, 88.8 percent, is virtually identical to that of the Hughes Court, 88.7, and slightly below that of its predecessor Court, 91.0 percent (see Table 5.5). The level of preferential and, to a less extent, precedential voting is also much higher in the Vinson Court than in its two predecessors as Tables 5.1, 5.3, and 5.5 show. A monotonically increasing proportion of the strongest level manifests itself across the three Courts: from 27.2 percent in the Hughes Court, 52.1 percent in Stone, to 60.8 percent in Vinson. Congruently, the Vinson Court also displays a higher proportion of weak preference voting than its predecessors: 32.9 versus 27.2 percent in Hughes and only 11.3 percent in Stone. Precedentially, neither the Hughes nor the Stone Court counts any strong precedent votes among their handful, while two of Vinson's total of ten are such. The Stone Court is weakest among the three overall, with five of seven votes falling in this category. Fourteen of Hughes's 16 are moderate, while the Vinson Court distributes its ten into two highest, six moderate, and two weak. The Vinson Court, however, does produce a marked decline in the number of votes per progeny, 1.82, as compared with 2.56 among the Hughes Court and 2.00 among the Stone Court.

Table 5.5.
Voting and opinion behavior: Vinson Court landmarks

Justice	Prefs/prec		%Prefs	Level of Expression					
				Preferences (%)			Precedent (%)		
				Strong (1)	Moderate (2)	Weak (3)	Strong (1)	Moderate (2)	Weak (3)
Douglas (Dou)	27	0	100.0	20 (74.1)	2 (7.4)	5 (18.5)			
Jackson (Jac)	4	0	100.0	2 (50.0)		2 (50.0)			
Rutledge (Ru)	2	0	100.0	2 (66.7)		0 (33.3)			
Murphy (Mur)	1	0	100.0	1 (100)					
Vinson (Vin)	1	0	100.0			1 (100)			
Black (Blk)	24	1	96.0	17 (70.8)	2 (8.3)	5 (20.8)	1 (100)		
Frankfurter (Frk)	14	3	82.4	5 (35.7)		9 (64.3)	1 (33.3)	2 (66.7)	
Reed (Re)	3	1	75.0		1 (33.3)	2 (66.7)		1 (100)	
Burton (Bur)	3	5	37.5	1 (50.0)		2 (50.0)		3 (60.0)	2 (40.0)
Totals	79	10	88.8	48 (60.8)	5 (6.3)	26 (32.9)	2 (20.0)	6 (60.0)	2 (20.0)

Precedent/progeny	Preferences	Precedent
Everson v. Board of Education (1947) **c**		
McCollum v. Board of Education (1948)	Bur-Frk-Jac-Ru-1	Bur-3
Zorach v. Clauson (1952)	Frk-Jac-1	
United Public Workers v. Mitchell (1947) **c**		
Adler v. Board of Education (1952)	Blk-Dou-1	
CSC v. Letter Carriers (1973)	Dou-1	
Broadrick v. Oklahoma (1973)	Dou-1	

Case		
		Frk-1 Re-2
United States v. California (1947) c	Frk-1 Re-2	
United States v. Louisiana (1950)	Frk-Re-3	
United States v. Texas (1950)	Frk-3	
Alabama v. Texas (1954)	Frk-3	
United States v. Louisiana (1960)		
United States v. Florida (1960)		
Fay v. New York (1947) c	Blk-Dou-Mur-Ru-1	
Moore v. New York (1948)	Dou-1	
Witherspoon v. Illinois (1968)		
McCollum v. Board of Education (1947) c	Re-3	
Zorach v. Clauson (1952)		
Terminiello v. Chicago (1949) c	Bur-Frk-Jack-Vin-3	
Beauharnais v. Illinois (1952)		
Wolf v. Colorado (1949) c	Dou-1	
Stefanelli v. Minard (1951)	Dou-1	
Rochin v. California (1952)	Dou-1	
Schwartz v. Texas (1952)	Dou-1	
Salsburg v. Maryland (1954)	Dou-1	
Irvine v. California (1954)	Dou-3	
Rea v. United States (1956)	Dou-1	
Frank v. Maryland (1959)	Dou-3	
Elkins v. United States (1960)	Dou-3	
Eaton v. Price (1960)	Dou-2	
Wilson v. Schnetler (1961)	Dou-2	
Pugach v. Dollinger (1961)	Dou-1	
Mapp v. Ohio (1961)		
United States v. Rabinowitz (1950) c	Blk-Frk-Jac-3	
United States v. Jeffers (1951)	Blk-Frk-3	
Giordenello v. United States (1958)	Blk-Frk-3	
Jones v. United States (1958)	Blk-2	
Abel v. United States (1960)	Blk-2 Frk-1	
Chapman v. United States (1961)		Frk-2

Table 5.5 (cont.)

Precedent/progeny	Preferences	Precedent
Chimel v. California (1969)		Blk-1
American Communications Assn. v. Douds (1950)　**c**		
Joint Anti-Fascist Committee v. McGrath (1951)		
Peters v. Hobby (1955)	Blk-1	
Yates v. United States (1957)	Blk-1	
Speiser v. Randall (1958)	Blk-1	
First Unitarian Church v. Los Angeles (1958)	Blk-1	
Killian v. United States (1961)	Blk-1	
United States v. Brown (1965)	Blk-1	
Dennis v. United States (1951)　**c**	Blk-1	
Yates v. United States (1957)	Blk-Dou-1	
Communist Party v. SACB (1961)	Blk-Dou-1	
Scales v. United States (1961)	Blk-Dou-1	
Gibson v. Florida Legislative Committee (1963)	Blk-Dou-1	
Brandenburg v. Ohio (1969)	Blk-Dou-1	
Garner v. Board of Public Works (1951)　**c**	Blk-Dou-1	
Adler v. Board of Education (1952)	Blk-Dou-1	Bur-2
Slochower v. Board of Education (1956)	Blk-Dou-Frk-1	Bur-3
Beilan v. Board of Education (1958)	Blk-Dou-1	Bur-Frk-2
Speiser v. Randall (1959)	Blk-Bur-Dou-Frk-3	
Carlson v. Landon (1952)　**c s**		
United States v. Witkovich (1957)	Blk-Dou-Frk-3	Bur-2

Legend: **c** = constitutional decision
　　　　s = statutory decision
　　　　= decision neither constitutionally nor statutorily based

Note: All progeny rest on the same decisional basis as the precedent unless otherwise indicated.

Nine of the 11 Vinson Court justices cast at least one vote in progeny of precedents from which they had dissented. As is true of the Stone Court, the liberals outdo the conservatives in preferential voting. Douglas, Black, Rutledge, and Murphy cast 54 of 55 votes compatibly with their dissents from landmark precedents (98.2 percent). The conservatives (Jackson, Vinson, Frankfurter, Reed, and Burton) vote preferences with 25 of their 34 votes (73.5 percent). Burton contributes five of the nine precedential votes. In casting fewer preferential than precedential votes we may conclude – tentatively, to be sure since we will confront further voting by Burton when we examine the Warren Court – that he, like Taft, appears guided by precedent. He does cast eight votes in toto, as compared with but four for Taft. Moreover, Burton's precedential votes occur in progeny of three separate landmarks: *Everson v. Board of Education* (1947), *Garner v. Board of Public Works* (1951), and *Carlson v. Landon* (1952).

Common Cases

Although dissenters from common Vinson Court precedents cast almost 50 percent more votes in progeny than did those of the Stone Court (40 versus 27), the same number of precedents occasioned these votes (5). The discrepancy in the votes in progeny stems from *Beauharnais v. Illinois* (1952), the progeny of which account for 25 of the Vinson Court's 40 votes.

The only case in the sample that warrants notice is *Darr v. Burford* (1950), the second leg in a four-step sequence of decisions, each of which overruled its predecessor.[31] With Douglas not participating, Black, Frankfurter, and Jackson dissented. The majority required a state convict to exhaust his direct appeals before petitioning a federal district court for collateral relief via a writ of habeas corpus. Including its demise in *Fay v. Noia, Darr* produced three progeny. In the first, *Frisbie v. Collins* (1952), Black, joined by the other dissenters, wrote the Court's opinion asserting the existence of the "special circumstances" that *Darr* exempted from its exhaustion requirement. In *Brown v. Allen* (1953), two dissenters maintained their preferences in a case in which the majority

---

[31]   As far as we know, no other issue in the Court's annals has been subject to an overruling of an overruling of an overruling. *Darr* overruled the original precedent, *Wade v. Mayo* (1948), which the Vinson Court also decided. *Wade*'s short life seems a result of the replacement of the liberal Murphy and Rutledge with Clark and Minton. The Warren Court case, *Fay v. Noia* (1963), voided *Darr. Fay*, in turn, met its fate at the hands of the Rehnquist Court decision, *Coleman v. Thompson* (1991). See Brenner and Spaeth (1995, 123, 125).

Table 5.6.
Voting and opinion behavior: Vinson Court ordinary cases

| | | | Level of Expression | | | | | |
| | | | Preferences (%) | | | Precedent (%) | | |
Justice	Prefs/prec	%Prefs	Strong (1)	Moderate (2)	Weak (3)	Strong (1)	Moderate (2)	Weak (3)
Black (Blk)	17	0	100.0	13 (76.5)	3 (17.6)	1 (5.9)			
Douglas (Dou)	15	0	100.0	14 (93.3)	1 (6.7)				
Frankfurter (Frk)	4	0	100.0	1 (25.0)	2 (50.0)	1 (25.0)			
Jackson (Jac)	2	2	66.7		1 (25.0)	1 (25.0)	2 (100)	–	–
Totals	38	2	95.0	28 (73.7)	7 (18.4)	3 (7.9)	2 (100)	–	–

Precedent/progeny	Preferences	Precedent
Farmers Reservoir & Irrigation v. McComb (1949) **s**	Jac-2	
Powell v. U.S. Cartridge Co. (1950)		Jac-1
Darr v. Buford (1950)		
Frisbie v. Collins (1952)	Blk-Frk-Jac-3	
Brown v. Allen (1953)	Blk-Frk-2	
Fay v. Noia (1963)	Blk-1	

Case		
Stefanelli v. Minard (1951)	Dou-1	
Pugach v. Dollinger (1961)	Dou-1	
Mapp v. Ohio (1961)	Dou-1	
Cleary v. Bolger (1963)		
Beauharnais v. Illinois (1952) **c**		Jac-1
Kedroff v. St. Nicholas Cathedral (1952)	Blk-Dou-2	
Roth v. United States (1957)	Blk-Dou-1	
Uphaus v. Wyman (1959)	Blk-Dou-1	
Kingsley Pictures Corp. v. Regents (1959)	Blk-Dou-1	
Smith v. California (1959)	Blk-Dou-1	
Braden v. United States (1961)	Blk-Dou-1	
Konigsberg v. State Bar (1961)	Blk-Dou-1	
A Quantity of Books v. Kansas (1964)	Blk-Dou-1	
Garrison v. Louisiana (1964)	Blk-Dou-1	
Rosenblatt v. Baer (1966)	Blk-Dou-1	
Ginsberg v. New York (1968)	Blk-Dou-1	
New York Times v. United States (1971)	Blk-Dou-1	
Heikkila v. Barber (1953) **s**		
Shaughnessy v. Pedreiro (1955)	Blk-Frk-1	
Brownell v. Tom We Shung (1956)	Blk-Frk-2	

Legend: **c** = constitutional decision
      s = statutory decision
      = decision neither constitutionally nor statutorily based
Note: All progeny rest on the same decisional basis as the precedent unless otherwise indicated.

ruled (1) that a federal district court will not, after Supreme Court denial of certiorari, reexamine federal questions meritoriously adjudicated by a state court, and (2) that failure to comply with local procedural rules precludes granting habeas even though failure to comply cost petitioners their right to full review of federal questions adversely decided by a state court. Only Black remained on the Court when *Fay* was decided. Needless to say, he joined the Court's opinion.

The Justices' Behavior

If there had been fairly substantial precedential voting prior to the Stone Court, its total absence from the Vinson Court might have signaled a breakdown of cooperative voting. But given the paucity of precedential voting throughout the Court's history, we continue to conclude that none of the legal models is explanatory, notwithstanding that only four of the Vinson Court justices cast any votes. Table 5.6 specifies this distribution.

No other Court or component of a Court's decisions except the Burger Court's landmark First Amendment decisions produces as high a proportion of strongly expressed votes as does the common litigation of the Vinson Court (78.6 percent versus 75.0). The progeny of four of the five precedents occasioned strong expressions, the only exception being the single progeny vote in the *Farmers Reservoir* precedent. We might ascribe this behavior to the four dissenting justices. But, if we do, what explains their failure to vote with similar intensity in the common decisions of the Hughes and Stone Courts? Of their 23 Hughes and Stone Court votes in progeny of precedents from which they dissented, only four were strongly expressed (17.4 percent), ten moderately (43.5 percent), and nine weakly (39.1 percent). These proportions stand in stark contrast to those of the Vinson Court. Theoretically, this suggests that the breakdown of consensual norms on the Court (Walker, Epstein, and Dixon 1988) was not limited to voting behavior.

CONCLUSION

Not much change occurs in the justices' landmark voting on these three Courts, as Table 5.7 and Figure 5.1 show. Indeed, not much difference exists between the landmark voting on these three Courts and that on those that preceded them except for the Taft Court. We do, however, find a continuation of the secular increase in preferential voting in ordinary litigation that has manifested itself throughout the Court's history. Granted, much of the upward tick results from the highly preferential

Table 5.7.
Preferential voting on the Hughes, Stone, and Vinson Courts

	Landmarks		Common cases	
Court	N	%	N	%
Hughes	125–16	88.7	16–7	69.6
Stone	71–7	91.0	23–4	85.2
Vinson	79–10	88.8	38–2	95.0
Totals	275–33	89.3	77–13	85.6

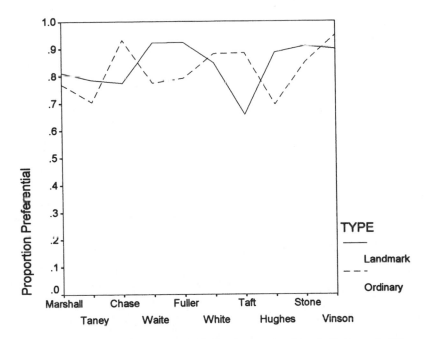

Figure 5.1. Precedential/preferential behavior on the Marshall through Vinson Courts.

voting of the Vinson Court justices. Nonetheless, the trend – though small in their totals – is upward.

At the landmark level on these three Courts, the total number of votes cast by dissenters from these decisions in their progeny exceeds 300.

Although the collective figures fall slightly below 90 percent, they beat those of the other two sets of Courts by approximately three and eleven points. (See Tables 3.7 and 4.9.)

These data clearly reveal that nonadherence to precedent pervades the entire premodern history of the Court, more so in landmark cases than in those of lesser significance. We turn now to the three most recent Courts – Warren, Burger, and Rehnquist – to ascertain the further manifestation of this pattern.

6

Precedential Behavior
in the Warren Court

At the 1952 Republican national convention, Governor Earl Warren of California, himself a contender for his party's nomination, sealed Dwight Eisenhower's victory over his chief rival, Robert Taft, by throwing the support of the California delegation behind Eisenhower in a credentials fight. Though Eisenhower would later label it "the biggest damn-fool mistake I ever made" (Warren 1977, p. 5), he repaid the debt by nominating Warren to the position of Chief Justice of the United States.

The Warren Court (1953–69) revolutionized American jurisprudence. Amazing as it might now seem, Robert Dahl was able to write in 1957, with a fair amount of accuracy, that the Supreme Court had never been a protector of minority rights. By the end of the Warren Court, Dahl's major assertions, that the Court rarely if ever acted in a counter-majoritarian fashion, that it was rarely successful when it did so, and that such actions were never at the behest of powerless minorities, could never again be plausibly claimed (Casper 1976).

Whether by divine intervention or not (see Chapter 5), the replacement of Vinson with Warren was essential to the Supreme Court's reaching a unanimous decision in *Brown v. Board of Education* (1954). With Reed supporting segregation and Jackson likely to write separately (Kluger 1975, pp. 682–83), Warren carefully avoided an explicit tally of votes immediately after the 1953 oral argument, so as not to cement positions. Nevertheless, the eventual conference vote still showed Reed dissenting.[1] Moreover, Jackson showed no signs of agreeing to the *opinion* being written. Fate, however, again intervened: Jackson suffered a heart attack at the end of March, reducing the likelihood that he would or could write separately. And in an institution not known for overt lobbying, twenty lunches between Warren and Reed helped convince the latter to do what was "the best thing for the country" (Kluger 1975, p. 698).

---

[1] Ulmer (1971) lists Frankfurter and Jackson, along with Reed, as voting to uphold segregation in the conference vote.

Beyond attacking state-sponsored segregation, the Warren Court unanimously upheld the authority of Congress to ban private discrimination through the commerce clause[2] and upheld the constitutionality of the Voting Rights Act.[3]

The Warren Court's egalitarianism also led it to overrule *Colegrove v. Green* (1946), which had held malapportionment to be nonjusticiable. The Court first ruled in 1962 that malapportionment challenged under the Fourteenth Amendment was not a "political question."[4] Two years later the Court decided the merits of federal and state reapportionment cases. In *Wesberry v. Sanders* (1964) the Court declared that the Constitution's command that representatives be chosen "by the People of the several States" means that all votes must have equal weight, in other words, one person, one vote. Thus, congressional districts within a given state must contain an equal number of people. Then, in *Reynolds v. Sims* (1964), the Court ruled that state legislative districts must be of approximately equal size. Despite the example of the U.S. Senate, even the upper house of state legislatures had to be apportioned on a one-person, one-vote basis.[5]

The Court expanded First Amendment rights by limiting the rights of states to prosecute sedition,[6] by limiting the reach of the Smith Act (see Chapter 5),[7] and by temporarily halting the inquisitions of the House Un-American Activities Committee.[8] But in the wake of threats to the Court's jurisdiction, Harlan and Frankfurter switched positions two years later, creating a majority upholding congressional authority.[9]

Other First Amendment decisions blocked organized prayer and Bible readings in public schools,[10] created strict standards for libel suits,[11] and reinvigorated the clear-and-present-danger test.[12]

In the realm of criminal justice, the Court in *Mapp v. Ohio* (1961) made the Fourth Amendment's exclusionary rule binding on the states, overruling *Wolf v. Colorado* (1949); in *Katz v. United States* (1967) held wiretaps to be within the scope of the Fourth Amendment, overruling *Olmstead v. United States* (1928); in *Malloy v. Hogan* (1964) made the Fifth Amendment's right against self-incrimination binding on the states,

---

[2]   *Heart of Atlanta Motel v. United States* (1964).
[3]   *South Carolina v. Katzenbach* (1966).
[4]   *Baker v. Carr* (1962).
[5]   *Lucas v. Forty-Fourth General Assembly* (1964).
[6]   *Pennsylvania v. Nelson* (1956).
[7]   *Yates v. United States* (1957).
[8]   *Watkins v. United States* (1957).
[9]   *Barenblatt v. United States* (1959).
[10] *Engel v. Vitale* (1962) and *Abington Township v. Schempp* (1963).
[11] *New York Times Co. v. Sullivan* (1964).   [12] *Brandenburg v. Ohio* (1969).

overruling *Adamson v. California* (1947); in *Benton v. Maryland* (1969) made the Fifth Amendment's right against double jeopardy binding on the states, overruling *Palko v. Connecticut* (1937); in *Gideon v. Wainwright* (1963) guaranteed the Sixth Amendment's right to counsel for all accused felons, overruling *Betts v. Brady* (1942); in *Duncan v. Louisiana* (1968) made the Sixth Amendment's guarantee of a jury trial in serious cases binding on the states, overruling *Maxwell v. Dow* (1900). Additionally, *Escobedo v. Illinois* (1964) and *Miranda v. Arizona* (1966) set specific limits on custodial interrogations by the police. Given these rulings, we expect to find little support for precedent among Warren Court justices.

Dissenters from the landmark decisions of the Warren Court produce approximately a quarter of all votes cast in the progeny of the landmarks that our source – the Congressional Quarterly (CQ) *Guide* (Witt 1990) – identifies.[13] Of a total of several dozen, 49 were decided nonunanimously, far more than in any earlier Court. Further increasing the number of votes is the fact that all but four of the Warren Court's nonunanimous landmarks produce progeny in which the dissenters participated. The first exception is *Elkins v. United States* (1960), which enunciated the silver platter doctrine. Inasmuch as *Elkins* rests on the inapplicability of the Fourth Amendment to the states, the opportunity for federal officials to use the silver platter doctrine became a dead letter one year later when the Court, in *Mapp v. Ohio* (1961), made the exclusionary rule binding on the states. Next, *United States v. Robel* (1967), an internal security case, held that the Subversive Activities Control Act violated freedom of association, effectively signaling the end of Court concern with this issue. In the third case, *Flast v. Cohen* (1968), not only did the sole dissenter, Justice Harlan, leave the Court two years later, but the case also pertained to taxpayers' suits, a matter of rare federal court concern. Finally, *Gaston County v. United States* (1969) also garnered but one dissenter – Justice Black – who left the Court two years later. Moreover, the issue, literacy tests, was not a recurring one.

Given the 424 votes dissenters from the Warren Court's leading decisions cast, we are able to divide these cases into six exhaustive subsets –

---

[13] The results we report for the Warren, Burger, and Rehnquist Courts differ slightly from those in our earlier work (Segal and Spaeth, 1996a) for three reasons: First, we have operationalized progeny in considerably greater detail in this book (see Chapter 2). Second, we completed the earlier identification of progeny three years before we finished that which this book contains. Third, as a result, the ending date of analysis is more current here. Notwithstanding these differences, and the fact that the earlier work only sampled the landmark decisions of the Warren, Burger, and Rehnquist Courts, the overall proportion of preferential/precedential votes differs by only 0.7 percent from those reported earlier.

civil rights, criminal procedure, First Amendment, internal security, re-apportionment, and miscellaneous. We were not able to do this for the decisions of earlier Courts because of the paucity of landmark cases. In our focus on each of these subsets, we will highlight precedential voting, limiting our attention to only the more interesting manifestations of preferential voting. By focusing on subsets we will also be able to zero in more closely on the justices' voting behavior.

THE FIRST AMENDMENT

One would impressionistically think that the Warren Court decided numerous First Amendment landmarks. Not so: There was a grand total of only five, of which one was unanimous, *New York Times v. Sullivan* (1964).[14] Moreover, one of the remaining four – the Warren Court's initial attempt to define obscenity, *Roth v. United States* (1957) – generated 54 of the 61 votes cast in progeny of First Amendment litigation. *Roth* brought dissents from Black, Douglas, and Harlan. In its numerous progeny – far more than those generated by any other Warren Court precedent – they never once failed to vote the preferences expressed in *Roth*. (See Table 6.1.) Indeed, more often than not they did so at the highest level (30 of 54 votes). Evidencing their undeviating adherence to their preferences is the fact that even in nonorally argued per curiam decisions based on *Roth*, all three dissenters persisted in their adherence to preferences.[15]

The second First Amendment landmark precedent is the school prayer case, *Engel v. Vitale* (1962). In the follow-up Bible reading case, *Abington School District v. Schempp* (1963), Stewart again emerged as the Court's sole dissenter. Also generating only a single progeny vote is *Tinker v. Des Moines Independent School District* (1969), the black armband case. With Harlan voting to dismiss in *Jones v. Board of Education* (1970), Black rested his vote on his *Tinker* dissent.

The remaining landmark based directly on the First Amendment is *NAACP v. Button* (1963), which brought dissents from Clark, Harlan, and Stewart, who viewed Virginia's statute related to barratry, mainte-nance, and champerty as a permissible regulation of the legal profession as applied to the solicitation of clients in school desegregation lawsuits financed by the National Association for the Advancement of Colored People (NAACP). With Stewart not participating, Clark and Harlan maintained their position in *Railroad Trainmen v. Virginia* (1964).

---

[14] Surprisingly, Witt does not list *Brandenburg v. Ohio* (1969) as a landmark case.
[15] There are 28 such summary per curiams. These may be found at 338 U.S. 434, 440–44, 446–50, 452, 454; 339 U.S. 47, 48, 50, 89, 573, 578; 390 U.S. 340; 392 U.S. 655; 396 U.S. 119; 397 U.S. 319, 699; 398 U.S. 278, 435; and 399 U.S. 525.

Harlan reaffirmed his *Button* vote in *United Mine Workers v. Illinois Bar* (1967). Stewart concurred in the result based upon the Court's decision in *Railroad Trainmen*, in which he did not participate. Inasmuch as this decision explictly rests on *Button*, in which Stewart did dissent, presumably his *United Mine Workers (UMW)* vote should count as preferential, though one step removed from the landmark progeny. Nonetheless, we exclude it from consideration as our decision rules do not cover this highly unusual situation. Stewart again failed to participate in *United Transportation Union v. Michigan State Bar* (1971). We count Harlan's vote as supporting his preferences even though he concurred in part and wrote – in reference to the two preceding progeny – "I accept their conclusion" (1971, 600). Harlan also labeled his vote as a partial dissent; he affirmed the decision below compatibly with his preferences; and he explictly referenced his opinion dissenting from the precedent; with regard to the progeny whose "conclusion" he accepted, he said, "I would not, however, extend those cases further than is required by their logic" (ibid.). In the remaining progeny, *In re Primus* (1978), Stewart did accede to precedent, voting with a liberal majority that adhered to *Button* and voided the public reprimand of a South Carolina lawyer who, after advising a group of women of their legal rights resulting from their sterilization as a condition of receiving public medical assistance, wrote one of them a letter informing her that the American Civil Liberties Union (ACLU) would provide her with free legal representation.

Table 6.1 presents the votes of the dissenting justices in this small, highly skewed set. The only surprise – if such it may be called – is the fact that Harlan shares the perfectly preferential consistency of Black and Douglas, both of whom are well known champions of the First Amendment. Indeed, Harlan registers one more preferential vote than Black, 19 versus 18.

CIVIL RIGHTS

Dissenters from the five nonunanimous landmark decisions of the Warren Court dealing with civil rights produced relatively few votes in their progeny, a grand total of 22. Clark, the sole dissenter in the first landmark, *Edwards v. South Carolina* (1963), persisted in his view that the sit-in demonstrations at issue did constitute a clear and present danger of breaching the peace in *Cox v. Louisiana* (1965) and *Brown v. Louisiana* (1966).[16] In *Adderley v. Florida* (1966), he silently joined the majority

---

[16] These cases all have a First Amendment component; but for their civil rights focus we would have included them there.

Table 6.1.
Voting and opinion behavior: Warren Court landmark First Amendment cases

| | | | | Level of Expression | | | | | |
| | | | | Preferences (%) | | | Precedent (%) | | |
Justice	Prefs/prec		%Prefs	Strong (1)	Moderate (2)	Weak (3)	Strong (1)	Moderate (2)	Weak (3)
Douglas (Dou)	21	0	100.0	16 (76.2)	3 (14.3)	2 (9.5)			
Harlan (Har)	19	0	100.0	8 (42.1)	4 (21.1)	7 (36.8)			
Black (Blk)	18	0	100.0	9 (50.0)	6 (33.3)	3 (16.7)			
Clark (Clk)	1	0	100.0		1 (100)				
Stewart (Stw)	1	1	50.0		1 (100)			1 (100)	
Totals	60	1	98.4	33 (55.0)	15 (25.0)	12 (20.0)	0	1 (100)	0

Precedent/progeny	Preferences	Precedent
Roth v. United States (1957) c	Blk-Dou-2	
Kingsley Books v. Brown (1957)	Blk-Dou-2 Har-1	
Kingsley Pictures v. Regents (1959)	Blk-3 Dou-Har-1	
Smith v. California (1959)	Blk-Dou-2 Har-1	
Times Film Corp. v. Chicago (1961)	Blk-Dou-2 Har-3	
Manual Enterprises v. Day (1962)	Blk-3 Dou-1 Har-3	
Bantam Books v. Sullivan (1963)	Blk-3 Dou-1 Har-3	
Jacobellis v. Ohio (1964)	Blk-Dou-Har-1	

Case	
A Quantity of Books v. Kansas (1964)	Blk-Dou-1 Har-3
Memoirs v. Massachusetts (1966)	Blk-2 Dou-1 Har-2
Ginzburg v. United States (1966)	Blk-2 Dou-Har-1
Mishkin v. New York (1967)	Blk-2 Dou-1 Har-2
Redrup v. New York (1967)	Blk-Dou-1 Har-2
Ginsberg v. New York (1968)	Blk-Dou-Har-1
Interstate Circuit v. Dallas (1968)	Blk-Dou-Har-1
Stanley v. Georgia (1969)	Blk-1 Dou-Har-3
United States v. Reidel (1971)	Blk-Dou-1 Har-3
United States v. 37 Photographs (1971)	Blk-Dou-1 Har-3
Miller v. California (1973)	Dou-1
Paris Adult Theatre I v. Slaton (1973)	Dou-1
Hamling v. United States (1974)	Dou-3
Jenkins v. Georgia (1974)	Dou-1
Engel v. Vitale (1962) **c**	
Abington School District v. Schempp (1963)	Stw-2
Tinker v. Des Moines School District (1969) **c**	
Jones v. Board of Education (1970)	Blk-1
NAACP v. Button (1963) **c**	
Railroad Trainmen v. Virginia State Bar (1964)	Clk-Har-2
UMW v. Illinois State Bar Assn. (1967)	Har-1
United Transportation Union v. MI State Bar (1971)	Har-1
In re Primus (1978)	Stw-2

Legend: **c** = constitutional decision
      s = statutory decision
      = decision neither constitutionally nor statutorily based

Note: All progeny rest on the same decisional basis as the precedent unless otherwise indicated.

opinion upholding the state's trespass law as applied to the premises of a county jail. But in each of these three progeny, Clark progressively diminished his level of opposition to the precedent from strongest to weakest.

The voting rights case, *Harper v. Virginia Board of Elections* (1966), which ruled that state poll taxes violated the equal protection clause, drew dissents from Black, Harlan, and Stewart. Although both the majority and the dissenters only marginally referenced *Harper* in the progeny, *Kramer v. Union School District* (1969), the position both sides took is on all fours with those in the precedent. The Court voided on equal protection grounds a New York statute that denied otherwise eligible persons the vote in school elections if they neither owned nor leased taxable realty nor were parents or guardians of children in public school.

In *Cipriano v. Houma* (1969), decided the same day as *Kramer*, Justice Harlan wrote that "while adhering to his views expressed in dissent" in *Harper*, he "consider[ed] himself bound by the Court's decision" and so "concurs in the result" (1969, 707). We count this vote as being precedential and as removing from consideration his preferential vote in *Kramer*. Harlan, however, treated his vote in *Williams v. Illinois* (1970), a criminal indigency case, as relevant to *Harper*. This vote comports with his dissent in the precedent and as such counts as preferential.

I attempted to expose the weakness in the precedential and jurisprudential foundation upon which the current doctrine of "equal protection" sits. . . . I need not retrace the views expressed in these cases, except to object once again to this rhetorical preoccupation with "equalizing" rather than analyzing the *rationality* of the legislative distinction in relation to legislative purpose. (1970, 260)

The final progeny in which any of the *Harper* dissenters participated, *Bullock v. Carter* (1972), saw Justice Stewart precedentially join a unanimous Court invalidating Texas's primary election filing-fee system.

Harlan and White dissented from the remaining civil rights precedent, *Jones v. Alfred H. Mayer Co.* (1968), in which the Court applied the Civil Rights Act of 1866 to private housing discrimination. In the first progeny, *Sullivan v. Little Hunting Park* (1969), they chastised the majority as "even more unwise than it was in *Jones*, in precipitately breathing still more life into [the 1866 Act], which is both vague and open-ended" (1969, 241). White followed up this vote with a precedential one in the unanimously decided *Tillman v. Wheaton-Haven Recreation Assn.* (1973), which held the 1866 Act to be violated. Thereafter, however, White reasserted his objections to *Jones* in *Runyon v. McCrary* (1976), *Cannon v. University of Chicago* (1979), and *Memphis v. Greene* (1981), while citing it as support for his conservative preferences in *Chapman v.*

Houston Welfare Rights Organization (1979) and *Jett v. Dallas Indepen-dent School District* (1989).

The only surprise that Table 6.2 presents is Justice White's high level of preferential voting. He was certainly perceived as a moderate during his tenure on the Warren Court (Spaeth 1979, 135–36). As noted, we could discount his precedential vote and rank him as the most preferen-tially voting of the justices in civil rights cases. On the other hand, all seven of his votes were cast in progeny of a single precedent, *Jones v. Alfred H. Mayer Co.* (1968).

REAPPORTIONMENT

Notwithstanding its specific focus, the progeny of each of the Warren Court's five reapportionment decisions produce at least one precedential vote. Because of this narrow focus, progeny of one of these landmarks also tend to be progeny of some of the others, decidedly unlike the other landmarks of this and earlier Courts. We consider them in chronological order.

Only Harlan served long enough to participate in the progeny of *Baker v. Carr* (1962), which overruled *Colegrove v. Green* (1946). Frankfurter, who wrote the plurality opinion in *Colegrove*, wrote the *Baker* dissent, which Harlan joined. Except for *Wesberry v. Sanders* (1964), requiring population equality among a state's congressional districts, and *Fortson v. Toombs* (1965), vacating and remanding to a district court its injunc-tion of an election pending reapportionment of the Georgia legislature, all of Harlan's nine votes attain the highest level of behavioral support. In *Wesberry*, he chose not to cite the *Baker* dissent, while in *Toombs*, he effectively supported the restraintist posture taken by the majority. In *Gray v. Sanders* (1963), voiding the Georgia county-unit system, and in *Reynolds v. Sims* (1964) and *WMCA v. Lomenzo* (1964), requiring equal population in the districts of both houses of state legislatures, Harlan referenced the *Baker* dissent, as well as those he himself wrote in *Gray* and *Wesberry*. But in *Fortson v. Dorsey* (1965), in which the majority said that an equitably apportioned legislature need not contain only single-member districts, Harlan – albeit irrelevantly – explicitly conformed to the one person, one vote doctrine (1965, 439–40). All parties had con-ceded the population equality of Georgia's senatorial districts. The ques-tion, rather, was whether the districts entitled to more than one senator could elect them at large. Evidencing Harlan's tactical, rather than sin-cere, accession to precedent in order to sustain a conservative decision is his behavior in the remaining three progeny in which he participated – *Avery v. Midland County* (1968), *Moore v. Ogilvie* (1969), and *Whitcomb*

Table 6.2.
Voting and opinion behavior: Warren Court landmark civil rights cases

| | | | Level of Expression | | | | | |
| | | | Preferences (%) | | | Precedent (%) | | |
Justice	Prefs/prec	%Prefs	Strong (1)	Moderate (2)	Weak (3)	Strong (1)	Moderate (2)	Weak (3)
Black (Blk)	5	0	100.0	4 (80.0)	1 (20.0)			
Clark (Clk)	3	0	100.0	1 (33.3)	1 (33.3)	1 (33.3)			
White (BW)	6	1	85.7	4 (66.7)	2 (33.3)				1 (100)
Harlan (Har)	4	1	80.0	2 (50.0)	1 (25.0)	1 (25.0)	1 (100)		
Stewart (Stw)	1	1	50.0		1 (100)			1 (100)	
Totals	19	3	86.4	11 (57.9)	6 (31.6)	2 (10.6)	1 (33.3)	1 (33.3)	1 (33.3)

Precedent/progeny	Preferences	Precedent
Edwards v. South Carolina (1963) **c**		
Cox v. Louisiana (1965)	Clk-1	
Brown v. Louisiana (1966)	Clk-2	
Adderley v. Florida (1966)	Clk-3	
Griffin v. Prince Edward County School Board (1964) **c**		
Palmer v. Thompson (1971)	Har-3	
South Carolina v. Katzenbach (1966) **c**		
Allen v. State Board of Elections (1969)	Blk-1	
Gaston County v. United States (1969)	Blk-1	
Oregon v. Mitchell (1970)	Blk-1	
Perkins v. Matthews (1971)	Blk-1	
Harper v. Virginia Board of Elections (1966) **c**		
Kramer v. Union School District (1969)	Blk-Har-Stw-2	Har-1
Cipriano v. Houma (1969)	Har-1	
Williams v. Illinois (1970)		
Bullock v. Carter (1972)		Stw-2
Jones v. Alfred H. Meyer Co. (1968) **s**		
Sullivan v. Little Hunting Park (1969)	Har-BW-1	BW-3
Tilman v. Wheaton-Haven Recreation Assn. (1973)		
Runyon v. McCrary (1976)	BW-1	
Chapman v. Houston WRO (1979)	BW-2	
Cannon v. University of Chicago (1979)	BW-1	
Memphis v. Greene (1981)	BW-1	
Jett v. Dallas Independent School District (1989)	BW-2	

Legend: **c** = constitutional decision
    s = statutory decision
    = decision neither constitutionally nor statutorily based

Note: All progeny rest on the same decisional basis as the precedent unless otherwise indicated.

v. Chavis (1971) – in all of which he expressly evoked opposition to *Baker* and its one person, one vote progeny. These votes counter his *Fortson v. Dorsey* vote.

Wesberry v. Sanders (1964), the congressional reapportionment case, drew dissents from Clark and Stewart, in addition to Harlan. Only Harlan used his *Wesberry* position as authority for his concurrence in *Wright v. Rockefeller* (1964). As we have seen, he protested the extension of the one person, one vote, standard to both houses of state legislatures in *Reynolds v. Sims* (1964). In his opinion (1964, 587–88), Clark denigrates the *Wesberry* holding; Stewart makes no reference to *Wesberry*, citing instead his dissent in another reapportionment case to support his position. After Clark's retirement, Stewart joined Harlan, concurring without opinion in *Sailors v. Board of Education* (1967), a progeny of *Gray*, as well as *Wesberry*. They further referenced their disapproval of *Wesberry* in *Kirkpatrick v. Preisler* (1969) and *Wells v. Rockefeller* (1969). But in *White v. Weiser* (1973), Stewart silently joined the majority in voiding congressional districting more mathematically equal than districts he had voted in dissent to uphold in *Kirkpatrick* and *Wells.*

Several of Harlan's dissents in the progeny of *Reynolds v. Sims* (1964) – *Fortson v. Dorsey, Carrington v. Rash, Avery v. Midland County, Moore v. Ogilvie,* and *Whitcomb v. Chavis* – also governed his dissents from other of the Warren Court's leading reapportionment decisions. He also used his *Reynolds* dissent to support his dissent in the landmark civil rights decision of *Harper v. Virginia Board of Elections* (1966). Although we count his vote in *Burns v. Richardson* (1966) as precedential, Harlan clearly adheres to his preferences as well:

> Because judicial responsibility requires me . . . to bow to the authority of *Reynolds v. Sims* despite my original and continuing belief that the decision was constitutionally wrong, I feel compelled to concur in the Court's disposition of this case. Even under *Reynolds*, however, I cannot agree with the rationale . . . of the Court's opinion [footnotes omitted]. (1964, 98)

Harlan took a similar position in *Hadley v. Junior College District* (1970), where he wrote, "I deem myself bound by *Reynolds* . . . despite my continued disagreement with them as constitutional holdings." But we count him here as voting preferences because "I do not think that [*Reynolds*] . . . or any other in this Court, justifies the present decision. I therefore dissent" (1970, 60).[17]

The remaining reapportionment decision, *Kirkpatrick v. Preisler* (1969), produces as many precedential votes as the other four combined:

---

[17] Harlan also adhered to his preferences in *Swann v. Adams* (1967), *Ely v. Klahr* (1971), and *Abate v. Mundt* (1971).

four. It also produces three preferential votes more than any of the others, 13. Harlan, Stewart, and White dissented from a ruling that a 3.1 percent variation in congressional district populations is unconstitutional. In *Wells v. Rockefeller* (1969) and *Abate v. Mundt* (1971), two decisions we have previously noted, they voted their antireapportionment preferences. After Harlan's retirement, Stewart and White continued to behave consistently in *Mahan v. Howell* (1973), *Gaffney v. Cummings* (1973), and *White v. Regester* (1973). But in *White v. Weiser* (1973) and *Chapman v. Meier* (1975), they adhered to precedent. White wrote the Court's opinion in *Weiser*, which Stewart joined. Three regularly concurring justices not on the Court when the precedent was decided – Burger, Powell, and Rehnquist – stated that "*Kirkpatrick* is virtually indistinguishable from this case" (1971, 798). In *Chapman v. Meier*, Stewart and White silently joined a unanimous Court in voiding a court ordered reapportionment plan with a 20 percent population variance. Although Stewart's votes in these two progeny may suggest a change of heart (he cast no others prior to his retirement), the same cannot be said for White. In *Karcher v. Daggett* (1983), White specifically referenced his *Kirkpatrick* dissent, arguing that if that decision compelled the result the *Karcher* majority reached, it ought to be overruled (1983, 766). On the other hand, White may have been moving in the direction of an accommodation of his views with those of the *Kirkpatrick* precedent. The maximum deviation in that case was 5.97 percent; here it was 0.70 percent, a difference of 3,674 in districts of more than 500,000 people.

Except for Black, the same justices as those dissenting from the civil rights cases are displayed here (see Table 6.3). Justice Harlan dominates their voting behavior, casting 35 of the 55 progeny votes. As noted, his three precedential votes could have been considered preferential. On the other hand, the pattern of Stewart's behavior suggests that at least in the area of reapportionment Stewart may have willingly acceded to the majority rather than maintain stubborn adherence to his own view.

INTERNAL SECURITY

The remaining sets of Warren Court decisions include most of its leading precedents: those dealing with internal security and criminal procedure. We assess internal security first, noting that even more than the civil rights cases do, many of them also pertain to First Amendment freedoms. All of the Warren Court's early landmarks through the *Scales* decision of 1961 concern internal security except the obscenity case, *Roth v. United States* (1957).

Table 6.3.
Voting and opinion behavior: Warren Court reapportionment cases

	Prefs/prec		%Prefs	Preferences (%)			Level of Expression		
							Precedent (%)		
Justice	Prefs	prec		Strong (1)	Moderate (2)	Weak (3)	Strong (1)	Moderate (2)	Weak (3)
Clark (Clk)	1	0	100.0	1 (100)					
Harlan (Ha)	32	3	91.4	22 (68.8)	4 (12.5)	6 (18.8)	3 (100)		
White (BW)	6	2	75.0	2 (33.3)	–	4 (66.7)	–	2 (100)	
Stewart (Stw)	8	3	72.7	3 (37.5)	–	5 (62.5)	–	3 (100)	
Totals	47	8	85.5	28 (59.6)	4 (8.5)	15 (31.9)	3 (37.5)	5 (62.5)	0

Precedent/progeny	Preferences	Precedent
Baker v. Carr (1962) c		
Gray v. Sanders (1963)	Har-1	
Wesberry v. Sanders (1964)	Har-2	
Reynolds v. Sims (1964)	Har-1	
WMCA v. Lomenzo (1964)	Har-1	
Fortson v. Dorsey (1965)	Har-3	
Fortson v. Toombs (1965)		Har-1

Case		
Avery v. Midland County (1968)	Har-1	
Moore v. Ogilvie (1969)	Har-1	
Whitcomb v. Chavis (1971)	Har-1	
***Wesberry v. Sanders* (1964)** c		
Wright v. Rockefeller (1964)	Har-1	
Reynolds v. Sims (1964)	Clk-Har-1	
Sailors v. Board of Education (1967)	Har-Stw-3	
Kirkpatrick v. Preisler (1969)	Har-Stw-1	
Wells v. Rockefeller (1969)	Har-Stw-1	
White v. Weiser (1973)		Stw-2
***Gray v. Sanders* (1963)** c		
Wesberry v. Sanders (1964)	Har-3	
Reynolds v. Sims (1964)	Har-1	Har-1
Fortson v. Dorsey (1965)	Har-1	
Carrington v. Rash (1965)	Har-3	
Fortson v. Morris (1966)	Har-3	
Sailors v. Board of Education (1967)	Har-1	
Moore v. Ogilvie (1969)	Har-1	
***Whitcombe v. Chavis* (1971)** c		
***Reynolds v. Sims* (1964)** c		
Fortson v. Dorey (1965)	Har-2	
Carrington v. Rash (1965)	Har-1	
Harper v. Virginia Board of Elections (1966)	Har-1	Har-1
Burns v. Richardson (1966)		

Table 6.3 (cont.)

Precedent/progeny	Preferences	Precedent
Swann v. Adams (1967)	Har-2	
Avery v. Midland County (1968)	Har-1	
Moore v. Ogilvie (1969)	Har-1	
Hadley v. Junior College District (1970)	Har-2	
Ely v. Klahr (1971)	Har-1	
Whitcomb v. Chavis (1971)	Har-1	
Abate v. Mundt (1971)	Har-1	
Kirkpatrick v. Preisler (1969) **c**		
Wells v. Rockefeller (1969)	Har-Stw-BW-1	
Abate v. Mundt (1971)	Har-Stw-BW-3	
Mahan v. Howell (1973)	Stw-BW-3	
Gaffney v. Cummings (1973)	Stw-BW-3	
White v. Regester (1973)	Stw-BW-3	
White v. Weiser (1973)		Stw-BW-2
Chapman v. Meier (1975)		Stw-BW-2
Karcher v. Daggett (1983)	BW-1	

Legend: **c** = constitutional decision
  s = statutory decision
     = decision neither constitutionally nor statutorily based

Note: All progeny rest on the same decisional basis as the precedent unless otherwise indicated.

We begin with *Watkins v. United States* (1957), which restricted congressional investigations to those serving legitimate legislative purposes. Clark, the solitary dissenter, interspersed his seven preferential votes with two that were precedential. (See Table 6.4.) In *Flaxer v. United States* (1958), he voted with the majority in a unanimous opinion written by Douglas ordering the acquittal of a subpoenaed witness who was not clearly informed of the date on which he was to produce certain membership lists. Clark's other precedential vote occurred when he joined another Douglas opinion in the last of the *Watkins* progeny in which he participated – the 6-to-3 decision in *DeGregory v. New Hampshire Attorney General* (1966). The Court reversed the appellant's contempt conviction for refusing to answer questions without invoking the self-incrimination clause because the state's asserted interest in protecting itself against subversion was too remote to override *DeGregory*'s political and associational privacy.

The liberal and conservative poles of the Court separately dissented in *Yates v. United States* (1957), the second of the major 1957 internal security decisions. Black and Douglas would go further than the majority and reverse the convictions of all the defendants for conspiracy to violate the Smith Act. Justice Clark would affirm the convictions. Black and Douglas did not treat the decisions in *Nowak v. United States* (1958) and *Maisenberg v. United States* (1958) as progeny of *Yates*. Clark, however, did, voting preferences in both. The decisions involved denaturalization decrees under the Nationality Act of 1940 and the Immigration and Naturalization Act of 1952, respectively. All three justices reaffirmed their *Yates* positions in *Speiser v. Randall* (1958), *Scales v. United States* (1961), and *Killian v. United States* (1961). But in *Noto v. United States* (1961), a case companion to *Scales*, Clark silently joined a unanimously liberal decision reversing a conviction under the membership clause of the Smith Act. The Court held the evidence insufficient to prove that the Communist Party advocated governmental overthrow other than as an abstract doctrine. A final progeny, *Law Students Research Council v. Wadmond* (1971), saw Black and Douglas rest their dissent on their opinions in *Yates* and other related internal security cases.

Kent v. Dulles (1958) shifted the internal security focus from domestic behavior to the right to travel abroad. Burton, Clark, Harlan, and Whittaker, eschewing consideration of constitutional questions, deemed the Secretary of State empowered to deny passports to petitioners. They reasserted this view in *Dayton v. Dulles* (1958), *Kent*'s companion case. After Burton's and Whittaker's departure, Clark and Harlan maintained their position in *Aptheker v. Secretary of State* (1964) and *Zemel v. Rusk* (1965). But in their final participation Clark and Harlan voted with their

Table 6.4.
Voting and opinion behavior: Warren Court internal security cases

Justice	Prefs/prec	%Prefs	Preferences (%) Strong (1)	Moderate (2)	Weak (3)	Level of Expression Precedent (%) Strong (1)	Moderate (2)	Weak (3)
Black (Blk)	19	0	100.0	13 (68.4)	3 (15.8)	3 (15.8)		
Douglas (Dou)	19	0	100.0	12 (63.2)	4 (21.1)	3 (15.8)		
Brennan (Brn)	7	0	100.0	2 (28.6)		5 (71.4)		
Warren (War)	7	0	100.0	2 (28.6)		5 (71.4)		
White (BW)	5	0	100.0		4 (80.0)	1 (20.0)		
Burton (Bur)	4	0	100.0	1 (25.0)	1 (25.0)	2 (50.0)		
Minton (Min)	3	0	100.0		1 (33.3)	2 (66.7)		
Stewart (Stw)	3	0	100.0		3 (100)			
Reed (Re)	1	0	100.0		1 (100)			
Whittaker (Wh)	1	0	100.0	1 (100)				
Harlan (Har)	14	1	93.7	2 (14.3)	5 (35.7)	7 (50.0)	–		1 (100)
Clark (Clk)	17	4	81.0	2 (11.8)	8 (47.1)	7 (41.2)		1 (25.0)	3 (75.0)
Totals	100	5	95.2	35 (35.0)	30 (30.0)	35 (35.0)	0	1 (20.0)	4 (80.0)

Precedent/progeny	Preferences	Precedent
Ullmann v. United States (1956) **c**	Blk-Dou-1	
Slochower v. Board of Higher Education (1956)	Dou-1	
Communist Party v. SACB (1961)	Blk-Dou-1	
United States v. Welden (1964)	Dou-1	
Kastigar v. United States (1972)	Dou-2	
Bellis v. United States (1974)		

Case		
Pennsylvania v. Nelson (1956)	Bur-Min-Re-2	
Uphaus v. Wyman (1959)		
Slochower v. Board of Higher Education (1956) **c**	Bur-Har-Min-3	
Beilan v. Board of Education (1958)	Bur-Har-Min-3	
Lerner v. Casey (1958)	Har-3	
Nelson v. Los Angeles County (1960) **c**		
Watkins v. United States (1957) **c**	Clk-1	Clk-3
Sweezy v. New Hampshire (1957)	Clk-3	
Flaxer v. United States (1958)	Clk-3	
Uphaus v. Wyman (1959)	Clk-3	
Barenblatt v. United States (1959)	Clk-2	
Wilkinson v. United States (1961)	Clk-3	
Deutch v. United States (1961)	Clk-2	
Hutcheson V. United States (1962)	Clk-3	
Russell v. United States (1962)	Clk-2	
DeGregory v. New Hampshire Attorney General (1966)		Clk-3
Yates v. United States (1957) **c**	Clk-2	
Nowak v. United States (1958)	Clk-2	
Maisenberg v. United States (1958)		
Speiser v. Randall (1958)	Blk-Dou-1 Clk-2	
Scales v. United States (1961)	Blk-Dou-2 Clk-2	
Noto v. United States (1961)	Blk-Dou-2	
Killian v. United States (1961)	Blk-Dou-2 Clk-3	
Law Students Research Council v. Wadmond (1971)	Blk-Dou-1	Clk-2
Kent v. Dulles (1958) **c**	Bur-Clk-Har-Wh-1	
Dayton v. Dulles (1958)	Clk-Har-2	
Aptheker v. Secretary of State (1964)	Clk-Har-3	
Zemel v. Rusk (1965)		
United States v. Laub (1967)		
Barenblatt v. United States (1959) **c**	Blk-Brn-Dou-War-1	Clk-Har-3
Wilkinson v. United States (1961)	Blk-Brn-Dou-War-1	
Braden v. United States (1961)	Blk-Brn-Dou-War-3	
Deutch v. United States (1961)		

Table 6.4 (*cont.*)

Precedent/progeny	Preferences	Precedent
Cramp v. Board of Public Instruction (1961)	Blk-Dou-1	
Gibson v. Florida Legislative Committee (1963)	Blk-Dou-1 Brn-War-3	
Gojack v. United States (1966)	Blk-1	
Communist Party v. SACB (1961) **c**		
Gibson v. Florida Legislative Committee (1963)	Blk-Dou-1	
Aptheker v. Secretary of State (1964)	Blk-1	
American Committee v. SACB (1964)	Blk-Dou-1 Brn-War-3	
United States v. Brown (1965)	Blk-Brn-Dou-War-3	
Albertson v. SACB (1965)	Blk-1	
Scales v. United States (1961) **c**		
United States v. Robel (1967)	Blk-Brn-Dou-War-3	
Aptheker v. Secretary of State (1964) **c**		
Zemel v. Rusk (1965)	Clk-Har-BW-3	
United States v. Robel (1967)	Har-BW-2	
Dombrowski v. Pfister (1965)		
Zwickler v. Koota (1967)	Har-1	
Cameron v. Johnson (1968)	Har-3	
Younger v. Harris (1971)	Har-3	
Elfbrandt v. Russell (1966) **c**		
Keyishian v. Board of Regents (1967)	Clk-Har-Stw-BW-2	
Whitehill v. Elkins (1967)	Har-Stw-BW-2	
Keyishian v. Board of Regents (1967) **c**		
Whitehill v. Elkins (1967)	Har-Stw-BW-2	

Legend: **c** = constitutional decision
        s = statutory decision
         = decision neither constitutionally nor statutorily based

Note: All progeny rest on the same decisional basis as the precedent unless otherwise indicated.

seven colleagues affirming the dismissal of an indictment alleging a conspiracy to promote and arrange travel to Cuba by citizens with passports not validated for travel there. These are the last of the precedential votes. Dissenters from the precedents set in the remaining landmark internal security cases of the Warren Court unfailingly voted preferentially in their progeny.

Black and Douglas, along with Brennan and Warren, dissented from the ruling in *Barenblatt v. United States* (1959) that Congress could, for reasons of public interest, limit the First Amendment rights of witnesses before it. The 19 votes the dissenters cast in progeny all supported their preferences, with 13 of the 19 votes bolstered at the highest level.

The four liberals also dissented from the decisions in *Communist Party v. Subversive Activities Control Board* (1961) and *Scales v. United States* (1961), decided the same day. The former held that the registration of the Communist Party under the Subversive Activities Control Act did not violate the First Amendment or constitute a bill of attainder. *Scales* said that knowing membership in subversive organizations did not violate the First Amendment. These two decisions marked the high water mark of conservative internal security decision making. One year later, Justice Goldberg would join the Court and provide the liberals with the fifth vote needed to reverse the Court's orientation and uproot the legacy of McCarthyism. Accordingly, all of the progeny of *Communist Party* and *Scales* were liberally decided with the liberals consistently voting their preferences. But even so, in half of these 16 votes Black and Douglas referenced their *Communist Party* dissents: in *Gibson v. Florida Legislative Committee* (1963) and *American Committee v. Subversive Activities Control Board*, and Black alone in *Aptheker v. Secretary of State* (1964) and *Albertson v. Subversive Activities Control Board* (1965). In the single progeny of *Scales*, *United States v. Robel* (1967), the liberal outcome did not occasion reference to any *Scales* dissent.

We may note that *Dombrowski v. Pfister* (1965) arguably should be considered a federalism case, rather than internal security. The Court ruled that federal court abstention is not required when a state statute is attacked as void on its face. We defend our categorization on the grounds (1) that the legislation whose constitutionality was challenged was two Louisiana internal security laws and (2) that the appellee, Pfister, was chair of the state un-American activities committee. If we did not place the case among the internal security decisions, it would have located among the miscellaneous ones.

Twelve of the 16 justices who sat during the time these landmarks were decided dissented from at least one of them and participated in at least one of their progeny. The only exceptions are Jackson, Minton,

Goldberg, and Fortas. Ten of them cast nothing but preferential votes. The preferential proportion reaches that of the mid-1990s. Moreover, although the liberal Black, Douglas, Brennan, and Warren locate in the four top positions on Table 6.4, they cast only three more preference votes than their nonliberal colleagues.

We may also note in passing that Burton's four preferential votes, pertaining to three different landmark precedents, substantially mitigate the perception, based on his Vinson Court behavior, that he might truly be motivated to adhere to precedent. Combining his Vinson and Warren votes does, however, find him casting four preferential votes more than those that were precedential, nine versus five.

CRIMINAL PROCEDURE

The final coherent set of Warren Court landmarks runs the gamut of criminal procedure. Whether because of its breadth or because of the variety of constitutional provisions at issue, these precedents produce 60 percent of the precedential votes cast by dissenters in their progeny (30 of 50). Like the last few of the internal security cases, the vast majority of the criminal procedure landmarks – overwhelmingly liberal in outcome (12 of 15) – see some combination of the justices unaffiliated with this wing of the Court dissent: Clark, Harlan, Stewart, and White.[18] The relatively large number of votes adhering to precedent superficially suggests that conservative justices – at least those on the Warren Court – may be more accepting of precedent than their more liberal colleagues. We will keep this focus in mind as we proceed through this set.

Because the number of votes is sufficiently large, we further subdivide criminal procedure into six exhaustive components. We start with *Miranda v. Arizona.*

Miranda v. Arizona

Not surprisingly, the progeny of *Miranda v. Arizona* (1966) generate a third of the votes cast in the criminal procedure set (56 of 168). An interesting pattern of behavior emerges. The dissenters initially reassert their opposition to *Miranda* at the highest level. But beginning in the middle years of the Burger Court, with a conservative majority securely ensconced on the Court,[19] the two remaining *Miranda* dissenters – Stewart and White – when voting their preferences invariably join con-

---

[18] The three conservative decisions pertain to search and seizure: *Ker v. California* (1963), *Warden v. Hayden* (1967), and *Terry v. Ohio* (1968).
[19] *Beckwith v. United States* (1976) marks the onset of this trend.

servative decisions explaining or distinguishing *Miranda*. The level of preferential support thus becomes muted, falling to the weakest level.

In the immediate aftermath of the *Miranda* decision, all four dissenters adhered to their preferences in *Johnson v. New Jersey* (1966); Clark and Harlan expressly disapproved of *Miranda* in *Davis v. North Carolina* (1966); while Harlan and Stewart cite their *Miranda* dissent as the basis for their regular concurrence in *Schmerber v. California* (1966). In the landmark juvenile case of *In re Gault* (1967), Stewart asserted that "I continue to believe [*Miranda*] was constitutionally erroneous" (1967, 81). In the lineup identification case of *United States v. Wade* (1967), White, speaking for himself, Harlan, and Stewart, wrote with reference to *Miranda*: "I objected then to what I thought was an uncritical and doctrinaire approach without satisfactory factual foundation. I have much the same view of the present ruling and therefore dissent" (1967, 250). Clark, however, in what would prove to be his final participation in a progeny of *Miranda*, stated, "I dissented in *Miranda* but I am bound by it now, as we all are" (1967, 243). Stewart clearly disagreed with Clark's statement that we are all bound by *Miranda* in his 57-word opinion in *Orozco v. Texas* (1969), which states in part, "It seems to me that those of us who dissented in *Miranda* . . . remain free not only to express our continuing disagreement with that decision, but also to oppose any broadening of its impact" (1069, 331). White had said the same a year earlier in an opinion that his two remaining dissenters also signed: "I continue to believe that the decision in *Miranda* was an extravagant and unwise interpretation of the Fifth Amendment, and I would prefer that *Miranda* be abandoned" (*Mathis v. United States* 1968, 5–6).

But in the same case where Stewart asserted his freedom to persist in his opposition to *Miranda*, Harlan came to the opposite conclusion:

> The passage of time has not made the *Miranda* case any more palatable to me than it was when the case was decided. . . .
> Yet, despite my strong inclination to join in the dissent of my Brother WHITE, I can find no acceptable avenue of escape from *Miranda* in judging this case. . . . Therefore, and purely out of respect for *stare decisis*, I reluctantly feel compelled to acquiesce in today's decision of the Court, at the same time observing that the constitutional condemnation of this perfectly understandable, sensible, proper, and indeed commendable piece of police work highlights the unsoundness of *Miranda*. (*Orozco v. Texas* 1969, 327–28)

According to our decision rules, this language supports precedent although Harlan could hardly have damned *Miranda* more vigorously. In *Jenkins v. Delaware* (1969), he echoed his *Orozco* position, "As one who has never agreed with the *Miranda* case but nonetheless felt bound by it" (1969, 222). Harlan, however, seems not to have been bound by the liberal *Miranda* precedent except for these two cases. In his remaining vote in *Miranda* progeny, *Harris v. New York* (1971), he joined Burger's conservative opinion of the Court conversely citing *Miranda* as authority that the admission of unwarned statements impeaches the credibility of the defendant's trial testimony.

Stewart and White account for the other five votes supporting the *Miranda* precedent. In *Brown v. Illinois* (1975), the Court unanimously reversed the conviction of a defendant arrested without either a warrant or probable cause. After being read the *Miranda* warnings, he made inculpatory statements. The Court held that the warnings did not break the causal chain of unconstitutional custody. In *Edwards v. Arizona* (1981), White, joined by Stewart, wrote the Court's opinion to the effect that notwithstanding the provision of *Miranda* warnings, once an accused requests an attorney, interrogation may not begin again without the attorney present. After Stewart's retirement, White joined the Court's opinion in another liberal decision unanimously affirming the reversal of an individual's conviction because of the prosecutor's use of his postarrest, post-*Miranda* silence as evidence of sanity (*Wainwright v. Greenfield* 1986).[20]

Search and Seizure

Of the four *Mapp v. Ohio* dissenters, only Harlan voted in its progeny. Of his seven votes, one supported the precedent: his opinion of the Court in *Mancusi v. DeForte* (1968). This case turned on questions antecedent to admissibility: an individual's standing to object to the search of his office and the reasonableness of the search itself. Harlan countered this vote by his opinion in *Coolidge v. New Hampshire* (1971), the last of *Mapp*'s progeny in which he participated, where he called for the "overruling" of *Mapp* (1971, 490).

The search and seizure decision that generated the most votes in its progeny, ten, is *Chimel v. California* (1969). In the process of narrowing the scope of a warrantless search incident to a lawful arrest,[21] the Court overruled the landmark Vinson Court decision, *United States v. Rabinowitz* (1950). Black and White dissented, objecting to the overruling of *Rabinowitz* and asserting that in their view "exigent circumstances" established the needed probable cause (1969, 783). In the first of *Chimel*'s progeny, *Vale v. Louisiana* (1970), White joined a liberal major-

---

[20]   The votes of the *Miranda* dissenters in progeny are as follows: White 25–3, Stewart 15–2, Harlan 6–2, and Clark 2–1; total: 48-8, 85.7 percent. Note that both of Harlan's votes precedentially supporting *Miranda* are open to question. If these be counted as preferences the proportion increases to 89.3 percent.

[21]   Here that it could not extend to the whole of the defendant's house.

ity voiding another warrantless search of a defendant's house. Eleven years later, in *New York v. Belton* (1981), he stated that this case comprises "an extreme extension of *Chimel* and one to which I cannot subscribe" (1981, 472) in a liberal dissent, which Justice Marshall joined, to a majority's decision that *Chimel* authorized the search of the defendant's jacket incident to his lawful warrantless arrest because the jacket was in the passenger compartment of the car that the defendant occupied. Thus, it was within the arrestee's "immediate control" as *Chimel* construed this phrase. However, nine years later, in *Maryland v. Buie* (1990), the only remaining progeny in this line of cases, White wrote the conservative opinion of the Court limiting the applicability of *Chimel*. Like *Chimel* and *Vale*, *Buie* involved the in-home search of the suspect incident to his warrantless arrest.

Totaling the votes of the justices in the search and seizure cases shows the following: Black and Douglas 8–0, Brennan 2–0, Warren and Goldberg 1–0, Harlan 6–1, and White 5–2: total 31–3, 91.2 percent.

Self-Incrimination

The progeny of the two self-incrimination landmarks – *Malloy v. Hogan* (1964) and *Griffin v. California* (1965) – produce almost a quarter of the precedential votes resulting from repudiated Warren Court dissents (12 of 50). Moreover, the precedential votes cast by the dissenters perfectly match those that are preferential (12). Over the dissents of Clark, Harlan, Stewart, and White, the Court in *Malloy* overruled the precedents of *Twining v. New Jersey* (1908) and *Adamson v. California* (1947) and held that the Fourteenth Amendment requires the states to adhere to the self-incrimination clause. In the first progeny, *Griffin v. California* (1965), which is also the other leading Warren Court self-incrimination decision, Stewart and White voted preferences. Clark silently joined the liberal majority that held that the clause does not permit prosecutorial comment on a defendant's silence. Harlan, concurring, reworded the reluctance with which he acceded to other precedents:

Given last term's decision in *Malloy* . . . I see no legitimate escape from today's decision and therefore concur in it. I do so, however, with great reluctance, since for me the decision exemplifies the creeping paralysis with which the Court's recent adoption of the "incorporation" doctrine is infecting the operation of the federal system. . . .
Although compelled [*sic!*] to concur in this decision . . . (1965, 615–16, 617)

The compulsion Harlan felt apparently dissipated within a year. In *Stevens v. Marks* (1966), he and Stewart exchanged positions with Clark and White, who adhered to precedent by silently joining a liberal majority. As noted, Stewart and White had voted their preferences in *Griffin*. Harlan, joined by Stewart, objected to the reversal of a police officer's citation and conviction for contempt after withdrawal of a waiver of immunity. In referring to *Malloy*, Harlan carpingly observed that it "could have a far more serious impact" than at an earlier time (1966, 250). In *Spevack v. Klein* (1967), Harlan, along with the other three, refused to extend *Malloy*'s protection to lawyers who were disbarred for refusing to turn over records they were required as attorneys to keep. But in the last of *Malloy*'s progeny, *Williams v. Florida* (1970), Harlan did expressly accept its applicability, Stewart grudgingly.[22]

In addition to being a progeny of *Malloy*, *Griffin v. California* (1965) is a leading decision in its own right, as we have pointed out. As in *Malloy*, its dissenters – Stewart and White – cast more precedential votes in its progeny than preferential ones, six out of ten. (See Table 6.5.) Disagreeing with the majority, who ruled that adverse prosecutorial comments about an accused's refusal to testify violate the self-incrimination clause, Stewart and White said, "The California comment rule is not a coercive device which impairs the right against self-incrimination, but rather a means of articulating and bringing into the light of rational discussion a fact inescapably impressed on the jury's consciousness" (1965, 622).

In *Chapman v. California* (1967), they agreed with the decision that adverse commentary on a defendant's failure to testify amounted to a harmless error. Although a subsequent progeny of *Griffin*, *United States v. Hasting* (1983), suggests that *Chapman* decided a question independent of *Griffin*, we nonetheless consider Stewart's and White's *Chapman* votes precedential. White silently joined the majority opinion, while Stewart's special concurrence does appear to accept the authority of *Griffin*: "Prosecutors are unlikely to indulge in clear violations . . . and if they do I see no reasons why the sanction of reversal should not be the result" (1967, 45). In *Brooks v. Tennessee* (1972), they voted with a liberal majority voiding a rule penalizing a silent defendant. In *Lakeside v. Oregon* (1978), they reaffirmed their preferences in an opinion by Stewart that read *Griffin* narrowly. But in *Carter v. Kentucky* (1981), in another opinion by Stewart, they supported the defendant in a case that answered a question "specifically anticipated and reserved" in *Griffin* as well as *Lakeside* (1981, 295). Arguably, this takes the case beyond

---

[22] At 119. White wrote the Court's opinion making no reference to *Malloy*. Stewart, while "substantially agree[ing] with the separate opinion" of Harlan, also observed that it "fully demonstrates some of the basic errors in a mechanistic 'incorporation' approach to the Fourteenth Amendment" (1971, 143).

Griffin's pale, but it does seem to us that the opinion does depend on *Griffin* – at least, *Shepard's Citations* thinks so, as their analysis column indicates that *Griffin* was followed. After Stewart's retirement, White twice voted preferentially with conservative majorities, in *United States v. Hasting* (1983) and *United States v. Robinson* (1988).

Although the votes in *Griffin's* progeny do not support precedent to the unequivocal extent that those of *Malloy* – the other self-incrimination case – do, they are sufficiently numerous to suggest that the legal model may have operated in Warren Court Fifth Amendment litigation.[23] We will further consider this possibility when we analyze the Burger Court's progeny. On the other hand, it may be less the Fifth Amendment that accounts for this behavior than the effort to incorporate various provisions of the Bill of Rights into the due process clause of the Fourteenth Amendment. In this connection, recall that only one of *Mapp's* seven votes supported precedent, a markedly smaller proportion than those in either *Malloy* or the case we next consider: *Benton v. Maryland* (1969).[24]

Double Jeopardy

No case produced a greater proportion of precedential votes than *Benton v. Maryland* (1969), 71.4 percent (five of seven). Although falsely asserting that "my usual practice is to adhere until the end of the Term to views I have expressed in dissent during the Term," Harlan did specifically adhere to *Benton* in a progeny decided the same day, *North Carolina v. Pearce* (1969): "I believe I should not proceed in these important cases as if *Benton* had turned out otherwise" (1969, 744). He repeated his acceptance of the precedent in his other participation, "having acceded in *North Carolina v. Pearce* . . . to the decision in *Benton v. Maryland* . . . which, over my dissent" (*Ashe v. Swenson* 1970, 448). Stewart, the other *Benton* dissenter, slightly less strongly repudiated his preferences by writing the Court's opinion in both *Pearce* and *Ashe v. Swenson*. In his three other pariticipations in progeny of *Benton*, Stewart sandwiched silent preferentially conservative votes in *Illinois v. Somerville* (1973) and *Swisher v. Brady* (1978) around another liberal opinion of the Court in *Crist v. Bretz* (1978).

---

[23] The dissenters' votes are White 5–4, Stewart 4–4, Harlan 2–2, and Clark 1–2.

[24] Dissenters in earlier cases concerning incorporation of the procedural guarantees of the Bill of Rights that produced progeny did not vote precedentially. The 21 such votes in *Betts v. Brady* (1942) and the twelve in *Wolf v. Colorado* (1949) were all preferential. The dissenters in *Palko v. Connecticut* (1937) and *Louisiana ex rel. Francis v. Resweber* (1947) had no opportunity to vote in progeny.

Jury Trial

Harlan's and Stewart's behavior in the progeny of *Duncan v. Louisiana* (1968) shatters any perception that they systematically adhered to precedent in cases incorporating procedural guarantees of the Bill of Rights into the due process clause of the Fourteenth Amendment. *Duncan* requires the states to provide a jury trial in all criminal cases that, if tried in a federal court, would require adherence to the Sixth Amendment's guarantee of trial by jury. Although Harlan acceded to precedent in the first of *Benton*'s progeny, he did not see fit to do so in the first of *Duncan*'s, *Bloom v. Illinois* (1968). Joined by Stewart, Harlan adhered to his preferential practice of reiterating his dissent: "I dissent for the reasons expressed in my dissenting opinion in *Duncan*" (1968, 215).

After concurring in the conservative decision in *Dyke v. Taylor Implement Co.* (1968), they specifically reiterated their adherence, in *Frank v. United States* (1969), to the two paragraph dissent in *Bloom*, which specifically rested on *Duncan*, quoted earlier. Admittedly, they did gratuitously assert that they were "bound by the decisions of the Court" (1969, 152), but this assertion does not lessen their fidelity to their preferences: *Frank* was a clearly conservative decision, one which the dissenters – Warren and Douglas – characterized as "an unfortunate retreat from our recent decisions enforcing the Constitution's command that those accused of criminal offenses be afforded their fundamental right to a jury trial" (1969, 152).

Indeed, Harlan uses his dissent in *Benton v. Maryland* to emphasize further the strength of his preferences. In a sentence detailing his antiincorporation position that began with *Mapp v. Ohio* in 1961, he concludes: "more particularly in the *Duncan* case I undertook to show that the 'selective incorporation' doctrine finds no support either in history or in reason" (1969, 808).[25] In *Dickey v. Florida* (1970), with the other seven justices agreeing with the language in Chief Justice Burger's opinion, Harlan felt the need to couple his join with the "following reservation" referencing his *Duncan* dissent – "This reservation reflects the hope that some day the Court will return to adjudicating state criminal cases in accordance with the historic meaning of the Due Process Clause" (1970, 39).

Not to be uncharitable or caustic, Harlan patently displays a schizophrenic approach to constitutional interpretation in *Baldwin v. New York* (1970) and *Williams v. Florida* (1970):

[25] In a footnote, Harlan does state, "In the interest of strict accuracy, it should be pointed out that MR. JUSTICE STEWART cannot and does not fully join in . . . [this] sentence of this opinion" (Id.).

I would sustain both the Florida and New York statutes on the constitutional premises discussed in my dissenting opinion in *Duncan*. . . . In taking that course in *Baldwin*, I cannot, in a matter that goes to the very pulse of sound constitutional adjudication, consider myself constricted by *stare decisis.*

Accordingly, I dissent in [*Baldwin*] and, as to the jury issue, concur in the result in [*Williams*]. Given *Malloy v. Hogan* . . . I join that part of the Court's opinion in [*Williams*] relating to the Florida "alibi" procedure. (1970, 118–19)

Harlan's only bow toward the *Duncan* precedent comes in a footnote at the end of the first paragraph quoted. There he references a Frankfurter opinion that precedent "embodies an important social policy." But as such, it is "not a mechanical formula of adherence" when it collides with a prior doctrine broader in scope, "intrinsically sounder, and verified by experience" (Id.). Given that the existence of such characteristics is inherently subjective, Harlan's supportive statement elevates minority will above the judicial majority.[26] In his two remaining participations, Harlan again reiterates attachment to preferences, and again at the strongest level by resting his votes on his *Duncan* dissent.[27] Indeed, all but three of the 16 votes cast by Harlan (9) and Stewart (7) in *Duncan*'s progeny manifest strong attachment to preferences. See Table 6.5.

Miscellaneous Criminal Procedure

The four remaining landmark criminal procedure decisions of the Warren Court address discrete issues.

1. In *Robinson v. California* (1962), involving cruel and unusual punishment in a non–death penalty case, White reasserted his preferences in its progeny, *Powell v. Texas* (1968).
2. The three dissenters from *Fay v. Noia* (1963) – Clark, Harlan, and Stewart – voted preferences at ten of eleven opportunities. The consistency of these justices occasions no surprise given the history of *Fay*. The Court ruled that habeas corpus was available to Noia, who was imprisoned as a result of an involuntary confession. New York admitted that his confession had been coerced. Although he had failed to exhaust his remedies under state law, thereby creating an adequate and independent ground for upholding the action of the

---

[26] Lest we implicitly mischaracterize him, Stewart, though he says, "I substantially agree," with Harlan's opinion in *Baldwin* and *Williams*, does add that "I cannot subscribe to his opinion in its entirety" because it relies on opinions "which I did not join" (1970, 143).

[27] *California v. Green* (1970) and *McKeiver v. Pennsylvania* (1971). In the latter case, he begins his concurrence as follows: "If I felt myself constrained to follow *Duncan v. Louisiana.*" (1971, 55). Stewart's votes in these cases, however, bear no relevance to *Duncan*. In his final participation, *Codispoti v. Pennsylvania* (1974), Stewart voted his preferences by joining Rehnquist's dissent.

state courts, the Supreme Court ruled that he could bypass them because forfeiture of remedies does not legitimize unconstitutional state conduct. In the process, the Court overruled the Vinson Court decision, *Darr v. Buford* (1950), which had overruled *Wade v. Mayo* (1948). The dissenters viewed *Fay* as "one of the most disquieting that the Court has rendered in a long time" (1963, 448). They asserted that the federal courts had no power to release Noia from custody because his confinement rested on a state ground that the federal courts are bound to respect. The dissenters' position ultimately prevailed – if "ultimately" is the correct word – 28 years later, when the Rehnquist Court overruled *Fay* in *Coleman v. Thompson* (1991). *Coleman* effectively forbids state prisoners collateral access to the federal courts – that is, via a writ of habeas corpus – if they failed to adhere to state procedural rules (Brenner and Spaeth 1995, 105). We know of no other issue that has culminated (thus far) in the overruling of an overruling of an overruling.[28]

3. *Escobedo v. Illinois* (1964) foreshadowed *Miranda*, holding that uncounseled incriminating statements are inadmissible because they violate the Sixth Amendment. The same four justices who dissented two years later in *Miranda* did so here: Clark, Harlan, Stewart, and White. Indeed, *Miranda* is the first of *Escobedo*'s progeny. The dissenters further asserted their preferences in *Johnson v. New Jersey* (1966), *Frazier v. Cupp* (1969), and *United States v. Gouveia* (1984).

4. Although it is technically not a criminal case per se, we include *In re Gault* (1967) in this set of miscellaneous Warren Court criminal landmarks. Due process, said the majority, requires that the right to counsel and protection against self-incrimination apply to juvenile proceedings. Stewart dissented, "believ[ing] the Court's decision is wholly unsound as a matter of constitutional law, and sadly unwise as a matter of judicial policy" (1967, 78). Harlan, dissenting in part, disapproved of the classification of juvenile proceedings as either criminal or civil. "Both formulae are simply too imprecise to permit reasoned analysis" (1967, 68). Stewart cited his opinion as authority for his dissent in the self-incrimination case, *Leary v. United States* (1969). Both voted their preferences in *In re Winship* (1969) and

---

[28] In *Fay*'s progeny, Harlan and Clark voted preferentially, with Stewart joining the liberal majority in *Sanders v. United States* (1963); they all voted preferences in *Henry v. Mississippi* (1965). After Clark's retirement, Harlan and Stewart reiterated their original objections in *Kaufman v. United States* (1969); Harlan did so in *Desist v. United States* (1969) and *Mackey v. United States* (1971), and Stewart joined the majority opinion in *Wainwright v. Sykes* (1977) rejecting *Fay*'s "sweeping language" (1977, 87).

McKeiver v. Pennsylvania (1970). Stewart adhered to precedant in the unanimously decided case of *Breed v. Jones* (1975), which precluded prosecution of a defendant as an adult after juvenile proceedings found him in violation of a criminal statute, but unfit for treatment as a juvenile. In his final vote, Stewart reverted to his preferences in *Swisher v. Brady* (1978), joining a conservative majority that the dissent says undercuts *Gault*.[29]

The Justices' Votes

Table 6.5 displays the votes of the justices who participated in progeny of the Warren Court's criminal procedure landmarks from which they had dissented. As is true of the other sets into which we have divided the Warren Court's landmarks, precedential voting is limited to the nonliberal members of the Court – some combination of Clark, Harlan, Stewart, and White. Although we found some evidence of adherence to precedent in the progeny of the pair of self-incrimination landmarks and those of the double jeopardy case of *Benton v. Maryland*, this evidence does not offset the overwhelming evidence of preferential voting. Over 82 percent of the total number of votes by dissenters in progeny adhere to preferences.

MISCELLANEOUS WARREN COURT PRECEDENTS

The three miscellaneous Warren Court landmark precedents need not detain us.

1. The first is the noncriminal non–death penalty cruel and unusual punishment case: *Trop v. Dulles* (1958). Burton, Clark, Frankfurter, and Harlan dissented from the ruling that expatriation for wartime desertion violated the Eighth Amendment. Clark and Harlan adhered to their preferences in the three progeny in which they participated: *Kennedy v. Mendoza-Martinez* (1963), *Schneider v. Rusk* (1964), and *Afroyim v. Rusk* (1967).
2. Although Justice Black had no occasion to participate in any of the progeny of *Griswold v. Connecticut* (1965), the famous right to privacy case, the other dissenter, Stewart, did. He initially adhered to precedent in *Eisenstadt v. Baird* (1972), but thereafter he voted his *Griswold* preferences in his opinions in *Whalen v. Roe* (1977) and *Moore v. East Cleveland* (1977).

---

[29] As Table 6.5 shows, the votes in this set are Harlan 10-0, White 5-0, Clark 4-0, and Stewart 10-2.

Table 6.5.
Voting and opinion behavior: Warren Court criminal procedure cases

Justice	Prefs/prec		%Prefs	Level of Expression					
				Preferences (%)			Precedent (%)		
				Strong (1)	Moderate (2)	Weak (3)	Strong (1)	Moderate (2)	Weak (3)
Black (Blk)	8	0	100.0	8 (80.0)					
Douglas (Dou)	8	0	100.0	5 (62.5)	1 (12.5)	2 (25.0)			
Brennan (Brn)	2	0	100.0			2 (100)			
Warren (War)	1	0	100.0			1 (100)			
Goldberg (Go)	1	0	100.0			1 (100)			
Harlan (Har)	33	7	84.1	23 (69.7)	7 (21.2)	3 (9.1)	6 (85.7)	1 (14.3)	
White (BW)	40	9	82.5	10 (25.0)	3 (7.5)	27 (67.5)		8 (88.9)	1 (11.1)
Stewart (Stw)	38	11	77.6	18 (47.4)	4 (10.5)	16 (42.1)		10 (90.9)	1 (9.1)
Clark (Clk)	7	3	70.0	5 (71.4)	2 (28.6)		1 (33.3)	2 (66.7)	–
Totals	138	30	82.1	69 (50.0)	17 (12.3)	52 (37.7)	7 (23.3)	21 (70.0)	2 (6.7)

Precedent/progeny	Preferences	Precedent
MIRANDA WARNINGS		
Miranda v. Arizona (1966) c		
Johnson v. New Jersey (1966)	Clk-Har-Stw-BW-1	
Davis v. North Carolina (1966)	Clk-Har-1	
Schmerber v. California (1966)	Har-Stw-1	
In re Gault (1967)	Stw-1	
United States v. Wade (1967)	Har-Stw-BW-1	Clk-1
Mathis v. United States (1968)	Har-Stw-BW-1	
Orozco v. Texas (1969)	Stw-BW-1	Har-1

Case		
Jenkins v. Delaware (1969)	Har-Stw-BW-3	
Harris v. New York (1971)	Stw-3 BW-1	Har-1
Michigan v. Tucker (1974)	Stw-BW-3	
Oregon v. Hass (1975)		Stw-BW-2
Brown v. Illinois (1975)	Stw-3 BW-2	
Michigan v. Mosley (1975)	Stw-BW-3	
Beckwith v. United States (1976)	BW-3	
United States v. Mandujano (1976)	Stw-BW-3	
North Carolina v. Butler (1979)	Stw-BW-3	
Fare v. Michael C. (1979)	Stw-BW-3	Stw-BW-2
Roberts v. United States (1980)	Stw-BW-3	
Rhode Island v. Innis (1980)	Stw-BW-3	
Edwards v. Arizona (1981)		
Minnesota v. Murphy (1984)	BW-3	BW-2
New York v. Quarles (1984)	BW-3	
Berkemer v. McCarty (1984)	BW-3	
Oregon v. Elstad (1985)	BW-3	
Wainwright v. Greenfield (1985)		
Moran v. Burbine (1986)	BW-3	
Colorado v. Connelly (1986)	BW-3	
Connecticut v. Barrett (1987)	BW-3	
Colorado v. Spring (1987)	BW-3	
Patterson v. Illinois (1988)	BW-3	
Duckworth v. Eagan (1989)	BW-3	
Illinois v. Perkins (1990)	BW-3	

SEARCH AND SEIZURE

Case		
Mapp v. Ohio (1961)	Har-2	
Ker v. California (1963)	Har-2	
Linkletter v. Walker (1965)	Har-2	
Berger v. New York (1967)	Har-2	
Massachusetts v. Painten (1968)	Har-2	
Mancusi v. DeForte (1968)		
Coolidge v. New Hampshire (1971)	Har-1	Har-2

Table 6.5 (cont.)

Precedent/progeny	Preferences	Precedent
Chimel v. California (1969) **c**		
Vale v. Louisiana (1970)	Blk-1	BW-2
Williams v. United States (1971)	Blk-1	
Coolidge v. New Hampshire (1971)	Blk-BW-1	
Cupp v. Murphy (1973)	BW-3	
United States v. Robinson (1973)	BW-3	
United States v. Edwards (1974)	BW-3	
New York v. Belton (1981)		BW-2
Maryland v. Buie (1990)	BW-3	
Ker v. California (1963) **c**		
Aguilar v. Texas (1964)	Brn-Dou-Go-War-3	
Coolidge v. New Hampshire (1971)	Brn-Dou-3	
Warden v. Hayden (1967) **c**		
Berger v. New York (1967)	Dou-1	
Couch v. United States (1973)	Dou-1	
Katz v. United States (1967) **c**		
Terry v. Ohio (1968)	Blk-1	
Alderman v. United States (1969)	Blk-1	
Desist v. United States (1969)	Blk-1	
Kaiser v. New York (1969)	Blk-1	
United States v. White (1971)	Blk-1	
Terry v. Ohio (1968) **c**		
Sibron v. New York (1968)	Dou-2	
Adams v. Williams (1972)	Dou-1	
United States v. Robinson (1973)	Dou-1	
United States v. Brignoni-Ponce (1975)	Dou-1	
SELF-INCRIMINATION		
Malloy v. Hogan (1964) **c**		

Case		
Griffin v. California (1965)	Stw-BW-2	Clk-2Har-1
Stevens v. Marks (1966)	Har-Stw-2	Clk-BW-2
Spevack v. Klein (1967)	Clk-Har-Stw-BW-2	
Williams v. Florida (1970)		Har-1 Stw-2
Griffin v. California (1965) **c**		
Chapman v. California (1967)		Stw-BW-2
Brooks v. Tennessee (1972)		Stw-BW-2
Lakeside v. Oregon (1978)	Stw-BW-3	
Kentucky v. Carter (1981)		Stw-BW-3
United States v. Hasting (1983)	BW-3	
United States v. Robinson (1988)	BW-3	
DOUBLE JEOPARDY		
Benton v. Maryland (1969) **c**		Har-1 Stw-2
North Carolina v. Pearce (1969)		Har-1 Stw-2
Ashe v. Swenson (1970)		Stw-2
Illinois v. Somerville (1973)	Stw-3	
Crist v. Bretz (1978)		
Swisher v. Brady (1978)	Stw-3	
JURY TRIAL		
Duncan v. Louisiana (1968) **c**	Har-Stw-1	
Bloom v. Illinois (1968)	Har-Stw-3	
Dyke v. Taylor Implement Co. (1968)	Har-Stw-1	
Frank v. United States (1969)	Har-Stw-1	
Benton v. Maryland (1969)	Har-1	
Dickey v. Florida (1970)	Har-Stw-1	
Baldwin v. New York (1970)	Har-Stw-1	
Williams v. Florida (1970)	Har-1	
California v. Green (1970)	Har-1	
McKeiver v. Pennsylvania (1971)	Stw-2	
Codispoti v. Pennsylvania (1974)		
MISCELLANEOUS CRIMINAL PROCEDURE		
Robinson v. California (1963) **c**	BW-1	
Powell v. Texas (1968)		

Table 6.5 (*cont.*)

Precedent/progeny	Preferences	Precedent
Fay v. Noia (1963)		Stw-2
Sanders v. United States (1963)	Clk-Har-1	
Henry v. Mississippi (1965)	Clk-Har-Stw-1	
Kaufman v. United States (1969)	Har-Stw-1	
Desist v. United States (1969)	Har-1	
Mackey v. United States (1971)	Har-1	
Wainwright v. Sykes (1977)	Stw-1	
Escobedo v. Illinois (1964) **c**		
Miranda v. Arizona (1966)	Clk-2 Har-Stw-BW-1	
Johnson v. New Jersey (1966)	Clk-Har-Stw-BW-1	
Frazier v. Cupp (1969)	Har-Stw-BW-3	
United States v. Gouveia (1984)	BW-2	
In re Gault (1967) **c**		
Leary v. United States (1969)	Stw-1	
In re Winship (1970)	Har-Stw-1	
McKeiver v. Pennsylvania (1971)	Har-1 Stw-3	
Breed v. Jones (1975)		Stw-2
Swisher v. Brady (1978)	Stw-3	

Legend: **c** = constitutional decision
      s = statutory decision
      = decision neither constitutionally nor statutorily based

Note: All progeny rest on the same decisional basis as the precedent unless otherwise indicated.

3. Warren associated himself with Black and Harlan in dissent in *Shapiro v. Thompson* (1969), which held that state residency requirements for welfare recipients violated the right to travel interstate as well as the equal protection clause. Unlike Black and Harlan, Warren departed the Court before the appearance of any cases to which his position in *Shapiro* was relevant. Harlan, however, reprised his original views in *Dandridge v. Williams* (1969) and *Williams v. Illinois* (1970). However, we count both Black and Harlan as precedential in *Graham v. Richardson* (1971). Although the case does not mention *Shapiro* in its summary, one may fairly conclude that the majority's opinion rests on it. Black did join it, while Harlan specially concurred. The issue parallels *Shapiro*: state residency requirements conditioning welfare benefits for aliens.

Table 6.6 displays the progeny and votes of the justices in these three landmarks. Although the voting of the four relevant justices falls somewhat below that on the other Warren Court tables (76.9 percent), it does not differ appreciably enough to warrant qualifying our conclusions about the overall behavior of the Warren Court justices, the matter to which we now turn.

CONCLUSION

In dividing this chapter into its components, we find considerable variation in the proportion of preferential and precedential votes, ranging from a preferential high of 98.4 percent in the First Amendment to a low of 76.9 percent in the three miscellaneous decisions – *Trop, Griswold*, and *Shapiro v. Thompson*. Figure 6.1 displays these differences. The First Amendment subset ranks highest because 54 of its 60 preferential votes were cast by the dissenters in the obscenity case, *Roth v. United States* (1957). Much more evenly distributed are the votes in the progeny of the Warren Court's internal security cases, which produce the second highest proportion of preference votes, 95.3 percent. Preferential proportions of the other subsets are civil rights, 86.4 percent; reapportionment 85.5; and criminal procedure 82.1.

Within the large criminal procedure set, the 31 votes in the miscellaneous subset result in 29 that are preferential (93.5 percent). This contrasts with the three noncriminal miscellaneous cases, which produced the lowest proportion of preferential voting of any of the six categories into which we have divided the Warren Court landmarks, 76.9 percent (10 of 13). No apparent reasons suggest themselves for the pronounced difference in proportions among the components of

Table 6.6.
Voting and opinion behavior: Warren Court miscellaneous cases

						Level of Expression			
				Preferences (%)			Precedent (%)		
Justice	Prefs/prec		%Prefs	Strong (1)	Moderate (2)	Weak (3)	Strong (1)	Moderate (2)	Weak (3)
Clark (Clk)	3	0	100.0		3 (100.0)				
Harlan (Har)	5	1	83.3	2 (40.0)	3 (60.0)			1 (100)	
Stewart (Stw)	2	1	66.7		2 (100)				1 (100)
Black (Blk)	0	1	0.0	–	–	–	–	–	1 (100)
Totals	10	3	76.9	2 (20.0)	8 (80.0)	0	0	1 (33.3)	2 (66.7)

Precedent/progeny	Preferences	Precedent
Trop v. Dulles (1958) **c**		
Kennedy v. Mendoza-Martinez (1963)	Clk-Har-2	
Schneider v. Rusk (1964)	Clk-Har-2	
Afroyim v. Rusk (1967)	Clk-Har-2	
Griswold v. Connecticut (1965) **c**		
Eisenstadt v. Baird (1972)	Stw-2	Stw-2
Whalen v. Roe (1977)	Stw-2	
Moore v. East Cleveland (1977)		
Shapiro v. Thompson (1969) **c**		
Dandridge v. Williams (1969)	Har-1	
Williams v. Illinois (1971)	Har-1	
Graham v. Richardson (1970)		Blk-Har-3

Legend: **c** = constitutional decision
     s = statutory decision
     = decision neither constitutionally nor statutorily based
Note: All progeny rest on the same decisional basis as the precedent unless otherwise indicated.

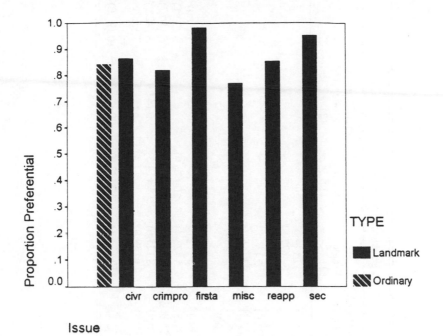

Figure 6.1. Precedential/preferential behavior on the Warrent Court.

criminal procedure. Why, for example, should only two of the seven votes in the progeny of *Benton v. Maryland* (1969) support preferences when all 16 of those in *Duncan v. Louisiana* (1968) do so? The same two justices dissented, and both cases involved incorporation of provisions of the Bill of Rights. Whatever the reason(s), *Benton*, plus the two self-incrimination cases (*Malloy v. Hogan* and *Griffin v. California*), deviate remarkably from the other criminal procedure categories, with ratios of 28.6 and 50 percent, respectively. The progeny of these three landmarks produce 57 percent of the precedentially sustaining votes in criminal procedure (17 of 30), but only 10 percent of those that support the dissenters' preferences (14 of 138).

For the overall voting of the individual dissenters in progeny of Warren Court landmarks, Table 6.7 provides the data. Thirteen of the 17 justices who sat on this Court voted. The briefly serving Jackson, Fortas, and Marshall, plus Frankfurter, did not. Overall, preferential voting in the Warren Court falls slightly below that of its predecessor Courts – Vinson, Stone, and Hughes. Table 6.7 shows these differences to be slight. Nevertheless, given the Warren Court's reputation as one that

Table 6.7.
Voting and opinion behavior: Warren Court landmarks

| Justice | Prefs/prec | | %Prefs | Level of Expression | | | | | |
| | | | | Preferences (%) | | | Precedent (%) | | |
				Strong (1)	Moderate (2)	Weak (3)	Strong (1)	Moderate (2)	Weak (3)
Douglas	48	0	100.0	33 (68.8)	8 (16.7)	7 (14.6)			
Brennan	9	0	100.0	2 (22.2)		7 (77.8)			
Warren	8	0	100.0	2 (25.0)		6 (75.0)			
Burton	4	0	100.0	1 (25.0)	1 (25.0)	2 (50.0)			
Minton	3	0	100.0		1 (33.3)	2 (66.7)			
Goldberg	1	0	100.0			1 (100)			
Reed	1	0	100.0		1 (100)				
Whittaker	1	0	100.0	1 (100)					
Black	50	1	98.0	34 (68.0)	10 (20.0)	6 (12.0)			1 (100)
Harlan	107	13	89.2	59 (55.1)	23 (21.5)	25 (23.4)			3 (23.1)
White	57	12	82.1	16 (28.1)	9 (15.8)	32 (56.1)	10 (76.9)	10 (83.3)	2 (16.7)
Clark	32	7	82.1	9 (28.1)	15 (46.9)	8 (25.0)	1 (14.3)	3 (42.9)	3 (42.9)
Stewart	53	17	75.7	21 (39.6)	11 (20.8)	21 (39.6)		16 (94.1)	1 (5.6)
Totals	374	50	88.2	178 (47.6)	79 (21.1)	117 (31.3)	11 (22.0)	29 (58.0)	10 (20.0)

shattered precedent rather indiscriminately, one might expect that those who most strenuously objected to the Court's path-breaking decisions – Harlan, Clark, Stewart, and White – to adhere to their dissenting positions somewhat more frequently than they did.

The number of preferential and precedential votes that dissenters from the Warren Court's landmark decisions cast in progeny are sufficient to allow for some comparison between them, as Table 6.7 does. The 374 votes supporting preferences divide as follows: 47.7 percent strong, 21.1 moderate, and 31.2 weak. The 50 votes adhering to precedent separate into 22.0 percent strong, 58.0 moderate, and 20.0 weak. Overall, then, the Warren Court dissenters behaved more intensely when voting their preferences than when they attached themselves to precedent. Strong preferential voting proportionately occurred twice as often as that supporting precedent. Complementarily, moderate voting was twice as frequent when justices voted precedent as when they followed their preferences.

An explanation for these differences probably depends on the idiosyncratic proclivities of specific justices: that certain of them are more or less adamant about their individual views, depending on whether they are preferentially or precedentially expressed. Assessment of the components of the criminal procedure landmarks suggests the existence of additional variables. Preferential votes in *Miranda*'s progeny were initially strongly expressed; in the later cases, they manifest themselves weakly. Undoubtedly, this reflects the shift of the Court's overall orientation from liberal to conservative. Warren Court liberalism peaked in the years following *Miranda*. Its dissenters understandably reiterated their objections rather emphatically. But once the Burger Court produced a conservative majority, the remaining dissenters had no need to flail away by mounting further objections. Rather, they simply became members of majorities that distinguished and narrowly applied *Miranda*, citing it as authority for a conservative result. Such behavior typifies weak preferential voting. Intensity instead characterizes members of the erstwhile majority. We also note that in the two criminal procedure subsets in which precedential voting matches and exceeds that supporting preferences, self-incrimination and *Benton v. Maryland*, strong preferential voting is utterly absent. Eight of the twelve preference votes in the former set are moderate in tone, the other four weak. The pair of *Benton* preference votes are both weak.

COMMON CASES

Notwithstanding the Court's 16 year life span, the sample of the Warren Court's ordinary litigation did not produce many votes in progeny by justices who dissented from these precedents, only 38. By contrast, the Vinson Court, of seven years' duration, produced forty. On the other hand, the 38 Warren Court votes are spread over ten precedents, the Vinson Court over only five. We discuss only three of these decisions.

In *Schulz v. Pennsylvania R. Co.* (1956), five justices held the evidence sufficient for submission to a jury in a Jones Act matter involving the drowning of a railroad's employee caused by the lack of a safe place to work. Burton, Minton, and Reed dissented without opinion. Frankfurter asserted that the writ of certiorari should have been dismissed as improvidently granted. After Minton's retirement, he referenced this dissent in *Rogers v. MP R. Co.* (1957).[30] Reed again dissented without opinion, and Burton at least indirectly acceded to the precedent by concurring without opinion. In *Schulz*'s final progeny, *Atlantic & Gulf Stevedores v. Ellerman Lines* (1962), Frankfurter objected to the majority's refusal to allow the court of appeals to correct the trial judge's instructions to the jury.

Clark and Burton dissented from the holding in *Reid v. Covert* (1957) declaring unconstitutional a provision of the Uniform Code of Military Justice that provided a peacetime court-martial for overseas dependents of military personnel accused of a capital offense. Clark subsequently reversed himself and wrote the Court's opinions in *Kinsella v. United States ex rel. Singleton* (1960), *Grisham v. Hagen* (1960), and *McElroy v. United States ex rel. Guagliardo* (1960), extending the precedent to noncapital offenses and to civilian employees of the armed forces.[31]

The final Warren Court precedent in progeny of which dissenters participated that warrants comment is *Haynes v. United States* (1968), from which Warren dissented. *Haynes* is also the last of the sampled Warren Court cases. The majority declared unconstitutional a provision of the National Firearms Act requiring registration of certain weapons. In *Grosso v. United States* (1968), Warren explained his reason for his *Haynes* dissent: "The impact of that decision on the efforts of Congress to enact much needed federal gun control laws is not consistent with

---

[30]　*Rogers* concerned the Federal Employers' Liability Act (FELA) rather than the Jones Act. The justices, however, treat them as fungible statutes, differing only as to the occupations of injured employees: on land or on sea.

　　Frankfurter favored *Rogers* rather than *Schulz* as authority for his writ improvidently granted (WIG) dissents in subsequent cases, such as *Baker v. T&P R. Co.* (1959). It is clear, however, that he consistently voted preferences in FELA and Jones Act cases involving the sufficiency of the evidence found by the fact finder. However, rather than count these, we maintain strict adherence to our decision rules.

[31]　In recounting *Reid*'s history, Clark candidly asserts, "The writer of this opinion wrote the [*Reid*] dissent" (1960, note 241). Burton had retired before the three progeny were decided. (See Schubert 1963.)

Table 6.8.
Voting and opinion behavior: Warren Court ordinary cases

| Justice | Prefs/prec | | %Prefs | Preferences (%) | | | Level of Expression | | |
| | | | | Strong (1) | Moderate (2) | Weak (3) | Precedent (%) | | |
							Strong (1)	Moderate (2)	Weak (3)
Black (Blk)	5	0	100.0	3 (60.0)	2 (40.0)				
Douglas (Dou)	5	0	100.0	2 (40.0)	3 (60.0)				
Frankfurter (Frk)	4	0	100.0	1 (25.0)	3 (75.0)				
Harlan (Har)	3	0	100.0		3 (100)				
Stewart (Stw)	3	0	100.0		2 (66.7)	1 (33.3)			
Brennan (Brn)	2	0	100.0	1 (50.0)	1 (50.0)				
Reed (Re)	1	0	100.0		1 (100)				
Warren (War)	4	2	66.7	2 (50.0)	2 (50.0)		2 (100)		
Clark (Clk)	5	3	52.5		2 (40.0)	3 (60.0)	3 (100)	1 (100)	
Burton (Bur)	0	1	0.0						
Totals	32	6	84.2	9 (28.1)	19 (59.4)	4 (12.5)	5 (83.3)	1 (16.7)	0

Precedent/progeny		Preferences	Precedent
Mastro Plastics Corp. v. NLRB (1956)	**s**		
NLRB v. Lion Oil Co. (1957)		Frk-Har-2	
Drake Bakeries v. Bakery Workers (1962)		Har-2	
Schulz v. Pennsylvania R. Co. (1956)	**s**		
Rogers v. MP R. Co. (1957)		Frk-1 Re-2	Bur-2
A & G Stevedores v. Ellerman Lines (1962)		Frk-2	
Roviaro v. United States (1957)		Clk-2	
Jencks v. United States (1957)		Clk-3	
Rugendorf v. United States (1964)			

Table 6.8 (cont.)

Precedent/progeny	Preferences	Precedent
McCray v. Illinois (1967)	Clk-3	
Lehmann v. United States ex rel. Carson (1957) **s**		
Mulcahy v. Catalanotte (1957)		
Reid v. Covert (1957) **c**	Blk-Dou-1	
Kinsella v. Singleton (1960)		Clk-1
Grisham v. Hagan (1960)		Clk-1
McElroy v. United States ex rel. Guagliardo (1960)		Clk-1
Sinkler v. MP R. Co. (1958) **s**		
Ward v. ACL R. Co. (1960)	Frk-Har-2	
Braden v. United States (1961) **c**		
Konigsberg v. State Bar (1961)	Blk-Brn-Dou-War-1	
In re Anastaplo (1961)	Blk-Brn-Dou-War-2	
Cohen v. Hurley (1961)	Blk-Dou-War-2	
Scales v. United States (1961)	Blk-1 Dou-2	
Rogers v. Richmond (1961) **s**		
Shotwell Mfg. Co. v. United States (1963)	Clk-Stw-3	
Jackson v. Denno (1964)	Clk-Stw-2	
Arnell v. United States (1966) **s**		
United States v. United Continental Tuna (1976)	Stw-2	
Haynes v. United States (1968) **c**		
Grosso v. United States (1968)	War-1	War-1
Leary v. United States (1969)		War-1
United States v. Covington (1969)		War-1

Legend: **c** = constitutional decision
    s = statutory decision
    = decision neither constitutionally nor statutorily based
Note: All progeny rest on the same decisional basis as the precedent unless otherwise indicated.

national safety" (1968, 84). But in the two remaining progeny – the companion cases *Leary v. United States* (1969) and *United States v. Covington* (1969) – Warren expressly adhered to the *Haynes* precedent. Leary had been indicted for knowingly transporting and facilitating the concealment of imported marijuana and for failing to pay the prescribed tax, Covington for obtaining marijuana without paying the tax. Not only did Warren adhere to the *Haynes* precedent, he also adhered to *Grosso*, the *Haynes* progeny from which he had dissented (1969, 54, 61).

The Justices' Behavior

The thirty-eight votes cast in progeny by dissenters from the Warren Court's ordinary precedents are distributed among ten justices. Table 6.8 displays their behavior. Seven justices cast only preferential votes. Five of the six precedential votes were cast by Clark and Warren. Although they pertained to only two precedents, all five votes were strongly expressed. No other Court or subset of any Court cast as high a percentage of strong votes adhering to precedent except for the two such votes cast among the 88 preferential votes in the Burger Court's landmark federalism cases. The Burger Court's death penalty set comes next closest, with 16 of its 24 votes supporting strongly expressed precedent (66.7 percent). Indeed, among the ten preceding Courts, ordinary precedents received only two strongly supportive votes, as compared with the five cast by Clark and Warren alone in the Warren Court's ordinary litigation. However, strong expression by no means characterizes the preferential voting of the Warren Court justices, unlike that of the Vinson Court. Granted that the vast majority of the strongly expressed preferential votes on the Vinson Court were cast by Black and Douglas, 90 percent (27 of 30), or 84 percent (27 of 32) of the total votes. Their proportion on the Warren Court, by contrast, reaches only 50 percent (5 of 10). While the numbers (N) are too small to admit of systematic comparison, we suspect the discrepancy results from the strength – or the lack thereof – of these justices' support for the policy aspects of the cases triggering the responses in question.

The ratio of preference to precedent votes (84.2 percent) approximates that of the White, Taft, and Stone Courts while falling below that of the 95 percent preferential Vinson Court and some 15 points above that of the Hughes Court. Clearly, the Warren Court neither invented nor perfected preferential decision making.

7

Precedential Behavior
in the Burger Court

Richard Nixon campaigned for the Presidency in 1968 against Hubert Humphrey, against Lyndon Johnson, and against the Warren Court. The Warren Court, he declared, had gone too far in protecting the criminal forces in society, as opposed to the peace forces. He wanted "strict constructionists" who would not read their preferred views of public policy into law.

Nixon soon got his chance. In June 1968, Earl Warren announced his intention to resign at "such time as a successor is qualified" to take his place. Johnson nominated his close friend and adviser Abe Fortas, who was already serving as associate justice, to be chief justice, and another crony, Homer Thornberry, to take Fortas's seat.

With a better than reasonable shot at a Nixon victory in November, a coalition of Republicans and Southern Democrats filibustered Fortas's nomination. With the vote on cloture failing to receive two-thirds support, Fortas's bid for promotion failed. But as Warren had not officially resigned, he chose to stay in office, stating, "Since they won't confirm Abe, they will have me" (Abraham 1985, p. 13).

The following spring, the 78-year-old Warren, who had wanted to see a liberal replace him (White 1982), gave in to the inevitable and resigned unconditionally, allowing Richard Nixon to name his successor. Nixon swiftly named Warren Burger to take Earl Warren's place. At the same time, *Life* magazine disclosed that in 1966 Fortas had accepted $20,000 as part of an annual consulting fee from Louis Wolfson, a millionaire businessman later convicted of stock manipulation. The ensuing controversy forced Fortas to resign.

On August 18, 1969, Nixon chose Circuit Court of Appeals Judge Clement Haynsworth, a Democrat from South Carolina, to replace Fortas. The selection of Haynsworth was part of Nixon's "Southern strategy," by which he hoped to win the votes of conservative white Democratic Southerners in 1972.

Haynsworth at first appeared certain of confirmation. Though the

Democrats controlled the Senate, Republicans and conservative Southern Democrats had a working majority. Confidence in Haynsworth began to erode when Judiciary Committee hearings began to focus on cases decided by Haynsworth in which he had a direct, albeit minor, financial interest. Ideological critics alleged that Haynsworth had compiled an antiunion, anti–civil rights record as an appellate judge. On November 21, 1969, the Senate rejected him by a vote of 55 to 45.

In angry reaction to Haynsworth's defeat, Nixon nominated G. Harrold Carswell, a little-known federal judge from Florida who had graduated from a local Southern law school. So poorly qualified was he that the dean of the Yale Law School was moved to declare that he "presents more slender credentials than any nominee put forth this century."[1] Even Carswell's Senate floor leader, Roman Hruska (Republican of Nebraska), declared, "Even if he were mediocre, there are a lot of mediocre judges, and people and lawyers. They are entitled to a little representation, aren't they, and a little chance" (Weaver 1970). But the most damaging blow to Carswell's candidacy occurred when a Florida television station found film of a 1948 speech in which he declared, "I yield to no man as a fellow candidate or as a fellow citizen in the firm vigorous belief in the principles of White Supremacy, and I shall always be so governed" ("Excerpts from Carswell Talk" 1970, A22).[2] Carswell was defeated in a surprisingly close vote, 51 to 45. Nixon eventually replaced Fortas with Harry Blackmun of Minnesota, claiming that the Senate would not confirm a Southerner. Yet barely a year later the Senate voted 89 to 1 to confirm Lewis Powell of Virginia to take Hugo Black's seat. Four days later it confirmed William Rehnquist to take Harlan's seat in a contentious (68 to 26) battle that centered on a memo Rehnquist wrote as a clerk for Justice Jackson supporting segregation in the *Brown* case.

With four new conservative justices seated, the Burger Court (1969–86) was expected by friend and foe alike to launch a counter revolution against liberal Warren Court precedents (see Blasi 1983; Funston 1977). Instead, it was the Burger Court (with the four Nixon justices only sometimes in dissent) that first created abortion rights,[3]

---

[1] U.S. Senate, *Hearings on the Nomination of G. Harold Carswell, of Florida, to Be Associate Justice of the Supreme Court of the United States*, 91st Congress, 2d Session, 1970, p. 242.

[2] Though this should have been enough to force Carswell's withdrawal, his nomination pressed forward. Assistant Attorney General William Rehnquist later commented that Carswell's support for white supremacy amounted to no more than "some rather thin evidence of personal hostility toward blacks" (Massaro 1990, p. 109).

[3] *Roe v. Wade* (1973). White and Rehnquist dissented.

struck death penalties,[4] protected women under the Fourteenth Amendment,[5] permitted school busing,[6] and accepted race-based affirmative action plans.[7]

Despite these decisions, the Burger Court cannot be considered an extension of the Warren Court: three years after *Furman* it upheld the constitutionality of the death penalty provided procedural safeguards were followed;[8] limited the reach of the *Mapp*[9] and *Miranda* decisions;[10] increased the ability of states to ban obscene materials;[11] refused to equalize state spending between school districts;[12] refused to extend the right to privacy to homosexual conduct;[13] and allowed programs within colleges and universities to discriminate without fear of the entire school's losing federal funds.[14]

Other major decisions of the Burger Court forced Nixon to hand over the Watergate tapes,[15] protected the press against prior censorship,[16] limited campaign finance reform,[17] and struck down the legislative veto.[18]

Although it has the same number of precedential votes as the Warren Court (49 versus 50), the Burger Court produces almost twice as many preferential votes in progeny by dissenters from its leading decisions (683 versus 374).[19] The Court's landmarks, like those of the Warren Court, may be divided into several discrete sets. Because of the appearance of new issues and the reconfiguration of old ones, the breakdown does not match that of the Warren Court. Criminal procedure, civil rights, and the First Amendment overlap, but their contents markedly differ.[20]

---

[4]   *Furman v. Georgia* (1972). All four Nixon appointees dissented.

[5]   The unanimously decided *Reed v. Reed* (1971).

[6]   The unanimously decided *Swann v. Charlotte-Mecklenburg Board of Education* (1971).

[7]   *Regents v. Bakke* (1978). Burger, Stewart, Rehnquist, and Stevens dissented from that part of the opinion upholding affirmative action.

[8]   *Gregg v. Georgia* (1976).

[9]   *Stone v. Powell* (1976) and *United States v. Leon* (1984).

[10] *New York v. Quarles* (1984).

[11] *Miller v. California* (1973).

[12] *San Antonio v. Rodriguez* (1973).

[13] *Bowers v. Hardwick* (1986).

[14] *Grove City College v. Bell* (1984).

[15] *United States v. Nixon* (1974).

[16] *New York Times Co. v. United States* (1971).

[17] *Buckley v. Valeo* (1976).

[18] *INS v. Chadha* (1983).

[19] For the reasons stated in Chapter 6, note 13, our results slightly differ from those reported in our original analysis of progeny. (See Segal and Spaeth 1996a.)

[20] Twenty-three leading decisions produce no progeny, as compared with four of the Warren Court's, notwithstanding that only four of the 23 contain a solo dissent. The relative recency of many of these cases and the nonrecurring character of others probably account for this discrepancy. Many of them, however, serve as progeny. The 23 cases are *Oregon v. Mitchell* (1970), *McKeiver v. Pennsylvania* (1971), *New York*

ABORTION

From a public perspective, certainly the most contentious, if not the most salient, issue confronting the Burger Court was abortion. The five leading decisions identified by our source generated dissents by Rehnquist and White (*Roe v. Wade* [1973]), plus O'Connor (*Akron v. Akron Center* (1983) and *Planned Parenthood v. Ashcroft* [1983]), plus Burger in *Thornburgh v. American College* (1986). Blackmun, the author of *Roe*, dissented in *Harris v. McRae* (1980), along with Brennan, Marshall, and Stevens. Not surprisingly, the 72 votes these justices cast in progeny all supported their preferences. See Table 7.1. The dissenters from the first two decisions, *Roe* and *Harris v. McRae*, were much more muted in their opinions than they were in the later three. Nineteen of the 21 progeny votes in *Akron* and all 15 in *Ashcroft* were strong expressions.

CRIMINAL PROCEDURE

The Burger Court decided the same number of nonunanimous criminal procedure landmarks as the Warren Court, 15. We break the criminal procedure cases into five small subsets: search and seizure, *Miranda*/self-incrimination, jury, juveniles, and miscellaneous. The progeny of these landmarks barely halve the number of Warren Court votes (97 versus 167). Preferential voting, however, exceeds that of the Warren Court (96.9 percent versus 82.1 percent). Inasmuch as the Burger Court's reputation does not rest on matters of criminal procedure, as did much of that of the Warren Court, one would have assumed more precedential voting on the Burger Court.

Search and Seizure

Eight of the 13 Burger Court justices dissented from one or more of these five decisions,[21] Rehnquist in three of them. *Nix* alone had fewer than three dissenters, two. Of the thirty-nine votes they cast in progeny,

---

Times v. United States (1971), Bigelow v. Virginia (1975), Pasadena City Board of Education v. Spangler (1976), United Jewish Organizations v. Carey (1977), Zurcher v. Stanford Daily (1978), Orr v. Orr (1979), United States v. Helstoski (1979), Hutchinson v. Proxmire (1979), H.L. v. Matheson (1981), Washington v. Gunther (1981), Rostker v. Goldberg (1981), Plyler v. Doe (1982), Board of Education v. Pico (1982), Bob Jones University v. United States (1983), Karcher v. Daggett (1983), Brown v. Thomson (1983), Solem v. Helm (1983), Firefighters v. Stotts (1984), Ake v. Oklahoma (1985), Vasquez v. Hillary (1986), and Bowers v. Hardwick (1986).

[21] Marshall v. Barlow's Inc. (1978), Payton v. New York (1980), Nix v. Williams (1984), United States v. Leon (1984), and Tennessee v. Garner (1985).

Table 7.1.
Voting and opinion behavior: Burger Court abortion cases

Justice	Prefs/prec		%Prefs	Preferences (%)			Level of Expression Precedent (%)		
				Strong (1)	Moderate (2)	Weak (3)	Strong (1)	Moderate (2)	Weak (3)
Rehnquist (Rhn)	25	0	100.0	15 (60.0)	4 (16.0)	6 (24.0)	0	0	0
White (BW)	25	0	100.0	15 (60.0)	4 (16.0)	6 (24.0)			
O'Connor (OC)	14	0	100.0	13 (92.9)		1 (7.1)			
Blackmun (Blm)	2	0	100.0	1 (50.0)		1 (50.0)			
Brennan (Brn)	2	0	100.0	1 (50.0)		1 (50.0)			
Marshall (Mar)	2	0	100.0	1 (50.0)		1 (50.0)			
Stevens (Stv)	2	0	100.0	1 (50.0)		1 (50.0)			
Totals	72	0	100.0	47 (65.3)	8 (11.1)	17 (23.6)	0	0	0

Precedent/progeny	Preferences	Precedent
Roe v. Wade (1973) **c**		
Planned Parenthood v. Danforth (1976)	Rhn-BW-2	
Beal v. Doe (1977)	Rhn-BW-3	
Maher v. Roe (1977)	Rhn-BW-3	
Poelker v. Doe (1977)	Rhn-BW-3	
Colautti v. Franklin (1979)	Rhn-BW-2	
Harris v. McRae (1980)	Rhn-BW-3	
Akron v. Akron Center (1983)	Rhn-BW-2	
Planned Parenthood v. Ashcroft (1983)	Rhn-BW-2	
Thornburgh v. American College (1986)	Rhn-BW-1	
Webster v. Reproductive Health Services (1989)	Rhn-BW-1	

	Rhn-BW-1
Planned Parenthood v. Casey (1992)	
Harris v. McRae (1980) **c**	
Akron v. Akron Center (1983)	Blm-Brn-Mar-Stv-3
Webster v. Reproductive Health Services (1989)	Blm-Brn-Mar-Stv-1
Akron v. Akron Center (1983) **c**	
Planned Parenthood v. Ashcroft (1983)	OC-Rhn-BW-1
Simopoulos v. Virginia (1983)	OC-Rhn-BW-1
Thornburgh v. American College (1986)	OC-Rhn-BW-1
Webster v. Reproductive Health Services (1989)	OC-1 Rhn-BW-3
Hodgson v. Minnesota (1990)	OC-Rhn-BW-1
Ohio v. Akron Center (1990)	OC-Rhn-BW-1
Planned Parenthood v. Casey (1992)	OC-Rhn-BW-1
Planned Parenthood v. Ashcroft (1983) **c**	
Simopoulos v. Virginia (1983)	OC-Rhn-BW-1
Thornburgh v. American College (1986)	OC-Rhn-BW-1
Hodgson v. Minnesota (1990)	OC-Rhn-BW-1
Ohio v. Akron Center (1990)	OC-Rhn-BW-1
Planned Parenthood v. Casey (1992)	OC-Rhn-BW-1
Thornburgh v. American College (1986) **c**	
Webster v. Reproductive Health Services (1989)	OC-Rhn-BW-3
Planned Parenthood v. Casey (1992)	OC-Rhn-BW-1

Legend: **c** = constitutional decision
       s = statutory decision
       = decision neither constitutionally nor statutorily based

Note: All progeny rest on the same decisional basis as the precedent unless otherwise indicated.

only two adhere to precedent. Both involve White's vote in progeny of *Payton v. New York*, in which he wrote a conservative dissent that Burger and Rehnquist joined. The majority had ruled that the Fourth Amendment prohibits police from making a warrantless and nonconsensual entry into a suspect's home in order to make a felony arrest. White subsequently wrote a liberal dissent in *Washington v. Chrisman*. A student carrying a bottle of gin was stopped by an officer, who requested identification. The officer accompanied the student to his room so that he might provide same. From the open door, he observed what he suspected to be marijuana and entered the room to confirm his suspicions. In *Tennessee v. Garner*, White wrote the Court's opinion voiding a statute that authorized the use of deadly force against a nondangerous fleeing suspect. Only if the officer has probable cause to believe that the suspect poses a significant threat of serious injury to the officer or others does the Fourth Amendment permit such action. White sandwiches both a weakly and a strongly preferential vote between these precedential ones.[22]

Tennessee v. Garner also forms a precedent for two 1989 decisions, *Brower v. Inyo County* and *Graham v. Conner*. We count the *Garner* dissenters – O'Connor and Rehnquist – as weakly preferential even though they silently join a liberal majority opinion in both cases. Each case also contains a special concurrence taking the majority to task for watering down the *Garner* precedent. In *Graham*, for example, Blackmun, speaking for himself, Brennan, and Marshall, wrote: "I see no reason for the Court . . . to reach out to decide that prearrest excessive force claims are to be analyzed under the Fourth Amendment *rather than* under a substantive due process standard. I also see no basis for the Court's suggestion . . . that . . . *Tennessee v. Garner* . . . implicitly so held" (1989, 399–400).

Interestingly, the distribution in the strength of the preferential votes closely matches that of the Warren Court. Seventeen of its votes were strong, five moderate, and 15 weak. On the Burger Court, the numbers are 15, 6, and 10, respectively.

Self-Incrimination

The progeny of the three self-incrimination cases – *Harris v. New York* (1971), *New York v. Quarles* (1984), and *Kastigar v. United States* (1972)

[22] In *Texas v. Brown* and *Welsh v. Wisconsin*, respectively. Joined only by Rehnquist, he wrote in the latter that "I continue to believe that the Court erred in *Payton* in requiring exigent circumstances to justify warrantless in-home felony arrests" (1984, 759). The majority ruled unconstitutional the warrantless nighttime entry of a suspect's home to arrest him for a civil nonjailable traffic offense.

– generate 23 votes in progeny by dissenters. *Harris* and *Quarles* are *Miranda* connected. The former holds unwarned statements admissible for the purpose of impeaching the defendant's credibility; the latter creates a public safety exception to providing the warnings. *Kastigar* decreed that the Organized Crime Control Act's narrowing of the scope of witness immunity does not violate the self-incrimination clause.

The 23 votes dissenters cast in the progeny all support their preferences (see Table 7.2). This is in marked contrast with the Warren Court self-incrimination set, in which only half the 24 votes support preferences. Neither did *Miranda* itself achieve especially high consistency, 85.7 percent. Twenty of the 23 Burger Court votes strongly reaffirm the justices' original dissent. This also contrasts markedly with the earlier set (see Table 6.5), in which two-thirds of the votes are moderate in tone, and another quarter weak. Only two Warren Court votes, both precedential, are strongly so. Moreover, *Miranda*'s preferential votes are roughly divided between strong and weak. Three precedential votes are strong; the other five, moderate.

Jury Trial

The three Burger Court jury landmarks parallel the self-incrimination cases: though their progeny produce only 14 votes, as compared with 23 in the self-incrimination progeny, all support the justices' preferences. In ten of the 14 votes, they voice themselves strongly, as compared with 20 of the 23 self-incrimination votes. Because the first of the landmarks, *Williams v. Florida* (1970), produces bifurcated dissents – Marshall objecting to a six-member jury, Black and Douglas to Florida's notice of alibi rule – we arguably should have counted Douglas's vote in *Wardius v. Oregon* as resting on self-incrimination, rather than trial by jury. But because Marshall cast the other four progeny votes, and did so on jury grounds, we deem it preferable to count Douglas's vote with his, rather than distinctively. The other two landmarks, *Johnson v. Louisiana* (1972) and *Apodaca v. Oregon* (1972), concern the constitutionality of less than unanimous verdicts. *Burch v. Louisiana* (1979) is progeny of both; *Ballew v. Georgia* (1978), of *Apoduca*.

Juveniles

The first of the Burger Court's juvenile landmarks, *In re Winship* (1970), holds that the standard, proof beyond a reasonable doubt, applies to juvenile actions that if committed by an adult would be criminal. Burger, Stewart, and Black dissented. The first two, in an opinion by Burger, preferred a less protective standard: "I cannot regard it as a manifesta-

Table 7.2.
Voting and opinion behavior: Burger Court criminal procedure cases

Justice	Prefs/prec		%Prefs	Preferences (%)			Level of Expression Precedent (%)		
				Strong (1)	Moderate (2)	Weak (3)	Strong (1)	Moderate (2)	Weak (3)
Marshall (Mar)	27	0	100.0	20 (74.1)	6 (22.2)	1 (3.7)			
Brennan (Brn)	19	0	100.0	14 (73.7)	4 (21.1)	1 (5.3)			
Stevens (Stv)	10	0	100.0	5 (50.0)	3 (30.0)	2 (20.0)			
Rehnquist (Rhn)	9	0	100.0	3 (33.3)		6 (66.7)			
Blackmun (Blm)	6	0	100.0	3 (50.0)		3 (50.0)			
Burger (Brg)	6	0	100.0	2 (33.3)	1 (16.7)	3 (50.0)			
Douglas (Dou)	5	0	100.0	4 (80.0)	1 (20.0)				
Stewart (Stw)	4	0	100.0	2 (50.0)	1 (25.0)	1 (25.0)			
O'Connor (OC)	2	0	100.0			2 (100)			
White (BW)	6	2	75.0	3 (50.0)		3 (50.0)		2 (100)	
Black (Blk)	0	1	0.0						1 (100)
Totals	94	3	96.9	56 (59.6)	16 (17.0)	22 (23.4)	0	2 (67.7)	1 (33.3)

Precedent/progeny	Preferences	Precedent
SEARCH AND SEIZURE		
Marshall v. Barlow's Inc. (1978) **c**	Blm-Rhn-3 Stv-1	
Donovan v. Dewey (1981)	Stv-1	
Michigan v. Clifford (1984)	Blm-Rhn-Stv-3	
New York v. Burger (1987)		
Payton v. New York (1980) **c**	Rhn-BW-1	
Steagald v. United States (1981)	Brg-Rhn-BW-3	BW-2
Michigan v. Summers (1981)		
Washington v. Chrisman (1982)	Brg-Rhn-BW-3	
Texas v. Brown (1983)	Rhn-BW-1	
Welsh v. Wisconsin (1984)	Brg-1	
Segura v. United States (1984)	Brg-Rhn-1	BW-2
Tennessee v. Garner (1985)		
Nix v. Williams (.984)	Mar-2	
Murray v. United States (1988)		
United States v. Leon (1984)	Brn-Mar-1	
Massachusetts v. Sheppard (1984)	Brn-Mar-1	
INS v. Lopez-Mendoza (1984)	Brn-Mar-1	
Oregon v. Elstad (1985)	Brn-Mar-1	
Maryland v. Macon (1985)	Brn-Mar-Stv-2	
Illinois v. Krull (1987)	Stv-2	
Arizona v. Evans (1995)		
Tennessee v. Garner (1985) **c**	OC-Rhn-3	
Brower v. Inyo County (1989)	OC-Rhn-3	
Graham v. Connor (1989)		

Table 7.2 (*cont.*)

Precedent/progeny	Preferences	Precedent
SELF-INCRIMINATION (*MIRANDA*)		
Harris v. New York (1971) **c**		
Michigan v. Tucker (1974)	Dou-2	
Oregon v. Hass (1975)	Brn-Mar-1	
Michigan v. Mosely (1975)	Brn-Mar-1	
United States v. Havens (1980)	Brn-Mar-2	
Jenkins v. Anderson (1980)	Brn-Mar-1	
Kastigar v. United States (1972) **c**		
Zicarelli v. New Jeresey Commission (1972)	Dou-Mar-1	
Sarno v. Illinois Crime Commission (1972)	Dou-Mar-1	
California Bankers v. Shultz (1974)	Dou-1	
Pillsbury Co. v. Conboy (1983)	Mar-1	
New York v. Quarles (1984) **c**		
Oregon v. Elstad (1985)	Brn-Mar-1	
Moran v. Burbine (1985)	Brn-Mar-Stv-1	
Duckworth v. Eagan (1989)	Brn-Mar-Stv-1	

JURY TRIAL

Case			
Williams v. Florida (1970) **c**	Mar-1		
Johnson v. Louisiana (1972)	Mar-1		
Apodaca v. Oregon (1972)	Dou-1		
Wardius v. Oregon (1973)	Mar-1		
Colegrove v. Battin (1973)	Mar-2		
Ballew v. Georgia (1978) **c**			
Johnson v. Louisiana (1972)		Brn-Mar-Stw-1	Blk-1
Burch v. Louisiana (1979)			
Apodaca v. Oregon (1972) **c**		Brn-Mar-Stw-1	
Ballew v. Georgia (1978)		Brn-Mar-Stw-2	
Burch v. Louisiana (1979)			

JUVENILES

Case		
In re Winship (1970) **c**		
McKeiver v. Pennsylvania (1971)	Brg-Stw-3	
Santosky v. Kramer (1982)	Brg-2	
Schall v. Martin (1983) **c**		
United States v. Salerno (1987)	Brn-Mar-Stv-2	

MISCELLANEOUS CRIMINAL PROCEDURE

Case		
Scott v. Illinois (1979) **c**		
Baldasar v. Illinois (1980)	Blm-Brn-Mar-1 Stv-3	
Nichols v. United States (1994)	Blm-Stv-1	
Gannett Co. v. DePasquale (1979) **c**		
Richmond Newspapers v. Virginia (1980)	Blm-Brn-Mar-BW-1	
Press-Enterprise Co. v. Superior Court (1986)	Blm-Brn-Mar-BW-3	

Legend: **c** = constitutional decision
      s = statutory decision
      = decision neither constitutionally nor statutorily based

Note: All progeny rest on the same decisional basis as the precedent unless otherwise indicated.

tion of progress to transform juvenile courts into criminal courts" (1970, 376). Black objected to the standard itself. Nowhere in the Constitution, he said, is it prescribed.

In determining the cases that are progeny of *Winship*, we exclude the large number that cite it as general authority for the use of the beyond reasonable doubt standard; instead we restrict its focus to juvenile proceedings. This reveals two progeny, *McKeiver v. Pennsylvania* (1971) and *Santosky v. Kramer* (1982).[23] Burger and Stewart joined the conservative plurality in *McKeiver*, while Black joined Douglas's dissent. We count Black's vote as precedential even though the opinion he joined rests on a juvenile's right to trial by jury rather than a standard of "guilt." This focus makes this dissent progeny of *In re Gault*, the Warren Court's juvenile landmark. Nonetheless, the dissent does supportively reference *Winship*: "We have held indeed that where a juvenile is charged with an act that would constitute a crime if committed by an adult, he is entitled to be tried under a standard of proof beyond a reasonable doubt" (1971, 560). This suffices to support precedent.

As we have seen time and again, the justices cite precedents of which they disapprove when doing so enables them to support their preferences. This is precisely the form in which our definition of a weak preferential vote most commonly manifests itself. Therefore, it should occasion no surprise if a justice who supports one policy (e.g., Black and jury trial) favorably cites a precedent which he opposes (e.g., Black and his opposition to proof beyond a reasonable doubt in juvenile proceedings) if it enhances attainment of the prior – and presumably more important – of the two objectives.

The other juvenile landmark, *Schall v. Martin* (1984), upholds the pretrial detention of juveniles against a challenge that it violates due process of law. The dissenters – Brennan, Marshall, and Stewart – adhere to their preferences in the single progeny, *United States v. Salerno* (1987). Accordingly, six of the seven votes in this small subset support preferences, although not especially strongly: four moderately, two weakly.

Miscellaneous Criminal Procedure

The two such cases, *Scott v. Illinois* (1979) and *Gannett Co. v. DePasquale* (1979), generated 14 votes by their dissenters, all of them preferential. Both landmarks concern the Sixth Amendment. *Scott* limits the right to appointed counsel to proceedings in which imprisonment was

---

[23]   Only Burger remained on the Court when *Santosky* was decided. He voted his preferences by joining Rehnquist's dissent supporting a standard that more readily allows states to terminate parental rights.

actually imposed. *DePasquale* maintains that the guarantee of a public trial is for the defendant's benefit, not for that of the public.

Five of the six votes in *Scott*'s progeny, *Baldasar v. Illinois* (1980) and *Nichols v. United States* (1994), strongly support preferences. That of Stevens in *Baldasar* is weakly such. The dissenters' votes in the first of *DePasquale*'s two progeny, *Richmond Newspapers v. Virginia* (1980), strongly support preferences, while those in *Press-Enterprise Co. v. Superior Court* (1986) do so weakly. These results show a tad less vigor than the Warren Court's set of miscellaneous criminal procedure cases.

The Justices' Votes

Overall, dissenters from the landmark criminal procedure cases cling to their preferences markedly more strongly than did their Warren Court colleagues: 96.9 percent versus 82.1 percent. Compare Table 7.2 with Table 6.5. This difference is also reflected in the strength with which the two Courts manifest their preferences. Almost 60 percent of the Burger Court votes show strong support as compared with barely half those of the Warren Court (50.0 percent). At the other extreme, less than a quarter of the Burger Court votes are weakly preferential as compared with almost 40 percent of the Warren Court's. On the precedential side, although the Burger Court justices so voted on only three occasions, their two-thirds moderate proportion accurately reflects that of the thirty Warren Court votes.

The holdover justices, Brennan and Douglas, continue their consistently preferential behavior. Black's single Burger Court vote – precedential – is the antithesis of those he cast on the Warren Court. The other holdovers, Stewart and White, increase and decrease, respectively, their preferential voting: Stewart from 77.6 to 100 percent; White, from 82.5 to 75 percent.

THE DEATH PENALTY

Although capital punishment concerns a relatively small number of Burger Court landmarks, seven, only two more than abortion, it generated an outpouring of progeny far exceeding that of any other component into which we have divided the Burger Court's landmark decisions. Fully half the precedential votes occur here: 25 of 50, as well as 20 percent of those supporting preferences: 136 of 682. These differences of proportions reveal that preferential voting falls markedly below that observed in the previous subsets, abortion and criminal procedure. Given the salience of this issue, as manifested in the total number of death penalty cases this Court decided, one would expect preferential voting to exceed 84.9 percent. See Table 7.3.

The 1972 and 1976 decisions, *Furman v. Georgia*, *Gregg v. Georgia*, and *Woodson v. North Carolina*, spawn the vast majority of the progeny votes: 116, including all 25 precedential votes. *Furman* voided the death penalty as it was then administered throughout the United States and drew dissents from the four then-conservative justices: Blackmun, Burger, Powell, and Rehnquist. *Gregg* resurrected the death penalty over the dissents of Brennan and Marshall. In a companion to *Gregg*, *Woodson v. North Carolina*, three of the *Furman* dissenters – Blackmun, Burger, and Rehnquist – joined by White, objected to voiding mandatory death penalties.

The first of *Furman*'s progeny, *Moore v. Illinois* (1972), found all four dissenters expressly accepting its holding. Two years later, in *Schick v. Reed* (1974), the dissenters, with the support of Stewart and White, cite *Furman* as authority for denying the petitioner relief from a no-parole condition of his commuted death sentence. The dissenters here – Brennan, Douglas, Marshall – chastise the majority for "paying only lip service" to *Furman* (1974, 268). In *Gregg* and two of its companions, *Profitt v. Florida* (1976) and *Jurek v. Texas* (1976), the *Furman* dissenters voted their preferences. Powell, however, split with his colleagues in *Woodson v. North Carolina* (1976) and *Roberts v. Louisiana* (1976), holding that mandatory death sentences "depart markedly from contemporary standards" (1976, 301) and fail "to provide a constitutionally tolerable response" to unbridled jury discretion (1976, 302). But, less than a year later, only Rehnquist adheres to his original position in *Gardner v. Florida* (1977). The other three vote to vacate and remand a decision in which the trial court judge based his death sentence in part on a presentence investigation report not disclosed to the parties' counsel.

Powell continued to vote precedentially in *Roberts v. Louisiana* (1977) and *Coker v. Georgia* (1977). In a footnote in *Coker*, Powell arguably says he is voting his preferences: "my opinion in *Furman* did emphasize that the proportionality test as to rape should be applied on a case-by-case basis, noting that in some cases the death sentence would be 'grossly excessive'" (1977, 602). But his vote supports precedent: reversal of the death sentence. Powell's action here is noteworthy because it inverts the typical disjunction between opinion and vote: verbally adhere to precedent while voting preferences.

The decision in *Coker* also warrants notice because it signals Blackmun's shift from his *Furman* pro–death penalty position. In all subsequent progeny he voted liberally, with the exception of *Pulley v. Harris* (1984). Here the Court ruled that the Constitution does not require that a defendant's sentence be compared with sentences imposed in similar capital cases to ascertain whether his was proportionate. Especially noteworthy is *California v. Brown* (1987), where Blackmun cites and quotes his conservative *Furman* opinion in *opposition* (*sic!*) to a conservative decision: "Long ago, when in dissent, I expressed my fear of legislation that would make the death penalty mandatory, and thus remove all discretion from the sentencer, I observed that such legislation would be 'regressive . . . , for it [would] eliminat[e] the element of mercy in the imposition of punishment'" (1987, 562).

Gregg v. Georgia (1976), which reinstituted the death penalty, drew dissents from Brennan and Marshall. In each of its progeny, totaling 58 votes, they reiterate their opposition to capital punishment. In only three cases did one or the other not explicitly reference his original position: both in *Roberts v. Louisiana* (1977), and Marshall in *Enmund v. Florida* (1982) and *Cabana v. Bullock* (1986). See Table 7.3.

The third of the major Burger Court death penalty cases, *Woodson v. North Carolina* (1976), is a companion to *Gregg*. In outlawing a statutorily mandated death sentence, Blackmun, Burger, Rehnquist, and White dissent. Blackmun bases his position on his *Furman* dissent. They all adhere to their respective *Woodson* views in another companion case, *Roberts v. Louisiana* (1976). But in *Gardner v. Florida* (1977), Blackmun and White cite the *Woodson* plurality opinion as authority for their anti–death penalty votes. Only Burger and Rehnquist cite *Woodson* to sustain their votes in *Coker v. Georgia* (1977), as do Rehnquist and White in *Lockett v. Ohio* (1978). Beginning with his vote and the opinion that he joined in *Caldwell v. Mississippi* (1985), Blackmun begins to manifest consistent opposition to capital punishment. Only twice thereafter did he cast a pro–death penalty vote.[24] *Woodson* remains the vehicle for his opposition in *California v. Brown* (1987). In *Sumner v. Shuman* (1987), Rehnquist and White continue to adhere to their *Woodson* dissents, as does Rehnquist in *Tuilaepa v. California* (1994). Of *Woodson*'s 20 progeny votes, 16 support the justices' preferences; four do not. All except Rehnquist's *Tuilaepa* vote are expressed strongly.

The four remaining death penalty landmarks produce only preferential votes. In *Rummel v. Estelle* (1980), the only progeny of *Coker*, Rehnquist, joined by Burger, uses the liberal *Coker* ruling to justify the Court's opinion upholding mandatory life sentences: "A more extensive intrusion into the basic line drawing process that is pre-eminently the province of the legislature would be difficult to square with the view expressed in *Coker* that the Court's Eighth Amendment's judgments

---

[24] In *Lowenfield v. Phelps* (1988) and *Franklin v. Lynaugh* (1988).

Table 7.3.
Voting and opinion behavior: Burger Court death penalty cases

| | | | Level of Expression | | | | | |
| | | | Preferences (%) | | | Precedent (%) | | |
Justice	Prefs/prec		%Prefs	Strong (1)	Moderate (2)	Weak (3)	Strong (1)	Moderate (2)	Weak (3)
Brennan (Brn)	31	0	100.0	29 (93.5)	1 (3.2)	1 (3.2)			
Marshall (Mar)	31	0	100.0	27 (87.1)	1 (3.2)	3 (9.7)			
O'Connor (OC)	4	0	100.0	1 (25.0)	1 (25.0)	2 (50.0)			
Stevens (Stv)	2	0	100.0	1 (50.0)	1 (50.0)				
Rehnquist (Rhn)	29	2	93.5	12 (41.4)	3 (10.3)	14 (48.3)	2 (100)		
Burger (Brg)	16	2	88.9	8 (50.0)	1 (6.3)	7 (43.8)	1 (50.0)		1 (50.0)
White (BW)	4	1	80.0	3 (75.0)	1 (25.0)		1 (100)		
Powell (Pow)	9	8	52.9			9 (100)	4 (50.0)		4 (50.0)
Blackmun (Blm)	10	12	45.5	8 (80.0)		2 (20.0)	8 (66.7)		4 (33.3)
Totals	136	25	84.9	89 (65.4)	9 (6.6)	38 (27.9)	16 (66.0)	0	9 (36.0)

Precedent/progeny	Preference	Precedent
Furman v. Georgia (1972) **c**		Blm-Brg-Pow-Rhn-1
Moore v. Illinois (1972)		
Schick v. Reed (1974)		
Gregg v. Georgia (1976)	Blm-Brg-Pow-Rhn-3	
Profitt v. Florida (1976)	Blm-1 Brg-Pow-Rhn-3	
Jurek v. Texas (1976)	Blm-1 Brg-Pow-Rhn-3	
Woodson v. North Carolina (1976)	Blm-Brg-1 Pow-Rhn-3	Pow-3
Roberts v. Louisiana (1976)	Blm-1 Brg-Rhn-3	Pow-3
Gardner v. Florida (1977)	Blm-Brg-1 Rhn-3	Blm-Brg-3 Pow-1
Roberts v. Louisiana (1977)	Rhn-2	Pow-3
Coker v. Georgia (1977)	Blm-Brg-Rhn-1	Blm-Pow-3
Lockett v. Ohio (1978)	Brg-Rhn-1	
Bell v. Ohio (1978)	Rhn-1	
	Rhn-1	
Godfrey v. Georgia (1980)	Brg-Rhn-2	Blm-Pow-1
Pulley v. Harris (1984)	Blm-Brg-Pow-Rhn-3	
California v. Brown (1987)	Pow-Rhn-3	Blm-1
McCleskey v. Kemp (1987)	Pow-Rhn-3	Blm-1
Sumner v. Shuman (1987)	Rhn-1	Blm-Pow-1
Maynard v. Cartwright (1988)		Blm-Rhn-1
Penry v. Lynaugh (1989)	Rhn-3	Blm-3
Gregg v. Georgia (1976) **c**	Brn-Mar-1	
Profitt v. Florida (1976)	Brn-Mar-1	
Jurek v. Texas (1976)	Brn-Mar-1	
Woodson v. North Carolina (1976)	Brn-Mar-1	
Roberts v. Louisiana (1976)	Brn-Mar-1	
Gardner v. Florida (1977)	Brn-Mar-1	
Roberts v. Louisiana (1977)	Brn-Mar-3	
Dobbert v. Florida (1977)	Brn-Mar-1	
Coker v. Georgia (1977)	Brn-Mar-1	

Table 7.3 (cont.)

Precedent/progeny	Preference	Precedent
Lockett v. Ohio (1978)	Mar-1	
Bell v. Ohio (1978)	Mar-1	
Godfrey v. Georgia (1980)	Brn-Mar-1	
Beck v. Alabama (1980)	Brn-Mar-1	
Adams v. Texas (1980)	Brn-Mar-1	
Eddings v. Oklahoma (1982)	Brn-1	
Zant v. Stephens (1982)	Brn-Mar-1	
Hopper v. Evans (1982)	Brn-Mar-1	
Enmund v. Florida (1982)	Brn-1 Mar-3	
Zant v. Stephens (1983)	Brn-Mar-1	
Pulley v. Harris (1984)	Brn-Mar-1	
Strickland v. Washington (1984)	Brn-Mar-1	
Wainwright v. Witt (1985)	Brn-Mar-1	
Baldwin v. Alabama (1985)	Brn-Mar-1	
Cabana v. Bullock (1986)	Brn-1 Mar-3	
Darden v. Wainwright (1986)	Brn-1	
California v. Brown (1987)	Brn-Mar-1	
Tison v. Arizona (1987)	Brn-Mar-1	
McCleskey v. Kemp (1987)	Brn-Mar-1	
Lowenfield v. Phelps (1988)	Brn-Mar-1	
Maynard v. Cartwright (1988)	Brn-Mar-1	
Johnson v. Mississippi (1988)	Brn-Mar-1	
Hildwin v. Florida (1989)	Brn-Mar-1	
Woodson v. North Carolina (1976) **c**		

Case		
Roberts v. Louisiana (1976)	Blm-Brg-Rhn-BW-1	Blm-BW-1
Gardner v. Florida (1977)	Rhn-1	
Roberts v. Louisiana (1977)	Blm-Brg-Rhn-BW-1	
Coker v. Georgia (1977)	Brg-Rhn-1	
Lockett v. Ohio (1978)	Rhn-BW-1	
Caldwell v. Mississippi (1985)		Blm-1
California v. Brown (1987)	Rhn-BW-1	Blm-1
Sumner v. Shuman (1987)	Rhn-3	
Tuilaepa v. California (1994)		
Coker v. Georgia (1977) **c**	Brg-Rhn-3	
Rummel v. Estelle (1980)		
Enmund v. Florida (1982) **c**	Brg-OC-Pow-Rhn-3	
Cabana v. Bullock (1986)	OC-Pow-Rhn-3	
Tison v. Arizona (1987)	OC-Rhn-1	
South Carolina v. Gathers (1989)		
Lockhart v. McCree (1986) **c**	Brn-Mar-Stv-1	
Buchanan v. Kentucky (1987)	Brn-Mar-Stv-2	
Holland v. Illinois (1990)		
Ford v. Wainwright (1986) **c**		
Penry v. Lynaugh (1989)	OC-Rhn-BW-2	

Legend: **c** = constitutional decision
s = statutory decision
= decision neither constitutionally nor statutorily based

Note: All progeny rest on the same decisional basis as the precedent unless otherwise indicated.

should neither be nor appear to be merely the subjective views of individual justices" (1980, 275).

Seven of the nine votes dissenters from *Enmund v. Florida* (1982), the felony murder rule case, cast are weakly preferential like the pair in *Coker*'s progeny: those of Burger, O'Connor, Powell, and Rehnquist in *Cabana v. Bullock* (1986), and, after Burger's retirement, those of the others in *Tison v. Arizona* (1987). O'Connor, however, joined by Rehnquist, references her *Enmund* opinion in *South Carolina v. Gathers* (1989).

Brennan, Marshall, and Stevens dissented from the decision in *Lockhart v. McCree* (1986), permitting the exclusion of anti–death penalty jurors from the guilt phase of a capital trial. In *Buchanan v. Kentucky* (1987), these justices again voice their opposition to death penalty–qualified juries, doing so moderately in *Holland v. Illinois* (1990). The majority decreed meritless a white defendant's Sixth Amendment challenge to the prosecution's peremptory exclusion of all black potential jurors.

Finally, in her opinion of the Court in *Penry v. Lynaugh* (1989), Justice O'Connor and the remaining dissenters from *Ford v. Wainwright* (1986) – Rehnquist and White – distinguished this precedent in order to sustain their preferences that death need not necessarily be disproportionate when inflicted on mentally retarded persons.

The Justices' Votes

Overall, dissenters from the Burger Court's capital punishment cases cast 161 progeny votes, 136 of which are preferential (84.9 percent). The liberals, however, as Table 7.3 shows, were inflexibly consistent (Brennan and Marshall, plus two votes from Stevens). All 64 of their votes support their preferences. By contrast, the conservatives (Blackmun, initially at least, and Burger, O'Connor, Powell, Rehnquist, and White) prove to be much more varied in their responses: 72 preference votes, 25 precedential (74.2 percent). Rehnquist and Burger support their preferences at about the 90 percent level, while Blackmun and Powell, remarkably considering the data we've seen so far, are closer to 50 percent. Arguably, precedent had some impact on these votes.

FEDERALISM

Capital punishment ends our focus on the Burger Court's criminal procedure landmarks. We turn now to federalism, an issue that did not warrant inclusion among the Warren Court's leading decisions. Although federal–state relationships excite the legal mind, they seem to have little effect on the public at large. Given its legalistic face, and the fact that issues of federalism are awash in technicalities, we expect that precedent may play a more important role than it does in other areas of Supreme Court decision making.

Douglas was the sole dissenter in *Younger v. Harris* (1971), the leading one of a number of cases that formulate the modern system of comity and its abstention doctrine. Federal courts, the majority held, will not interfere with ongoing state criminal proceedings except under the most grave circumstances. Douglas's objection was twofold: first, many of these state prosecutions adversely affect the exercise of First Amendment freedoms. Second, federal courts exist to vindicate federal rights. Litigants should not be required to run the gauntlet of state court proceedings before seeking vindication in federal courts. In twelve subsequent cases, Douglas adhered to his original stance. He stated his position well in *Huffman v. Pursue, Ltd.* (1975):

MR. JUSTICE DOUGLAS . . . wishes to make clear that he adheres to the view he expressed in *Younger v. Harris* . . . that federal abstention from interference with state criminal prosecutions is inconsistent with the demands of our federalism where important and overriding civil rights (such as those involved in the First Amendment) are about to be sacrificed. (1975, 618)

The dissenters from *Edelman v. Jordan* (1974) cast almost half the votes in this federalism set, 41 of 90. An Eleventh Amendment case, *Edelman* bars private suits imposing liability on states payable from public funds. Overruling four precedential decisions, the majority said that immunity garbs a state against a class action seeking retroactive payment for violations of the federal–state program of Aid to the Aged, Blind, and Disabled. In addition to overruling precedents, the majority limited the applicability of *Ex parte Young* (1908), the landmark Eleventh Amendment decision of the Fuller Court, to prospective relief only.

Lending credence to our assumption that cases pertaining to federalism would manifest more adherence to precedent than other more salient issues is the fact that the *Ex parte Young* dissenter, Justice Harlan, observed precedent in two of his three votes in progeny. That, however, does not prove to be the situation in *Edelman*. Of the 41 votes the *Edelman* dissenters cast, only two support precedent: those cast by Blackmun and Marshall in *Florida Department v. Treasure Salvors* (1982). But in joining the Court's judgment, they did so most strongly. Although the plurality ruled that the Eleventh Amendment did not bar the process the federal court employed, thereby supporting Blackmun's and Marshall's preferences, the opinion also said, "It is clear that the relief sought in this case is consistent with the principles of *Edelman v. Jordan*" (1982, 697). All the votes they otherwise cast, as well as those by Brennan, support their preferences.[25] Over 60 percent of these *Edelman* preference votes effectively reach strong preferential levels.

Probably generating more public attention than any of the other federalism landmarks of the Burger Court are the pair of cases involving the constitutionality of provisions of the Fair Labor Standards Act (FLSA), the maximum hour and minimum wage law of the federal government. In *National League of Cities v. Usery* (1976), the five-member majority declared unconstitutional FLSA amendments extending wage and hour provisions to most state and local government employees. Overruling *Maryland v. Wirtz* (1969), the majority ruled that the amendment directly displaces state ability to structure traditional governmental employee relationships, thereby exceeding the scope of the commerce clause. Justice Blackmun cast the swing vote and wrote a one paragraph concurring opinion:

Although I am not untroubled by certain possible implications of the Court's opinion . . . the result with respect to the statute under challenge here is necessarily correct. I may misinterpret the Court's opinion, but it seems to me that it adopts a balancing approach, and does not outlaw federal power in areas such as environmental protection, where the federal interest is demonstrably greater. (1976, 856)

Nine years later, Blackmun apparently had second thoughts and wrote the Court's opinion for himself and the *Usery* dissenters that the wage and hour requirements of the FLSA contravene no affirmative limit on Congress's power under the commerce clause as applied to a federally subsidized public mass-transit authority: *Garcia v. SAMTA* (1985).

In the four progeny of *Usery*, the dissenters voted their preferences: *Hodel v. Virginia Surface Mining* (1981), *United Transportation Union v. LI R. Co.* (1982), *EEOC v. Wyoming* (1983), and of course *SAMTA* itself. *SAMTA*, in turn, produced only one vote by a dissenter: that of O'Connor in *South Carolina v. Baker* (1988). Burger and Powell had retired, and Rehnquist specifically wrote in *Baker* that *SAMTA* was irrelevant, inasmuch as the Court's decision here rested on the Tenth Amendment rather than the commerce clause.

The last of the Burger Court's federalism landmarks, *Stone v. Powell* (1976), was decided the same year as *National League of Cities* and garners dissents from Brennan, Marshall, and White. Although the decision arguably contains enough of a criminal law dimension to warrant its inclusion among those cases, we chose not to include it therewith because the precedent does not address the merits of these controversies. It

---

[25] Douglas, the fourth dissenter, departed the Court before participating in any progeny.

focuses instead on the extent to which state *habeas* petitioners have access to a federal forum. The three dissenters evenly split their votes among *Stone*'s progeny, consistently reiterating their objections to the stringent conditions *Stone* imposed on such access.

The Justices' Votes

Notwithstanding its relatively low salience vis-à-vis the other subsets into which we have divided the Burger Court's decisions, only two of the 90 votes that dissenting justices cast in the progeny of the federalism landmarks support the precedent in question, a preferential proportion of 97.8 percent. The strength of the preferential votes divides 61–8–31 percent, respectively, as Table 7.4 shows.

CIVIL RIGHTS

The Burger Court's civil rights landmarks, not surprisingly, outnumber those of any other category into which we have divided these cases: 25. Because they lend themselves to subdivision, we will proceed accordingly.

School Segregation

San Antonio Independent School District v. Rodriguez (1973) holds that the Fourteenth Amendment could not equalize interdistrict discrepancies in school financing. White, Brennan, Douglas, and Marshall dissented on the basis that Texas's scheme was not rational. Except for White, they also viewed education as a fundamental – that is, constitutional – right. In *Massachusetts v. Murgia* (1976), *Maher v. Roe* (1977), and *Plyler v. Doe* (1982), Marshall explicitly adhered to his *Rodriguez* dissent. In *Plyler*, White separated himself from the other *Rodriguez* dissenters, citing the case as authority for no heightened scrutiny, a matter that White did not address in his *Rodriguez* dissent. As noted, his focus there was the irrationality of Texas's school financing. Nonetheless, we count White's *Plyler* vote as precedential because the *Plyler* scheme is clearly less rational than that in *Rodriguez*, the denial of public education to illegal immigrant alien children. We also count White's majority vote in *Kadrmas v. Dickinson Public Schools* (1988) as precedential.[26]

---

[26] Although we counted his vote as preferential in our earlier analysis (Segal and Spaeth 1996a, 982), reconsideration counsels reversal. While *Kadrmas* involves inequality markedly less severe than that in *Rodriguez*, the action of a local school board to charge a fee for busing children to school, the *Kadrmas* decision is conservative, and White's vote in *Rodriguez* was liberal, and nothing in the opinion overcomes this fact.

Table 7.4.
Voting and opinion behavior: Burger Court federalism cases

Justice	Prefs/prec		%Prefs	Level of Expression					
				Preferences (%)			Precedent (%)		
				Strong (1)	Moderate (2)	Weak (3)	Strong (1)	Moderate (2)	Weak (3)
Brennan (Brn)	24	0	100.0	16 (66.7)	1 (4.2)	7 (29.2)			
Douglas (Dou)	12	0	100.0	12 (100)					
White (BW)	10	0	100.0	4 (40.0)		6 (60.0)			
Stevens (Stv)	4	0	100.0	1 (25.0)		3 (75.0)			
O'Connor (OC)	1	0	100.0	1 (100)					
Marshall (Mar)	25	1	96.2	13 (52.0)	4 (16.0)	8 (32.0)	1 (100)		
Blackmun (Blm)	12	1	92.3	7 (58.3)	2 (16.7)	3 (25.0)	1 (100)		
Totals	88	2	97.8	54 (61.4)	7 (8.0)	27 (30.7)	2 (100)	0	0

Precedent/progeny	Preferences	Precedent
Younger v. Harris (1971)	Dou-1	
Boyle v. Landry (1971)	Dou-1	
Perez v. Ledesma (1971)	Dou-1	
Dyson v. Stein (1971)	Dou-1	
Lake Carriers' v. MacMullan (1972)	Dou-3	
Mitchum v. Foster (1972)	Dou-3	
O'Shea v. Littleton (1974)	Dou-2	
Steffel v. Thompson (1974)	Dou-3	
Huffman v. Pursue (1975)	Dou-1	
MTM v. Baxley (1975)	Dou-2	
Hicks v. Miranda (1975)	Dou-3	
Roe v. Norton (1975)	Dou-1	
Doran v. Salem Inn. (1975)	Dou-1	
Edelman v. Jordan (1974) c	Blm-Mar-2 Brn-1	
Fitzpatrick v. Bitzer (1976)	Brn-Blm-Mar-3	
Milliken v. Bradley (1977)	Blm-Mar-3 Brn-1	
Hutto v. Finney (1978)	Mar-2	
Cory v. White (1982)	Brn-1	Blm-Mar-1
Florida Dept. v. Treasure Salvors (1982)	Mar-2	
Guardians Assn. v. New York City CSC (1983)	Blm-Brn-Mar-2	
Pennhurst Hospital v. Halderman (1984)	Brn-Mar-1	
Oneida County v. Oneida Nation (1985)	Blm-Brn-Mar-1	
Atascadero Hospital v. Scanlon (1985)	Blm-Brn-Mar-1	
Green v. Mansour (1985)	Blm-Brn-Mar-1	
Papasan v. Allain (1985)	Blm-Brn-Mar-1	
Welch v. Texas Department (1986)	Blm-Brn-Mar-1	
Dellmuth v. Muth (1987)	Blm-Brn-Mar-1	
Missouri v. Jenkins (1989)	Blm-Brn-Mar-3	
PATH v. Feeney (1990)	Blm-Brn-Mar-1	
PR Authority v. Metcalf & Eddy (1993)	Blm-1	

Table 7.4 (cont.)

Precedent/progeny	Preferences	Precedent
National League of Cities v. Usury (1976) **c**		
Hodel v. Virginia Surface Mining (1981)	Brn-Mar-Stv-BW-3	
UTU v. LI R. Co. (1982)	Brn-Mar-Stv-BW-3	
EEOC v. Wyoming (1983)	Brn-Mar-Stv-BW-3	
Garcia v. SAMTA (1985)	Brn-Mar-Stv-BW-1	
Garcia v. SAMTA (1985) **c**		
South Carolina v. Baker (1988)	OC-1	
Stone v. Powell (1976)		
United States v. Janis (1976)	Brn-Mar-1	
United States v. Martinez-Fuerte (1976)	Brn-Mar-1	
Juidice v. Vail (1977)	Brn-Mar-1	
Mincey v. Arizona (1978)	Brn-Mar-1	
Rokas v. Illinois (1978)	Brn-Mar-BW-1	
Rose v. Mitchell (1979)	Brn-Mar-BW-3	
Illinois v. Gates (1983)	BW-1	
Kimmelman v. Morrison (1986)	Brn-Mar-BW-3	
Brecht v. Abrahamson (1993)	BW-1	
Withrow v. Williams (1993)	BW-3	

Legend: **c** = constitutional decision
  s = statutory decision
     = decision neither constitutionally nor statutorily based
Note: All progeny rest on the same decisional basis as the precedent unless otherwise indicated.

In the Burger Court's two remaining school cases, *Runyon v. McCrary* (1976) and *Columbus Board of Education v. Penick* (1979), Rehnquist dissented with White and Powell, respectively, The former concerns the compatibility of racially specific private schools under the 1866 Civil Rights Act; the latter, the affirmative duty to end unconstitutional segregation even though not mandated at the time the case began. The dissenters in both cases adhered to their preferences in the progeny:[27] *McDonald v. Santa Fe Transportation Co.* (1976), *General Bldg. Contractors v. Pennsylvania* (1982), *Patterson v. McLean Credit Union* (1989), *Estes v. Dallas NAACP* (1980), and *Washington v. Seattle School District* (1982).[28]

Affirmative Action

Regents v. Bakke (1978) accounts for 24 of the 48 votes cast by dissenters in progeny of the Burger Court's affirmative action decisions. Because of the peculiar division in *Bakke*,[29] we rather formalistically confine our specification of progeny votes to those where the justices cite either their own *Bakke* opinion or one that counters the position they took in that case. Accordingly, we count Blackmun, Brennan, and Marshall as strongly reasserting their preferences in *Fullilove v. Klutznick* (1980), *Guardians Assn. v. New York City CSC* (1983), *Firefighters v. Stotts* (1984), *Wygant v. Jackson Board of Education* (1986), *United States v. Paradise* (1987), and *Richmond v. J.A. Croson Co.* (1989); Rehnquist likewise in *Guardians Assn.* By contrast, Stevens and White strongly support an outcome opposite to their *Bakke* position in *Guardians Assn.* White also weakly does so in *Stotts*. White, however, strongly reverts to his *Bakke* position in *Wygant*, as does Stevens in *Johnson v. Transportation Agency* (1987).

As between affirmative action and the other major racial component of the Burger Court's civil rights decisions, school segregation, only half a percentage point separates their preferential voting: 94.3 percent in schools and 93.8 percent in affirmative action. However, the preferences

[27]   The votes of the justices in the school segregation cases are Marshall 10–0, Rehnquist 9–0, Brennan 5–0, Powell 2–0, and White 7–2.

[28]   *Patterson* classically illustrates weak preferential voting. The dissenters joined the majority opinion, which supported the conservative votes they cast in the *Runyon* precedent. This majority opinion flatly stated that *Runyon* controlled their decision because *stare decisis* so decrees (1989, 170–79). Dissenters in the progeny, who were members of the precedent's majority, vigorously protested the "needlessly cramped interpretation" and "most pinched reading" (1989, 189) of the precedent, which emasculated it while only formalistically adhering to precedent.

[29]   Four justices relied on the statute's plain meaning to void the racial preference plan; four others upheld the use of nonstigmatic racial classifications.

in the latter are much more forcefully expressed than in the school cases: 38 strong, 6 moderate, and 1 weak. In the former, 19 strong, 3 moderate, and 11 weak.[30]

Sex Discrimination

Although the Burger Court's sex discrimination landmarks are as numerous (five) as those pertaining to school desegregation and affirmative action (five and six, respectively), dissenters cast far fewer votes in progeny than in the other two sets.

In *General Electric Co. v. Gilbert* (1976), Brennan and Marshall adhere to the position they took in *Geduldig v. Aiello* (1974), that the equal protection clause requires a state to include normal pregnancy-related disabilities in its insurance program. In *Duren v. Missouri* (1979), Rehnquist reiterated the opposition he alone voiced in *Taylor v. Louisiana* (1975) to the automatic exemption of women from jury service. Joined by Burger, he referenced *Reed v. Reed* (1971) in his plurality opinion in *Michael M. v. Superior Court* (1981) rather than the landmark, *Craig v. Boren* (1976), which formulates the intermediate scrutiny test for purposeful discrimination based on sex. In *Craig*, he and Burger had insisted that the traditional "rational basis" test used in *Reed* suffices.[31]

Akin to the division in *Regents v. Bakke* (1978), the justices in *Arizona Governing Committee v. Norris* (1983) found themselves split into two four-member coalitions, with Justice O'Connor occupying the position of Powell in *Bakke*. Although the opinion of Marshall – the relevant part of which Brennan, Stevens, and White joined – is not labeled a dissent, whereas that of Powell, which, in relevant part, *five* justices joined, is identified as "dissenting in part and concurring part" (1983, 1095), we nonetheless must construe it as a dissent because of the opinions in *Florida v. Long* (1988), the sole progeny of *Norris*. The precedent holds that pension benefits may not vary on the basis of the recipient's sex when all employees pay the same premiums. Marshall and company objected to the majority's refusal to extend relief to contributions antedating the Court's decision. In the progeny, Marshall, Brennan, and Stevens object to the majority's refusal to treat sufficiently preferentially the victimized employees (1988, 244–45). White, however, voted precedentially, acceding to the nonpreferential aspects of *Norris*.

---

[30] The justices' votes are Rehnquist 10–0; Blackmun, Brennan, and Marshall 7–0, O'Connor 3–0; Burger 2–0; Stewart 1–0; Stevens 3–1; and White 5–2.

[31] Notwithstanding the heavy incidence of sex discrimination cases since the mid-1970s, most references to *Craig* cite it as authority for *jus tertii* standing rather than for its impact on women.

The final sexual landmark, *Grove City College v. Bell* (1984), held over the dissents of Brennan and Marshall that Title IX of the Educational Amendments of 1972 applies only to specific discriminatory programs, not to all those operated by the culpable institution.[32] In *Department of Transportation v. Paralyzed Veterans* (1986), the dissenters object to the use of *Grove City* to construe narrowly the prohibitions of the Rehabilitation Act of 1973.

Although the Burger Court's sex discrimination cases produce a preferential voting proportion a few points below that of school segregation and affirmative action, it still exceeds 90 percent (90.9). The intensity of expression, however, is markedly less than that in the other two sets, equally divided between strong and moderate voting.

Reapportionment and Voting

The single reapportionment and two voting cases occasioned the casting of 23 votes by dissenters in their progeny, all of which supported the justices' preferences. Brennan, Marshall, and Douglas, dissenting from the decision in *Mahan v. Howell* (1973) that upheld a 16 percent population variance in a state's legislative districts, vote consistently in *Gaffney v. Cummings* (1973), *White v. Regester* (1973), *Chapman v. Meier* (1975), *Connor v. Finch* (1977), and *Brown v. Thomson* (1983).

In the first of the two voting cases, *Mobile v. Bolden* (1980), Brennan, Marshall, and White dissent from the constitutionality of a city's at-large election system. They adhere to their preferences in *Williams v. Brown* (1980), *Rogers v. Lodge* (1982), and *Thornburg v. Gingles* (1986). In the last of these, Brennan wrote the opinion of the Court upholding Congress's amendment of the Voting Rights Act of 1965 that overturned *Mobile v. Bolden*, the precedent to which Brennan, Marshall, and White objected. In *Davis v. Bandemer* (1986), the majority held that political gerrymandering presents a justiciable question, but that its unconstitutionality initially requires a prima facie showing of vote dilution. In *Davis*'s single progeny, *Shaw v. Reno* (1993), Stevens reiterates his view disapproving of grotesquely shaped districts designed to deprive voters of electoral power.[33]

---

[32] Note may be made that *Grove City* is a favorite example of social choice theorists who focus on separation of powers games involving cases of statutory interpretation (Marks 1988; Gely and Spiller 1990; Segal 1997, 33).

[33] The strength of preferential voting mirrors that of school segregation: lower than affirmative action, but higher than sex discrimination: strong 13, moderate 2, weak 8.

Miscellaneous Civil Rights

Although these six cases cover a range of issues, their proportion of preferential voting reflects that of the preceding sections of the Burger Court's landmarks, 92.3 percent (36 of 39). One may quarrel with our inclusion of *Monell v. Dept. of Social Services* (1978) here rather than with federalism. Admittedly, it is a close question. The dissenters, Burger and Rehnquist, anchor the conservative spectrum on both dimensions. We give the nod to civil rights because the damage suits to which *Monell* subjects local officials arise under the Civil Rights Act of 1871. Inclusion in either category does not appreciably affect the resulting proportion of preferential voting.

In *Washington v. Davis* (1976) the majority ruled that more than disparate impact is necessary to establish discriminatory intent and thus a violation of the equal protection clause. Brennan and Marshall dissented, asserting that the statutory standards of Title VII are not met in job tests that far more blacks than whites failed. They maintain their expansive reading of civil rights liability in *Arlington Heights v. Metropolitan Housing Corp.* (1977), *Personnel Administrator v. Feeney* (1979), *Columbus Board of Education v. Penick* (1979), *Memphis v. Greene* (1981), and *Hernandez v. New York* (1991).

Arlington Heights v. Metropolitan Housing Corp. (1977), a progeny of *Washington v. Davis* (1976), is a precedent in its own right, albeit a problematic one as far as our purposes are concerned. The majority held that violations of the equal protection clause require a showing of discriminatory purpose or intent. Brennan and Marshall dissent in part, desiring that the entire case be remanded to the court of appeals because they view that court as better qualified to evaluate the record in light of the Court's decision in *Arlington Heights* and in *Washington v. Davis*. White also dissented, objecting to the majority's discussion of the standard for proving a racial discriminatory purpose. Given these procedural objections, we view the votes of Brennan, Marshall, and White in the progeny of the related case of *Washington v. Davis*, just discussed, as inapposite for consideration here.[34] Accordingly, we find only one prog-

---

[34] Two other cases arguably constitute precedents. In the unanimously liberal decision of *Hunter v. Underwood* (1985), the Court ruled that Alabama's disenfranchisement of persons convicted of certain crimes runs afoul of the purposeful discrimination established in *Arlington Heights*. We exclude this decision from consideration because the *Arlington Heights* dissenters objected procedurally, rather than substantively. We also exclude from consideration *Batson v. Kentucky* (1986), involving the use of peremptory challenges to exclude blacks from juries. We do so because the *Arlington Heights* dissenters do not disagree with that part of this decision the *Batson* Court relied on.

Inclusion of these cases and those mentioned in the text would produce none but preferential votes, however.

eny of *Arlington Heights: New York Authority v. Beazer* (1979). Here the dissent was grounded procedurally, with White asserting for himself, Marshall, and Brennan that *"Arlington Heights . . .* involved nearly identical circumstances" (1979, 598).

As mentioned, *Monell v. Department of Social Services* (1978) subjected local officials to liability for civil rights violations. In the process, it overruled the Warren Court's decision in *Monroe v. Pape* (1961) and of necessity revoked the absolute immunity of local governments. In its progeny, Burger and Rehnquist behaved preferentially except for Rehnquist's vote in *Canton v. Harris* (1989). Here he took a position more supportive of the city than the dissenters O'Connor, Scalia, and Kennedy. Hence, we count his vote as precedential even though it does allow the city another bite of the apple.

Conclusion

Little difference occurs across the subsets of the Burger Court's civil rights decisions in the level of preferential voting. Fewer than 10 percentage points separate the 100 percent of reapportionment/voting and the 90.9 percent of the small sex discrimination set. The overall average is 94.2 percent (147 of 156 votes). Markedly more variance characterizes the levels of preferential voting. Almost 85 percent of the affirmative action votes are strongly expressed, with only one of 45 votes weakly preferential (2.2 percent). School segregation and reapportionment/voting also exceed 50 percent strongly preferential (56.5 and 54.2 percent, respectively). Half of the ten preference votes in the small sex discrimination set strongly supports this behavior. Lowest are the miscellaneous civil rights landmarks, where fewer than a third of the preference votes are strongly so. At the other extreme, all but one of the weak preference votes locate in reapportionment/voting, school segregation, and miscellaneous civil rights, with respective percentages of 37.5, 33.3, and 26.5 percent.

The Justices' Votes

Eleven of the 13 justices who dissent from landmark civil rights decisions of the Burger Court participate in their progeny, as Table 7.5 indicates. Only Black and Harlan, who served for only the first two terms of the Court's existence, do not appear. Justice White accounts for over half the precedential votes (5 of 9). White also accounts for the majority of the precedential votes in the criminal procedure set (2 of 3). No other justice produces such a disproportionate share. But on the other hand,

Table 7.5.
Voting and opinion behavior: Burger Court civil rights cases

Justice	Prefs/prec		%Prefs	Preferences (%)			Level of Expression		
				Strong (1)	Moderate (2)	Weak (3)	Precedent (%) Strong (1)	Moderate (2)	Weak (3)
Marshall (Mar)	34	0	100.0	23 (67.6)	5 (14.7)	6 (17.6)			
Brennan (Brn)	28	0	100.0	17 (60.7)	5 (17.9)	6 (21.4)			
Blackmun (Blm)	7	0	100.0	7 (100)					
Douglas (Dou)	3	0	100.0	1 (50.0)		2 (50.0)			
Powell (Pow)	4	0	100.0	3 (75.0)		1 (25.0)			
O'Connor (OC)	3	0	100.0	2 (66.7)	1 (33.3)				
Stewart (Stw)	2	0	100.0	2 (100)					
Rehnquist (Rhn)	33	2	94.3	13 (39.4)	11 (33.3)	9 (27.3)		2 (100)	
Burger (Brg)	12	1	92.3	3 (25.0)	7 (58.3)	2 (16.7)		1 (100)	
Stevens (Stv)	5	1	83.3	4 (80.0)	1 (20.0)		1 (100)		
White (BW)	16	5	76.2	10 (62.5)	1 (6.3)	5 (31.3)	1 (20.0)	1 (20.0)	3 (60.0)
Totals	147	9	94.2	85 (57.8)	31 (21.1)	31 (21.1)	2 (22.2)	4 (44.4)	3 (33.3)

SCHOOL DESEGREGATION

Precedent/progeny	Preferences	Precedent
San Antonio Independent School Dist. v. Rodriguez (1973) c		
Massachusetts v. Murgia (1976)	Mar-1	
Maher v. Roe (1977)	Mar-1	BW-3
Plyler v. Doe (1982)	Mar-1	
Martinez v. Bynum (1983)	Mar-1	
Cleburne v. Cleburne Living Center (1985)	Mar-1	
Papasan v. Allain (1986)	Brn-Mar-BW-3	
Kadrmas v. Dickinson Public Schools (1988) c	Brn-Mar-1	BW-3
Keyes v. Denver School District (1973)	Rhn-3	
Milliken v. Bradley (1974)	Rhn-2	
Columbus Bd. of Education v. Penick (1979)	Rhn-2	
Dayton Bd. of Education v. Brinkman (1979)	Rhn-2	
Estes v. Dallas NAACP (1980)		
Milliken v. Bradley (1974) c	Brn-Mar-BW-1	
Hills v. Gautreaux (1976)	Brn-Mar-BW-3	
Milliken v. Bradley (1977)	Brn-Mar-BW-1	
Washington v. Seattle School Dist. (1982) s		
Runyon v. McCrary (1976) s	Rhn-BW-1	
McDonald v. Santa Fe Transp. Co. (1976)	Rhn-BW-3	
Genl. Bldg Contractors v. PA (1982)	Rhn-BW-3	
Patterson v. McLean Credit Union (1989) c		
Columbus Bd. of Education v. Penick (1979) c		
Estes v. Dallas NAACP (1980)	Pow-Rhn-1	
Washington v. Seattle School Dist. (1982)	Pow-Rhn-1	

Table 7.5 (*cont.*)

Precedent/progeny	Preferences	Precedent
AFFIRMATIVE ACTION		
Regents v. Bakke (1978) **c**		
Fullilove v. Klutznick (1980)	Blm-Brn-Mar-1	Stv-BW-1
Guardians Assn. v. New York City CSC (1983)	Blm-Brn-Mar-Rhn-1	BW-3
Firefighters v. Stotts (1984)	Blm-Brn-Mar-1	
Wygant v. Jackson Bd. of Education (1986)	Blm-Brn-Mar-BW-1	
United States v. Paradise (1987)	Stv-1	
Johnson v. Transportation Agency (1987)	Blm-Brn-Mar-1	
Richmond v. J.A. Croson Co. (1989) **s**		
Steelworkers v. Weber (1979) **s**		
Firefighters v. Cleveland (1986)	Bgr-Rhn-2	
Johnson v. Transportation Agency (1987)	Rhn-2	
Fullilove v. Klutznick (1980) **c**		
Minnick v. California Dept. (1981)	Rhn-Stw-1	
Richmond v. J.A. Croson Co. (1989)	Rhn-3 Stv-1	
Wygant v. Jackson Bd. of Education (1986) **c**		
Richmond v. J.A. Croson Co. (1989)	Blm-Brn-Mar-Stv-1	
Sheet Metal Workers v. EEOC (1986) **s**		
United States v. Paradise (1987)	OC-Rhn-BW-2	
Johnson v. Transportation Agency (1987)	OC-Rhn-BW-1	
Richmond v. J.A. Croson Co. (1989)	OC-Rhn-BW-1	
Firefighters v. Cleveland (1986) **s**		
Sheet Metal Workers v. EEOC (1986)	Brg-Rhn-1	
Johnson v. Transportation Agency (1987)	Rhn-BW-1	

SEX DISCRIMINATION

Gelduldig v. Aiello (1974) **c**	
GE Co. v. Gilbert (1976)	
Taylor v. Louisiana (1975) **c**	
Duren v. Missouri (1979)	
Craig v. Boren (1976) **c**	Brn-Mar-1
Michael M. v. Superior Court (1981)	Rhn-1
Arizona Committee v. Norris (1983) **s**	
Florida v. Long (1988)	Brg-Rhn-2
Grove City College v. Bell (1984) **s**	Brn-Mar-1 Stv-2 BW-2
Dept. of Transp. v. Paralyzed Vets (1986) **s**	Brn-Mar-2

REAPPORTIONMENT AND VOTING

Mahan v. Howell (1973) **c**	
Gaffney v. Cummings (1973)	Brn-Dou-Mar-1
White v. Regester (1973)	Brn-Dou-Mar-1
Chapman v. Meier (1975)	Brn-Dou-Mar-3
Connor v. Finch (1977)	Brn-Mar-3
Brown v. Thompson (1983)	Brn-Mar-2
Mobile v. Bolden (1980) **c**	
Williams v. Brown (1980)	Brn-Mar-BW-1
Rogers v. Lodge (1982)	Brn-Mar-BW-3
Thornburgh v. Gingles (1986)	Brn-Mar-BW-1
Davis v. Bandemer (1986) **c**	
Shaw v. Reno (1993)	Stv-1

Table 7.5 (cont.)

Precedent/progeny	Preferences	Precedent
MISCELLANEOUS CIVIL RIGHTS		
Albemarle Paper Co. v. Moody (1975) s		
Franks v. Bowman Transp. Co. (1976)	Brg-2	
Teamsters v. United States (1977)		Brg-2
Occidental Life Ins. Co. v. EEOC (1977)	Brg-2	
Los Angeles Dept. v. Manhart (1978)	Brg-2	
Washington v. Davis (1976) s		
Arlington Heights v. Metro Housing (1977)	Brn-Mar-2	
Personnel Administrator v. Feeney (1979)	Brn-Mar-2	
Columbus Bd. of Education v. Penick (1979)	Brn-Mar-3	
Memphis v. Greene (1981)	Brn-Mar-2	
Hernandez v. New York (1991)	Mar-1	
Arlington Heights v. Metro Housing (1977) c		
New York Transit Authority v. Beazer (1979)	Brn-Mar-BW-1	

Case		
Monell v. Dept. of Social Services (1978) **s**	Brg-Rhn-1	
Owen v. City of Independence (1980)	Brg-Rhn-1	
Maine v. Thiboutot (1980)	Brg-Rhn-3	
Newport v. Fact Concerts (1981)	Rhn-2	
Brandon v. Holt (1985)	Brg-Rhn-3	
Oklahoma City v. Tuttle (1985)	Brg-Rhn-2	
Pembaur v. Cincinnati (1986)	Rhn-2	
Springfield v. Kibbe (1987)		Rhn-3
Canton v. Harris (1989)	Rhn-3	
Will v. Michigan State Police (1989)		
Davis v. Passman (1979) **c**	Brg-2 Pow-Stw-1	
Carlson v. Green (1980)	Pow-Rhn-3	
United States v. Stanley (1987)		
Batson v. Kentucky (1986) **c**		
Hernandez v. New York (1991)	Rhn-3	
Edmondson v. Leesville Concrete Co. (1991)	Rhn-2	
Georgia v. McCollum (1992)		
J.E.B. v. Alabama (1994)	Rhn-1	Rhn-2

Legend: **c** = constitutional decision

s = statutory decision

= decision neither constitutionally nor statutorily based

Note: All progeny rest on the same decisional basis as the precedent unless otherwise indicated.

White voted completely preferentially in abortion (25 of 25) and federalism (10 of 10).

FIRST AMENDMENT

The eleven nonunanimous First Amendment landmarks of the Burger Court divide themselves into three categories: religion, campaign spending, and miscellaneous. As in the other sets of Burger Court decisions that we have considered, preferential voting remains high, 96.9 percent.

Religion

All four of the religion cases concern the establishment clause rather than free exercise, and they all produce nothing but preferential votes in their progeny. *Mueller v. Allen* (1983), upholding a state income tax deduction for tuition, textbooks, and transportation paid by parents of all schoolchildren against an establishment clause challenge, drew dissents from Brennan, Marshall, Blackmun, and Stevens. In its sole progeny, *Zobrest v. Catalina Foothills School District* (1993), Blackmun and Stevens adhere to their original position.[35] The second of the religion cases, *Lynch v. Donnelly* (1984), upheld the display of a municipally erected nativity scene. The dissenters – Brennan, Marshall, Blackmun, and Stevens – reiterated their position in *Allegheny County v. Greater Pittsburgh ACLU* (1990) and *Lee v. Weisman* (1992).

The other two religion cases are closely interrelated. The second, *Aguilar v. Felton* (1985), is a progeny of the first, *Wallace v. Jaffree* (1985); it is also a precedent itself; and both cases share the same progeny with one exception. The dissenters in *Wallace v. Jaffree* (1985), the moment of classroom silence case, cite it as authority for their votes in its equally salient progeny: *Grand Rapids v. Ball* (1985), *Aguilar v. Felton* (1985), *Edwards v. Aguillard* (1987), *Allegheny County v. Greater Pittsburgh ACLU* (1990), *Lee v. Weisman* (1992), and *Kiryas Joel Board of Education v. Grumet* (1994).

The three *Jaffree* dissenters, Burger, Rehnquist, and White, added O'Connor as a fourth member and used their *Aguilar* dissents to support their votes in the same progeny as applies to *Jaffree* except *Edwards v.*

[35] Although the three concurring opinions in *Witters v. Washington Department* (1986) all criticize the majority – which includes the four *Mueller* dissenters – for their failure to reference that decision, which they said "strongly supports the result we reach today" (1986, 490), we do not consider it a progeny of *Mueller* precisely because – compatibly with our decision rules – the majority opinion views it as inapposite. Not only does the syllabus not reference it, the majority opinion cites it only once, and then solely to quote a brief passage from *Lemon v. Kurtzman*.

Aguillard. This case voided a Louisiana requirement that forbade the teaching of evolution unless accompanied by instruction in "creation science." *Aguilar*, by contrast, pertains to the employment of public remedial and counseling personnel in parochial schools.[36]

Campaign Spending

The first of the three landmark campaign spending cases is the original one that the Court decided: the highly fractionalized decision in *Buckley v. Valeo* (1976). Justice White dissented from the holding that Federal Election Campaign Act limits on candidate spending violate the First Amendment. Blackmun and Burger dissented from the ruling that candidate spending limits imposed on individuals and organizations do not violate the First Amendment. Rehnquist and Burger dissented from the public financing of presidential elections. Although Rehnquist cast no relevant vote in any of *Buckley*'s progeny, the other three dissenters did. All of these were preferentially consistent: Blackmun in *California Medical Assn. v. FEC* (1981),[37] White in *Citizens Against Rent Control v. Berkeley* (1981) and *Steelworkers v. Sadlowski* (1982), Burger and White in *FEC v. National Conservative PAC* (1985), and White and Blackmun in *FEC v. Massachusetts Citizens for Life* (1987).

The four justices who dissented in *First National Bank v. Bellotti* (1978), which declared unconstitutional a state law prohibiting corporate campaign expenditures – Brennan, Marshall, White, and Rehnquist – never voted together in dissent in any other case during the 19 years they all served on the Supreme Court (1972–1990). This may explain why their votes in *Bellotti*'s progeny do not sustain their preferences especially well. Brennan cast two precedential votes, and Marshall one, out of the total of 19 that the four collectively cast.

Although *Central Hudson G&E Co. v. PSC* (1980) does not concern campaign spending, Rehnquist bases his opinion directly on his *Bellotti* dissent. Hence, we count his vote. On the other hand, we exclude

---

[36] The votes of the justices in the religion cases are Rehnquist 10–0, White 5–0, Blackmun and Stevens 3–0, O'Connor and Burger 2–0, and Brennan and Marshall 1–0.

[37] Blackmun in his opinion in this case makes an insubstantial bow in the direction of precedent:

> Although I dissented in part in *Buckley* ... I am willing to accept as binding the Court's judgment ... that the contribution limitations challenged there were constitutional. But it does not follow that I must concur in the plurality conclusion today that political contributions are not entitled to full First Amendment protection. ... It was to such language that I referred when I suggested in my dissent that the Court had failed to make a principled constitutional distinction between expenditure and contribution limits [footnotes omitted]. (1981, 202)

Consolidated Edison v. New York PSC (1980) from consideration even though it cites *Bellotti* in its syllabus. We omit it because it does not pertain to campaign spending, but rather to purely commercial speech,[38] and because *Bellotti* merely serves as a convenient, but by no means necessary, negative premise from which to commence analysis: that is, a state may not confine corporate speech to specified issues (1980, 533). The Court, rather, "must consider whether the State can demonstrate that its regulation is constitutionally permissible" (Id. 535).

Unlike the other *Bellotti* dissenters, Rehnquist specifically says his *Bellotti* opinion "does not come into play" in *Citizens Against Rent Control v. Berkeley* (1981, 300); therefore, we exclude him. On its face, however, his *Berkeley* vote supports his *Bellotti* preferences. *Berkeley* concerned an ordinance limiting to $250 contributions to committees supporting or opposing ballot initiatives. White and Marshall voted their *Bellotti* preferences, while Brennan adhered to precedent by silently joining the majority that voided the ordinance.

The *Bellotti* dissenters maintained their preferences in *FEC v. National Right to Work Committee* (1987), *FEC v. NCPAC* (1985), and *Austin v. Michigan Chamber of Commerce* (1990), except for Rehnquist in *NCPAC*, where he again disclaimed reliance on *Bellotti*. But in *FEC v. Massachusetts Citizens for Life* (1987), though Brennan's opinion of the Court, which Marshall joined, feebly attempts to distinguish *Bellotti*, they nonetheless fail to sustain their original position, thereby voting precedentially.

FEC v. NCPAC (1985), a progeny of *Bellotti*, is also a precedent in its own right. Over the dissents of Marshall and White,[39] the majority voided a $1000 limit on political action committee (PAC) contributions to publicly funded presidential campaigns. White said that congressional authority overrides the First Amendment because the government's interest meets strict scrutiny (1985, 507–8), an assertion with which Marshall essentially agreed (Id. 521).

In *Austin v. Michigan Chamber of Commerce* (1990), which is also a progeny of *Bellotti*, Marshall and White adhere to their preferences, as does White in *FEC v. Massachusetts Citizens for Life* (1986). In the latter case, Marshall silently joins the Court's opinion, which distinguished *NCPAC*. Although we counted Marshall's vote as supporting precedent

---

[38]   A regulation that prohibited public utilities from including with their monthly bills inserts discussing various public policy issues. Moreover, the three separate opinions make only a single nonsubstantive reference to *Bellotti*.

[39]   Brennan also dissented, but only that the Democratic Party lacked standing to sue, a matter not relevant to any of the case's progeny in which Brennan participated.

in our original analysis (Segal and Spaeth 1996a, 995), reconsideration counsels against counting Marshall's vote as either precedent or preference.[40] The opinion which he joined presents three reasons for the irrelevance of *Citizens for Life* (1986, 259): (1) The organization does not pose the potential for unfair deployment of wealth for political purposes; (2) it was formed to disseminate political ideas, not to amass capital; (3) it differs from organizations that have been the focus of campaign spending regulation.

Miscellaneous First Amendment Landmarks

The progeny of the four miscellaneous First Amendment landmarks show only one precedential vote, that of Burger in *Branti v. Finkel* (1980), a progeny of *Elrod v. Burns* (1976). Burger, along with Rehnquist and Powell, disagreed with the *Elrod* majority that freedom of association precludes patronage dismissals of public employees. The dissenters voted consistently in the other progeny: Rehnquist in *Abood v. Detroit Board of Education* (1977) and *Rutan v. Illinois GOP* (1990); all three in *Davis v. Passman* (1979); and Powell and Rehnquist in *Branti v. Finkel* (1980).

Generating the vast majority of votes by dissenters is the celebrated obscenity case, *Miller v. California* (1973), all 61 of which not surprisingly upheld the dissenters' preferences. Of the Burger Court landmarks, only the 63 progeny votes of *Furman v. Georgia* (1972) exceeded the number spawned by *Miller*.[41]

The other two miscellaneous First Amendment cases each produce a pair of progeny, in which all six votes cast support the dissenters' preferences. *Branzburg v. Hayes* (1972), which denied journalists a First Amendment right to refuse to disclose confidential sources of information, is cited by Stewart and Marshall as authority in *Zurcher v. Stanford Daily* (1978) and by Stewart and Brennan in *Houchins v. KQED* (1978). Rehnquist, dissenting alone in *Richmond Newspapers v. Virginia* (1980), which asserted that the First Amendment afforded the public a right of access to criminal trials, maintains his position in *Globe Newspaper Co. v. Superior Court* (1982) and *Press-Enterprise v. Superior Court* (1986).

---

[40] We counted White's vote, however, because he ignored the differences between *NCPAC* and *Citizens for Life* by explicitly resting his vote on his *NCPAC* dissent (1986, 271).

[41] The Warren Court's leading obscenity case, *Roth v. United States* (1957), also produces a disproportionate number of votes in progeny, 54. Only *Miranda v. Arizona* has more, 56.

Conclusion

Collectively, the three components of the Burger Court's First Amendment landmarks do not appreciably vary from the proportion of preferential votes produced by dissenters in the other categories into which we have divided these decisions. (See Tables 7.1–7.6.) The percent preferential ties criminal procedure at 96.9 percent, slightly behind the perfectly preferential abortion set and federalism at 97.8 percent. Notably, perhaps, the preferences of the First Amendment dissenters are expressed markedly more strongly than those of any other set. Almost 80 percent of these votes are strongly supported, as Table 7.6 shows. This result obtains because 59 of these 99 votes are cast in progeny of *Miller v. California*, the obscenity case. Without *Miller*, the proportion of strong preferences decreases to 61.5 percent. This brings it into line with the other preceding sets, which range between 65.3 and 54.5 percent.

The Justices' Votes

As in civil rights cases, all but the two most briefly serving members of the Burger Court participated in the progeny of the Court's landmark First Amendment decisions – Black and Harlan. Table 7.6 displays the justices' votes. The rankings of the justices at the preference/precedent extremes of Tables 7.5 and 7.6 are somewhat inverted. Whereas Marshall and Brennan are first and second on civil rights, only Burger ranks lower than they on the First Amendment. This, of course, results because they cast three of the four precedential votes in the First Amendment set (all in progeny of *First National Bank v. Bellotti* [1978]), a campaign spending case. At the other extreme, Rehnquist, Stewart, and White – who occupy three of the bottom five positions on civil rights (again because of a preponderance of precedential votes) – locate at the top of the First Amendment cases, where they collectively cast naught but preferential votes (51).

GOVERNMENTAL IMMUNITY

Although four of the Burger Court's landmarks concern governmental immunity, this set contains far fewer votes in progeny than any of the others, 20. Only the two separation of powers decisions, the succeeding set, have fewer, seven votes. Also distinguishing governmental immunity decisions is the markedly lower proportion of preferential votes, 75 percent.

In the single progeny of *United States v. Brewster* (1972), the two participating dissenters split their votes. *Brewster* holds that the speech or debate clause does not apply to senators who solicit bribes. In *United States v. Helstoski* (1979), Brennan reiterates his *Brewster* views, while White silently joins the majority's opinion, which favorably cites the *Brewster* precedent.

Butz v. Economou (1978) accounts for half the votes cast in the progeny of the governmental immunity decisions. The Court ruled that absolute immunity does not cloak federal officials from liability for violations of constitutional rights. They have only qualified immunity. Of the three dissenters who participate in *Butz*'s progeny – Burger, Rehnquist, and Stevens – Stevens accounts for all three of the precedential votes that the progeny produces. Indeed, with but a single exception, *Nixon v. Fitzgerald* (1982), he adheres to the *Butz* precedent in these cases. In none of the cases in which he upholds precedent does he articulate his reasons for doing so. In each, he silently joins the majority opinion. Burger and Rehnquist vote consistently in *Nixon*, *Harlow*, and *Cleavenger*. We do not count their votes or that of Stewart in *Davis v. Passman* because Burger and Rehnquist view the case as turning on separation of powers rather than the speech or debate clause (1979, 249). Stewart does not reach the question of immunity. Because the respondent was a member of Congress, the threshold question for him is the applicability of the speech or debate clause to Passman's conduct.

The adjacent cases of *Nixon v. Fitzgerald* (1982) and *Harlow v. Fitzgerald* (1982) are the two remaining precedents in this set. *Nixon* holds the President to be absolutely immune from civil damages for his official actions; *Harlow*, that only qualified immunity protects presidential aides. *Harlow* serves as a progeny of *Nixon* in that all four dissenters vote preferentially: Brennan, Marshall, Blackmun, and White. Burger, the sole dissenter in *Harlow*, votes his preferences in three of its four progeny. He supports the precedent – albeit marginally – in the last of this series of cases, *Malley v. Briggs* (1986).

Notwithstanding the very small number of votes in this set, only the death penalty and civil rights produce a higher absolute number of precedential votes than governmental immunity. Reflecting this fact is its ratio of one precedential vote for every three supporting preferences. Only the remaining set, separation of powers, with but seven progeny votes, displays proportionately more precedential voting. Perhaps the conjunction of the issue with other constitutional provisions explains the relatively high incidence of precedential voting, or the novelty of these cases in comparison with such conventional matters as criminal procedure and First Amendment freedom. Table 7.7 contains the votes of the justices.

Table 7.6.
Voting and opinion behavior: Burger Court First Amendment cases

| | | | | Level of Expression | | | | | |
| | | | | Preferences (%) | | | Precedent (%) | | |
Justice	Prefs/prec		%Prefs	Strong (1)	Moderate (2)	Weak (3)	Strong (1)	Moderate (2)	Weak (3)
Rehnquist (Rhn)	20	0	100.0	15 (75.0)	3 (15.0)	2 (10.0)			
Stewart (Stw)	16	0	100.0	16 (100)					
White (BW)	15	0	100.0	9 (60.0)	2 (13.3)	4 (26.7)			
Douglas (Dou)	9	0	100.0	7 (77.8)	2 (22.2)				
Blackmun (Blm)	5	0	100.0	2 (40.0)	1 (20.0)	2 (40.0)			
Stevens (Stv)	3	0	100.0	1 (33.3)	1 (33.3)	1 (33.3)			
O'Connor (OC)	2	0	100.0	2 (100)					
Powell (Pow)	2	0	100.0	2 (100)					
Marshall (Mar)	26	1	96.3	21 (80.8)	1 (3.8)	4 (15.4)			1 (100)
Brennan (Brn)	24	2	92.3	21 (87.5)		3 (12.5)			2 (100)
Burger (Brg)	4	1	80.0	3 (75.0)		1 (25.0)	0	1 (100)	
Totals	126	4	96.9	99 (78.6)	10 (7.9)	17 (13.5)	0	1 (25.0)	3 (75.0)

Precedent/progeny	Preferences	Precedent
RELIGION		
Mueller v. Allen (1983) **c**	Blm-Stv-2	
Zobrest v. Catalina Foothills Sch. Dist. (1993)		
Lynch v. Donnelly (1984) **c**	Blm-Brn-Mar-Stv-1	
Allegheny County v. Grtr. Pittsburgh ACLU (1990)	Blm-Stv-3	
Lee v. Weisman (1992)		
Wallace v. Jaffree (1985) **c**		
Grand Rapids v. Ball (1985)	Rhn-1	
Aguilar v. Felton (1985)	Brg-Rhn-1	
Edwards v. Aguillard (1987)	Rhn-1	
Allegheny County v. Grtr. Pittsburgh ACLU (1990)	Rhn-BW-1	
Lee v. Weisman (1992)	Rhn-BW-1	
Kiryas Joel Bd. of Education v. Grumet (1994)	Rhn-BW-1	
Aguilar v. Felton (1985) **c**	Brg-OC-1 Rhn-2	
Grand Rapids Sch. Dist. v. Ball (1985)	Rhn-BW-1	
Allegheny County v. Grtr. Pittsburgh ACLU (1990)	Rhn-BW-1	
Lee v. Weisman (1992)	OC-Rhn-1	
Kiryas Joel Bd. of Education v. Grumet (1994)		
CAMPAIGN SPENDING		
Buckley v. Valeo (1976) **c**	Blm-1	
California Medical Assn. v. FEC (1981)	BW-1	
Citizens v. Berkeley (1981)	BW-2	
Steelworkers v. Sadlowski (1982)	Brg-3 BW-1	
FEC v. Natl. Conservative PAC (1985)	Blm-3 BW-1	
FEC v. Citizens for Life		

Table 7.6 (cont.)

Precedent/progeny	Preferences	Precedent
1st National Bank v. Bellotti (1978) **c**	Rhn-1	
Central Hudson G&E v. PSC (1980)	Mar-2 BW-1	Brn-3
Citizens v. Berkeley (1981)	Brn-Mar-Rhn-BW-3	
FEC v. Natl. Right to Work Comtee. (1982)	Brn-Mar-BW-3	
FEC v. NCPAC (1985)	Rhn-1 BW-2	Brn-Mar-3
FEC v. Citizens for Life (1987)	Brn-Mar-Rhn-BW-3	
Austin v. Michigan C. of C. (1990)		
FEC v. NCPAC (1985) **c**	BW-1	
FEC v. Citizens for Life (1986)	Mar-BW-3	
Austin v. Michigan C. of C. (1990)		
MISCELLANEOUS		
Branzburg v. Hayes (1972) **c**	Mar-Stw-1	
Zurcher v. Stanford Daily (1978)	Brn-Stw-1	
Houchins v. KQED (1978)		
Miller v. California (1973) **c**		
Paris Adult Theatre I v. Slaton (1973)	Brn-Dou-Mar-Stw-1	
Kaplan v. California	Brn-Dou-Mar-Stw-1	
United States v. 12 200-Ft Reels (1973)	Brn-Dou-Mar-Stw-1	
United States v. Orito (1973)	Brn-Mar-Stw-1 Dou-2	
Heller v. New York (1973)	Brn-Dou-Mar-Stw-1	
Alexander v. Virginia (1973)	Brn-Dou-Mar-Stw-1	
Hamling v. United States (1974)	Brn-Mar-Stw-1 Dou-2	

Case		
Jenkins v. Georgia (1974)	Brn-Dou-Mar-Stw-1	
Erznoznik v. Jacksonville (1975)	Dou-1	
McKinney v. Alabama (1976)	Brn-Mar-Stw-1	
Marks v. United States (1977)	Brn-Mar-Stw-1	
Smith v. United States (1977)	Brn-Mar-Stw-1	
Splawn v. California (1977)	Brn-Mar-Stw-1	
Ward v. Illinois (1977)	Brn-Mar-Stw-1	
Pinkus v. United States (1978)	Brn-Mar-Stw-1	
New York v. Ferber (1982)	Brn-Mar-1	
Maryland v. Macon (1985)	Brn-Mar-1	
Pope v. Illinois (1987)	Brn-Mar-1	
Fort Wayne Books v. Indiana (1989)	Brn-Mar-1	
Sable Communications v. FCC (1989)	Brn-Mar-1	
Elrod v. Burns (1976) **c**	Rhn-1	
Abood v. Detroit Bd. of Education (1977)	Brg-Pow-Rhn-1	
Davis v. Passman (1979)	Pow-Rhn-1	Brg-2
Branti v. Finkel (1980)	Rhn-1	
Rutan v. Illinois GOP (1990)		
Richmond Newspapers v. Virginia (1980) **c**		
Globe News Co. v. Superior Court (1982)	Rhn-2	
Press-Enterprise v. Superior Court (1986)	Rhn-2	

Legend: **c** = constitutional decision

  s = statutory decision

  = decision neither constitutionally nor statutorily based

Note: All progeny rest on the same decisional basis as the precedent unless otherwise indicated.

Table 7.7.
Voting and opinion behavior: Burger Court governmental immunity cases

Justice	Prefs/prec		%Prefs	Preferences (%) Strong (1)	Moderate (2)	Weak (3)	Level of Expression — Precedent (%) Strong (1)	Moderate (2)	Weak (3)
Rehnquist (Rhn)	3	0	100.0		2 (66.7)	1 (33.3)			
Brennan (Brn)	2	0	100.0	2 (100)					
Blackmun (Blm)	1	0	100.0	1 (100)					
Marshall (Mar)	1	0	100.0	1 (100)					
Burger (Brg)	6	1	85.7	1 (16.7)	3 (50.0)	2 (33.3)			1 (100)
White (BW)	1	1	50.0	1 (100)				1 (100)	
Stevens (Stv)	1	3	25.0			1 (100)			3 (100)
Totals	15	5	75.0	6 (40.0)	5 (33.3)	4 (27.7)	0	1 (20.0)	4 (80.0)

Precedent/progeny	Preferences	Precedent
United States v. Brewster (1972) **c**	Brn-1	BW-2
United States v. Helstoski (1979)		
Butz v. Economou (1978)		Stv-3
Davis v. Passman (1979)	Brg-Rhn-Stv-3	
Nixon v. Fitzgerald (1982)	Brg-Rhn-2	Stv-3
Harlow v. Fitzgerald (1982)	Brg-Rhn-2	Stv-3
Cleavenger v. Saxner (1985)		
Nixon v. Fitzgerald (1982)	Blm-Brn-Mar-BW-1	
Harlow v. Fitzgerald (1982)		
Harlow v. Fitzgerald (1982)	Brg-3	
Davis v. Scherer (1984)	Brg-1	
Mitchell v. Forsyth (1985)	Brg-2	
Cleavenger v. Saxner (1985)		
Malley v. Briggs (1986)		Brg-3

Legend: **c** = constitutional decision

s = statutory decision

= decision neither constitutionally nor statutorily based

Note: All progeny rest on the same decisional basis as the precedent unless otherwise indicated.

SEPARATION OF POWERS

Only two of the nonunanimous Burger Court landmark decisions pertain to separation of powers, *INS v. Chadha* (1983) and *Bowsher v. Synar* (1986). In both cases, the Court declared congressional laws unconstitutional. *Chadha* voided the one-house legislative veto; *Bowsher*, a progeny of *Chadha*, the authorization of the comptroller general to perform certain executive functions.

White and Rehnquist separately dissent in *Chadha*: White on the main issue in the case and on the question of the severability of the unconstitutional provision from the rest of the statute; Rehnquist, only on severability. In *Bowsher*, the first of *Chadha*'s two progeny, White again dissents. Citing *Chadha*, he says, "I have expressed my view that the Court's recent efforts to police the separation of powers have rested on untenable constitutional propositions leading to regrettable results. . . . Today's result is even more misguided" (1986, 759). Because *Bowsher* involves no severability issue, Rehnquist's vote is irrelevant.

The other progeny of *Chadha* is *Alaska Airlines v. Brock* (1987). In a unanimous decision, the justices all hold that a legislative veto provision of the Airline Deregulation Act of 1978 pertaining to the right of furloughed employees to be rehired first is severable from other provisions. Neither White nor Rehnquist disagrees. Hence, both votes are precedential.

Blackmun, rather than Rehnquist, joins White in dissent in *Bowsher*. Their separate opinions echo one another. White: "The Court's decision rests on a feature of the legislative scheme that is of minimal practical significance and that presents no substantial threat to the basic scheme of separation of powers" (1986, 759). Blackmun: "I cannot see the sense of invalidating legislation of this magnitude in order to preserve a cumbersome, 65-year-old removal power that has never been exercised and appears to have been forgotten until this legislation" (1986, 778). In the two progeny, *Morrison v. Olson* (1989) and *Mistretta v. United States* (1989), both justices vote compatibly with their *Bowsher* position that no violation of separation of powers occurred.

This small set, presaging perhaps Supreme Court oversight of legislative–executive relationships, produces the lowest proportion of preferential voting, 71.4 percent. Only the next smallest set, immunity, approximates this percentage (75.0 percent). Moreover, four of the five preferential votes, along with both precedential votes, are weakly so. No other Burger Court set even remotely matches this low level. The three relevant justices voted as follows: Blackmun 2–0, White 3–1, and Rehnquist 0–1.

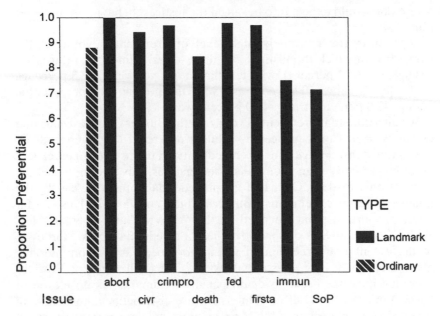

Figure 7.1. Precedential/preferential behavior on the Burger Court.

CONCLUSION

The proportion of preferential votes cast by dissenting justices in the progeny of landmark cases of the Burger Court exceeds – albeit slightly – that of any other Court: 93.2 percent. Closest to it are the Waite and Fuller Courts, 92.3 and 92.4 percent, respectively. As Figure 7.1 shows, five of the eight sets into which we divide these cases show preferential voting well above 90 percent: abortion, 100; federalism, 97.8, criminal procedure and First Amendment, 96.9; and civil rights, 94.3 percent. Only the two smallest sets, immunity and separation of powers, deviate appreciably from this pattern, at 75.0 and 71.4 percent, respectively. The relatively low levels of preferential voting in this pair of sets may result from the novelty of these issues. Rarely did earlier Courts consider these types of questions.

The death penalty positions itself midway between the foregoing extremes, at 84.9 percent. Twenty-one of the 25 precedential votes, however, are cast in progeny of *Furman v. Georgia* (1972). If we exclude *Furman* from consideration, 94 of the remaining 98 votes support the relevant justices' preferences, 95.9 percent. This places this category where one would expect it to be, given the justices' behavior in the other salient sets.

Supporting the extremely high level of preferential voting is the strength with which the justices cast these votes. Almost two-thirds are strongly so (64.2 percent), with less than a quarter weak (23.3 percent), as Table 7.8 shows. This contrasts with the intensity of precedential voting: 42.0 percent strong, 44.0 percent weak.

We also note that preferential voting on the Burger Court exceeds that of the Warren Court justices by a full five percent (93.2 versus 88.2). Given that conservative courts reputedly attach themselves to precedent more consistently than their liberal adversaries, this finding belies the conventional wisdom. Over half the precedential votes were cast by the nonliberal justices Rehnquist, Burger, White, and Powell. This is a far lower proportion than prevailed on the Warren Court where Harlan, White, Clark, and Stewart cast 50 of the 51 precedential votes. Moreover, to the extent that precedential voting does occur, it is nonrandomly distributed to a very substantial extent. Thus, all eight of Powell's precedential votes occur in death penalty landmarks, as do eleven of Blackmun's twelve. Half of White's ten are civil rights connected, and three of Stevens's occur in the progeny of a single governmental immunity landmark.

We also note some fluctuation in the behavior of the holdover justices from the Warren Court. Douglas again cast no precedential votes, and Brennan only two among his 132. White, though increasing his proportion of preferential votes on the Burger Court, remains relatively low: 82.1 to 88.9 percent. Most deviant, other than Black with his single Burger Court vote, is Stewart. Lowest on the Warren Court with a preferential ratio of 75.7 percent, all 22 of his Burger Court votes supported his preferences. A large part of the explanation results from his votes (14) in progeny of the obscenity case, *Miller v. California* (1973).

COMMON LITIGATION

Although the Burger Court existed for only a year longer than the Warren Court, our sample of ordinary litigation contains 36 cases, as compared with 24 for the Warren Court. More substantially, 22 precedents produce progeny in which the precedent's dissenters participated, as opposed to ten such Warren Court cases. But most significantly, these Burger Court precedents generate 125 votes, almost six per precedent, as contrasted with only 38 in the Warren Court, fewer than four per precedent.

The initial Burger Court precedent producing dissenters' votes in

Table 7.8.
Voting and opinion behavior: Burger Court landmarks

				Level of Expression					
				Preferences (%)			Precedent (%)		
Justice	Prefs/prec		%Prefs	Strong (1)	Moderate (2)	Weak (3)	Strong (1)	Moderate (2)	Weak (3)
Douglas (Dou)	29	0	100.0	24 (83.3)	3 (10.0)	2 (6.7)			
O'Connor (OC)	26	0	100.0	19 (73.1)	2 (7.7)	5 (19.2)			
Stewart (Stw)	22	0	100.0	20 (90.9)	1 (4.5)	1 (4.5)			
Marshall (Mar)	146	2	98.6	106 (72.6)	17 (11.6)	23 (15.8)	1 (50.0)		1 (50.0)
Brennan (Brn)	130	2	98.5	100 (76.9)	11 (8.5)	19 (14.6)			2 (100)
Rehnquist (Rhn)	117	5	95.9	58 (48.7)	22 (19.3)	37 (31.9)	2 (40.0)	2 (40.0)	1 (20.0)
Burger (Brg)	44	5	89.8	17 (38.6)	12 (27.3)	15 (34.1)	1 (20.0)	2 (40.0)	2 (40.0)
White (BW)	80	10	88.9	46 (57.5)	8 (10.0)	26 (32.5)	3 (30.0)	3 (30.0)	4 (40.0)
Stevens (Stv)	27	4	87.1	13 (48.1)	6 (22.2)	8 (29.6)	1 (25.0)		3 (75.0)
Blackmun (Blm)	45	13	79.3	29 (64.4)	3 (6.7)	13 (28.9)	9 (69.2)		4 (30.8)
Powell (Pow)	15	8	65.2	5 (33.3)		10 (66.7)	4 (50.0)		4 (50.0)
Black (Blk)	0	1	0.0						1 (100)
Totals	681	50	93.2	437 (64.2)	85 (12.5)	159 (23.3)	21 (42.0)	7 (14.0)	22 (44.0)

progeny is *Rosenbloom v. Metromedia* (1971), a libel action in which a radio broadcast allegedly defamed the plaintiff. Unable to reach an opinion, the majority essentially concluded that the *New York Times* (1964) standard of actual malice applied because the plaintiff, though not a public figure, was involved in a newsworthy event. The dissenters – Harlan, Marshall, and Stewart – objected to the extension of private libels to the *New York Times* rule if they arise out of events of "public or general concern" (1971, 62). This results, said Marshall, in "ad hoc balancing of the two interests involved. The Court is required to weigh the nuances of each particular circumstance on its scale of values regarding the relative importance of society's interest in protecting individuals from defamation against the importance of a free press" (Id. 81).

After Harlan's retirement, Marshall and Stewart joined the majority opinion in *Gertz v. Robert Welch, Inc.* (1974), which favorably cited Marshall's dissent in the precedent. In *Time, Inc. v. Firestone* (1975), Marshall dissented, while Stewart joined a regular concurrence. Both, however, voted their preferences. Marshall expressly referenced his *Rosenbloom* dissent, while Stewart "adheres to the principles of *Gertz*" (1975, 464), a progeny of the precedent in which, as noted, he clearly voted his preferences. In *Herbert v. Lando* (1979), in separate dissenting opinions, Marshall and Stewart disapproved of the apparently untrammeled discovery into the editorial processes of the publisher the majority allowed the plaintiff. *Wolston v. Reader's Digest* (1979) saw Stewart and Marshall join the majority opinion and decision coalitions, respectively. Stewart associated himself with language referencing the *Rosenbloom* proposition that *Gertz* and *Firestone* "repudiated . . . and we reject it again today" (1979, 167). After Stewart's retirement, Marshall continued to adhere to his preferences by dissenting in *Dun & Bradstreet v. Greenmoss Builders* (1985).

Jimenez v. Weinberger (1974) concerns the right of illegitimate children to disability benefits under the Social Security Act. Their disabled father was entitled to such benefits. The majority declared the statutory provisions governing eligibility unconstitutional. Rehnquist dissented, viewing the criteria at issue to be rationally based: "I frankly find the Court's opinion in this case a perplexing three-legged stool. The holding is clearly founded on notions of equal protection . . . and the Court speaks specifically of improper 'discrimination.' Yet the opinion has strong due process overtones as well, at times appearing to pay homage to the still novel, and I think unsupportable, theory that 'irrebuttable presumptions' violate due process" (1974, 638).

Rehnquist adhered to his preferences in *Jimenez*'s five progeny. He wrote the conservative opinion of the Court in *Weinberger v. Salfi* (1975), which the dissenters said "*is* flatly contrary to several recent decisions, specifically... *Jimenez*" (1975, 802). He joined Blackmun's opinion of the Court in *Mathews v. Lucas* (1976), distinguishing *Jimenez*, and *Norton v. Mathews* (1976), both of which involved the statutory classifications under which illegitimate children could inherit from their father's estate. He dissented in *Trimble v. Gordon* (1977), where a minimum winning majority voided Illinois's law allowing illegitimate children to inherit only from intestate mothers, not fathers. Finally, he wrote the Court's opinion for a minimum winning majority in *Califano v. Boles* (1979), upholding the Social Security Act's survivor's benefits to widows and divorced wives, but not to mothers of illegitimate children.

Burger and White dissented from *Wingo v. Wedding* (1974), in which the majority ruled that federal magistrates may not conduct evidentiary hearings in habeas corpus proceedings. Burger wrote the Court's opinion in *United States v. Raddatz* (1980), a case that concerned amendments to the Federal Magistrates Act enacted in response to the decision in the *Wingo* precedent.[42] Burger, joined by White, construed the new language defining magistrates' authority more broadly than did the dissent.[43]

United States v. Miller (1976) holds that bank patrons have no expectation of privacy in copies of checks, deposit slips, and other material relating to their accounts; that these materials are banks' business records, not patrons' private papers; and that consequently patrons have no Fourth Amendment interest vindicable against subpoenas. Brennan and Marshall dissented.

Specially concurring in *Fisher v. United States* (1976), they cite the precedent as evidence of the "denigration of privacy principles" (1976, 414), this time in the context of taxpayers' self-incrimination challenge to the production of tax-related documents in their accountants' hands. In *Andresen v. Maryland* (1976) they reiterate their concern about "the recent trend of decisions to eviscerate Fourth Amendment protections" (1976, 485, note 1). In *United States v. Martinez-Fuerte* (1976), they assert that the decision "virtually empties the [Fourth] Amendment of its reasonableness requirement" (1976, 568). In *Smith v. Maryland* (1979),

---

[42]   *Thomas v. Arn* (1985) states that the amendments "were prompted" by the *Wingo* decision (1985, 152, note 12). *Gomez v. United States* (1989) corroborates: "In part, Congress intended to overturn judicial opinions limiting the scope of the Act, including *Wingo v. Wedding*" (1989, 867, note 14).

[43]   A de novo determination, as distinct from a de novo hearing, violates neither Article III nor the due process clause according to *Raddatz* (1980, 674). This construction satisfies Article III by reserving ultimate adjudicatory authority to federal district court judges and effects a "proper balance" (Id. 683) between the requirements of procedural due process and the constraints of Article III. The dissenters argued that the failure of the district court judge personally to hear controverted testimony concerning credibility crucial to the outcome violates due process.

"that constitutional protections are not abrogated whenever a person apprises another of facts valuable in criminal investigations" (1979, 748), here the warrantless installation of a pen register. In *United States v. Payner* (1980), they object to a holding that "effectively turns the standing rules created by this Court for assertions of Fourth Amendment violations into a sword to be used by the Government to permit it deliberately to invade one person's Fourth Amendment rights in order to obtain evidence against another" (1980, 738). Finally, they dissent from the substantial extension of the private-search doctrine in *United States v. Jacobsen* (1984).

The first case from our Burger Court sample to produce precedential votes in its progeny is *TVA v. Hill* (1978), the famous snail darter case. Highly publicized, it has symbolic, if not much legal, significance. Blackmun, Powell, and Rehnquist dissented from the decision construing the Endangered Species Act to prohibit impoundment of the Little Tennessee River by the Tellico Dam. Said Powell: The act "cannot reasonably be interpreted as applying to a project that is completed or substantially completed when its threat to an endangered species is discovered. Nor can I believe that Congress could have intended this Act to produce the 'absurd result' – in the words of the District Court – of this case. . . . Where the statutory language and legislative history . . . need not be construed to reach such a result, I view it as the duty of this Court to adopt a permissible construction that accords with some modicum of common sense and the public weal" (1978, 196). To which the majority opinion retorted: "The commitment to the separation of powers is too fundamental for us to pre-empt congressional action by judicially decreeing what accords with 'common sense and the public weal'" (Id. 195).[44]

In *Hill*'s first progeny, *Weinberger v. Romero-Barcelo* (1982), the majority took pains to distinguish the precedent and allow the district court broad discretion in ordering the Navy to comply with the provisions of the Federal Water Pollution Control Act. Powell, the only vocal member of *Hill*'s dissenting trio, emphasized in his opinion concurring with the majority that the district court's "thorough opinion demonstrates the reasonableness of its decision in light of all pertinent factors" (1982, 321, note *). *Hill*'s other progeny, *Kelly v. Robinson* (1986), is a debatable one, given that it addresses an issue distinct from the precedent. None-

---

[44] Congress amended the Endangered Species Act after *Hill*. See *Chemical Mfrs Assn. v. Natural Resources Defense Council* (1985, 160, note 7). The "swiftly granted relief" that Congress granted the TVA precluded judicial modification. See *Federal Reserve System v. Dimension Financial Corp.* (1986, 374, note 7). In explaining the *Hill* decision, the Court rationalized its construction of legislative intent as sometimes producing "anomalies," because "explicit language" may effect "a curious result" (Id.).

theless, we count it as such because its majority opinion – which the dissenters joined – relies directly on Powell's *Hill* dissent.

Among the sample of common litigation of the Burger Court, *United States v. LaSalle National Bank* (1978) exhibits the highest ratio of precedent to preference votes, 5 to 1. Burger, Rehnquist, Stevens, and Stewart dissented, supporting lower court decisions denying enforcement to Internal Revenue Service (IRS) summonses issued solely for the purpose of unearthing evidence of criminal conduct. In *United States v. Euge* (1980), the *LaSalle* dissenters, except Stevens, joined a majority that holds the summons authority at issue in *LaSalle* extends to handwriting exemplars. In *United States v. Stuart* (1989), the remaining dissenters, Rehnquist and Stevens, voted with the other justices reaffirming the *LaSalle* precedent. They did not make clear whether they felt obliged to adhere to the precedent or complied because Congress had codified the *LaSalle* holding (1989, 363). Our decision rules do not distinguish between these motivations. It suffices that they affirmed the precedent from which they had dissented.

Bacchus Imports Ltd. v. Dias (1984) holds that a state tax exemption on locally manufactured alcoholic beverages violates the commerce clause. The dissenters – O'Connor, Rehnquist, and Stevens – said it violates the Twenty-first Amendment. The conjunction of state taxation, the commerce clause, and the Twenty-first Amendment – with the equal protection clause and the state action exemption from the antitrust laws lurking in the background – gives rise to a convoluted set of progeny that make the identification of precedent and preference votes problematic if not impossible. We identify five progeny containing a total of 13 votes, more than any other common Burger Court decision except *Goss v. Lopez*. Wary of pitfalls, we identify eight of these 13 votes as supporting preferences; five, precedent.

Stevens voted precedentially by joining the majority in the first of *Bacchus*'s progeny, *Metropolitan Life Insurance Co. v. Ward* (1985). This decision distinguishes the precedent and holds that the equal protection clause precludes a state from using its tax power to promote a domestic insurance company. According to the majority this is not a legitimate state purpose (1985, 882); according to the dissent it is an "astonishing" holding (Id. 883). In the next progeny, *Brown-Forman Distillers Corp. v. New York Liquor Authority* (1986), Rehnquist continues to vote his pro-state preferences, while O'Connor and Stevens changed their positions: O'Connor voting precedent, Stevens preferences. Not only does the majority rule that the state's beverage control law violates the commerce clause because it forbids distillers and producers from selling to in-state wholesalers at a price higher than the lowest price charged wholesalers elsewhere in the United States, it also overrules the Warren Court precedent, *Joseph E. Seagram & Sons v. Hostetter* (1966).

New York law is again at issue in the next of *Bacchus*'s progeny, *324 Liquor Corp. v. Duffy* (1987). O'Connor and Rehnquist again view the Twenty-first Amendment as controlling, while Stevens and the other justices view the state action exemption from the antitrust laws as determinative. The provision at issue required liquor retailers to charge 112 percent of the "posted" wholesale price, while wholesalers could sell to retailers at less than the "posted" price.[45] In the penultimate progeny, *Tyler Pipe v. Washington Dept. of Revenue* (1987), we treat O'Connor's vote as inapposite, as we did Stevens's in *324 Liquor Corp.* In her brief concurrence, O'Connor joins the majority opinion on narrow grounds unrelated to *Bacchus.* Stevens adheres to precedent by voting with the majority, while Rehnquist continues to follow his pro-state proclivities. The Court held that the state's manufacturing tax violated the commerce clause because exemptions limited assessment to locally manufactured products sold out-of-state. Finally, Rehnquist continues his pro-state voting in *West Lynn Creamery, Inc. v. Healy* (1994), while O'Connor and Stevens adhere to the *Bacchus* precedent along with five of their colleagues. *West Lynn* concerned an assessment on all milk dealers selling to Massachusetts retailers, the proceeds of which were distributed to the state's dairy farmers.

Brennan, Marshall, and Stevens dissented from *Mitsubishi Motors Corp. v. Soler Chrysler-Plymouth, Inc.* (1985), which holds that neither the antitrust laws nor concerns of international comity preclude arbitration; indeed, the latter requires enforcement of the clause in question. The dissenters hold, inter alia, that the Federal Arbitration Act does not apply to antitrust claims. They also dissented in *Shearson/American Express, Inc. v. McMahon* (1987), where the Court ruled that the strong federal policy favoring arbitration warrants such resolution notwithstanding the antifraud provisions of the Securities Exchange Act. Stevens separated himself from Brennan and Marshall and joined the Court's opinion in *Volt Information Services v. Stanford University* (1989), which applied the precedent to an arbitration clause under which contractual disputes would be governed by the law of the place where the contract is performed. Brennan and Marshall viewed the choice of law clause reviewable "to guard against arbitrary denials of federal claims" (1989, 482). The final progeny, *Rodriguez de Quijas v. Shearson/*

---

[45] We consider Stevens's vote as neither precedent nor preference. The majority opinion, which he joined, makes no reference to *Bacchus*, and the basis for decision, the state action exemption to the antitrust laws, does not strictly speaking turn on pro-state or antistate sentiments.

Table 7.9.
Voting and opinion behavior: Burger Court ordinary cases

Justice	Prefs/prec	%Prefs	Preferences (%)			Level of Expression Precedent (%)		
			Strong (1)	Moderate (2)	Weak (3)	Strong (1)	Moderate (2)	Weak (3)
Marshall (Mar)	24	100.0	7 (29.2)	12 (50.0)	5 (20.8)			1 (100)
Brennan (Brn)	19	100.0	6 (31.6)	8 (42.1)	5 (26.3)			1 (100)
Douglas (Dou)	2	100.0	1 (50.0)	1 (50.0)				1 (100)
White (BW)	1	100.0		1 (100)				1 (100)
Powell (Pow)	9	90.0	3 (33.3)	1 (11.1)	5 (55.6)			1 (100)
Blackmun (Blm)	8	88.9	2 (25.0)	2 (25.0)	4 (50.0)			1 (100)
Burger (Brg)	8	88.9	1 (12.5)	3 (37.5)	4 (50.0)			1 (100)
Rehnquist (Rhn)	21	87.5	4 (19.0)	8 (38.1)	9 (42.9)			3 (100)
Stewart (Stw)	7	87.5	2 (28.6)	3 (42.9)	2 (28.6)			1 (100)
Stevens (Str)	9	60.0	1 (11.1)	7 (77.8)	1 (11.1)	1 (16.7)	2 (33.3)	3 (50.0)
O'Connor (OC)	2	50.0	1 (50.0)	1 (50.0)			1 (50.0)	1 (50.0)
Totals	110 15	88.0	28 (25.5)	47 (42.7)	35 (31.8)	1 (6.7)	3 (20.0)	11 (73.3)

Table 7.9 (*cont.*)

Precedent/progeny	Preferences	Precedent
Rosenbloom v. Metromedia (1971) **c**		
Gertz v. Welch (1974)	Mar-Stw-1	
Time v. Firestone (1976)	Mar-1 Stw-2	
Herbert v. Lando (1979)	Mar-Stw-2	
Wolston v. Reader's Digest (1979)	Mar-Stw-2	
Dun & Bradstreet v. Greenmoss Bldrs. (1985)	Mar-2	
United States v. Midwest Video Corp. (1979) **s**		
FCC v. Midwest Video Corp. (1979)	Pow-Rhn-Stw-3	
Heller v. New York (1973) **c**		
Alexander v. Virginia (1973)	Brn-Dou-Mar-Stw-1	
American Party of Texas v. White (1974) **c**		
Storer v. Brown (1974)	Dou-2	
Jimenez v. Weinberger (1974) **c**		
Weinberger v. Salfi (1975)	Rhn-3	
Mathews v. Lucas (1976)	Rhn-3	
Norton v. Mathews (1976)	Rhn-3	
Trimble v. Gordon (1977)	Rhn-2	
Califano v. Boles (1979)	Rhn-3	
Wingo v. Wedding (1974) **s**		
United States v. Raddatz (1980)	Brg-BW-2	
Goss v. Lopez (1975) **c**		
Wood v. Strickland (1975)	Blm-Brg-Pow-Rhn-1	
Paul v. Davis (1976)	Blm-Brg-Pow-Rhn-3	
Ingraham v. Wright (1977)	Blm-Brg-Pow-Rhn-3	
Board of Curators v. Horowitz (1978)	Blm-Brg-Pow-Rhn-3	

Case		
United States v. Miller (1976) c	Brn-Mar-1	
Fisher v. United States (1976)	Brn-Mar-1	
Andresen v. Maryland (1976)	Brn-Mar-1	
United States v. Martinez-Fuerte (1976)	Brn-Mar-1	
Smith v. Maryland (1979)	Brn-Mar-2	
United States v. Payner (1980)	Brn-Mar-2	
United States v. Jacobsen (1984)		
Castaneda v. Partida (1977) c	Brg-2 Pow-Rhn-1 Stw-3	
Rose v. Mitchell (1979)	Brg-Pow-Rhn-3	
Wayte v. United States (1985)	Brg-Pow-Rhn-2	
Vasquez v. Hillary (1986)		
United States v. Washington (1977) c	Brn-Mar-1	
Minnesota v. Murphy (1984)		Blm-Pow-Rhn-3
Massachusetts v. United States (1978) c	Rhn-2	
American Trucking Assns. v. Scheiner (1987)		Brg-Rhn-Stw-3
TVA v. Hill (1978) s		Rhn-Stv-3
Weinberger v. Romero-Barcelo (1982)	Blm-Pow-Rhn-1	
Kelly v. Robinson (1986)		Stv-1
United States v. LaSalle Natl. Bank (1978) s	Stv-2	
United States v. Euge (1980)		
United States v. Stuart (1989)		
Regents v. Tomanio (1980) s	Brn-Mar-3	
Chardon v. Fumero Soto (1983)	Brn-Mar-3	
Burnett v. Grattan (1984)	Brn-Mar-3	
Wilson v. Garcia (1985)	Brn-Mar-3	
Hardin v. Straub (1989)		
American Tobacco Co. v. Patterson (1982) s	Stv-1	
Pullman-Standard v. Swint (1982)	Blm-Brn-Mar-2	
Lorance v. AT&T Technologies (1989)		
Rice v. Rehner (1983) s		
California v. Cabazon Band (1987)	Blm-Brn-Mar-3	

Table 7.9 (cont.)

Precedent/progeny	Preferences	Precedent
Bacchus Imports Ltd. v. Dias (1984) **c**		
Metropolitan Life Ins. Co. v. Ward (1985)	OC-Rhn-2	Stv-3
Brown-Forman v. NY Liquor Auth. (1986)	Stv-Rhn-2	OC-2
324 Liquor Corp. v. Duffy (1987)	OC-Rhn-1	
Tyler Pipe v. Washington Dept. (1987)	Rhn-2	Stv-3
West Lynn Creamery v. Healy (1994)	Rhn-2	OC-Stv-2
Maryland v. Macon (1985) **c**		
New York v. P.J. Video (1986)	Brn-Mar-2	
Mitsubishi Motors v. Soler Chrysler (1985) **s**		
Shearson/Amer. Express v. McMahon (1987)	Brn-Mar-Stv-2	Stv-2
Volt Information v. Stanford U. (1989)	Brn-Mar-2	
Rodriguez de Quijas v. Shearson/Amer. (1989)	Brn-Mar-Stv-2	
Cabana v. Bullock (1986)		
Tison v. Arizona (1987)	Blm-Brn-Mar-Stv-2	
Turner v. Murray (1986) **c**		
Morgan v. Illinois (1992)	Rhn-2	
Kuhlman v. Wilson (1986) **c**		
Sawyer v. Whitley (1992)	Stv-2	
Herrera v. Collins (1993)	Stv-2	
Schlup v. Delo (1995)	Stv-3	

Legend: **c** = constitutional decision
       s = statutory decision
       = decision neither constitutionally nor statutorily based
Note: All progeny rest on the same decisional basis as the precedent unless otherwise indicated.

American Express (1989), saw the three dissenters reunited, again in dissent, from a decision overruling an early Warren Court precedent, *Wilko v. Swan* (1953). The majority ruled that a predispute arbitration agreement under the Securities Act of 1933 does not require a judicial forum for resolution. Given the dissenters' overall behavior, Stevens's dissent, which Brennan and Marshall, along with Blackmun, joined, is markedly ironic – and arguably was written tongue in cheek:

We, of course, are not subject to the same restraint when asked to upset one of our own precedents. But when our earlier opinion gives a statutory provision concrete meaning, which Congress elects not to amend during the ensuing $3\frac{1}{2}$ decades, our duty to respect Congress' work product is strikingly similar to the duty of other federal courts to respect our work product.

The Justices' Behavior

The preferential proportion of the justices' common case voting, 88.0 percent, closely conforms to that of the other twentieth century Courts. Only the 69.6 percent of the Hughes Court and the perfectly preferential behavior of the Vinson Court justices deviate as much as four percentage points from the preferential proportion of the Burger Court. Very little difference separates the Warren from the Burger Court. The expressive distribution, however, does differ markedly from that of the other twentieth century Courts. Table 7.9 displays the justices' behavior.

Eleven of the 13 Burger Court justices voted in at least one of the progeny from which they had dissented. Only the two justices serving the briefest period did not participate, Black and Harlan. No other Court attains as high a proportion of participants except that containing the Burger Court's landmark decisions, when all but Harlan participated. We note little difference in the justices' behavior between the landmark and common cases except for Stevens and O'Connor. Stevens drops from 87.1 to 60.0 percent on the ordinary cases, O'Connor from 100 to 50.0 percent. However, she cast only four votes in the common set. Overall, the most marked difference between the two sets is the markedly higher proportion of strong preference votes in the landmark cases (64.0 versus 25.5 percent) and the corresponding decrease in weak voting (23.5 versus 31.8 percent).

8

Precedential Behavior
in the Rehnquist Court

Resignations from the Court for reasons other than retirement are not unusual. John Jay resigned in 1795 to become Governor of New York. James Byrnes resigned in 1942 to aid the war effort as director of the Office of Economic Stabilization. Arthur Goldberg resigned in 1965 to become U.S. Ambassador to the United Nations.[1] While Court watchers may consider these demotions of one sort or another, none approximates Burger's decision in 1986 to resign in order to head the Commission on the Bicentennial of the Constitution.

President Reagan nominated the Court's premier conservative, William Rehnquist, to take Burger's spot, and one of the nation's most conservative appellate court judges, Antonin Scalia, to take Rehnquist's spot. With the retirements of Brennan in 1990 and Marshall in 1991, the Court, bereft of any liberals, is currently split between moderates and conservatives.

The Rehnquist Court (1986–), unlike the Burger Court, has launched an explicit attack on liberal precedents. In *Payne v. Tennessee* (1991), the Court upheld the use of victim impact statements in death penalty cases, overruling *Booth v. Maryland* (1987) and *South Carolina v. Gathers* (1989). According to the opinion authored by Rehnquist, *stare decisis* should apply to economic decisions with especial force because people need stability in their business affairs. But in cases involving "procedural and evidentiary rules," the essence of due process, equal protection, and the Fourth through the Eighth Amendments, "the opposite is true" (p. 737).

Similarly, the Court in *Agostini v. Felton* (1997) overruled another liberal decision, A*guilar v. Felton* (1985), by recognizing an even longerstanding judicially created constraint on *stare decisis*: its limited standing in constitutional cases:

---

[1]   Under conditions suggesting blackmail. See Stebenne (1996).

The doctrine of *stare decisis* does not preclude us from recognizing the change in our law and overruling *Aguilar* and those portions of *Ball* inconsistent with our more recent decisions. As we have often noted, "*[s]tare decisis* is not an inexorable command," *Payne v. Tennessee* ... but instead reflects a policy judgment that "in most matters it is more important that the applicable rule of law be settled than that it be settled right," *Burnet v. Coronado Oil & Gas Co.* ... (Brandeis, J., dissenting). That policy is at its weakest when we interpret the Constitution because our interpretation can be altered only by constitutional amendment or by overruling our prior decisions. (1997, 422)

The Rehnquist Court has been not only conservative, but activist,[2] using its powers to strike congressional legislation as outside the scope of the commerce clause. In *United States v. Lopez* (1995), the Court voided prohibitions on the possession of guns at or near school grounds. In *Printz v. United States* (1997) the Court struck that part of the Brady Bill requiring local law enforcement officials to conduct background checks on firearm purchasers. Against Justice Stevens's claim that "there is not a clause, sentence, or paragraph in the entire text of the Constitution of the United States that supports the proposition that a local police officer can ignore a command contained in a statute enacted by Congress pursuant to an express delegation of power enumerated in Article I," Justice Scalia wrote for the Court:

We held in *New York* that Congress cannot compel the States to enact or enforce a federal regulatory program. Today we hold that Congress cannot circumvent that prohibition by conscripting the State's officers directly. The Federal Government may neither issue directives requiring the States to address particular problems, nor command the States' officers, or those of their political subdivisions, to administer or enforce a federal regulatory program. It matters not whether policymaking is involved, and no case-by-case weighing of the burdens or benefits is necessary; such commands are fundamentally incompatible with our constitutional system of dual sovereignty. (1997, 944–45)

In more moderate decisions, it limited but did not ban abortion rights,[3] minority gerrymandered districts,[4] affirmative action programs,[5] and mandatory drug tests,[6] with Justice O'Connor often holding the swing vote.

Finally, despite its conservative majority, the Court has strongly

---

[2] At the close of the 1996 term the Court struck down three separate pieces of legislation in one week, the Communications Decency Act (CDA), the Religious Freedom Restoration Act, and the Brady Bill, something it had never done before. Striking the CDA, of course, cannot be considered a conservative decision.

[3] *Planned Parenthood v. Casey* (1992).

[4] *Miller v. Johnson* (1995).

[5] *Adarand Constructors v. Pena* (1995).   [6] *Chandler v. Miller* (1997).

upheld First Amendment rights (except when abortion is at issue),[7] striking congressional efforts to ban flag burning[8] and censoring the Internet.[9]

LANDMARK DECISIONS

As of the time of this writing, the Rehnquist Court has existed for eleven years. Hence, its opportunity to generate progeny of leading decisions is appreciably less than that of earlier Courts, notwithstanding the tendency of our source for leading decisions – the CQ *Guide* (Witt 1990) – to identify recent cases as such. Moreover, the source itself was compiled after only five terms of Rehnquist Court decisions. A compilation closer to the time of our writing, however, would not markedly increase the number of analyzable progeny because of the lag between the establishment of a precedent and the appearance of its progeny.

Accordingly, although our source lists 19 nonunanimous Rehnquist Court decisions as landmarks, only ten of them produce progeny.[10] Although the paucity of progeny militates against formal categorization, these ten cases fit into six of the eight categories into which we divided the decisions of the Burger Court: abortion, criminal procedure, death penalty, civil rights, First Amendment, and separation of powers. Clearly, then, the major case agenda of the Rehnquist Court continues the pattern manifest on the Burger Court.

We begin this short chapter with *Webster v. Reproductive Health Services* (1989), which holds that restrictions on the use of public employees in nontherapeutic abortions does not contravene the Constitution. The dissenters – Blackmun, Brennan, Marshall, and Stevens – collectively cast eight preferential votes in *Webster*'s progeny: *Hodgson v. Minnesota* (1990), *Rust v. Sullivan* (1991), and *Planned Parenthood v. Casey* (1992).

Three Rehnquist Court landmarks pertain to criminal procedure. *United States v. Salerno* (1987) upholds preventive detention of arrestees charged with serious felonies on the government's showing that their release threatens public safety. In *Foucha v. Louisiana* (1992), Stevens

---

[7] *Rust v. Sullivan* (1991), upholding a gag order on doctors working at clinics receiving federal funds, and *Madsen v. Women's Health Center* (1994), sustaining certain limits on pro-life protests.

[8] *United States v. Eichman* (1990).

[9] *Reno v. ACLU* (1997).

[10] The progenyless precedents are *Tashjian v. Connecticut GOP* (1986), *United States v. Paradise* (1987), *Johnson v. Transportation Agency* (1987), *Tison v. Arizona* (1987), *McCleskey v. Kemp* (1987), *Edwards v. Aguillard* (1987), *Thompson v. Oklahoma* (1988), *South Carolina v. Baker* (1988), and *Wards Cove v. Atonio* (1989).

voted his preferences in a case that invalidated a state statute permitting indefinite confinement of persons not guilty by reason of insanity until they prove they are dangerous neither to themselves nor to others. In *Skinner v. Railway Labor Executives, Assn.* (1989), Brennan and Marshall dissented from a ruling that the Fourth Amendment does not preclude toxicological testing of railroad employees after an accident. They adhered to their dissent in *United States v. Sokolow* (1989) and *Conrail v. Railway Labor Executives' Assn.* (1989). In *National Treasury Employees Union v. Von Raab* (1989), a case related to *Skinner*, the majority ruled that a urinalysis test of Customs Service employees who seek transfers or promotions does not violate the Fourth Amendment. Brennan, Marshall, and Stevens reiterated their objections in *Michigan State Police v. Sitz* (1990).

The adjacent death penalty cases of *Penry v. Lynaugh* (1989) and *Stanford v. Kentucky* (1989) reciprocally serve as precedent and progeny to one another. Brennan and Marshall referenced their dissent in *Stanford*, in which the majority concluded that the imposition of death on persons aged 16 or 17 does not constitute cruel and unusual punishment. In *Penry*, Blackmun and Stevens joined Brennan and Marshall in dissenting from a decision upholding the death sentence of a mentally retarded person, which dissents they applied to *Stanford*. After the resignations of Brennan and Marshall, Blackmun and Stevens voted their *Penry* preferences in *Graham v. Collins* (1993) and *Johnson v. Texas* (1993).

The first of the Rehnquist Court's important affirmative action cases, *Richmond v. J.A. Croson Co.* (1989), generated one progeny in which the dissenters – Brennan, Marshall, and Blackmun – participated before retirement: *Metro Broadcasting v. FCC* (1990). White and Stevens joined them in a short-lived opinion by Brennan that held that benign race-conscious remedies mandated by Congress – as distinct from those established by state and local governments – need only meet intermediate, rather than strict, scrutiny.[11]

The Rehnquist Court's First Amendment landmark is the flag desecration case, *Texas v. Johnson* (1989). Its progeny, of course, is its federal counterpart, *United States v. Eichman* (1990), in which the same four justices dissented: O'Connor, Rehnquist, Stevens, and White.[12]

---

[11] *Adarand Constructors v. Pena* (1995) overruled *Metro Broadcasting* and required all affirmative action programs, state and federal, to meet strict scrutiny.

[12] On the rare occasion when *Shepard's* fails to cite a case that appears in a subsequent decision its omission is egregious. *Texas v. Johnson* exemplifies. It is fully cited on the first page of the majority opinion in *Eichman* (312), and as *Johnson* on every page thereafter (313–19). Every page but one of the *Eichman* dissent contains the full cite

Generating the most progeny of any Rehnquist Court precedent, four, is *Allegheny County v. Greater Pittsburgh ACLU* (1989). A sequel to the conservatively decided Burger Court nativity scene case, *Lynch v. Donnelly* (1984), it drew dissents from Kennedy, Rehnquist, Scalia, and White, as a result of Justice O'Connor's switching her vote from conservative to liberal. The first of its progeny, *Lee v. Weisman* (1992), produced an interesting exchange among the justices. The case concerns a clerically rendered invocation and benediction at a public high school graduation. Speaking for himself and four colleagues, including O'Connor, Justice Kennedy initially asserted the irrelevance of the *Allegheny County* precedent to his decision: "This case does not require us to revisit the difficult questions dividing us in recent cases, questions of the definition and full scope of the principles governing the extent of permitted accommodation by the State for the religious beliefs and practices of many of its citizens" (1992, 586). He thereupon proceeds to cite his *Allegheny County* dissent supportively, although with a liberal rather than a conservative twist:[13]

Our decisions . . . recognize . . . that prayer exercises in public schools carry a particular risk of indirect coercion. The concern may not be limited to the context of schools, but it is most pronounced there. See *Allegheny County*. . . . What to most believers may seem nothing more than a reasonable request that the nonbeliever respect their religious practices, in a school context may appear to the nonbeliever or dissenter to be an attempt to employ the machinery of the State to enforce a religious orthodoxy. (Id. 592)

Justice Souter, after emphasizing that he, Stevens, and O'Connor "join the whole of the Court's opinion, and fully agree that prayers at public school graduation ceremonies indirectly coerce religious observance" (Id. 609), surveyed a lengthy list of precedents and concluded: "Such is the settled law. Here, as elsewhere, we should stick to it absent some

---

(319, 321–24). The fact that *Shepard's* references only full citations certainly does not minimize its failure to reference even a single page of *Johnson*.

A similar situation prevailed as between the Burger Court governmental immunity decisions of *Nixon v. Fitzgerald* (1981) and *Harlow v. Fitzgerald* (1981). The full *Nixon* cite appears throughout the majority and two of the four separate opinions in *Harlow*, again with nary a reference in *Shepard's*.

Moreover, the *Texas* and *Nixon* cases are, respectively, cited in the syllabus of *Eichman* and *Harlow*. And although *Shepard's* does not give the syllabus formal attention, a case cited there presumably would catch the eye of *Shepard's* coders.

13 Strictly speaking, we should count Kennedy's vote as supporting precedent since he used his dissent from the precedent to achieve an opposite outcome. On the other hand, compatibly with our decision rules, he does specifically reference his *Allegheny County* special opinion, and nowhere in his opinion of the Court in *Weisman* does he recant his *Allegheny County* views or accede to the majority's holding in that case. Indeed, in pertinent part, he says in *Allegheny County*: "The majority['s] . . . view of the Establishment Clause reflects an unjustifiable hostility toward religion, a hostility inconsistent with our history and our precedents, and I dissent from this holding" (1989, 535).

compelling reason to discard it" (Id. 611). Superficially this is an unexceptional statement, but given the behavior we have documented in this and the preceding four chapters of this book, Souter's assertion accurately characterizes the old saw: Do as I say, not as I do.[14]

We conclude our discussion of *Weisman* with an excerpt from Scalia's dissent. He, along with Rehnquist and White, had joined Kennedy's separate opinion in the precedent, *Allegheny County*. Scalia not only adheres to his previous position, but also cites and castigates Kennedy for his use of his opinion to justify the switch from conservative to liberal:

> Three Terms ago, I joined an opinion recognizing that the Establishment Clause must be construed in light of the "[g]overnment policies of accommodation, acknowledgment, and support for religion [that] are an accepted part of our political and cultural heritage." That opinion affirmed that "the meaning of the Clause is to be determined by reference to historical practices and understandings." It said that "[a] test for implementing the protections of the Establishment Clause that, if applied with consistency, would invalidate longstanding traditions cannot be a proper reading of the Clause." *Allegheny County . . .*
>
> These views of course prevent me from joining today's opinion, which is conspicuously bereft of any reference to history. (Id. 631)

The *Allegheny County* dissenters behaved consistently with their preferences in its other progeny: *Westside Community Board of Education v. Mergens* (1990), *Kiryas Joel Board of Education v. Grumet* (1994), and *Capital Square Review Board v. Pinette* (1995).

The last of the Rehnquist Court landmark precedents is *Morrison v. Olson* (1988). The case raised a question of congressional power to vest the appointment of an independent investigatory counsel in the judiciary, and that such action does not violate separation of powers by impermissibly interfering with the functions of the executive branch. Scalia, at inordinate length, alone dissented. He adhered to his strict separation position in *Mistretta v. United States* (1989) and *Evans v. United States* (1992).

CONCLUSION

Whether we count all of the votes in the progeny of the Rehnquist Court's landmark decisions as supporting the dissenters' preferences or count Kennedy's vote in *Lee v. Weisman* (1992), a progeny of *Allegheny County v. Greater Pittsburgh ACLU* (1989), as precedential, a higher proportion of this Court's votes support preferences – either all 45 or 44 of 45 (97.8 percent) – than do those of any other Court. Next most

[14] Admittedly, we have identified no instances where Souter does not practice what he preaches. Absent contrary evidence, we will give him the benefit of the doubt, although not those who joined his concurrence.

supportive of preferences is the Burger Court's 93.2 percent. But whether we can ascribe this unusually high degree of preferential voting behavior to the fact that these are conservative Courts or to the fact that liberals maintain their disapproval of conservative decisions in the progeny of these precedents will be examined in Chapter 9. The latter seems an incomplete explanation inasmuch as the conservative justices vote as preferentially as their colleagues, as Table 8.1 shows.

Coupled with the perfectly preferential voting is a higher incidence of strong manifestations of preferences than obtains on any other Court, 71.1 percent. Indeed, every one of the nine participating justices expresses his or her preferences strongly more than half the time. In the Burger and Warren Courts, by comparison, only 7 of 12 and 4 of 13 do so.

COMMON LITIGATION

The number of votes cast by dissenters in the progeny of the Rehnquist Court's common cases, 25, approximates those of the Taft, Hughes, and Stone Courts, far below those of the Taney, Waite, Fuller, and Burger Courts. This paucity, however, extends over six precedents, the first of which is *Colorado v. Bertine* (1987), in which Brennan and Marshall dissented. The case concerned an inventory search of the van of a person arrested for driving while under the influence of alcohol. The majority ruled that the rules regulating inventory searches governed the facts rather than those governing searches of closed containers conducted solely for the purpose of investigating criminal conduct. The dissenters alleged that the majority made inventory searches a talisman to avoid compliance with the Fourth Amendment (1987, 387). They adhered to their preferences in *Florida v. Wells* (1990), another inventory search case.

The two dissenters still on the Court when the initial progeny of *INS v. Cardoza-Fonseca* (1987) was decided, Rehnquist and White, reasserted their preferences in *NLRB v. Food & Commercial Workers* (1987). In the precedent the majority ruled, over the objections of the INS, that distinctive standards governed the two types of relief statutes afforded deportable aliens, asylum and the withholding of deportation. The dissenters deferred to the Bureau of Immigration Appeals that there was no practical difference from the evidence aliens must submit to become eligible for relief. Although the progeny, *Food & Commercial Workers*, concerned an issue different from the precedent, an unfair labor practice, the majority opinion specifically asserted its adherence to the precedent (1987, 124, 125). Rehnquist and White, regularly concurring, disparaged the dicta of the precedent. The other progeny, *INS v. Elias-Zacarias* (1992), found the precedent's dissenters in the majority in a case denying asylum to an alien whom a guerrilla organization attempted to coerce into military service.

O'Lone v. Estate of Shabazz (1987) held that denying prisoners of the Islamic faith attendance at a Friday afternoon religious service on security grounds did not violate their free exercise of religion. Blackmun, Brennan, Marshall, and Stevens dissented. All but Blackmun adhered to their preferences in the progeny, *Thornburgh v. Abbott* (1989), by quoting their *O'Lone* dissent expressing concern "that the Court today too readily 'substitute[s] the rhetoric of judicial deference for meaningful scrutiny of constitutional claims in the prison setting'" (Id. 429). Blackmun voted precedent and wrote the Court's opinion.

Stevens, the sole dissenter in *Doe v. United States* (1988), adhered to the precedent in its single progeny, *Baltimore Social Services v. Bouknight* (1990). Doe was held in contempt for refusing to comply with a court order requiring him to authorize foreign banks to disclose records of his accounts. The majority ruled that inasmuch as the consent directive was not testimonial his protection against self-incrimination did not apply. Stevens distinguished the forced production in this case from the physical evidence of other cases because the target is "compelled to use his mind to assist the Government in developing its case" (1988, 220). In *Bouknight*, he silently joined the majority compelling a mother to produce her abused child.[15]

Like *Doe*, *Hernandez v. Commissioner* (1989) also produced no preference votes in its single progeny. O'Connor and Scalia dissented from a holding that the Internal Revenue Code does not permit taxpayers to deduct as a charitable contribution payments to branches of the Scientology Church for services known as "auditing" and "training." For herself and Scalia, O'Connor asserted that the IRS unconstitutionally discriminated by its refusal "to allow payments for the religious service of auditing to be deducted as charitable contributions in the same way it has allowed fixed payments to other religions to be deducted" (1989, 713). O'Connor wrote the Court's opinion, which all the justices silently joined, in *Swaggart v. California Board of Equalization* (1990), holding that sales and use taxes on in-state sales and out-of-state purchases of

---

[15] Whether Stevens compromised his preferences by his *Bouknight* vote is a close question. Arguably, surrendering one's child does not entail the mental activity required to authorize a bank to produce the subject's records. Moreover, unlike the *Doe* situation, production of a child is part of a "noncriminal regulatory regime" (1990, 556). We have chosen, however, to treat Stevens's vote as precedential because of the majority opinion's reliance on the *Doe* precedent.

Table 8.1.
Voting and opinion behavior: Rehnquist Court landmarks

Justice	Prefs/prec	%Prefs	Preferences (%) Strong (1)	Moderate (2)	Weak (3)	Level of Expression Precedent (%) Strong (1)	Moderate (2)	Weak (3)
Marshall (Mar)	8	0	100.0	6 (75.0)	1 (12.5)	1 (12.5)			
Stevens (Stv)	8	0	100.0	5 (62.5)	2 (25.0)	1 (12.5)			
Blackmun (Blm)	7	0	100.0	4 (57.1)	2 (28.6)	1 (14.3)			
Brennan (Brn)	7	0	100.0	5 (71.4)	1 (14.3)	1 (14.3)			
Scalia (Sca)	5	0	100.0	4 (80.0)	1 (20.0)				
Kennedy (Ken)	4	0	100.0	3 (75.0)	1 (25.0)				
Rehnquist (Rhn)	3	0	100.0	2 (66.7)	1 (33.3)				
White (BW)	2	0	100.0	2 (100)					
O'Connor (OC)	1	0	100.0	1 (100)					
Totals	45	0	100.0	32 (71.1)	9 (20.0)	4 (8.9)	0	0	0

Precedent/progeny	Preferences	Precedent
Morrison v. Olson (1988) **c**		
Mistretta v. United States (1989)	Sca-1	
Evans v. United States (1992)	Sca-1	
United States v. Salerno (1987) **c**		
Foucha v. Louisiana (1992)	Stv-3	

Case	Precedent basis
Webster v. Reproductive Health Services (1989) **c**	Blm-Brn-Mar-1
Hodgson v. Minnesota (1990)	Blm-Mar-Stv-1
Rust v. Sullivan (1991)	Blm-Stv-1
Planned Parenthood v. Casey (1992)	
Skinner v. Railway Labor Executives Assn. (1989) **c**	Brn-Mar-1
United States v. Sokolow (1989)	Brn-Mar-2
Conrail v. Railway Labor Executives (1989)	
Natl. Treasury Employees Union v. Von Raab (1989) **c**	Brn-Mar-Stv-1
Michigan State Police v. Sitz (1990)	
Stanford v. Kentucky (1989) **c**	Brn-Mar-1
Penry v. Lynaugh (1989)	
Penry v. Lynaugh (1989) **c**	Blm-Brn-Mar-Stv-1
Stanford v. Kentucky (1989)	Blm-Stv-2
Graham v. Collins (1993)	Blm-Stv-2
Johnson v. Texas (1993)	
Richmond v. J.A. Croson Co. (1989) **c**	Blm-Brn-Mar-3
Metro Broadcasting v. FCC (1990)	
Texas v. Johnson (1989) **c**	OC-Rhn-Stv-BW-1
United States v. Eichman (1990)	
Allegheny v. Greater Pittsburgh ACLU (1989) **c**	Ken-Sca-1
Westside Community Bd. of Ed. v. Mergens (1990)	Ken-Rhn-Sca-BW-1
Lee v. Weisman (1992)	Ken-1
Kiryas Joel Bd. of Ed. v. Grumet (1994)	Ken-Rhn-Sca-2
Capital Square Board v. Pinette (1995)	

Legend: **c** = constitutional decision
 s = statutory decision
 = decision neither constitutionally nor statutorily based

Note: All progeny rest on the same decisional basis as the precedent unless otherwise indicated.

Table 8.2.
Voting and opinion behavior: Rehnquist Court ordinary cases

| | | | Level of Expression | | | | | |
| | | | Preferences (%) | | | Precedent (%) | | |
Justice	Prefs/prec	%Prefs	Strong (1)	Moderate (2)	Weak (3)	Strong (1)	Moderate (2)	Weak (3)
Brennan (Brn)	4	0	100.0	2 (50.0)	2 (50.0)			
Marshall (Mar)	4	0	100.0	2 (50.0)	2 (50.0)			
Rehnquist (Rhn)	2	0	100.0		1 (50.0)	1 (50.0)		
White (BW)	2	0	100.0		1 (5000)	1 (50.0)		
Stevens (Stv)	4	2	66.7	2 (50.0)		2 (50.0)		2 (100)
Blackmun (Blm)	3	2	60.0	1 (33.3)	1 (33.3)	1 (33.3)		2 (100)
O'Connor (OC)	0	1	0.0					1 (100)
Scalia (Sca)	0	1	0.0					1 (100)
Totals	19	6	76.0	7 (36.8)	7 (36.8)	5 (26.3)	0	6 (100)	0

Precedent/progeny	Preferences	Precedent
Colorado v. Bertine (1987) **c**		
Florida v. Wells (1990)	Brn-Mar-2	
INS v. Cardoza-Fonseca (1987) **s**		
NLRB v. Food & Commercial Workers (1987)	Rhn-BW-2	
INS v. Elias-Zacarias (1992)	Rhn-BW-3	
O'Lone v. Estate of Shabazz (1987) **c**		Blm-2
Thornburgh v. Abbott (1989)	Brn-Mar-Stv-1	
Doe v. United States (1988) **c**		
Baltimore Social Svcs. v. Bouknight (1990)		Stv-2
Hernandez v. IRC (1989) **s**		
Swaggart v. California Board (1990)		OC-Sca-2
Will v. Michigan State Police (1989) **s**		
Dellmuth v. Muth (1989)	Blm-Brn-Mar-Stv-1	
Ngiraingas v. Sanchez (1990)	Brn-Mar-2	Blm-Stv-2
Hafer v. Melo (1991)	Blm-Stv-3	
Hilton v. South Carolina Commission (1991)	Blm-2 Stv-3	

Legend: **c** = constitutional decision

       s = statutory decision

       = decision neither constitutionally nor statutorily based

Note: All progeny rest on the same decisional basis as the precedent unless otherwise indicated.

religious goods by its residents did not contravene the religion clauses of the First Amendment. Not only does O'Connor cite and quote the *Hernandez* majority opinion, she also quotes her dissent in that case as authority for the decision in the *Swaggart* progeny. In none of the several hundred progeny that we have analyzed do we find another instance where the progeny cites as authority for a majority decision a precedent along with the dissent therefrom.

A minimum winning coalition in *Will v. Michigan State Police* (1989) ruled that neither a state nor a state official acting in an official capacity is a "person" for purposes of a Reconstruction Civil Rights Act (42 U.S.C. §1983). The dissenters – Blackmun, Brennan, Marshall, and Stevens – reaffirmed their position in *Dellmuth v. Muth* (1989), in which the majority held states immune from federal court suits for violations of the Education for the Handicapped Act. In *Ngiraingas v. Sanchez* (1990), the dissenters split. Blackmun wrote the Court's opinion, which Stevens joined, stating that neither territories nor their officers are "persons" for 42 U.S.C. §1983 purposes. Brennan and Marshall demurred. After the retirement of Brennan and Marshall, Blackmun and Stevens reasserted their preferences in *Hafer v. Melo* (1991) and *Hilton v. South Carolina Commission* (1991). In *Hafer*, the Court unanimously ruled that state officers may be personally liable for damages under §1983 for actions taken in their official capacity. In *Hilton*, the majority heavily relied on *Will* by analogizing the cases to one another insofar as both concerned a question of statutory construction. Substantively, the *Hilton* Court ruled that the Federal Employers' Liability Act creates a cause of action against a state-owned railroad enforceable in state court. The Court further stated that *Will* did not overrule the 1964 precedent on which the *Hilton* cause of action rested.

We do not include *Hilton* as the only progeny of a final Rehnquist Court decision, *Gregory v. Ashcroft* (1991), notwithstanding its formal compliance with our decision rules. The Court ruled that Missouri's mandatory retirement age for judges does not violate the Age Discrimination in Employment Act. Blackmun and Marshall dissented.[16] After Marshall's retirement, Blackmun concurred without opinion to the Court's decision in *Hilton*, which as we have seen is also a progeny of *Will v. Michigan State Police*. We exclude Blackmun's *Hilton* vote from consideration not only because we cannot determine whether it is

---

[16] In the course of his opinion Blackmun indicated disagreement with the dictionary's definition of policy making insofar as judges are concerned. Actually, all of the justices waffled on judges as policy makers except Stevens and White, who labeled them for what they are. See Segal and Spaeth (1993, 6–7). The issue arose because the ADEA excludes from its coverage employees on a policy-making level (1991, 456).

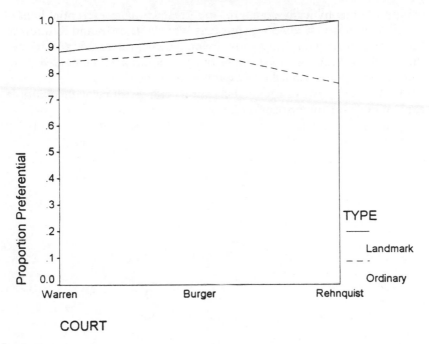

Figure 8.1. Precedential/preferential behavior on the Warren, Burger, and Rehnquist Courts.

precedential or preferential, but also – and more important – because the *Gregory* precedent is cited only as authority for a rule of statutory construction (1991, 210), not for the decision on the merits.

The Justices' Behavior

Notwithstanding its small size, only two of the thirteen Courts whose ordinary decisions we have sampled had as high a proportion of precedential votes as the 24 percent of the Rehnquist Court (see Table 8.2): the 30.4 percent of the Hughes Court and the 29.5 percent of the Taney Court. Does this partial and relatively minimal resurgence of precedential voting in the Rehnquist Court's ordinary litigation bode operational relevance for one of the precedential models of decision making? We hardly think so, given the fact that the landmark decisions of the Rehnquist Court produced naught but preferential votes. A more likely explanation is that this small sample merely generated an insignificant nonrandom blip on the screen of preferential voting.

Figure 8.1 graphically compares the precedential/preferential behavior of the last three Courts we consider: Warren, Burger, and Rehnquist. Three of the four data points show an increase in preferential voting over that of the preceding Court. Only the Rehnquist Court's behavior toward ordinary litigation shows a preferential decrease.

In Chapter 9, we examine the overall trends along with plausible explanations for the justices' behavior.

9

The Supreme Court
and *Stare Decisis*

We began this book with the assumption that for precedent to be an *influence* on the behavior of justices, it must lead them to a result they would not otherwise have reached. Thus, if a justice agrees with the establishment of a precedent, it is impossible to determine whether that justice was influenced by the precedent in subsequent cases, for her preferences, whatever their cause, coincide with the precedent.[1] But for justices who disagree with the established precedent, such as those who dissent from it, we can attempt to determine whether they are influenced by the precedent by examining whether their behavior shifts toward the position taken in that precedent in subsequent cases. Using this strategy, we examined the influence of precedent by studying 2,425 votes and opinions cast by 77 justices in 1,206 progeny of 341 cases. We have found that precedent rarely influences United States Supreme Court justices. In this chapter we summarize the complete dataset, explore alternative explanations for our results, and examine possible systematic explanations for the relatively few instances where justices are influenced by precedent.

DATA DESCRIPTION AND SUMMARY

Of our 2,425 votes and opinions, 288, or 11.9 percent, fall into one of our precedential categories,[2] while 2,137, or 88.1 percent, fall into one of our preferential categories.[3] We will break these out into landmarks versus

---

[1]   To argue for precedential impact in such cases is to argue that the justice would have changed her position but was forestalled from doing so by the precedent she helped establish. While this might occasionally happen, we imagine that such circumstances are rather rare.

[2]   We find 2.6 percent in our strong precedential category, 7.4 percent in our moderate precedential category, and 1.9 percent in our weak precedential category. Rounding prevents this calculation from totaling 11.8 percent.

[3]   We found 25.0 percent in our strong preferential category, 21.8 percent in the moderate preferential category, and 41.4 percent in the weak preferential category.

ordinary cases and apportion them among a number of other factors. Though there may be some subset of justices or some types of issues or some periods within our sample where precedential behavior might be greater, we can state our overall conclusion straightforwardly: the justices are rarely influenced by *stare decisis*. This holds even without comparisons to changing behavior by justices who originally supported the precedents in question (discussed later). If our choice is among the precedential models, moderate models, and preferential models discussed in Chapter 1, the data we collected are most consistent with the expectations of the preferential models. The levels of precedential behavior that we find at the United States Supreme Court are simply not consistent with the empirical manifestations of the sort of arguments we find, for example, in Dworkin (1978). For example:

- That judges are not free to "pick and choose amongst the principles and policies that make up" the doctrine of *stare decisis* (p. 38)
- That a judge cannot apply extralegal principles "according to his own lights" (p. 39)
- That judges "do not have discretion in the matter of principles" (p. 47)
- That when a new case falls within the scope of a previous decision, the earlier case has an "enactment force" that binds judges

Even recognizing the lesser pull of precedent on higher courts, the notions that there are correct answers to hard legal questions, that the judge's job is to find these answers, and that precedents constitute major guideposts of this search make the empirical fit of Dworkin's model to the U.S. Supreme Court a rather poor one.

Though our conclusions are limited to the impact of precedent, and not to other forms of law oriented behavior, the levels of precedential behavior we find do not support Pritchett's statement "Judges make choices, but they are not the 'free' choices of congressmen" (1969, p. 42). Indeed, given the extraordinary constraints on representatives imposed by constituents (Fiorina 1974) and party (Cox and McCubbins 1993), we would conversely argue that members of Congress make choices, but they are not the free choices of Supreme Court justices. And while Murphy is indeed correct that precedents are rarely overruled, this hardly means that justices are constrained by precedent. As we have noted, the overall levels of precedential behavior are so low that only the preferential models discussed in Chapter 1 appear to be in the right ballpark. We discuss these models further in the material that follows.

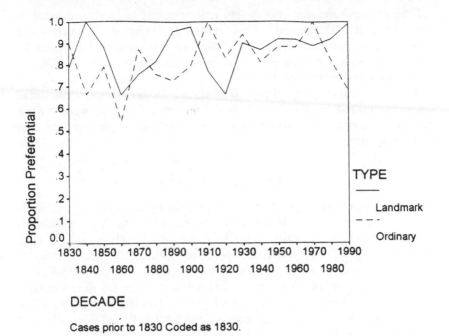

DECADE

Cases prior to 1830 Coded as 1830.

Figure 9.1. Precedential/preferential behavior by decade.

Precedent over Time

We present our findings diachronically in Figure 9.1. Here we aggregate cases by decade according to the year of the progeny, with five landmarks and four ordinary cases from before 1830 coded with the 1830s. As can readily be seen, while levels fluctuate around the mean levels, there is not much of a pattern over time. Preferential behavior in landmark cases peaks in the 1840s (100 percent), in the first decade of the twentieth century (97.7 percent), and again at the end of the century (99.0 percent). Precedential behavior in landmarks peaks at fairly moderate levels during the 1860s (33.3 percent precedential)[4] and again in the 1920s (again 33.3 percent). The sharp rise in the 1930s might suggest that as the Court gained control over its jurisdiction in the 1920s, the percentage of cases with legal discretion increased, but the low levels of precedential behavior in virtually all previous decades belie this conclusion.

[4] The *n* here is only six cases, compared with 17 in the 1850s and 46 in the 1870s.

Preferential behavior in ordinary cases peaked in 1910, and again in the 1970s, at 100 percent.[5] Precedential behavior in ordinary cases peaked at 45.5 percent during the 1860s, suggesting that the results for the landmarks during that decade were not accidental, and, surprisingly, at 31.8 percent during the 1990s.

What is clear beyond doubt is that the modern Supreme Courts, heavily criticized for their activism, did not invent or even perfect preferential behavior; it has been with us since Washington packed the Court with Federalists.

The Justices' Behavior

Table 9.1 presents the summary voting scores for each justice for whom we have at least one vote to consider in either a landmark or an ordinary case. As noted in Chapter 1, we label justices "preferential" if their preferential scores are above 66.7 percent, "moderately preferential" if their scores are between 33.3 and 66.7 percent, and "precedential" if their scores are below 33.3 percent. In landmark cases, for the 34 justices deciding ten or more cases, no justice can be labeled a precedentialist, but two, Harold Burton (69.2 percent preferential) and Lewis Powell (65.2 percent preferential), can be labeled moderates. We also note that Taft voted precedentially in three of his four landmark progeny, while Nathan Clifford, a Buchanan appointee who squeaked through the Senate in a twenty-six to twenty-three vote, voted precedentially in three of his seven.

Five justices voted their preferences in every landmark progeny they decided: Benjamin Harrison appointee David Brewer, Arthur appointee Horace Gray, Cleveland appointee Wheeler Peckham, and two modern-era justices, William O. Douglas (to no one's surprise, we are sure) and Sandra O'Connor (confirming our speculative judgment in Chapter 1, in contrast to the conventional wisdom noted there). We especially note Douglas's record, which was consistent through 120 decisions! O'Connor is a distant second with 27. Honorable mention goes to Warren Court stalwarts Hugo Black (96.8 percent preferential), William Brennan (98.6 percent), and Thurgood Marshall (98.7 percent), as well as William Rehnquist (96.1 percent) for surpassing the 95 percent preferential level.

In ordinary cases there are fewer justices who decided ten or more cases. Of the 22 who did, none can be labeled precedentialist, but three can be labeled moderates: Chief Justice Fuller, who is right on the border

---

[5]   Again, we have only six cases in the 1910s. The preferential perfection demonstrated in the 1970s is based on 52 cases.

Table 9.1.
Justices' precedential behavior by case type

					TYPE		
JUSTICE					Landmark	Ordinary	Total
Baldwin	VOTE	preferences	Count			1	1
			Percent			100.0%	100.0%
	Total		Count			1	1
			Percent			100.0%	100.0%
Barbour	VOTE	preferences	Count		1		1
			Percent		100.0%		100.0%
	Total		Count		1		1
			Percent		100.0%		100.0%
Black	VOTE	precedent	Count		3		3
			Percent		3.2%		2.5%
		preferences	Count		90	29	119
			Percent		96.8%	100.0%	97.5%
	Total		Count		93	29	122
			Percent		100.0%	100.0%	100.0%
Blackmun	VOTE	precedent	Count		13	3	16
			Percent		20.0%	21.4%	20.3%
		preferences	Count		52	11	63
			Percent		80.0%	78.6%	79.7%
	Total		Count		65	14	79
			Percent		100.0%	100.0%	100.0%
Bradley	VOTE	precedent	Count			2	2
			Percent			22.2%	20.0%
		preferences	Count		1	7	8
			Percent		100.0%	77.8%	80.0%
	Total		Count		1	9	10
			Percent		100.0%	100.0%	100.0%
Brandeis	VOTE	precedent	Count		2		2
			Percent		10.0%		7.1%
		preferences	Count		18	8	26
			Percent		90.0%	100.0%	92.9%
	Total		Count		20	8	28
			Percent		100.0%	100.0%	100.0%
Brennan	VOTE	precedent	Count		2		2
			Percent		1.4%		1.2%
		preferences	Count		146	25	171
			Percent		98.6%	100.0%	98.8%
	Total		Count		148	25	173
			Percent		100.0%	100.0%	100.0%
Brewer	VOTE	precedent	Count			1	1
			Percent			14.3%	4.5%
		preferences	Count		15	6	21
			Percent		100.0%	85.7%	95.5%
	Total		Count		15	7	22
			Percent		100.0%	100.0%	100.0%

Table 9.1 (*cont.*)

JUSTICE				TYPE		
				Landmark	Ordinary	Total
Brown	VOTE	precedent	Count	1	3	4
			Percent	25.0%	60.0%	44.4%
		preferences	Count	3	2	5
			Percent	75.0%	40.0%	55.6%
	Total		Count	4	5	9
			Percent	100.0%	100.0%	100.0%
Burger	VOTE	precedent	Count	5	1	6
			Percent	10.2%	11.1%	10.3%
		preferences	Count	44	8	52
			Percent	89.8%	88.9%	89.7%
	Total		Count	49	9	58
			Percent	100.0%	100.0%	100.0%
Burton	VOTE	precedent	Count	4	1	5
			Percent	33.3%	100.0%	38.5%
		preferences	Count	9		9
			Percent	69.2%		64.3%
	Total		Count	13	1	14
			Percent	100.0%	100.0%	100.0%
Butler	VOTE	precedent	Count	4		4
			Percent	12.1%		11.1%
		preferences	Count	29	3	32
			Percent	87.9%	100.0%	88.9%
	Total		Count	33	3	36
			Percent	100.0%	100.0%	100.0%
Campbell	VOTE	preferences	Count	2	5	7
			Percent	100.0%	100.0%	100.0%
	Total		Count	2	5	7
			Percent	100.0%	100.0%	100.0%
Cardozo	VOTE	precedent	Count	1		1
			Percent	16.7%		16.7%
		preferences	Count	5		5
			Percent	83.3%		83.3%
	Total		Count	6		6
			Percent	100.0%		100.0%
Catron	VOTE	precedent	Count	3	6	9
			Percent	33.3%	42.9%	39.1%
		preferences	Count	6	8	14
			Percent	66.7%	57.1%	60.9%
	Total		Count	9	14	23
			Percent	100.0%	100.0%	100.0%
Chase, S.P.	VOTE	preferences	Count	5	2	7
			Percent	100.0%	100.0%	100.0%
	Total		Count	5	· 2	7
			Percent	100.0%	100.0%	100.0%

Table 9.1 (*cont.*)

JUSTICE				TYPE		
				Landmark	Ordinary	Total
Clark	VOTE	precedent	Count	7	3	10
			Percent	17.9%	33.3%	20.8%
		preferences	Count	32	5	38
			Percent	82.1%	66.7%	79.2%
	Total		Count	39	9	48
			Percent	100.0%	100.0%	100.0%
Clarke	VOTE	precedent	Count		1	1
			Percent		25.0%	14.3%
		preferences	Count	3	3	6
			Percent	100.0%	75.0%	85.7%
	Total		Count	3	4	7
			Percent	100.0%	100.0%	100.0%
Clifford	VOTE	precedent	Count	3	4	7
			Percent	42.9%	50.0%	46.7%
		preferences	Count	4	4	8
			Percent	57.1%	50.0%	53.3%
	Total		Count	7	8	15
			Percent	100.0%	100.0%	100.0%
Daniel	VOTE	preferences	Count	5	14	19
			Percent	100.0%	100.0%	100.0%
	Total		Count	5	14	19
			Percent	100.0%	100.0%	100.0%
Davis	VOTE	precedent	Count	2	1	3
			Percent	28.6%	16.7%	23.1%
		preferences	Count	5	5	10
			Percent	71.4%	83.3%	76.9%
	Total		Count	7	6	13
			Percent	100.0%	100.0%	100.0%
Day	VOTE	preferences	Count	2	2	4
			Percent	100.0%	100.0%	100.0%
	Total		Count	2	2	4
			Percent	100.0%	100.0%	100.0%
Douglas	VOTE	precedent	Count		1	1
			Percent		3.4%	0.7%
		preferences	Count	120	28	148
			Percent	100.0%	96.6%	99.3%
	Total		Count	120	29	149
			Percent	100.0%	100.0%	100.0%
Field	VOTE	precedent	Count	2	10	12
			Percent	8.3%	25.6%	19.0%
		preferences	Count	22	29	51
			Percent	91.7%	74.4%	81.0%
	Total		Count	24	39	63
			Percent	100.0%	100.0%	100.0%

Table 9.1 (*cont.*)

JUSTICE				TYPE		
				Landmark	Ordinary	Total
Frankfurter	VOTE	precedent	Count	5	1	6
			Percent	18.5%	6.7%	14.3%
		preferences	Count	22	14	36
			Percent	81.5%	93.3%	85.7%
	Total		Count	27	15	42
			Percent	100.0%	100.0%	100.0%
Fuller	VOTE	precedent	Count	2	8	10
			Percent	13.3%	33.3%	25.6%
		preferences	Count	13	16	29
			Percent	86.7%	66.7%	74.4%
	Total		Count	15	24	39
			Percent	100.0%	100.0%	100.0%
Goldberg	VOTE	preferences	Count	1		1
			Percent	100.0%		100.0%
	Total		Count	1		1
			Percent	100.0%		100.0%
Gray	VOTE	preferences	Count	12	4	16
			Percent	100.0%	100.0%	100.0%
	Total		Count	12	4	16
			Percent	100.0%	100.0%	100.0%
Grier	VOTE	precedent	Count		4	4
			Percent		50.0%	50.0%
		preferences	Count		4	4
			Percent		50.0%	50.0%
	Total		Count		8	8
			Percent		100.0%	100.0%
Harlan I	VOTE	precedent	Count	3	2	5
			Percent	8.3%	5.3%	6.8%
		preferences	Count	33	36	69
			Percent	91.7%	94.7%	93.2%
	Total		Count	36	38	74
			Percent	100.0%	100.0%	100.0%
Harlan II	VOTE	precedent	Count	13		13
			Percent	10.8%		10.6%
		preferences	Count	107	3	110
			Percent	89.2%	100.0%	89.4%
	Total		Count	120	3	123
			Percent	100.0%	100.0%	100.0%
Holmes	VOTE	precedent	Count	4	1	5
			Percent	14.3%	25.0%	15.6%
		preferences	Count	24	3	27
			Percent	85.7%	75.0%	84.4%
	Total		Count	28	4	32
			Percent	100.0%	100.0%	100.0%

Table 9.1 (*cont.*)

| JUSTICE | | | | TYPE | | |
				Landmark	Ordinary	Total
Hughes	VOTE	precedent	Count		2	2
			Percent		66.7%	25.0%
		preferences	Count	5	1	6
			Percent	100.0%	33.3%	75.0%
	Total		Count	5	3	8
			Percent	100.0%	100.0%	100.0%
Iredell	VOTE	preferences	Count	1		1
			Percent	100.0%		100.0%
	Total		Count	1		1
			Percent	100.0%		100.0%
Jackson	VOTE	precedent	Count	1	3	4
			Percent	8.3%	33.3%	19.0%
		preferences	Count	11	6	17
			Percent	91.7%	66.7%	81.0%
	Total		Count	12	9	21
			Percent	100.0%	100.0%	100.0%
Johnson	VOTE	precedent	Count		1	1
			Percent		25.0%	11.1%
		preferences	Count	5	3	8
			Percent	100.0%	75.0%	88.9%
	Total		Count	5	4	9
			Percent	100.0%	100.0%	100.0%
Kennedy	VOTE	preferences	Count	4		4
			Percent	100.0%		100.0%
	Total		Count	4		4
			Percent	100.0%		100.0%
Lamar, L.	VOTE	preferences	Count	1		1
			Percent	100.0%		100.0%
	Total		Count	1		1
			Percent	100.0%		100.0%
Livingston	VOTE	preferences	Count		1	1
			Percent		100.0%	100.0%
	Total		Count		1	1
			Percent		100.0%	100.0%
Marshall, T.	VOTE	precedent	Count	2		2
			Percent	1.3%		1.1%
		preferences	Count	154	28	182
			Percent	98.7%	100.0%	98.9%
	Total		Count	156	28	184
			Percent	100.0%	100.0%	100.0%
McKenna	VOTE	precedent	Count	3		3
			Percent	20.0%		13.6%
		preferences	Count	12	7	19
			Percent	80.0%	100.0%	86.4%
	Total		Count	15	7	22
			Percent	100.0%	100.0%	100.0%

Table 9.1 (*cont.*)

JUSTICE				TYPE		
				Landmark	Ordinary	Total
McKinley	VOTE	precedent	Count		1	1
			Percent		100.0%	100.0%
	Total		Count		1	1
			Percent		100.0%	100.0%
McLean	VOTE	precedent	Count	1	5	6
			Percent	25.0%	35.7%	33.3%
		preferences	Count	3	9	12
			Percent	75.0%	64.3%	66.7%
	Total		Count	4	14	18
			Percent	100.0%	100.0%	100.0%
McReynolds	VOTE	precedent	Count	7	2	9
			Percent	14.6%	18.2%	15.3%
		preferences	Count	41	9	50
			Percent	85.4%	81.8%	84.7%
	Total		Count	48	11	59
			Percent	100.0%	100.0%	100.0%
Miller	VOTE	precedent	Count	2	5	7
			Percent	33.3%	22.7%	25.0%
		preferences	Count	4	17	21
			Percent	66.7%	77.3%	75.0%
	Total		Count	6	22	28
			Percent	100.0%	100.0%	100.0%
Minton	VOTE	preferences	Count	3		3
			Percent	100.0%		100.0%
	Total		Count	3		3
			Percent	100.0%		100.0%
Murphy	VOTE	precedent	Count	3	1	4
			Percent	27.3%	33.3%	28.6%
		preferences	Count	8	2	10
			Percent	72.7%	66.7%	71.4%
	Total		Count	11	3	14
			Percent	100.0%	100.0%	100.0%
Nelson	VOTE	precedent	Count	2	2	4
			Percent	66.7%	50.0%	57.1%
		preferences	Count	1	2	3
			Percent	33.3%	50.0%	42.9%
	Total		Count	3	4	7
			Percent	100.0%	100.0%	100.0%
O'Connor	VOTE	precedent	Count		3	3
			Percent		60.0%	9.4%
		preferences	Count	27	2	29
			Percent	100.0%	40.0%	90.6%
	Total		Count	27	5	32
			Percent	100.0%	100.0%	100.0%

Table 9.1 (*cont.*)

JUSTICE				TYPE		
				Landmark	Ordinary	Total
Peckham	VOTE	precedent	Count		1	1
			Percent		50.0%	7.7%
		preferences	Count	11	1	12
			Percent	100.0%	50.0%	92.3%
	Total		Count	11	2	13
			Percent	100.0%	100.0%	100.0%
Pitney	VOTE	preferences	Count	1	2	3
			Percent	100.0%	100.0%	100.0%
	Total		Count	1	2	3
			Percent	100.0%	100.0%	100.0%
Powell	VOTE	precedent	Count	8	1	9
			Percent	34.8%	10.0%	27.3%
		preferences	Count	15	9	24
			Percent	65.2%	90.0%	72.7%
	Total		Count	23	10	33
			Percent	100.0%	100.0%	100.0%
Reed	VOTE	precedent	Count	3	1	4
			Percent	15.0%	16.7%	15.4%
		preferences	Count	17	5	22
			Percent	85.0%	83.3%	84.6%
	Total		Count	20	6	26
			Percent	100.0%	100.0%	100.0%
Rehnquist	VOTE	precedent	Count	5	3	8
			Percent	3.9%	11.5%	5.2%
		preferences	Count	122	23	145
			Percent	96.1%	88.5%	94.8%
	Total		Count	127	26	153
			Percent	100.0%	100.0%	100.0%
Roberts	VOTE	precedent	Count	1	3	4
			Percent	14.3%	33.3%	25.0%
		preferences	Count	6	6	12
			Percent	85.7%	66.7%	75.0%
	Total		Count	7	9	16
			Percent	100.0%	100.0%	100.0%
Rutledge, W.	VOTE	preferences	Count	4		4
			Percent	100.0%		100.0%
	Total		Count	4		4
			Percent	100.0%		100.0%
Sanford	VOTE	precedent	Count	2		2
			Percent	50.0%		50.0%
		preferences	Count	2		2
			Percent	50.0%		50.0%
	Total		Count	4		4
			Percent	100.0%		100.0%

Table 9.1 (*cont.*)

JUSTICE				Landmark	Ordinary	Total
				TYPE		
Scalia	VOTE	precedent	Count		1	1
			Percent		100.0%	16.7%
		preferences	Count	5		5
			Percent	100.0%		83.3%
	Total		Count	5	1	6
			Percent	100.0%	100.0%	100.0%
Shiras	VOTE	preferences	Count	6		6
			Percent	100.0%		100.0%
	Total		Count	6		6
			Percent	100.0%		100.0%
Stevens	VOTE	precedent	Count	4	8	12
			Percent	10.3%	38.1%	20.0%
		preferences	Count	35	13	48
			Percent	89.7%	61.9%	80.0%
	Total		Count	39	21	60
			Percent	100.0%	100.0%	100.0%
Stewart	VOTE	precedent	Count	17	1	18
			Percent	18.5%	9.1%	17.5%
		preferences	Count	75	10	85
			Percent	81.5%	90.9%	82.5%
	Total		Count	92	11	103
			Percent	100.0%	100.0%	100.0%
Stone	VOTE	precedent	Count	1	1	2
			Percent	5.6%	33.3%	9.5%
		preferences	Count	17	2	19
			Percent	94.4%	66.7%	90.5%
	Total		Count	18	3	21
			Percent	100.0%	100.0%	100.0%
Story	VOTE	preferences	Count		2	2
			Percent		100.0%	100.0%
	Total		Count		2	2
			Percent		100.0%	100.0%
Strong	VOTE	precedent	Count		1	1
			Percent		14.3%	8.3%
		preferences	Count	5	6	11
			Percent	100.0%	85.7%	91.7%
	Total		Count	5	7	12
			Percent	100.0%	100.0%	100.0%
Sutherland	VOTE	precedent	Count	4		4
			Percent	19.0%		16.7%
		preferences	Count	17	3	20
			Percent	81.0%	100.0%	83.3%
	Total		Count	21	3	24
			Percent	100.0%	100.0%	100.0%

Table 9.1 (*cont.*)

JUSTICE				TYPE		
				Landmark	Ordinary	Total
Swayne	VOTE	precedent	Count	2	1	3
			Percent	28.6%	11.1%	18.8%
		preferences	Count	5	8	13
			Percent	71.4%	88.9%	81.3%
	Total		Count	7	9	16
			Percent	100.0%	100.0%	100.0%
Taft	VOTE	precedent	Count	3		3
			Percent	75.0%		75.0%
		preferences	Count	1		1
			Percent	25.0%		25.0%
	Total		Count	4		4
			Percent	100.0%		100.0%
Taney	VOTE	precedent	Count	1		1
			Percent	14.3%		12.5%
		preferences	Count	6	1	7
			Percent	85.7%	100.0%	87.5%
	Total		Count	7	1	8
			Percent	100.0%	100.0%	100.0%
Thompson	VOTE	precedent	Count	2		2
			Percent	28.6%		25.0%
		preferences	Count	5	1	6
			Percent	71.4%	100.0%	75.0%
	Total		Count	7	1	8
			Percent	100.0%	100.0%	100.0%
VanDevanter	VOTE	precedent	Count	6	1	7
			Percent	22.2%	12.5%	20.0%
		preferences	Count	21	7	28
			Percent	77.8%	87.5%	80.0%
	Total		Count	27	8	35
			Percent	100.0%	100.0%	100.0%
Vinson	VOTE	preferences	Count	1		1
			Percent	100.0%		100.0%
	Total		Count	1		1
			Percent	100.0%		100.0%
Warren	VOTE	precedent	Count		2	2
			Percent		33.3%	14.3%
		preferences	Count	8	4	12
			Percent	100.0%	66.7%	85.7%
	Total		Count	8	6	14
			Percent	100.0%	100.0%	100.0%
Washington	VOTE	preferences	Count	1		1
			Percent	100.0%		100.0%
	Total		Count	1		1
			Percent	100.0%		100.0%

Table 9.1 (*cont.*)

JUSTICE				Landmark	Ordinary	Total
				TYPE		
Wayne	VOTE	precedent	Count		2	2
			Percent		50.0%	50.0%
		preferences	Count		2	2
			Percent		50.0%	50.0%
	Total		Count		4	4
			Percent		100.0%	100.0%
White, B.	VOTE	precedent	Count	22		22
			Percent	13.7%		13.4%
		preferences	Count	139	3	142
			Percent	86.3%	100.0%	86.6%
	Total		Count	161	3	164
			Percent	100.0%	100.0%	100.0%
White, E.	VOTE	precedent	Count	1	2	3
			Percent	8.3%	18.2%	13.0%
		preferences	Count	11	9	20
			Percent	91.7%	81.8%	87.0%
	Total		Count	12	11	23
			Percent	100.0%	100.0%	100.0%
Whittaker	VOTE	preferences	Count	1		1
			Percent	100.0%		100.0%
	Total		Count	1		1
			Percent	100.0%		100.0%

at 66.7 percent preferential; Jackson's first appointee, John McLean (64.3 percent); and from the modern era, the moderate Republican John Paul Stevens (61.9 percent). If we lowered the number of cases needed for classification, we could add the Polk appointee Robert Grier and, again, Nathan Clifford, both with four of eight votes falling in the precedential category. At the other end of the spectrum, Black, Brennan, and Marshall are 100 percent preferential, with Douglas gaining honorable mention at 96.6 percent.

Indeed, if we categorize precedents as being liberal or conservative, something we are able to do for all civil liberties and economics cases since the 1937 term,[6] we find that dissenters from conservative landmarks switched their positions in those cases' progeny only 15 times out of 640 opportunities (2.3 percent) (see Table 9.2). Alternatively, dissenters

[6] From the 1946 term forward we use Spaeth's U.S. Supreme Court database, as expanded to cover the Vinson Court. For the 1937–45 terms, we use data from a separate project (NSF grant SBR9320509, Lee Epstein, Carol Mershon, Jeffrey Segal, and Harold Spaeth, principal investigators) to categorize cases.

Table 9.2.
Precedential behavior by direction of precedent, civil liberties, and
economics cases, 1937–1995

				Liberal	Conserv.	Total
				\multicolumn{3} Direction of Prec.		
TYPE				Liberal	Conserv.	Total
Landmark	VOTE	precedent	Count	99	15	114
			Percent	13.9%	2.3%	8.4%
		preferences	Count	612	625	1237
			Percent	86.1%	97.7%	91.6%
	Total		Count	711	640	1351
			Percent	100.0%	100.0%	100.0%
Ordinary	VOTE	precedent	Count	18	13	31
			Percent	16.7%	10.3%	13.2%
		preferences	Count	90	113	203
			Percent	83.3%	89.7%	86.8%
	Total		Count	108	126	234
			Percent	100.0%	100.0%	100.0%

from liberal landmarks switched their positions 99 times out of 711
opportunities (13.9 percent).[7] If we examine those justices who served
since the start of the Roosevelt Court and participated in ten or more
progeny of landmark cases, those justices who are relatively more liberal
(above the mean of .16 in the Segal–Cover ideology scores) voted
precedentially 10.0 percent of the time, while those who are relatively
more conservative voted precedentially 15.9 percent of the time. Thus,
there exists some evidence that in these cases for these years the old
canard might in fact be true: conservative justices are more restrained,
toward precedent at least, than are liberal justices.

TESTING ALTERNATIVE EXPLANATIONS

Our research design treats justices as supporting precedent whenever
they shift positions to support a precedent they had opposed. In such
cases, we have a prima facie case that the change in the justices' behavior
is due to precedent, but it is clear that other factors might explain this

[7]   To the extent that critical legal theorists expect a conservative bias to law, they might
expect that liberal outcomes, when they are achieved, will soon be limited or overturned. Thus conservative dissenters might be most likely to stick to their preferences.
This is the opposite of what we observe.

shift as well. For example, Justice Blackmun's shift toward support for *Furman v. Georgia* (1972) in the 1980s undoubtedly had little to do with precedential support for *Furman*, which he explicitly rejected through much of the 1970s, and much to do with his increasing liberalism. In this section we establish a baseline for the amount of shifting we would expect even without the newly established precedent, and then examine two alternative explanations for such behavior: changing personal preferences over time and changing political constraints over time.

Establishing a Baseline

In our study we have found that when a newly established precedent diverges from a justice's previously revealed preferences, the justice will shift positions and support the precedent about 12 percent of the time in subsequent cases. About 10 percent of the total cases represent the strongest manifestations of precedential behavior (strong or moderate), whereby justices either explicitly accede to the precedent they had dissented from or sign opinions explicitly citing the original precedent as authority for their opinion. But this amount of changing behavior could readily result from a series of other factors that need not have anything to do with the establishment of the precedent. That is, some proportion of the changing behavior we have observed would have happened anyway. The question is, how much?

We answer that by examining the behavior of those justices who originally joined the majority opinion of the established precedent. To establish a baseline of normal behavioral changes by justices, we took a 30 percent random sample of our cases[8] and assessed the future behavior of the justices who sided with the majority in the established precedents. Compared to dissenting justices who *explicitly* switched positions 10 percent of the time, justices who sided with the majority explicitly switched positions only 0.9 percent of the time. This quasi experiment, holding the cases, the progeny, and the periods constant, and "manipulating" which side of the case the justice was on, demonstrates that the overwhelming majority of explicitly precedential behavior that we find is in fact precedential. Though the absolute levels are low, justices who dissent from a precedent are much more likely to change positions explicitly than are those justices who originally supported the precedent.

At the same time, we must take a more cautious view if we try to examine *all* manifestations of precedential behavior. The problem here

---

[8]   Actually, we attempted a 25 percent sample, but SPSS's pseudorandom number generator returned 29.7 percent of the cases.

is that the weakest manifestation of precedential behavior turns on direction, which is a function of the dissenters' votes. In attempting to identify the majority's behavior in progeny, direction is not always clear[9] and thus we are hesitant about making too much of these results. Nevertheless, for the sake of completeness, we find justices in the original majority switching positions 9.7 percent of the time, compared to 11.8 percent of the time for justices who dissented. While these differences are statistically significant from each other,[10] suggesting a substantively small (perhaps minute) but statistically significant impact of precedent, the results, given our concerns about these data, suggest that we should at least be wary of the small percentage of our cases that fall into the weak precedential category.

Changing Preferences

On the aggregate level, the amount of consistent behavior by justices in the majority clearly suggests that much of the (low levels of) explicitly precedential behavior is in fact real precedential behavior. Yet this aggregate finding might mask particular types of cases where other factors might lead to apparently precedential behavior that is actually caused by other factors.

Our first alternative explanation for the specific switches in the justices' behavior that we observe in our cases may simply be attitude change. At least in recent years, a fair number of justices have become either more liberal or more conservative over time (Epstein, Hoekstra, Segal, and Spaeth 1998), and we have no reason to doubt that this occurred in earlier years as well. If this is the case, as the time between the precedential case and the progeny increases, the likelihood of switching positions might increase regardless of whether one supports the doctrine of *stare decisis* or not.

We examine this hypothesis in Figure 9.2.[11] As can readily be seen, there is no support for this alternative explanation. In landmark cases, preferential behavior hovers around 90 percent for the entire period. The ordinary cases show more variability, but precedential behavior is higher after one year (31.6 percent) than it is at 21+ years (16.7 percent).

---

[9]   For example, the dissent may take a liberal position. This, by definition, makes the majority conservative, even though a dissent by another subset of justices to the right of the majority's position would cause us to identify the majority as liberal.

[10] $P < .05$.

[11]   Because there are fewer and fewer justices around to decide progeny with each passing year, we collapsed years 10–15 into the value 10, 16–20 into the value 16, and 21–26 (the maximum) into the value 21.

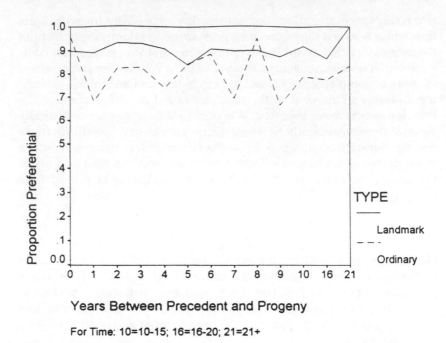

Years Between Precedent and Progeny

For Time: 10=10-15; 16=16-20; 21=21+

Figure 9.2. Precedential/preferential behavior by years since precedent.

The changing behavior that we observe and label precedential shows no systematic sign of actually constituting long-term changes in sincere preferences.

Separation of Powers

In *Regents v. Bakke* (1978), Justice Stewart joined dissenting Justices Burger, Rehnquist, and Stevens in holding that Title VI of the Civil Rights Act prohibited all race-conscious college admissions decisions. But in 1979, Stewart joined the majority holding in *Steelworkers v. Weber*, upholding race-conscious promotions under Title VII of the same act. To positive political theorists such as William Eskridge (1991), such behavior represents not the influence of *stare decisis*, but that of strategic factors in a separation-of-powers game, where the justices seek to maximize their policy preferences *subject to the constraints imposed by Congress and the President*. Accordingly, much of what we have labeled precedential behavior may in reality be sophisticated behavior by strategic justices, behavior that has nothing to do with *stare decisis*.

Under these models (see Chapter 1), if the political environment stays the same, there is little reason to expect sitting justices to shift positions on an issue, regardless of the establishment of a precedent. But if the political environment changes, justices may have to respond to those changes to avoid being overruled, especially (if not exclusively) in statutory cases.

According to these models, the justices may need to change positions because of a single change in the political environment, such as when the Senate moved from Republican to Democratic after the 1986 election (Segal 1997). That switch should have freed liberal justices from the constraints imposed by the Republican dominated environment that had existed since 1981. But if the entire political environment shifts, as it did between 1950 and 1953, then we should observe virtually all justices shifting in a conservative direction (ibid.): liberals who were free through 1950 would now be constrained, while conservatives who were constrained through 1950 would now be free.

To examine whether some of the purportedly precedential nature we observe in the justices' behavior might in fact be sophisticated strategies in a separation-of-powers game, we coded each precedential case and each progeny by the political environment in which it occurred, as captured by the partisan control of the House, Senate, and Presidency. We then measured whether there was *any* change in the political environment between the precedent and the progeny, and whether there was *complete* change in the political environment (that is, from complete party domination by one party to complete party domination by another) from the precedent to the progeny. If rather than picking up precedential behavior, we are picking up sophisticated behavior, then our precedential scores should be higher within our set of statutory cases when there is any change in the political environment, and higher still when there is a complete change in the political environment.

We coded each of our precedential cases as based on constitutional grounds, statutory grounds, both, or neither. This resulted in 1,830 votes in the progeny of cases that were predominantly constitutional, 303 votes in the progeny of cases that were predominantly statutory, 287 votes in the progeny of cases that dealt with neither statutes nor the Constitution (such as common law, or oversight of federal courts), and 5 votes in the progeny of cases that were both statutory and constitutional.

We next coded partisan control of government. While such control is relatively easy to assess today, such was not the case in the early years of the Republic. For example, Federalists controlled the first Congress, even though there was as yet no Federalist Party. Reference books can help, but they sometimes obscure as much as they enlighten. For example, the authoritative Congressional Quarterly (CQ) *Guide to Congress* (1991) states on page 688 that from 1801 the Democratic-Republicans "occupied the White House and controlled Congress until 1829." Just three paragraphs later it states that the outgrowth "Democrats captured control of Congress in 1826." Adding to the confusion, CQ's chart of party affiliation in Congress lists the Nineteenth Congress (1825–27) as under control of the "Administration Party," and the Twentieth Congress (1827–29) as under the control of the Jeffersonian Party. Neither of these parties shows up in the listing of American political parties in the companion CQ *Guide to U.S. Elections* (1994). Despite these problems, we believe we can make reasonably legitimate decision rules as to partisan control of the national political environment.

First, we started with the table of partisan affiliation in Congress and the Presidency in the *Guide to Congress* (1991, p. 93-A). We then made the following changes so as to avoid coding nominal changes in the political environment as actual changes: we coded the Administration Party of 1789 as Federalist; the Administration Party of 1825 as National Republican; the Democratic-Republican (1801–25) and Jeffersonian (1827–29) Parties as Democratic; and the Union Party (1865) as Republican. We additionally changed the coding of three Presidents: John Quincy Adams from Democratic-Republican to National Republican;[12] John Tyler from Whig to Democrat;[13] and Andrew Johnson from Republican to Democrat.[14]

We present our results in Figures 9.3 and 9.4. Figure 9.3 shows precedential behavior in statutory cases given any change in the political environment. In landmark cases, there is virtually no change (5.0 percent versus 5.9 percent), while in ordinary cases, where the Court should be least concerned about congressional interference, there is a visibly perceptible (19.2 percent versus 23.7 percent) but statistically insignificant ($p < .3$) increase.

We have even less of a story in Figure 9.4, which presents our results for situations where there was a complete change in the political environment. Here, precedential behavior in landmark cases drops from 5.7 to

---

[12] Adams was elected as a Democratic-Republican, but his branch of the party quickly split off into the National Republican Party. Coding him as a Democratic-Republican would mean that his Party did not control Congress, whereas it did.

[13] Tyler, a Democrat, was elected Vice President on William Henry Harrison's Whig ticket. Tyler replaced Harrison's cabinet with Democrats and subsequently sought the Democratic presidential nomination.

[14] Johnson, a Democrat, was elected Vice President on Lincoln's Union (Republican) ticket. Given the battles that ensued between Johnson and Congress, it would be nearly impossible to code Johnson as a Republican and thus claim that the same party controlled the White House and Congress.

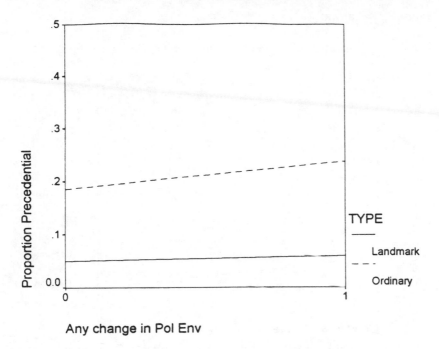

Any change in Pol Env

Figure 9.3. Precedential behavior by any change in the political environment.

0.0 percent, while in ordinary cases it drops from 21.3 to 18.2 percent.[15] Whether or not sophisticated voting occurs on the Supreme Court except in the rarest of circumstances, the data hardly suggest that the little precedential behavior we do observe is in reality part of a separation-of-powers game.

In conclusion, we do not and cannot know that all of the behavior that we label precedential is in fact due to the influence of precedent. But we have tested other potential causes of such behavior and found little evidence that they cause the shifts that we have observed.

TOWARD AN EXPLANATION OF PRECEDENTIAL BEHAVIOR

At this point, we might be tempted to conclude that we have relatively clear evidence, at least compared to prior studies, of low levels of

[15] Interestingly, we observe a statistically significant increase is precedential behavior in the progeny of landmark *constitutional* cases when there was a complete change in the political environment, from 10.3 to 22.2 percent. But five of the eight shifts in these cases moved *away* from the direction of the political environment. As such, this cannot constitute support for the SOP model.

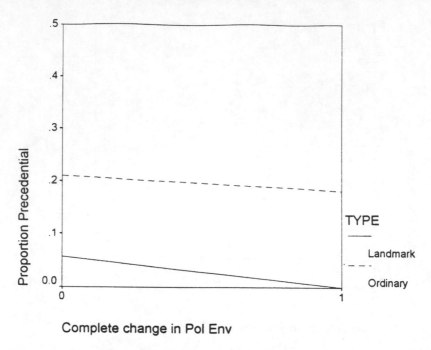

Complete change in Pol Env

Figure 9.4. Precedential behavior by complete change in political environment.

precedential behavior and leave it at that. On the other hand, even though precedential behavior seems fairly rare, it is important enough to attempt to inquire why it exists at all.

Salience

To be sure, as attitudinalists, we would not have predicted anything but low levels of precedential behavior. Yet if such behavior does exist, even at low levels, it should be *relatively* more likely to exist in low-salience cases (see, e.g., Segal and Spaeth 1993, ch. 7). Conversely, preferential behavior, though conceivably dominating all aspects of the decision on the merits, might be *relatively* more dominant in high-salience cases. This is our primary explanatory hypothesis. That is, to the (minor) extent that justices do defer to precedent, they should be relatively more likely to do so in cases that are less important. Of course these would include ordinary cases over landmark cases. Among cases not designated as landmarks, this might include statutory cases over constitutional cases, and since the Roosevelt Court, economic cases over civil liberties cases. We

Table 9.3.
Precedential behavior by type of case

			TYPE		Total
			Landmark	Ordinary	
VOTE	precedent	Count	183	105	288
		Percent	10.0%	17.6%	11.9%
	preferences	Count	1646	491	2137
		Percent	90.0%	82.4%	88.1%
Total		Count	1829	596	2425
		Percent	100.0%	100.0%	100.0%

will examine these predictions, and then proceed with predictions from alternative theoretical perspectives.

We begin with the distinction between landmark and ordinary cases. As Table 9.3 shows, of our 2,425 votes and opinions, 1,829 were from our population of landmark cases from *Witt*. The remaining 596 come from our stratified random sample of ordinary Supreme Court cases with dissent. Cumulatively, in cases where the justices' preferences conflicted with the relevant precedent, the justices supported the precedent in just 10 percent of landmark cases and 17.6 percent of ordinary cases. The results are significant at $p < .001$. This relationship holds through much of the Court's history. The exceptions, as Figure 9.1 demonstrates, are the 1830s, the 1870s, the 1910s–30s, and the 1970s.

We next examined the justices' behavior as a function of the level of interpretation (discussed earlier). We expect that precedential behavior should be higher in statutory cases, where the stakes are typically lower, than in constitutional cases, which make up the core of the Court's policy-making powers. This hypothesis coincides, though for slightly different reasons, with some of the Court's rhetoric about precedent. As the Court noted in *Patterson v. McLean Credit Union*, "Considerations of *stare decisis* have special force in the area of statutory interpretation, for here, unlike in the context of constitutional interpretation, the legislative power is implicated, and Congress remains free to alter what we have done" (1989, at 172–73). Justice Scalia echoed Justice Douglas's statement "A judge looking at a constitutional decision may have compulsions to revere past history and accept what was once written. But he remembers above all else that it is the Constitution which he swore to

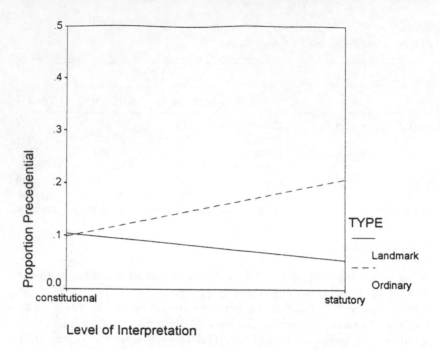

Level of Interpretation

Figure 9.5. Precedential behavior by type of interpretation.

support and defend, not the gloss which his predecessors have put on it"
(*South Carolina v. Gathers* 1989, at 825).

We might conceivably distinguish our explanation from the Court's in
that under the Court's explanation the difference between statutory and
constitutional cases should hold regardless of whether we are dealing
with landmark or ordinary cases. But if salience is the key to the difference, then landmark statutory cases may be just as preferentially driven
as landmark constitutional cases; ordinary statutory cases may be where
precedential behavior is maximized.

Figure 9.5 presents our results. Among landmark cases, there is little
difference between precedential levels in constitutional and statutory
cases; indeed, the relationship is in the opposite direction of what we
predicted (and the Court claims), but the results are not statistically
distinguishable from one another at conventional levels.[16] Alternatively,
we see a substantial increase in precedential behavior in statutory deci-

---

[16] The χ^2 is significant at $p < .10$.

sions of ordinary litigation. The precedential level of 21.1 percent is significantly higher than the constitutional level of ordinary litigation (9.9 percent)[17] and the statutory level of constitutional litigation (5.5 percent).[18] That is, in the least salient of these cases, but only in the least salient, do we find relative increases in precedential behavior, though even here the absolute levels remain fairly low.

Finally, for the period since the start of the Roosevelt Court, we know that civil liberties have been more salient to the Court than economic cases. If this is so, then we should expect relatively higher levels of precedential behavior in economic cases. This hypothesis is also consistent with Justice Rehnquist's "preferred precedents doctrine," whereby "Considerations in favor of *stare decisis* are at their acme in cases involving property and contract rights, where reliance interests are involved," but "the opposite is true in cases such as the present one involving procedural and evidentiary rules" (*Payne v. Tennessee* 1991, at 828). Again, if Rehnquist has accurately described the Court's behavior, we should find this relationship in both ordinary and landmark cases, but if salience is what drives the relationship then any increase in precedential behavior should be most pronounced in ordinary economic cases.

We tested this hypothesis by categorizing cases involving civil liberties or economic issues using Spaeth's U.S. Supreme Court database for the Vinson through Rehnquist Courts, and data from a separate project to categorize cases from the 1937 through 1945 terms (see footnote 3). We present the results in Figure 9.6.

Again, there is no difference in precedential behavior between economic (11.1 percent precedential) and civil liberties cases (8.3 percent precedential) among the progeny of landmark decisions ($p < .6$). But among the progeny of ordinary decisions, the difference is striking: 21.3 percent for economic cases versus 9.2 percent for civil liberties ($p < .02$).

In sum, our first shot at providing an explanation of the low levels of precedential behavior has proved successful. To the (minor) extent that precedential behavior exists, it is more likely to be found in cases of the lowest salience: ordinary cases compared to landmark cases; and among ordinary cases, statutory cases over constitutional cases and modern economic cases over modern civil liberties cases. The influence of precedent appears to be quite minor, but despite an earlier claim we made (Segal and Spaeth 1993, p. 363), it does not appear to be completely idiosyncratic.

---

[17] $p < .001.$ [18] $p < .001.$

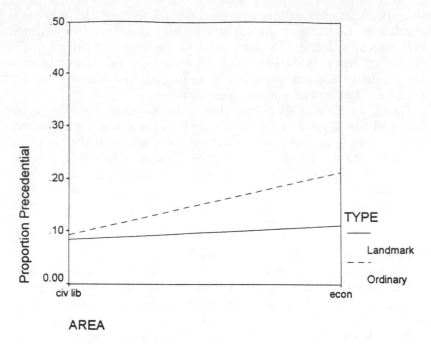

Figure 9.6. Precedential behavior by issue area.

Docket Control

As noted in Chapter 1, neoinstitutionalists argue that the Supreme Court is more likely to be able to ignore the strictures of the legal model than are other courts because the Supreme Court is a court of last resort and thus cannot be judicially reversed and has docket control and thus does not have to decide legally clear cases that lower courts often do (Segal and Spaeth 1993).[19]

We can test one aspect of the neoinstitutional approach by examining the change in precedential behavior before and after the Court gained control over its jurisdiction in 1925. Figure 9.7 presents preferential behavior in the three half decades before and after 1925. The data refute the hypothesis. While preferential behavior in ordinary cases jumps substantially after passage of the Judges Bill, the numbers are not out of line with historic trends (see Figure 9.1). More important, in landmark cases, the passage of the Judges Bill precedes a substantial drop in

---

[19] Neoinstitutionalists also argue that the Court is not politically constrained because of life tenure for the justices and the difficulty of passing override legislation. See Segal 1997.

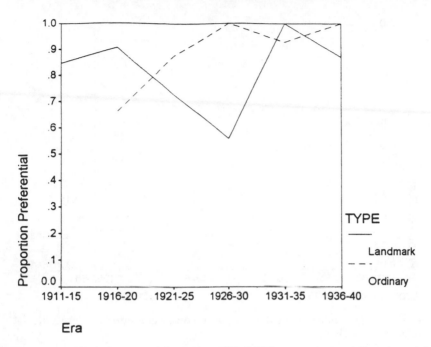

Figure 9.7. The influence of the Judges Bill (1925) on precedential/preferential behavior.

preferential behavior in the five subsequent years, a finding masked by the decade-by-decade grouping of the data in Figure 9.1.

Though these findings appear to refute the notion that preferential decision making requires docket control, the findings do not refute neoinstitutionalism per se. A long list of studies demonstrates that while lower court decisions are influenced in part by the judges' attitudes (for example, Carp and Rowland 1983; Songer, Segal, and Cameron 1994), they are also, unlike those of the Supreme Court, influenced by the commands of *stare decisis* (for example, Baum 1978; Songer 1987; Songer, Segal, and Cameron 1994). If lower courts are indeed constrained by higher courts in their choices, then it is hard to imagine what it could be other than its institutional environment that makes the Supreme Court unique.

Decline of Consensual Norms

If 1925 begins one period where we might have expected an increase in preferential behavior, 1941 represents another. With the ascension of

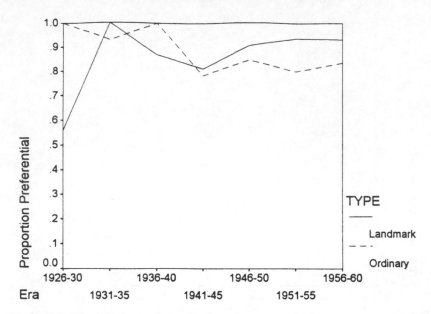

Figure 9.8. The influence of the demise of consensual norms on precedential/ preferential behavior.

Harlan Fiske Stone to the Chief Justiceship, the norm disfavoring dissenting opinions quickly eroded. If this form of cooperative behavior so quickly devolved, so might the sort of cooperative behavior that might lead to a norm favoring precedent.

As with the influence of the Judges Bill, we can quickly refute this hypothesis. Figure 9.8 presents preferential behavior in the periods before and after 1941. Though a cooperative hypothesis might have led to a prediction of increasing preferential behavior between 1936–40 and 1941–45, we actually observe the opposite. Again, this doesn't mean that cooperative behavior doesn't explain some of the precedential behavior that we observe, but our only clear *prior* prediction of when this might have devolved does not pan out.

CONCLUSIONS

Stare decisis is the lifeblood of the legal model, and the legal model is still the lifeblood of most legal scholars' thinking about law. Yet there has been virtually no real testing of the model, perhaps because creating falsifiable hypotheses about precedent and the legal model is not an easy task. Indeed, a June 1997 post to the Law and Courts listserve[20] asking legal academics how the legal model could be tested drew not a single suggestion from the hundreds of scholars who subscribe, many of whom, like one of the authors of this book, are willing to use the listserve to debate law and politics *ad infinitum*. Entering that void we have attempted the first falsifiable, systematic test of the influence of *stare decisis* on the behavior of U.S. Supreme Court justices. We do not expect this first word to be the last word, and we urge those who believe they can better test these models to do so. But for now, we must conclude this book with what the data so strongly suggest: in the realm of *stare decisis*, minority will does not defer to majority rule.

[20]   lawcourts-l@usc.edu.

References

Abraham, Henry A. 1985. *Justices and Presidents*, 2nd ed. New York: Oxford.

Ackerman, Bruce. 1991. *We the People*. Cambridge, MA: Harvard University Press.

Adamany, David. 1973. "Legitimacy, Realigning Elections and the Supreme Court." *Wisconsin Law Review* 790–846.

Axelrod, Robert. 1984. *The Evolution of Cooperation*. New York: Basic Books.

Barrett, Paul M. 1992. "Split Decision." *Wall Street Journal* June 30, A1.

Baum, Lawrence. 1978. "Lower Court Response to Supreme Court Decisions: Reconsidering a Negative Picture." *Justice System Journal* 3:208–219.

   1997. *The Puzzle of Judicial Behavior*. Ann Arbor: University of Michigan Press.

Baumeister, Roy, and Leonard Newman. 1994. "Self-Regulation of Cognitive Inference and Decision Processes." *Personality and Social Psychology Bulletin* 20:3–19.

Bendor, Jonathan, and Piotr Swistak. 1997. "The Evolutionary Stability of Cooperation." *American Political Science Review* 91:290–307.

Bickel, Alexander M. 1962. *The Least Dangerous Branch*. Indianapolis: Bobbs-Merrill.

Blackstone, Sir William. 1979. *Commentaries on the Laws of England: A Facsimile of the First Edition of 1765–1769*. Chicago: University of Chicago Press.

Blasi, Victor. 1983. *The Burger Court: The Counter-Revolution That Wasn't*. New Haven, CT: Yale University Press.

Brace, Paul, and Melinda Gann Hall. 1990. "Neo-Institutionalism and Dissent in State Supreme Courts." *Journal of Politics* 52:54–70.

Brennan, William J. 1985. Remarks of Justice William J. Brennan, Jr. In *The Great Debate*. Washington DC: The Federalist Society. pp. 11–25.

Brenner, Saul, and Harold J. Spaeth. 1995. *Stare Indecisis: The Alteration of Precedent on the Supreme Court, 1946–1992*. New York: Cambridge University Press.

Brenner, Saul, and Marc Stier. 1996. "Retesting Segal and Spaeth's *Stare Decisis* Model." *American Journal of Political Science* 40:1036–1048.

Cardozo, Benjamin N. 1921. *The Nature of the Judicial Process*. New Haven, Conn.: Yale University Press.

Carp, Robert A., and C.K. Rowland. 1983. *Policymaking and Politics in the Federal District Courts*. Knoxville: University of Tennessee Press.

Casper, Jonathan D. 1976. "The Supreme Court and National Policy Making." *American Political Science Review* 70:50–63.

Cox, Gary W., and Matthew D. McCubbins. 1993. *Legislative Leviathan: Party Government in the House*. Berkeley: University of California Press.

Dahl, Robert. 1957. "Decision-Making in a Democracy: The Supreme Court as a National Policy-Maker." *Journal of Public Law* 6:179–295.

Daly, Erin. 1995. "Reconsidering Abortion Law: Liberty, Equality, and the Rhetoric of Planned Parenthood v. Casey." *American University Law Review* 45:77–145.

Dworkin, Ronald. 1978. *Taking Rights Seriously*. Cambridge, MA: Harvard University Press.

1986. *Law's Empire*. Cambridge, MA: Harvard University Press.

Epstein, Lee. 1996. Personal correspondence with authors.

Epstein, Lee, Valerie Hoekstra, Jeffrey A. Segal, and Harold J. Spaeth. 1998. "Do Political Preferences Change? A Longitudinal Study of U.S. Supreme Court Justices." *Journal of Politics* 60:801–18.

Epstein, Lee, and Jack Knight. 1997. *Choices Justices Make*. Washington DC: Congressional Quarterly Press.

Epstein, Lee, and Joseph F. Kobylka. 1992. *The Supreme Court and Legal Change: Abortion and the Death Penalty*. Chapel Hill: The University of North Carolina Press.

Epstein, Lee, Jeffrey A. Segal, Harold J. Spaeth, and Thomas G. Walker. 1994. *The Supreme Court Compendium*. Washington DC: Congressional Quarterly Press.

Epstein, Lee, Jeffrey A. Segal, Harold J. Spaeth, and Thomas G. Walker. 1996. *The Supreme Court Compendium*, 2nd ed. Washington DC: Congressional Quarterly Press.

Epstein, Lee, and Thomas G. Walker. 1995. "The Role of the Supreme Court in American Society: Playing the Reconstruction Game." In

Lee Epstein, Ed., *Contemplating Courts*. Washington, DC: Congressional Quarterly Press.

Eskridge, William N., Jr. 1991. "Reneging on History? Playing the Court/Congress/President Civil Rights Game." *California Law Review* 79:613–684.

"Excerpts from Carswell Talk." 1970. *New York Times* January 22, 1970, p. A22.

Ferejohn, John, and Barry Weingast. 1992. "A Positive Theory of Statutory Interpretation." *International Review of Law and Economics* 12:263–279.

Fiorina, Morris. 1974. *Representatives, Roll Calls, and Constituencies*. Lexington, MA: D.C. Heath.

Fiss, Owen M. 1992. "Brewer, David Josiah." In Kermit L. Hall, ed., *The Oxford Companion to the Supreme Court of the United States*. New York: Oxford University Press, pp. 89–91.

Frank, Jerome. 1930. *Law and the Modern Mind*. New York: Brentano's. 1932. "What Courts Do in Fact." *Illinois Law Review* 26:645–666. 1949. *Law and the Modern Mind*. New York: Coward-McCann.

Funston, Richard Y. 1977. *Constitutional Counterrevolution*. New York: John Wiley & Sons.

Gabel, Peter. 1980. "Reification in Legal Reasoning." *Research in Law and Sociology* 3:25–51.

Gely, Rafael, and Pablo T. Spiller. 1990. "A Rational Choice Theory of Supreme Court Decision Making with Applications to the *State Form* and *Grove City* Cases." *Journal of Law, Economics, and Organizations* 6:263–300.

Gerhart, Eugene C. 1958. *America's Advocate: Robert H. Jackson*. Indianapolis, IN: Bobbs-Merrill.

Gillman, Howard. 1993. *The Constitution Besieged: The Rise and Demise of Lochner Era Police Power Jurisprudence*. Durhan, NC: Duke University Press.

Gray, John Chipman. 1931. *The Nature and Sources of Law*, 2nd ed. New York: Macmillan.

Greenhouse, Linda. 1988. "Precedent for Lower Courts: Tyrant or Teacher." *New York Times* January 29, 12. 1992a. "High Court, 5–4, Affirms Right to Abortion but Allows Most of Pennsylvania's Limits." *New York Times* June 30, A1. 1992b. "A Telling Court Opinion." *New York Times* July 1, A1.

Guide to Congress, 4th ed. 1991. Washington DC: Congressional Quarterly Press.

Guide to U.S. Elections, 3rd ed. 1994. Washington DC: Congressional Quarterly Press.

Haines, Charles Grove. 1922. "General Observations on the Effects of Personal, Political, and Economic Influences in the Decisions of Judges." *Illinois Law Review* 17:96–116.

Holmes, O.W. 1897. "The Path of the Law." *Harvard Law Review* 10:457–478.

Howard, C. Elaine. 1993. "The Roe'd to Confusion: Planned Parenthood v. Casey." *Houston Law Review* 30:1457–1490.

"It's About Time." *Los Angeles Times* September 13, 1981.

Kahneman, Daniel, and Amos Tversky. 1979. "Prospect Theory: An Analysis of Decision Under Risk." *Econometrica* 47:263–291.

———. 1984. "Choices, Values, and Frames." *American Psychologist* 39:341–350.

Kairys, David (ed.). 1982. *The Politics of Law: A Progressive Critique.* New York: Pantheon.

Kemper, Mark. 1998. "An Event-History Model of Supreme Court Precedent." Paper presented at the annual meetings of the Midwest Political Science Issue.

Kennedy, Duncan. 1980. "Toward an Historical Understanding of Legal Consciousness: The Case of Classical Legal Thought in America." *Research in Law and Sociology* 3:3–24.

King, Willard L. 1967. *Melville Weston Fuller.* Chicago: Phoenix Books.

Kluger, Richard. 1975. *Simple Justice.* New York: Knopf.

Knight, Jack. 1994. "Symposium: The Supreme Court and the Attitudinal Model." *Law and Courts* 4:5–6.

Knight, Jack, and Lee Epstein. 1996. "The Norm of Stare Decisis." *American Journal of Political Science* 40:1018–1035.

Kunda, Ziva. 1990. "The Case for Motivated Reasoning." *Psychological Bulletin* 108:480–498.

Levi, Edward H. 1949. *Introduction to Legal Reasoning.* Chicago: University of Chicago Press.

Lewis, Anthony. 1988. "Who Is George Bush." *New York Times* November 6, E25.

Lewis, Neil A. 1990. "Souter Is Linked to Anti-Abortion Brief." *New York Times* July 31, A12.

———. 1991. "Court Nominee Is Linked to Anti-Abortion Stand." *New York Times* July 3, A1.

Llewellyn, Karl N. 1931. "Some Realism About Realism: Responding to Dean Pound." *Harvard Law Review* 44:1222–1264.

———. 1951. *The Bramble Bush.* New York: Oceana Publications.

Maltz, Earl M. 1992. "Abortion, Precedent and the Constitution: A Comment on Planned Parenthood of Southeastern Pennsylvania v. Casey." *Notre Dame Law Review* 68:11–32.

Marcus, Ruth. 1992. "5–4 Court Declines to Overruled Roe." *Washington Post* June 30, A1.

Marks, Brian A. 1988. *A Model of Judicial Influence on Congressional Policy Making: Grove City College v. Bell*, Working Papers in Political Science. Palo Alto, CA: The Hoover Institution, Stanford University.

Massaro, John. 1990. *Supremely Political*. New York: State University of New York Press.

McCloskey, Robert. 1960. *The American Supreme Court*. Chicago: University of Chicago Press.

McKenna, Marian C. 1992. "McKenna, Joseph." In Kermit L. Hall, ed., *Oxford Companion to the Supreme Court of the United States*. New York: Oxford University Press, pp. 539–540.

Melone, Albert P. 1990. *Researching Constitutional Law*. Glenview, IL: Scott, Foresman/Little, Brown.

Mendelson, Wallace. 1961. *Justices Black and Frankfurter: Conflict in the Court*. Chicago: University of Chicago Press.

Morgan, Donald G. 1954. *Justice William Johnson: The First Dissenter*. Columbia: University of South Carolina Press.

Morrow, James D. 1994. *Game Theory for Political Scientists*. Princeton, NJ: Princeton University Press.

Murphy, Walter F., James E. Fleming, and William F. Harris, II. 1986. *American Constitutional Interpretation*. New York: Foundation Press.

Neikirk, William, and Glen Elsasser. 1992. "Top Court May Face Backlash." *Chicago Tribune* July 1, 1.

Orth, John V. 1992. "Young, Ex Parte." In Kermit L. Hall, ed., *The Oxford Companion to the Supreme Court of the United States*. New York: Oxford University Press, p. 949.

Phelps, Glenn A., and John B. Gates. 1991. "The Myth of Jurisprudence: Interpretive Theory in the Constitutional Opinions of Justices Rehnquist and Brennan." *Santa Clara Law Review*, 31:567–596.

Pringle, Henry F. 1939. *The Life and Times of William Howard Taft*, Vol. II. New York: Farrar & Rinehart.

Pritchett, C. Herman. 1948. *The Roosevelt Court*. New York: Macmillan.

1969. "The Development of Judicial Research." In Joel Grossman and Joseph Tanenhaus, eds., *Frontiers of Judicial Research*. New York: Wiley.

1977. *The American Constitution*, 3rd ed. New York: McGraw-Hill.

Rohde, David, and Harold Spaeth. 1976. *Supreme Court Decision Making*. San Francisco: W.H. Freeman.

Rosenberg, Gerald. 1994. "Symposium: The Supreme Court and the Attitudinal Model." *Law and Courts* 4:6–8.

Savage, David G. 1992. "The Rescue of Roe v. Wade." *Los Angeles Times* December 13, A1.

Scheb, John M. II. 1992. "Catron, John." In Kermit L. Hall, ed., *The Oxford Companion to the Supreme Court of the United States*. New York: Oxford University Press, pp. 129–130.

Schlesinger, Joseph A. 1966. *Ambition in Politics*. Chicago: Rand McNally.

Schubert, Glendon. 1963. "Civilian Control and Stare Decisis in the Warren Court." In Glendon Schubert, ed., *Judicial Decision Making*. New York: The Free Press of Glencoe.

Schwartz, Bernard. 1993. *A History of the Supreme Court*. New York: Oxford University Press.

Segal, Jeffrey A. 1997. "Separation of Power Games in the Positive Theory of Congress and Courts." *American Political Science Review* 91:28–44.

Segal, Jeffrey A., and Harold J. Spaeth. 1993. *The Supreme Court and the Attitudinal Model*. New York: Cambridge University Press.

1996a. "The Influence of *Stare Decisis* on the Votes of United States Supreme Court Justices." *American Journal of Political Science* 40:971–1003.

1996b. "Norms, Dragons, and Stare Decisis." *American Journal of Political Science* 40:1064–1082.

Shapiro, Martin. 1964. *Law and Politics in the Supreme Court*. New York: The Free Press.

1972. "Toward a Theory of Stare Decisis." *Journal of Legal Studies* 1:125.

Solan, Lawrence M. 1993. *The Language of Judges*. Chicago: University of Chicago Press.

Songer, Donald R. 1987. "The Impact of the Supreme Court on Trends in Economic Policy Making in the United States Courts of Appeals." *Journal of Politics* 49:830–844.

Songer, Donald R., and Stefanie A. Lindquist. 1996. "Not the Whole Story: The Impact of Justices' Values on Supreme Court Decision Making." *American Journal of Political Science* 40:1049–1063.

Songer, Donald R., Jeffrey A. Segal, and Charles M. Cameron. 1994. "The Hierarchy of Justice: Testing a Principal–Agent Model of Supreme Court–Circuit Court Interactions." *American Journal of Political Science* 38:673–696.

Spaeth, Harold. 1979. *Supreme Court Policy Making*. San Francisco: W.H. Freeman.

Spiller, Pablo T., and Rafael Gely. 1992. "Congressional Control or Judicial Independence: The Determinants of U.S. Supreme Court Labor–Relations Decisions, 1949–1988." *RAND Journal of Economics* 23:463–492.

Stebenne, David L. 1996. *Arthur J. Goldberg: New Deal Liberal*. New York: Oxford University Press.

Stern, Robert L., Eugene Gressman, and Stephen M. Shapiro. 1986. *Supreme Court Practice*, 6th ed. Washington, DC: Bureau of National Affairs.

Tushnet, Mark. 1979. "Truth, Justice, and the American Way." *Texas Law Review* 57:1307–1359.

   1988. *Red, White, and Blue: A Critical Analysis of Constitutional Law*. Cambridge, MA: Harvard University Press.

Tversky, Amos, and Daniel Kahneman. 1986. "Rational Choice and the Framing of Decisions." *The Journal of Business* 59:251–278.

Ulmer, S. Sidney. 1971. "Earl Warren and the *Brown* Decision." *Journal of Politics*, 32:689–702.

Walker, Thomas, Lee Epstein, and William Dixon. 1988. "On the Mysterious Demise of Consensual Norms in the United States Supreme Court." *Journal of Politics* 50:361–389.

Warren, Charles. 1923. *The Supreme Court in United States History*. Boston: Little, Brown.

Warren, Earl. 1977. *The Memoirs of Earl Warren*. New York: Doubleday.

Weaver, Warren Jr. 1970. "Carswell Nomination Attacked and Defended as Senate Opens Debate on Nomination." *New York Times* March 17, A21.

Wechsler, Herbert. 1961. *Principles, Politics and Fundamental Law*. Cambridge, MA: Harvard University Press.

White, G. Edward. 1982. *Earl Warren: A Public Life*. New York: Oxford University Press.

Witt, Elder. 1981. *The Supreme Court and Its Work*. Washington, DC: Congressional Quarterly Press.

   1990. *Guide to the U.S. Supreme Court*. Washington, DC: Congressional Quarterly Press.

Yalof, Devid A. 1997. *Choosing Supreme Court Nominees: Selection Politics from Truman to Reagan*. Unpublished Ph.D. dissertation. The Johns Hopkins University.

Yntema, Hessel. 1934. "Legal Science and Reform." *Columbia Law Review* 34:209–229.

Table of Cases

Index